W. A. Lemly
Winston-Salem
N. C.

MARK TWAIN

A BIOGRAPHY

VOLUME II

Mark Twain

MARK TWAIN AT 36

MARK TWAIN

A BIOGRAPHY

THE PERSONAL AND LITERARY LIFE OF
SAMUEL LANGHORNE CLEMENS

BY
ALBERT BIGELOW PAINE

WITH LETTERS, COMMENTS AND INCIDENTAL
WRITINGS HITHERTO UNPUBLISHED; ALSO
NEW EPISODES, ANECDOTES, ETC.

FOUR VOLUMES
FULLY ILLUSTRATED

VOLUME II

HARPER & BROTHERS PUBLISHERS
NEW YORK AND LONDON
MCMXII

PRINTED IN THE UNITED STATES OF AMERICA

I-M

CONTENTS

CONTENTS

CONTENTS

ILLUSTRATIONS

MARK TWAIN
A BIOGRAPHY

LXXV

AS TO DESTINY

IF any reader has followed these chapters thus far, he may have wondered, even if vaguely, at the seeming fatality of events. Mark Twain had but to review his own life for justification of his doctrine of inevitability—an unbroken and immutable sequence of cause and effect from the beginning. Once he said:

"When the first living atom found itself afloat on the great Laurentian sea the first act of that first atom led to the *second* act of that first atom, and so on down through the succeeding ages of all life, until, if the steps could be traced, it would be shown that the first act of that first atom has led inevitably to the act of my standing here in my dressing-gown at this instant talking to you."

It seemed the clearest presentment ever offered in the matter of predestined circumstance—predestined from the instant when that primal atom felt the vital thrill. Mark Twain's early life, however imperfectly recorded, exemplifies this postulate. If through the years still ahead of us the course of destiny seems less clearly defined, it is only because thronging events make the threads less easy to trace. The web becomes richer, the pattern more intricate and confusing, but the line of fate neither breaks nor falters, to the end.

LXXVI

ON THE BUFFALO "EXPRESS"

WITH the beginning of life in Buffalo, Mark Twain had become already a world character—a man of large consequence and events. He had no proper realization of this, no real sense of the size of his conquest; he still regarded himself merely as a lecturer and journalist, temporarily popular, but with no warrant to a permanent seat in the world's literary congress. He thought his success something of an accident. The fact that he was prepared to settle down as an editorial contributor to a newspaper in what was then only a big village is the best evidence of a modest estimate of his talents.

He "worked like a horse," is the verdict of those who were closely associated with him on the *Express*. His hours were not regular, but they were long. Often he was at his desk at eight in the morning, and remained there until ten or eleven at night.

His working costume was suited to comfort rather than show. With coat, vest, collar, and tie usually removed (sometimes even his shoes), he lounged in his chair, in any attitude that afforded the larger ease, pulling over the exchanges; scribbling paragraphs, editorials, humorous skits, and what not, as the notion came upon him. J. L. Larned, his co-worker (he sat on the opposite side of the same table), remembers that Mark Twain enjoyed his work as he went along—the humor of it—and that he frequently laughed as some whimsicality or new absurdity came into his mind.

"I doubt," writes Larned, "if he ever enjoyed anything more than the jackknife engraving that he did on a piece of board of a military map of the siege of Paris, which was printed in the *Express* from his original plate, with accompanying explanations and comments. His half-day of whittling and laughter that went with it are something that I find pleasant to remember. Indeed, my whole experience of association with him is a happy memory, which I am fortunate in having. . . . What one saw of him was always the actual Mark Twain, acting out of his own nature simply, frankly, without pretense, and almost without reserve. It was that simplicity and naturalness in the man which carried his greatest charm."

Larned, like many others, likens Mark Twain to Lincoln in various of his characteristics. The two worked harmoniously together: Larned attending to the political direction of the journal, Clemens to the literary, and what might be termed the sentimental side. There was no friction in the division of labor, never anything but good feeling between them. Clemens had a poor opinion of his own comprehension of politics, and perhaps as little regard for Larned's conception of humor. Once when the latter attempted something in the way of pleasantry his associate said:

"Better leave the humor on this paper to me, Larned"; and once when Larned was away attending the Republican State Convention at Saratoga, and some editorial comment seemed necessary, Clemens thought it best to sign the utterance, and to make humor of his shortcomings.

I do not know much about politics, and am not sitting up nights to learn. . . .

I am satisfied that these nominations are all right and sound, and that they are the only ones that can bring peace to our distracted country (the only political phrase I am perfectly familiar with and competent to hurl at the public with fearless confidence—the other editor is full of them), but being merely satisfied is not enough. I always like to *know* before I shout. But I go for Mr. Curtis with all my strength! Being certain of him, I hereby shout all I know how. But the others may be a split ticket, or a scratched ticket, or whatever you call it.

I will let it alone for the present. It will keep. The other young man will be back to-morrow, and *he* will shout for it, split or no split, rest assured of that. He will prance into this political ring with his tomahawk and his war-whoop, and then you will hear a crash and see the scalps fly. He has none of my diffidence. He knows all about these nominees, and if he don't he will let on to in such a natural way as to deceive the most critical. He knows everything—he knows more than Webster's Unabridged and the American Encyclopedia—but whether he knows anything about a subject or not he is perfectly willing to discuss it. When he gets back he will tell you all about these candidates as serenely as if he had been acquainted with them a hundred years, though, speaking confidentially, I doubt if he ever heard of any of them till to-day. I am right well satisfied it is a good, sound, sensible ticket, and a ticket to win; but wait till *he* comes.

In the mean time I go for *George William Curtis* and take the chances.

MARK TWAIN.

He had become what Mr. Howells calls entirely "de-Southernized" by this time. From having been of slave-holding stock, and a Confederate soldier, he had become a most positive Republican, a rampant abolitionist—had there been anything left to abolish. His sympathy had been always with the oppressed, and he had now become their defender. His work on the paper revealed this more and more. He wrote fewer sketches and more editorials, and the editorials were likely to be either savage assaults upon some human abuse, or fierce espousals of the weak. They were fearless, scathing, terrific. Of some farmers of Cohocton, who had taken the law into their own hands to punish a couple whom they believed to be a detriment to the community, he wrote:

"The men who did that deed are capable of doing any

low, sneaking, cowardly villainy that could be invented in perdition. They are the very bastards of the devil."

He appended a full list of their names, and added:

"If the *farmers* of Cohocton are of this complexion, what on earth must a Cohocton rough be like?"

But all this happened a long time ago, and we need not detail those various old interests and labors here. It is enough to say that Mark Twain on the *Express* was what he had been from the beginning, and would be to the end—the zealous champion of justice and liberty; violent and sometimes wrong in his viewpoint, but never less than fearless and sincere. Invariably he was for the oppressed. He had a natural instinct for the right, but, right or wrong, he was for the under dog.

Among the best of his editorial contributions is a tribute to Anson Burlingame, who died February 23, 1870, at St. Petersburg, on his trip around the world as special ambassador for the Chinese Empire. In this editorial Clemens endeavored to pay something of his debt to the noble statesman. He reviewed Burlingame's astonishing career—the career which had closed at forty-seven, and read like a fairy-tale—and he dwelt lovingly on his hero's nobility of character. At the close he said:

"He was a good man, and a very, very great man. America lost a son, and all the world a servant, when he died."

Among those early contributions to the *Express* is a series called "Around the World," an attempt at collaboration with Prof. D. R. Ford, who did the actual traveling, while Mark Twain, writing in the first person, gave the letters his literary stamp. At least some of the contributions were written in this way, such as "Adventures in Hayti," "The Pacific," and "Japan." These letters exist to-day only in the old files of the *Express*, and indeed this is the case with most of Clemens's work for that paper. It was mainly ephemeral or timely work, and its larger value has disappeared. Here and there is a sentence worth remembering. Of two practical jokers who sent in a marriage notice of persons not even contemplating matrimony, he said: "This deceit has been practised maliciously by a couple of men whose small souls will escape through their pores some day if they do not varnish their hides."

Some of the sketches have been preserved. "Journalism in Tennessee," one of the best of his wilder burlesques, is as enjoyable to-day as when written. "A Curious Dream" made a lasting impression on his Buffalo readers, and you are pretty certain to hear of it when you mention Mark Twain in that city to-day. It vividly called attention to the neglect of the old North Street graveyard. The gruesome vision of the ancestors deserting with their coffins on their backs was even more humiliating than amusing, and inspired a movement for reform. It has been effective elsewhere since then, and may still be read with profit—or satisfaction—for in a note at the end the reader is assured that if the cemeteries of his town are kept in good order the dream is not leveled at his town at all, but "particularly and venomously at the next town."

LXXVII

THE "GALAXY"

MARK TWAIN'S work on the *Express* represented only a portion of his literary activities during his Buffalo residence. The *Galaxy*, an ambitious New York magazine of that day [published by Sheldon & Co. at 498 and 500 Broadway], proposed to him that he conduct for them a humorous department. They would pay $2,400 a year for the work, and allow him a free hand. There was some discussion as to book rights, but the arrangement was concluded, and his first instalment, under the general title of "Memoranda," appeared in the May number, 1870. In his Introductory he outlined what the reader might expect, such as "exhaustive statistical tables," "Patent Office reports," and "complete instructions about farming, even from the grafting of the seed to the harrowing of the matured crops." He declared that he would throw a pathos into the subject of agriculture that would surprise and delight the world. He added that the "Memoranda" was not necessarily a humorous department.

I would not conduct an exclusively and professedly humorous department for any one. I would always prefer to have the privilege of printing a serious and sensible remark, in case one occurred to me, without the reader's feeling obliged to consider himself outraged. . . . Puns cannot be allowed a place in this department . . . No circumstance, however dismal, will ever be considered a sufficient excuse for the admission of that last and saddest evidence of intellectual poverty, the pun.

The *Galaxy* was really a fine magazine, with the best contributors obtainable; among them Justin McCarthy, S. M. B. Piatt, Richard Grant White, and many others well known in that day, with names that still flicker here and there in its literary twilight. The new department appealed to Clemens, and very soon he was writing most of his sketches for it. They were better literature, as a rule, than those published in his own paper.

The first number of the "Memoranda" was fairly representative of those that followed it. "The Facts in the Case of the Great Beef Contract," a manuscript which he had undertaken three years before and mislaid, was its initial contribution. Besides the "Beef Contract," there was a tribute to George Wakeman, a well-known journalist of those days; a stricture on the Rev. T. DeWitt Talmage, who had delivered from the pulpit an argument against workingmen occupying pews in fashionable churches; a presentment of the Chinese situation in San Francisco, depicting the cruel treatment of the Celestial immigrant; a burlesque of the Sunday-school "good little boy" story,[1] and several shorter skits and anecdotes, ten pages in all; a rather generous contract.

Mark Twain's comment on Talmage was prompted by an article in which Talmage had assumed the premise that if workingmen attended the churches it would drive the better class of worshipers away. Among other things he said:

> I have a good Christian friend who, if he sat in the front pew in church, and a workingman should enter the door at the other end, would smell him instantly. My friend is not to blame for the sensitiveness of his nose, any more than you would flog a pointer for being keener on the scent than a stupid watch-dog.

[1] "The Story of the Good Little Boy Who Did Not Prosper" and the "Beef Contract" are included in *Sketches New and Old;* also the Chinese sketch, under the title, "Disgraceful Persecution of a Boy."

The fact is, if you had all the churches free, by reason of the mixing of the common people with the uncommon, you would keep one-half of Christendom sick at their stomach. If you are going to kill the church thus with bad smells I will have nothing to do with this work of evangelization.

Commenting on this Mark Twain said—well, he said a good deal more than we have room for here, but a portion of his closing paragraphs is worth preserving. He compares the Reverend Mr. Talmage with the early disciples of Christ—Paul and Peter and the others; or, rather, he contrasts him with them.

They healed the very beggars, and held intercourse with people of a villainous odor every day. If the subject of these remarks had been chosen among the original Twelve Apostles he would not have associated with the rest, because he could not have stood the fishy smell of some of his comrades who came from around the Sea of Galilee. He would have resigned his commission with some such remark as he makes in the extract quoted above: "Master, if thou art going to kill the church thus with bad smells I will have nothing to do with this work of evangelization." He is a disciple, and makes that remark to the Master; the only difference is that he makes it in the nineteenth instead of the first century.

Talmage was immensely popular at this time, and Mark Twain's open attack on him must have shocked a good many *Galaxy* readers, as perhaps his article on the Chinese cruelties offended the citizens of San Francisco. It did not matter. He was not likely to worry over the friends he would lose because of any stand taken for human justice. Larned said of him: "He was very far from being one who tried in any way to make himself popular." Certainly he never made any such attempt at the expense of his convictions.

The first *Galaxy* instalment was a sort of platform of principles for the campaign that was to follow. Not that each month's contribution contained personal criticism, or a defense of the Chinese (of whom he was always the champion as long as he lived), but a good many of them did. In the October number he began a series of letters under the general title of "Goldsmith's Friend Abroad Again," supposed to have been written by a Chinese immigrant in San Francisco, detailing his experience there. In a note the author says: "No experience is set down in the following letters which had to be invented. Fancy is not needed to give variety to the history of the Chinaman's sojourn in America. Plain fact is amply sufficient." The letters show how the supposed Chinese writer of them had set out for America, believing it to be a land whose government was based on the principle that all men are created equal, and treated accordingly; how, upon arriving in San Francisco, he was kicked and bruised and beaten, and set upon by dogs, flung into jail, tried and condemned without witnesses, his own race not being allowed to testify against Americans—Irish-Americans—in the San Francisco court. They are scathing, powerful letters, and one cannot read them, even in this day of improved conditions, without feeling the hot waves of resentment and indignation which Mark Twain must have felt when he penned them.

Reverend Mr. Talmage was not the only divine to receive attention in the "Memoranda." The Reverend Mr. Sabine, of New York, who had declined to hold a church burial service for the old actor, George Holland, came in for the most caustic as well as the most artistic stricture of the entire series. It deserves preservation to-day, not only for its literary value, but because no finer defense of the drama, no more searching sermon on self-righteousness, has ever been put into concrete form.[1]

[1] "The Indignity Put Upon the Remains of George Holland by the Rev. Mr. Sabine"; *Galaxy* for February, 1871. The reader will find it complete under Appendix J, at the end of last volume.

The "Little Church Around the Corner" on Twenty-ninth Street received that happy title from this incident. "There is a little church around the corner that will, perhaps, permit the service," Mr. Sabine had said to Holland's friends.

The little church did permit the service, and there was conferred upon it the new name, which it still bears. It has sheltered a long line of actor folk and their friends since then, earning thereby reverence, gratitude, and immortal memory.[1]

Of the *Galaxy* contributions a number are preserved in *Sketches New and Old*. "How I Edited an Agricultural Paper" is one of the best of these—an excellent example of Mark Twain's more extravagant style of humor. It is perennially delightful; in France it has been dramatized, and is still played.

A successful *Galaxy* feature, also preserved in the *Sketches*, was the "Burlesque Map of Paris," reprinted from the *Express*. The Franco-Prussian War was in progress, and this travesty was particularly timely. It creates only a smile of amusement to-day, but it was all fresh and delightful then. Schuyler Colfax, by this time Vice-President, wrote to him: "I have had the heartiest possible laugh over it, and so have all my family. You are a wicked, conscienceless wag, who ought to be punished severely."

The "Official Commendations," which accompany the map, are its chief charm. They are from Grant, Bismarck, Brigham Young, and others, the best one coming from one J. Smith, who says:

> My wife was for years afflicted with freckles, and though everything was done for her relief that could be done, all was in

[1] Church of the Transfiguration. Memorial services were held there for Joseph Jefferson; and a memorial window, by John La Farge, has been placed there in memory of Edwin Booth.

vain. But, sir, since her first glance at your map they have entirely left her. She has nothing but convulsions now.

It is said that the "Map of Paris" found its way to Berlin, where the American students in the beer-halls used to pretend to quarrel over it until they attracted the attention of the German soldiers that might be present. Then they would wander away and leave it on the table and watch results. The soldiers would pounce upon it and lose their tempers over it; then finally abuse it and revile its author, to the satisfaction of everybody.

The larger number of "Memoranda" sketches have properly found oblivion to-day. They were all, or nearly all, collected by a Canadian pirate, C. A. Backas, in a volume bearing the title of *Memoranda*,[1] a book long ago suppressed. Only about twenty of the *Galaxy* contributions found place in *Sketches New and Old*, five years later, and some of these might have been spared as literature. "To Raise Poultry," "John Chinaman in New York," and "History Repeats Itself" are valuable only as examples of his work at that period. The reader may consult them for himself.

[1] Also by a harpy named John Camden Hotten (of London), of whom we shall hear again. Hotten had already pirated *The Innocents*, and had it on the market before Routledge could bring out the authorized edition. Routledge later published the "Memoranda" under the title of *Sketches*, including the contents of the *Jumping Frog* book.

LXXVIII

THE PRIMROSE PATH

BUT we are losing sight of more important things. From the very beginning Mark Twain's home meant always more to him than his work. The life at 472 Delaware Avenue had begun with as fair a promise as any matrimonial journey ever undertaken. There seemed nothing lacking: a beautiful home, sufficient income, bright prospects—these things, with health and love, constitute married happiness. Mrs. Clemens wrote to her sister, Mrs. Crane, at the end of February: "Sue, we are two as happy people as you ever saw. Our days seem to be made up of only bright sunlight, with no shadow in them." In the same letter the husband added: "Livy pines and pines every day for you, and I pine and pine every day for you, and when we both of us are pining at once you would think it was a whole pine forest let loose."

To Redpath, who was urging lecture engagements for the coming season, he wrote:

DEAR RED,—I am not going to lecture any more forever. I have got things ciphered down to a fraction now. I know just about what it will cost to live, and I can make the money without lecturing. Therefore, old man, count me out.

And still later, in May:

I guess I am out of the field permanently. Have got a lovely wife, a lovely house, bewitchingly furnished, a lovely carriage, and a coachman whose style and dignity are simply awe-in-spiring, nothing less; and I am making more money than necessary, by considerable, and therefore why crucify myself nightly on the platform? The subscriber will have to be excused for the present season at least.

So they were very happy during those early months, acquiring pleasantly the education which any matrimonial experience is sure to furnish, accustoming themselves to the uses of housekeeping, to life in partnership, with all the discoveries and mental and spiritual adaptations that belong to the close association of marriage. They were far, very far, apart on many subjects. He was unpolished, untrained, impulsive, sometimes violent. Twichell remembers that in the earlier days of their acquaintance he wore a slouch hat pulled down in front, and smoked a cigar that sometimes tilted up and touched the brim of it. The atmosphere and customs of frontier life, the Westernisms of that day, still clung to him. Mrs. Clemens, on the other hand, was conservative, dainty, cultured, spiritual. He adored her as little less than a saint, and she became, indeed, his saving grace. She had all the personal refinement which he lacked, and she undertook the work of polishing and purifying her life companion. She had no wish to destroy his personality, to make him over, but only to preserve his best, and she set about it in the right way—gently, and with a tender gratitude in each achievement.

She did not entirely approve of certain lines of his reading; or, rather, she did not understand them in those days. That he should be fond of history and the sciences was natural enough, but when the *Life of P. T. Barnum, Written by Himself*, appeared, and he sat up nights to absorb it, and woke early and lighted the lamp to follow the career of the great showman, she was at a loss to comprehend this particular literary passion, and indeed was rather jealous of it. She did not realize then his vast interest in the study of human nature, or that such a book contained what Mr. Howells calls "the root of the human matter," the inner revelation of the human being at first hand.

Concerning his religious observances her task in the beginning was easy enough. Clemens had not at that time formulated any particular doctrines of his own. His natural kindness of heart, and especially his love for his wife, inclined him toward the teachings and customs of her Christian faith—unorthodox but sincere, as Christianity in the Langdon family was likely to be. It took very little persuasion on his wife's part to establish family prayers in their home, grace before meals, and the morning reading of a Bible chapter. Joe Goodman, who made a trip East, and visited them during the early days of their married life, was dumfounded to see Mark Twain ask a blessing and join in family worship. Just how long these forms continued cannot be known to-day; the time of their abandonment has perished from the recollection of any one now living.

It would seem to have been the Bible-reading that wrought the change. The prayer and the blessing were to him sincere and gracious; but as the readings continued he realized that he had never before considered the Bible from a doctrinal point of view, as a guide to spiritual salvation. To his logical reasoning mind, a large portion of it seemed absurd: a mass of fables and traditions, mere mythology. From such material humanity had built its mightiest edifice of hope, the doctrines of its faith. After a little while he could stand it no longer.

"Livy," he said one day, "you may keep this up if you want to, but I must ask you to excuse me from it. It is making me a hypocrite. I don't believe in this Bible. It contradicts my reason. I can't sit here and listen to it, letting you believe that I regard it, as you do, in the light of gospel, the word of God."

He was moved to write an article on the human idea of God, ancient and modern. It contained these paragraphs:

The difference in importance, between the God of the Bible and the God of the present day, cannot be described, it can only be vaguely and inadequately figured to the mind. . . . If you make figures to represent the earth and moon, and allow a space of one inch between them, to represent the four hundred thousand miles of distance which lies between the two bodies, the map will have to be eleven miles long in order to bring in the nearest fixed star.[1] So one cannot put the modern heavens on a map, nor the modern God; but the Bible God and the Bible heavens can be set down on a slate and yet not be discommoded. . . .

The difference between that universe and the modern one revealed by science is as the difference between a dust-flecked ray in a barn and the sublime arch of the Milky Way in the skies. Its God was strictly proportioned to its dimensions. His sole solicitude was about a handful of truculent nomads. He worried and fretted over them in a peculiarly and distractingly human way. One day he coaxed and petted them beyond their due, the next he harried and lashed them beyond their deserts. He sulked, he cursed, he raged, he grieved, according to his mood and the circumstances, but all to no purpose; his efforts were all vain, he could not govern them. When the fury was on him he was blind to all reason—he not only slaughtered the offender, but even his harmless little children and dumb cattle. . . .

To trust the God of the Bible is to trust an irascible, vindictive, fierce and ever fickle and changeful master; to trust the true God is to trust a Being who has uttered no promises, but whose beneficent, exact, and changeless ordering of the machinery of his colossal universe is proof that he is at least steadfast to his purposes; whose unwritten laws, so far as they affect man, being equal and impartial, show that he is just and fair; these

[1] His figures were far too small. A map drawn on the scale of 400,000 miles to the inch would need to be 1,100 miles long to take in both the earth and the nearest fixed star. On such a map the earth would be one-fiftieth of an inch in diameter—the size of a small grain of sand.

things, taken together, suggest that if he shall ordain us to live hereafter, he will still be steadfast, just, and fair toward us. We shall not need to require anything more.

It seems mild enough, obvious, even orthodox, now—so far have we traveled in forty years. But such a declaration then would have shocked a great number of sincerely devout persons. His wife prevailed upon him not to print it. She respected his honesty—even his reasoning, but his doubts were a long grief to her, nevertheless. In time she saw more clearly with his vision, but this was long after, when she had lived more with the world, had become more familiar with its larger needs, and the proportions of created things.

They did not mingle much or long with the social life of Buffalo. They received and returned calls, attended an occasional reception; but neither of them found such things especially attractive in those days, so they remained more and more in their own environment. There is an anecdote which seems to belong here.

One Sunday morning Clemens noticed smoke pouring from the upper window of the house across the street. The owner and his wife, comparatively newcomers, were seated upon the veranda, evidently not aware of impending danger. The Clemens household thus far had delayed calling on them, but Clemens himself now stepped briskly across the street. Bowing with leisurely politeness, he said:

"My name is Clemens; we ought to have called on you before, and I beg your pardon for intruding now in this informal way, but your house is on fire."

Almost the only intimate friends they had in Buffalo were in the family of David Gray, the poet-editor of the *Courier*. Gray was a gentle, lovable man. "The gentlest spirit and the loveliest that ever went clothed in clay, since Sir Galahad laid him to rest," Mark Twain once said of him. Both Gray and Clemens were friends of John Hay, and their families soon became intimate. Perhaps, in time, the Clemens household would have found other as good friends in the Buffalo circles; but heavy clouds that had lain unseen just beyond the horizon during those earlier months of marriage rose suddenly into view, and the social life, whatever it might have become, was no longer a consideration.

LXXIX

THE OLD HUMAN STORY

JERVIS LANGDON was never able to accept his son-in-law's invitation to the new home. His health began to fail that spring, and at the end of March, with his physician and Mrs. Langdon, he made a trip to the South. In a letter written at Richmond he said, "I have thrown off all care," and named a list of the four great interests in which he was involved. Under "number 5," he included "everything," adding, "so you see how good I am to follow the counsel of my children." He closed: "Samuel, I love your wife and she loves me. I think it is only fair that you should know it, but you need not flare up. I loved her before you did, and she loved me before she did you, and has not ceased since. I see no way but for you to make the most of it." He was already a very ill man, and this cheerful letter was among the last he ever wrote.

He was absent six weeks and seemed to improve, but suffered an attack early in May; in June his condition became critical. Clemens and his wife were summoned to Elmira, and joined in the nursing, day and night. Clemens surprised every one by his ability as a nurse. His delicacy and thoughtfulness were unfailing; his original ways of doing things always amused and interested the patient. In later years Mark Twain once said:

"How much of the nursing did I do? My main watch was from midnight to four in the morning, nearly four hours. My other watch was a midday watch, and

I think it was nearly three hours. The two sisters divided the remaining seventeen hours of the twenty-four hours between them, and each of them tried generously and persistently to swindle the other out of a part of her watch. I went to bed early every night, and tried to get sleep enough by midnight to fit me for my work, but it was always a failure. I went on watch sleepy and remained miserable, sleepy, and wretched, straight along through the four hours. I can still see myself sitting by that bed in the melancholy stillness of the sweltering night, mechanically waving a palm-leaf fan over the drawn, white face of the patient. I can still recall my noddings, my fleeting unconsciousness, when the fan would come to a standstill in my hand, and I woke up with a start and a hideous shock. During all that dreary time I began to watch for the dawn long before it came. When the first faint gray showed through the window-blinds I felt as no doubt a castaway feels when the dim threads of the looked-for ship appear against the sky. I was well and strong, but I was a man, afflicted with a man's infirmity—lack of endurance."

He always dealt with himself in this unsparing way; but those who were about him then have left a different story.

It was all without avail. Mr. Langdon rallied, and early in July there was hope for his recovery. He failed again, and on the afternoon of the 6th of August he died. To Mrs. Clemens, delicate and greatly worn with the anxiety and strain of watching, the blow was a crushing one. It was the beginning of a series of disasters which would mark the entire remaining period of their Buffalo residence.

There had been a partial plan for spending the summer in England, and a more definite one for joining the Twichells in the Adirondacks. Both of these projects were now abandoned. Mrs. Clemens concluded that she would be better at home than anywhere else, and invited an old school friend, a Miss Emma Nye, to visit her.

But the shadow of death had not been lifted from the Clemens household. Miss Nye presently fell ill with typhoid fever. There followed another long period of anxiety and nursing, ending with the death of the visitor in the new home, September 29th. The young wife was now in very delicate health; genuinely ill, in fact. The happy home had become a place of sorrow—of troubled nights and days. Another friend came to cheer them, and on this friend's departure Mrs. Clemens drove to the railway station. It was a hurried trip over rough streets to catch the train. She was prostrated on her return, and a little later, November 7, 1870, her first child, Langdon, was prematurely born. A dangerous illness followed, and complete recovery was long delayed. But on the 12th the crisis seemed passed, and the new father wrote a playful letter to the Twichells, as coming from the late arrival:

DEAR UNCLE AND AUNT,—I came into the world on the 7th inst., and consequently am about five days old now. I have had wretched health ever since I made my appearance . . . I am not corpulent, nor am I robust in any way. At birth I only weighed four and one-half pounds with my clothes on—and the clothes were the chief feature of the weight, too, I am obliged to confess, but I am doing finely, all things considered. . . . My little mother is very bright and cheery, and I guess she is pretty happy, but I don't know what about. She laughs a great deal, notwithstanding she is sick abed.

P. S.—Father says I had better write because you will be more interested in me, just now, than in the rest of the family.

A week later Clemens, as himself, wrote:

Livy is up and the prince keeps her busy and anxious these latter days and nights, but I am a bachelor up-stairs and don't have to jump up and get the soothing sirup, though I would as soon do it as not, I assure you. (Livy will be certain to read this letter.)

Tell Harmony that I do hold the baby, and do it pretty handily too, though with occasional apprehensions that his loose head will fall off. I don't have to quiet him; he hardly ever utters a cry. He is always thinking about something. He is a patient, good little baby.

Further along he refers to one of his reforms:

Smoke? I always smoke from three till five on Sunday afternoons, and in New York, the other day, I smoked a week, day and night. But when Livy is well I smoke only those two hours on Sunday. I'm boss of the habit now, and shall never let it boss me any more. Originally I quit solely on Livy's account (not that I believed there was the faintest *reason* in the matter, but just as I would deprive myself of sugar in my coffee if she wished it, or quit wearing socks if she thought them immoral), and I stick to it yet on Livy's account, and shall always continue to do so without a pang. But somehow it seems a pity that *you* quit, for Mrs. T. didn't mind it, if I remember rightly. Ah, it is turning one's back upon a kindly Providence to spurn away from us the good creature he sent to make the breath of life a *luxury* as well as a necessity, *enjoyable* as well as useful. To go quit smoking, when there ain't any sufficient excuse for it!—why, my old boy, when they used to tell me I would shorten my life ten years by smoking, they little knew the devotee they were wasting their puerile words upon; they little knew how trivial and valueless I would regard a decade that had no smoking in it! But I won't persuade you, Twichell—I won't until I see you again—but then we'll smoke for a week together, and then shut off again.

LXXX

LITERARY PROJECTS

THE success of the *Innocents* naturally made a thrifty publisher like Bliss anxious for a second experiment. He had begun early in the year to talk about another book, but nothing had come of it beyond a project or two, more or less hazy and unpursued. Clemens at one time developed a plan for a Noah's Ark book, which was to detail the cruise of the Ark in diaries kept by various members of it—Shem, Ham, and the others. He really wrote some of it at the time, and it was an idea he never entirely lost track of. All along among his manuscripts appear fragments from those ancient voyagers. One of the earlier entries will show the style and purpose of the undertaking. It is from Shem's record:

Friday: Papa's birthday. He is 600 years old. We celebrated it in a big, black tent. Principal men of the tribe present. Afterward they were shown over the ark, which was looking desolate and empty and dreary on account of a misunderstanding with the workmen about wages. Methuselah was as free with his criticisms as usual, and as voluble and familiar, which I and my brothers do not like; for we are past our one hundredth year and married. He still calls me Shemmy, just as he did when I was a child of sixty. I am still but a youth, it is true, but youth has its feelings, and I do not like this. . . .

Saturday: Keeping the Sabbath.

Sunday: Papa has yielded the advance and everybody is hard at work. The shipyard is so crowded that the men hinder each other; everybody hurrying or being hurried; the rush and confusion and shouting and wrangling are astonishing to our family, who have always been used to a quiet, country life.

It was from this germ that in a later day grew the diaries of Adam and Eve, though nothing very satisfactory ever came of this preliminary attempt. The author had faith in it, however. To Bliss he wrote:

I mean to take plenty of time and pains with the Noah's Ark book; maybe it will be several years before it is all written, but it will be a perfect lightning striker when it is done.

You can have the *first* say (that is plain enough) on that or any other book I may prepare for the press, as long as you deal in a fair, open, and honorable way with *me*. I do not think you will ever find me doing otherwise with you. I can get a book ready for you any time you want it; but you can't want one before this time next year, so I have plenty of time.

Bliss was only temporarily appeased. He realized that to get a book ready by the time he wanted it—a book of sufficient size and importance to maintain the pace set by the *Innocents*—meant rather more immediate action than his author seemed to contemplate. Futhermore, he knew that other publishers were besieging the author of the *Innocents;* a disquieting thought. In early July, when Mr. Langdon's condition had temporarily improved, Bliss had come to Elmira and proposed a book which should relate the author's travels and experiences in the Far West. It was an inviting subject, and Clemens, by this time more attracted by the idea of authorship and its rewards, readily enough agreed to undertake the volume. He had been offered half profits, and suggested that the new contract be arranged upon these terms. Bliss, figuring on a sale of 100,000 copies, proposed seven and one-half per cent. royalty as an equivalent, and the contract was so arranged. In after-years, when the cost of manufacture and paper had become greatly reduced,

Clemens, with but a confused notion of business details, believed he had been misled by Bliss in this contract, and was bitter and resentful accordingly. The figures remain, however, to show that Bliss dealt fairly. Seven and one-half per cent. of a subscription book did represent half profits up to 100,000 copies when the contract was drawn; but it required ten years to sell that quantity, and in that time conditions had changed. Bliss could hardly foresee that these things would be so, and as he was dead when the book touched the 100,000 mark he could not explain or readjust matters, whatever might have been his inclination.

Clemens was pleased enough with the contract when it was made. To Orion he wrote July 15 (1870):

> Per contract I must have another six-hundred-page book ready for my publisher January 1st, and I only began it to-day. The subject of it is a secret, because I may possibly change it. But as it stands I propose to do up Nevada and California, beginning with the trip across the country in the stage. Have you a memorandum of the route we took, or the names of any of the stations we stopped at? Do you remember any of the scenes, names, incidents, or adventures of the coach trip?—for I remember next to *nothing* about the matter. Jot down a foolscap page of items for me. I wish I could have two days' talk with you.
>
> I suppose I am to get the biggest copyright this time ever paid on a subscription book in this country.

The work so promptly begun made little progress. Hard days of illness and sorrow followed, and it was not until September that it was really under way. His natural enthusiasm over any new undertaking possessed him. On the 4th he wrote Bliss:

> During the past week I have written the first four chapters of the book, and I tell you *The Innocents Abroad* will have to get up early to beat it. It will be a book that will jump straight into continental celebrity the first month it is issued.

He prophesied a sale of 90,000 copies during the first twelve months and declared, "I see the capabilities of the subject."

But further disasters, even then impending, made continued effort impossible; the prospect of the new book for a time became gloomy, the idea of it less inspiring. Other plans presented themselves, and at one time he thought of letting the *Galaxy* publishers get out a volume of his sketches. In October he wrote Bliss that he was "driveling along tolerably fair on the book, getting off from twelve to twenty pages of manuscript a day." Bliss naturally discouraged the *Galaxy* idea, and realizing that the new book might be long delayed, agreed to get out a volume of miscellany sufficiently large and important for subscription sales. He was doubtful of the wisdom of this plan, and when Clemens suddenly proposed a brand-new scheme his publisher very readily agreed to hold back the publication of *Sketches* indefinitely.

The new book was to be adventures in the diamond mines of South Africa, then newly opened and of wide public interest. Clemens did not propose to visit the mines himself, but to let another man do the traveling, make the notes, and write or tell him the story, after which Clemens would enlarge and elaborate it in his own fashion. His adaptation of the letters of Professor Ford, a year earlier, had convinced him that his plan would work out successfully on a larger scale; he fixed upon his old friend, J. H. Riley, of Washington[1] (earlier of San Francisco), as the proper person to do the traveling. At the end of November he wrote Bliss:

> I have put my greedy hands upon the best man in America for my purpose, and *shall start him to the diamond field in South Africa within a fortnight at my expense . . . that the book will have a perfectly beautiful sale.*

[1] "Riley—Newspaper Correspondent." See *Sketches*.

He suggested that Bliss advance Riley's expense money, the amount to be deducted from the first royalty returns; also he proposed an increased royalty, probably in view of the startling splendor of the new idea. Bliss was duly impressed, and the agreement was finally made on a basis of eight and one-half per cent., with an advance of royalty sufficient to see Riley to South Africa and return.

Clemens had not yet heard from Riley definitely when he wrote his glowing letter to Bliss. He took it for granted that Riley, always an adventurous sort, would go. When Riley wrote him that he felt morally bound to the *Alta*, of which he was then Washington correspondent, also in certain other directions till the end of the session, Clemens wrote him at great length, detailing his scheme in full and urging him to write instantly to the *Alta* and others, asking a release on the ground of being offered a rare opportunity to improve his fortunes.

> You know right well that I would not have you depart a hair from any obligation for any money. The boundless confidence that I have in you is *born* of a conviction of your integrity in small as well as in great things. I know plenty of men whose integrity I would trust to here, but not off yonder in Africa.

His proposal, in brief, to Riley was that the latter should make the trip to Africa without expense to himself, collect memoranda, and such diamond mines as might be found lying about handy. Upon his return he was to take up temporary residence in the Clemens household until the book was finished, after which large benefits were to accrue to everybody concerned. In the end Riley obtained a release from his obligations and was off for the diamond mines and fortune.

Poor fellow! He was faithful in his mission, and it is said that he really located a mining claim that would have made him and his independent for all time to come; but returning home with his precious memoranda and the news of good fortune, he accidentally wounded himself with a fork while eating; blood-poisoning set in (they called it cancer then), and he was only able to get home to die. His memoranda were never used, his mining claim was never identified. Certainly, death was closely associated with Mark Twain's fortunes during those earlier days of his married life.

On the whole the Buffalo residence was mainly a gloomy one; its ventures were attended by ill-fortune. For some reason Mark Twain's connection with the *Express*, while it had given the paper a wide reputation, had not largely increased its subscription. Perhaps his work on it was too varied and erratic. Nasby, who had popularized the Toledo *Blade*, kept steadily to one line. His farmer public knew always just what to expect when their weekly edition arrived.

Clemens and his wife dreamed of a new habitation, amid new faces and surroundings. They agreed to offer their home and his interests in the *Express* for sale. They began to talk of Hartford, where Twichell lived, and where Orion Clemens and his wife had recently located.

Mark Twain's new fortunes had wrought changes in the affairs of his relatives. Already, before his marriage, he had prospected towns here and there with a view to finding an Eastern residence for his mother and sister, and he had kept Orion's welfare always in mind. When Pamela and her daughter came to his wedding he told them of a little city by the name of Fredonia (New York), not far from Buffalo, where he thought they might find a pleasant home.

"I went in there by night and out by night," he said, "so I saw none of it, but I had an intelligent, attractive audience. Prospect Fredonia and let me know what it is like. Try to select a place where a good many funerals pass. Ma likes funerals. If you can pick a good funeral corner she will be happy."

It was in her later life that Jane Clemens had developed this particular passion. She would consult the morning paper for any notice of obsequies and attend those that were easy of access. Watching the processions go by gave her a peculiar joy. Mrs. Moffett and her daughter did go to Fredonia immediately following the wedding. They found it residentially attractive, and rented a house before returning to St. Louis, a promptness that somewhat alarmed the old lady, who did not altogether fancy the idea of being suddenly set down in a strange house, in a strange land, even though it would be within hailing distance of Sam and his new wife. Perhaps the Fredonia funerals were sufficiently numerous and attractive, for she soon became attached to the place, and entered into the spirit of the life there, joining its temperance crusades, and the like, with zest and enjoyment.

Orion remained in St. Louis, but when Bliss established a paper called *The Publisher*, and wanted an editor, he was chosen for the place, originally offered to his brother; the latter, writing to Orion, said:

If you take the place with an air of *perfect confidence* in yourself, never once letting anything show in your bearing but a quiet, modest, entire, and perfect confidence in your ability to do *pretty much anything in the world*, Bliss will think you are the very man he needs; but *don't* show any shadow of timidity or unsoldierly diffidence, for that sort of thing is fatal to advancement.

I warn you thus because you are naturally given to knocking your pot over in this way, when a little judicious conduct would make it boil.

LXXXI

SOME FURTHER LITERARY MATTERS

MEANTIME *The Innocents Abroad* had continued to prosper. Its author ranked mainly as a humorist, but of such colossal proportions that his contemporaries had seemed to dwindle; the mighty note of the "Frog of Calaveras" had dwarfed a score of smaller peepers. At the end of a year from its date of publication the book had sold up to 67,000, and was continuing at the rate of several thousand monthly.

"You are running it in staving, tiptop, first-class style," Clemens wrote to Bliss. "On the average ten people a day come and hunt me up to tell me I am a benefactor! I guess that is a part of the program we didn't expect, in the first place."

Apparently the book appealed to readers of every grade. One hundred and fifteen copies were in constant circulation at the Mercantile Library, in New York, while in the most remote cabins of America it was read and quoted. Jack Van Nostrand, making a long horseback tour of Colorado, wrote:

> I stopped a week ago in a ranch hut a hundred miles from nowhere. The occupant had just two books: the Bible and *The Innocents Abroad*—the former in good repair.

Across the ocean the book had found no less favor, and was being translated into many and strange tongues. By what seems now some veritable magic its author's fame had become literally universal. The consul at

Hongkong, discussing English literature with a Chinese acquaintance, a mandarin, mentioned *The Pilgrim's Progress.*

"Yes, indeed, I have read it!" the mandarin said, eagerly. "We are enjoying it in China, and shall have it soon in our own language. It is by Mark Twain."

In England the book had an amazing vogue from the beginning, and English readers were endeavoring to outdo the Americans in appreciation. Indeed, as a rule, English readers of culture, critical readers, rose to an understanding of Mark Twain's literary value with greater promptness than did the same class of readers at home. There were exceptions, of course. There were English critics who did not take Mark Twain seriously, there were American critics who did. Among the latter was a certain William Ward, an editor of a paper down in Macon, Georgia—*The Beacon.* Ward did not hold a place with the great magazine arbiters of literary rank. He was only an obscure country editor, but he wrote like a prophet. His article—too long to quote in full—concerned American humorists in general, from Washington Irving, through John Phœnix, Philander Doesticks, Sut Lovingwood, Artemus Ward, Josh Billings and Petroleum V. Nasby, down to Mark Twain. With the exception of the first and last named he says of them:

> They have all had, or will have, their day. Some of them are resting beneath the sod, and others still live whose work will scarcely survive them. Since Irving no humorist in prose has held the foundation of a permanent fame except it be Mark Twain, and this, as in the case of Irving, is because he is a pure writer. Aside from any subtle mirth that lurks through his composition, the grace and finish of his more didactic and descriptive sentences indicate more than mediocrity.

The writer then refers to Mark Twain's description of the Sphinx, comparing it with Bulwer's, which he thinks may have influenced it. He was mistaken in this, for Clemens had not read Bulwer—never *could* read him at any length.

Of the English opinions, that of *The Saturday Review* was perhaps most doubtful. It came along late in 1870, and would hardly be worth recalling if it were not for a resulting, or collateral, interest. Clemens saw notice of this review before he saw the review itself. A paragraph in the Boston *Advertiser* spoke of *The Saturday Review* as treating the absurdities of the *Innocents* from a serious standpoint. The paragraph closed:

> We can imagine the delight of the humorist in reading this tribute to his power; and indeed it is so amusing in itself that he can hardly do better than reproduce the article in full in his next monthly "Memoranda."

The old temptation to hoax his readers prompted Mark Twain to "reproduce" in the *Galaxy*, not the *Review* article, which he had not yet seen, but an *imaginary Review* article, an article in which the imaginary reviewer would be utterly devoid of any sense of humor and treat the most absurd incidents of *The New Pilgrim's Progress* as if set down by the author in solemn and serious earnest. The pretended review began:

> Lord Macaulay died too soon. We never felt this so deeply as when we finished the last chapter of the above-named extravagant work. Macaulay died too soon; for none but he could mete out complete and comprehensive justice to the insolence, the impudence, the presumption, the mendacity, and, above all, the majestic ignorance of this author.

The review goes on to cite cases of the author's gross deception. It says:

> Let the cultivated English student of human nature picture to himself this Mark Twain as a person capable of doing the fol-

lowing described things; and not only doing them, but, with incredible innocence, printing them tranquilly and calmly in a book. For instance:

He states that he entered a hair-dresser's in Paris to get a shave, and the first "rake" the barber gave him with his razor it loosened his "hide," and lifted him out of the chair.

This is unquestionably extravagant. In Florence he was so annoyed by beggars that he pretends to have seized and eaten one in a frantic spirit of revenge. There is, of course, no truth in this. He gives at full length the theatrical program, seventeen or eighteen hundred years old, which he professes to have found in the ruins of the Colosseum, among the dirt and mold and rubbish. It is a sufficient comment upon this subject to remark that even a cast-iron program would not have lasted so long under the circumstances.

There were two and one-half pages of this really delightful burlesque which the author had written with huge enjoyment, partly as a joke on the *Review*, partly to trick American editors, who he believed would accept it as a fresh and startling proof of the traditional English lack of humor.

But, as in the early sage-brush hoaxes, he rather overdid the thing. Readers and editors readily enough accepted it as genuine, so far as having come from *The Saturday Review*; but most of them regarded it as a delicious bit of humor which Mark Twain himself had taken seriously, and was therefore the one sold. This was certainly startling, and by no means gratifying. In the next issue he undertook that saddest of all performances with tongue or pen: he explained his joke, and insisted on the truth of the explanation. Then he said:

If any man doubts my word now I will kill him. No, I will not kill him; I will win his money. I will bet him twenty to one, and let any New York publisher hold the stakes, that the statements I have above made as to the authorship of the article in question are entirely true.

But the Cincinnati *Enquirer* persisted in continuing the joke—in "rubbing it in," as we say now. The *Enquirer* declared that Mark Twain had been intensely mortified at having been so badly taken in; that his explanation in the *Galaxy* was "ingenious, but unfortunately not true." The *Enquirer* maintained that *The Saturday Review* of October 8, 1870, did contain the article exactly as printed in the "Memoranda," and advised Mark Twain to admit that he was sold, and say no more about it.

This was enraging. Mark Twain had his own ideas as to how far a joke might be carried without violence, and this was a good way beyond the limits. He denounced the *Enquirer's* statement as a "pitiful, deliberate falsehood," in his anger falling into the old-time phrasing of newspaper editorial abuse. He offered to bet them a thousand dollars in cash that they could not prove their assertions, and asked pointedly, in conclusion: "Will they swallow that falsehood ignominiously, or will they send an agent to the *Galaxy* office? I think the Cincinnati *Enquirer* must be edited by children." He promised that if they did not accept his financial proposition he would expose them in the next issue.

The incident closed there. He was prevented, by illness in his household, from contributing to the next issue, and the second issue following was his final "Memoranda" instalment. So the matter perished and was forgotten. It was his last editorial hoax. Perhaps he concluded that hoaxes in any form were dangerous playthings; they were too likely to go off at the wrong end.

It was with the April number (1871) that he concluded his relations with the *Galaxy*. In a brief valedictory he gave his reasons:

> I have now written for the *Galaxy* a year. For the last eight months, with hardly an interval, I have had for my fellows and comrades, night and day, doctors and watchers of the sick! During these eight months death has taken two members of my

home circle and malignantly threatened two others. All this I have experienced, yet all the time have been under contract to furnish "humorous" matter, once a month, for this magazine. I am speaking the exact truth in the above details. Please to put yourself in my place and contemplate the grisly grotesqueness of the situation. I think that some of the "humor" I have written during this period could have been injected into a funeral sermon without disturbing the solemnity of the occasion.

The "Memoranda" will cease permanently with this issue of the magazine. To be a pirate on a low salary, and with no share in the profits of the business, used to be my idea of an uncomfortable occupation, but I have other views now. To be a monthly humorist in a cheerless time is drearier.

Without doubt he felt a glad relief in being rid of this recurrent, imperative demand. He wrote to Orion that he had told the *Galaxy* people he would not write another article, long or short, for less than $500, and preferred not to do it at all.

The *Galaxy* department and the work on the *Express* were Mark Twain's farewell to journalism; for the "Memoranda" was essentially journalistic, almost as much so, and as liberally, as his old-time *Enterprise* position. Apparently he wrote with absolute freedom, unhampered by editorial policy or restriction. The result was not always pleasant, and it was not always refined. We may be certain that it was because of Mrs. Clemens's heavy burdens that year, and her consequent inability to exert a beneficent censorship, that more than one—more than a dozen—of the "Memoranda" contributions were permitted to see the light of print.

As a whole, the literary result of Mark Twain's Buffalo period does not reach the high standard of *The Innocents Abroad.* It was a retrogression—in some measure a return to his earlier form. It had been done under pressure, under heavy stress of mind, as he said. Also there was another reason; neither the subject treated nor the environment of labor had afforded that lofty inspiration which glorified every step of the *Quaker City* journey. Buffalo was a progressive city—a beautiful city, as American cities go—but it was hardly an inspiring city for literature, and a dull, dingy newspaper office was far, very far, from the pleasant decks of the *Quaker City*, the camp-fires of Syria, the blue sky and sea of the Mediterranean.

LXXXII

THE WRITING OF "ROUGHING IT"

THE third book published by Mark Twain was not the Western book he was preparing for Bliss. It was a small volume, issued by Sheldon & Co., entitled *Mark Twain's Autobiography* (Burlesque) *and First Romance*. The *Romance* was the "Awful, Terrible Medieval Romance" which had appeared in the *Express* at the beginning of 1870. The burlesque autobiography had not previously appeared. The two made a thin little book, which, in addition to its literary features, had running through it a series of full-page, irrelevant pictures—cartoons of the Erie Railroad Ring, presented as illustrations of a slightly modified version of "The House That Jack Built." The "House" was the Erie headquarters, the purpose being to illustrate the swindling methods of the Ring. The faces of Jay Gould, James Fisk, Jr., John T. Hoffman, and others of the combination, are chiefly conspicuous. The publication was not important, from any standpoint. Literary burlesque is rarely important, and it was far from Mark Twain's best form of expression. A year or two later he realized the mistake of this book, bought in the plates and destroyed them.

Meantime the new Western book was at a standstill. To Orion, in March, he wrote:

I am still nursing Livy night and day. I am nearly worn out. We shall go to Elmira ten days hence (if Livy can travel on a mattress then), and stay there until I finish the California book, say three months. But I can't begin work right away when I get there; must have a week's rest, for I have been through thirty days' terrific siege.

He promised to forward some of the manuscript soon.

Hold on four or five days and I will see if I can get a few chapters fixed to send to Bliss. . . .

I have offered this house and the *Express* for sale, and when we go to Elmira we leave here for good. I shall not select a new home till the book is finished, but we have little doubt that Hartford will be the place.

He disposed of his interest in the *Express* in April, at a sacrifice of $10,000 on the purchase price. Mrs. Clemens and the baby were able to travel, and without further delay he took them to Elmira, to Quarry Farm.

Quarry Farm, the home of Mrs. Clemens's sister, Mrs. Theodore Crane, is a beautiful hilltop, with a wide green slope, overlooking the hazy city and the Chemung River, beyond which are the distant hills. It was bought quite incidentally by Mr. and Mrs. Langdon, who, driving by one evening, stopped to water the horses and decided that it would make a happy summer retreat, where the families could combine their housekeeping arrangements during vacation days. When the place had first been purchased, they had debated on a name for it. They had tried several, among them "Go-as-you-please Hall," "Crane's Nest," and had finally agreed upon "Rest and Be Thankful." But this was only its official name. There was an abandoned quarry up the hill, a little way from the house, and the title suggested by Thomas K. Beecher came more naturally to the tongue. The place became Quarry Farm, and so remains.

Clemens and his wife had fully made up their minds to live in Hartford. They had both conceived an affection for the place, Clemens mainly because of Twichell, while both of them yearned for the congenial literary and social atmosphere, and the welcome which they felt awaited them. Hartford was precisely what Buffalo in that day was not—a home for the literary man. It held a distinguished group of writers, most of whom the Clemenses already knew. Furthermore, with Bliss as publisher of the Mark Twain books, it held their chief business interests.

Their plans for going were not very definite as to time. Clemens found that his work went better at the farm, and that Mrs. Clemens and the delicate baby daily improved. They decided to remain at Quarry Farm for the summer, their first summer in that beautiful place which would mean so much to them in the years to come.

It was really Joe Goodman, as much as anything, that stirred a fresh enthusiasm in the new book. Goodman arrived just when the author's spirits were at low ebb.

"Joe," he said, "I guess I'm done for. I don't appear to be able to get along at all with my work, and what I do write does not seem valuable. I'm afraid I'll never be able to reach the standard of *The Innocents Abroad* again. Here is what I have written, Joe. Read it, and see if that is your opinion."

Goodman took the manuscript and seated himself in a chair, while Clemens went over to a table and pretended to work. Goodman read page after page, critically, and was presently absorbed in it. Clemens watched him furtively, till he could stand it no longer. Then he threw down his pen, exclaiming:

"I knew it! I knew it! I am writing nothing but rot. You have sat there all this time reading without a smile, and pitying the ass I am making of myself. But I am not wholly to blame. I am not strong enough to fight against fate. I have been trying to write a funny book, with dead people and sickness everywhere. Mr.

Langdon died first, then a young lady in our house, and now Mrs. Clemens and the baby have been at the point of death all winter! Oh, Joe, I wish to God I could die myself!"

"Mark," said Joe, "I was reading critically, not for amusement, and so far as I have read, and can judge, this is one of the best things you have ever written. I have found it perfectly absorbing. You are doing a great book!"

Clemens knew that Goodman never spoke except from conviction, and the verdict was to him like a message of life handed down by an archangel. He was a changed man instantly. He was all enthusiasm, full of his subject, eager to go on. He proposed to pay Goodman a salary to stay there and keep him company and furnish him with inspiration—the Pacific coast atmosphere and vernacular, which he feared had slipped away from him. Goodman declined the salary, but extended his visit as long as his plans would permit, and the two had a happy time together, recalling old Comstock days. Every morning, for a month or more, they used to tramp over the farm. They fell into the habit of visiting the old quarry and pawing over the fragments in search of fossil specimens. Both of them had a poetic interest in geology, its infinite remotenesses and its testimonies. Without scientific knowledge, they took a deep pleasure in accumulating a collection, which they arranged on boards torn from an old fence, until they had enough specimens to fill a small museum. They imagined they could distinguish certain geological relations and families, and would talk about trilobites, the Old Red Sandstone period, and the azoic age, or follow random speculation to far-lying conclusions, developing vague humors of phrase and fancy, having altogether a joyful good time.

Another interest that developed during Goodman's stay was in one Ruloff, who was under death sentence for a particularly atrocious murder. The papers were full of Ruloff's prodigious learning. It was said that he had in preparation a work showing the unity of all languages. Goodman and Clemens agreed that Ruloff's death would be a great loss to mankind, even though he was clearly a villain and deserved his sentence. They decided that justice would be served just as well if some stupid person were hung in his place, and following out this fancy Clemens one morning put aside his regular work and wrote an article to the *Tribune*, offering to supply a substitute for Ruloff. He signed it simply "Samuel Langhorne," and it was published as a serious communication, without comment, so far as the *Tribune* was concerned. Other papers, however, took it up and it was widely copied and commented upon. Apparently no one ever identified Mark Twain with the authorship of the letter, which, by the way, does not appear to have prolonged Ruloff's earthly usefulness.[1]

Life at the farm may have furnished agricultural inspiration, for Clemens wrote something about Horace Greeley's farming, also a skit concerning Henry Ward Beecher's efforts in that direction. Of Mr. Beecher's farming he said:

"His strawberries would be a comfortable success if robins would eat turnips."

The article amused Beecher, and perhaps Greeley was amused too, for he wrote:

MARK,—You are mistaken as to my criticisms on your farming. I never publicly made any, while you have undertaken to tell the exact cost per pint of my potatoes and cabbages, truly enough the inspiration of genius. If you will really betake yourself to farming, or even to telling what you know about it, rather than what you don't know about mine,

[1] The reader will find the Ruloff letter in full under Appendix K, at the end of last volume.

I will not only refrain from disparaging criticism, but will give you my blessing.

Yours, HORACE GREELEY.

The letter is in Mr. Greeley's characteristic scrawl, and no doubt furnished inspiration for the turnip story in *Roughing It*, also the model for the pretended facsimile of Greeley's writing.

Altogether that was a busy, enterprising summer at Quarry Farm. By the middle of May, Clemens wrote to Bliss that he had twelve hundred manuscript pages of the new book already written, and that he was turning out the remainder at the rate of from thirty to sixty-five per day. He was in high spirits by this time. The family health had improved, and prospects were bright.

I have enough manuscript on hand now to make (allowing for engravings) about four hundred pages of the book, consequently am two-thirds done. I intended to run up to Hartford about the middle of the week and take it along, but I find myself so thoroughly interested in my work now (a thing I have not experienced for months) that I can't bear to lose a single moment of the inspiration. So I will stay here and peg away as long as it lasts. My present idea is to write as much more as I have already written, and then collect from the mass the very best chapters and discard the rest. When I get it done I want to see the man who will begin to read it and not finish it. Nothing grieves me now; nothing troubles me, nothing bothers me or gets my attention. I don't think of anything but the book, and don't have an hour's unhappiness about anything, and don't care two cents whether school keeps or not. The book will be done soon now. It will be a starchy book; the dedication will be worth the price of the volume. Thus:

TO THE LATE CAIN

THIS BOOK IS DEDICATED

not on account of respect for his memory, for it merits little respect; not on account of sympathy for him, for his bloody deed

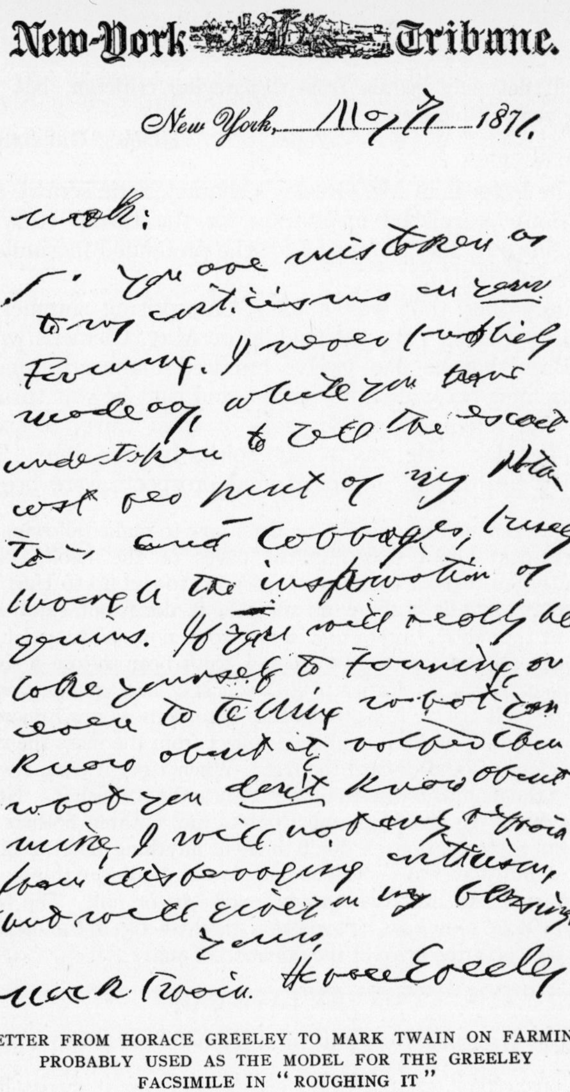

New-York Tribune.

New York, 1871.

LETTER FROM HORACE GREELEY TO MARK TWAIN ON FARMING. PROBABLY USED AS THE MODEL FOR THE GREELEY FACSIMILE IN "ROUGHING IT"

places him without the pale of sympathy, strictly speaking, but out of a mere humane commiseration for him, in that it was his misfortune to live in a dark age that knew not the beneficent insanity plea.

Probably Mrs. Clemens diverted this picturesque dedication in favor of the Higbie inscription, or perhaps the author never really intended the literary tribute to Cain. The impulse that inspired it, however, was characteristic.

In a postscript to this letter he adds:

My stock is looking up. I am getting the bulliest offers for books and almanacs; am flooded with lecture invitations, and one periodical offers me $6,000 cash for twelve articles of any length, and on any subject, treated humorously or otherwise.

He set in to make hay while the sun was shining. In addition to the California book, which was now fast nearing completion, he discussed a scheme with Goodman for a six-hundred-page work which they were to do jointly; he planned and wrote one or two scenes from a Western play, to be built from episodes in the new book (one of them was the "Arkansas" incident, related in Chapter XXXI); he perfected one of his several inventions—an automatically adjusting vest-strap; he wrote a number of sketches, made an occasional business trip to New York and Hartford; prospected the latter place for a new home. The shadow which had hung over the sojourn in Buffalo seemed to have lifted.

He had promised Bliss some contributions for his new paper, and in June he sent three sketches. In an accompanying letter he says:

Here are three articles which you may have if you will pay $125 for the lot. If you don't want them I'll sell them to the *Galaxy*, but not for a cent less than three times the money. . . .

If you take them pay one-tenth of the $125 in weekly instalments to Orion till he has received it all.

He reconsidered his resolution not to lecture again, and closed with Redpath for the coming season. He found himself in a lecture-writing fever. He wrote three of them in succession: one on Artemus Ward, another on "Reminiscences of Some Pleasant Characters I Have Met," and a third one based on chapters from the new book. Of the "Reminiscence" lecture he wrote Redpath:

"It covers my whole acquaintance; kings, lunatics, idiots, and all." Immediately afterward he wrote that he had prepared still another lecture, " title to be announced later."

"During July I'll decide which one I like best," he said. He instructed Redpath not to make engagements for him to lecture in churches. "I never made a success of a lecture in a church yet. People are afraid to laugh in a church."

Redpath was having difficulties in arranging a circuit to suit him. Clemens had prejudices against certain towns and localities, prejudices that were likely to change overnight. In August he wrote:

DEAR RED,—I am different from other women; my mind changes oftener. People who have no mind can easily be steadfast and firm, but when a man is loaded down to the guards with it, as I am, every heavy sea of foreboding or inclination, maybe of indolence, shifts the cargo. See? Therefore, if you will notice, one week I am likely to give rigid instructions to confine me to New England; the next week send me to Arizona; the next week withdraw my name; the next week give you full, untrammeled swing; and the week following modify it. You must try to keep the run of my mind, Redpath; it is your business, being the agent, and it always was too many for me. . . . Now about the West this week, I am willing that you shall retain all the Western engagements. But what I shall want next week is still with God. Yours, MARK.

He was in Hartford when this letter was written, arranging for residence there and the removal of his belongings. He finally leased the fine Hooker house on Ford Street, in that pleasant seclusion known as Nook Farm—the literary part of Hartford, which included the residence of Charles Dudley Warner and Harriet Beecher Stowe. He arranged for possession of the premises October 1st. So the new home was settled upon; then learning that Nasby was to be in Boston, he ran over to that city for a few days of recreation after his season's labors.

Preparations for removal to Hartford were not delayed. The Buffalo property was disposed of, the furnishings were packed and shipped away. The house which as bride and groom they had entered so happily was left empty and deserted, never to be entered by them again. In the year and a half of their occupancy it had seen well-nigh all the human round, all that goes to make up the happiness and the sorrow of life.

LXXXIII

LECTURING DAYS

LIFE in Hartford, in the autumn of 1871, began in the letter, rather than in the spirit. The newcomers were received with a wide, neighborly welcome, but the disorder of establishment and the almost immediate departure of the head of the household on a protracted lecturing tour were disquieting things; the atmosphere of the Clemens home during those early Hartford days gave only a faint promise of its future loveliness.

As in a far later period, Mark Twain had resorted to lecturing to pay off debt. He still owed a portion of his share in the *Express;* also he had been obliged to obtain an advance from the lecture bureau. He dreaded, as always, the tedium of travel, the clatter of hotel life, the monotony of entertainment, while, more than most men, he loved the tender luxury of home. It was only that he could not afford to lose the profit offered on the platform.

His season opened at Bethlehem, Pennsylvania, October 16th, and his schedule carried him hither and thither, to and fro, over distances that lie between Boston and Chicago. There were opportunities to run into Hartford now and then, when he was not too far away, and in November he lectured there on Artemus Ward.

He changed his entertainment at least twice that season. He began with the "Reminiscences," the lecture which he said would treat of all those whom he had met, "idiots, lunatics, and kings," but he did not like it, or it did not go well. He wrote Redpath of the Artemus Ward address:

"It suits me, and I'll never deliver the nasty, nauseous 'Reminiscences' any more."

But the Ward lecture was good for little more than a month, for on December 8th he wrote again:

> Notify all hands that from this time I shall talk nothing but selections from my forthcoming book, *Roughing It.* Tried it twice last night; suits me tiptop.

And somewhat later:

> Had a splendid time with a splendid audience in Indianapolis last night; a perfectly jammed house, just as I have all the time out here. . . . I don't care now to have any appointments canceled. I'll even "fetch" those Dutch Pennsylvanians with this lecture.
>
> Have paid up $4,000 indebtedness. You are the last on my list. Shall begin to pay you in a few days, and then I shall be a free man again.

Undoubtedly he reveled in the triumphs of a platform tour, though at no time did he regard it as a pleasure excursion. During those early weeks the proofs of his new book, chasing him from place to place, did not add to his comfort. Still, with large, substantial rewards in hand and in prospect, one could endure much.

In the neighborhood of Boston there were other compensations. He could spend a good part of his days at the Lyceum headquarters, in School Street, where there was always congenial fellowship—Nasby, Josh Billings, and the rest of the peripatetic group that about the end of the year collected there. Their lectures were never tried immediately in Boston, but in the outlying towns; tried and perfected—or discarded. When the provincial audiences were finally satisfied, then the final test in the Boston Music Hall was made, and if this proved successful the rest of the season was safe. Redpath's lecturers put up at Young's Hotel, and spent their days at the bureau, smoking and spinning yarns, or talking shop. Early in the evening they scattered to the outlying towns, Lowell, Lexington, Concord, New Bedford. There is no such a condition to-day: lecturers are few, lecture bureaus obscure; there are no great reputations made on the platform.

Neither is there any such distinct group of humorists as the one just mentioned. Humor has become universal since then. Few writers of this age would confess to taking their work so seriously as to be at all times unsmiling in it; only about as many, in fact, as in that day would confess to taking their work so lightly that they could regard life's sterner phases and philosophies with a smile.

Josh Billings was one of the gentlest and loveliest of our pioneers of laughter. The present generation is not over-familiar even with his name, but both the name and sayings of that quaint soul were on everybody's lips at the time of which we are writing. His true name was Henry W. Shaw, and he was a genuine, smiling philosopher, who might have built up a more permanent and serious reputation had he not been induced to disfigure his maxims with ridiculous spelling in order to popularize them and make them bring a living price. It did not matter so much with Nasby's work. An assumed illiteracy belonged with the side of life which he presented; but it is pathetic now to consider some of the really masterly sayings of Josh Billings presented in that uncouth form which was regarded as a part of humor a generation ago. Even the aphorisms that were essentially humorous lose value in that degraded spelling.

"When a man starts down hill everything is greased for the occasion," could hardly be improved upon by distorted orthography, and here are a few more gems which have survived that deadly blight.

"Some folks mistake vivacity for wit; whereas the

difference between vivacity and wit is the same as the difference between the lightning-bug and the lightning."

"Don't take the bull by the horns—take him by the tail; then you can let go when you want to."

"The difficulty is not that we know so much, but that we know so much that isn't so."

Josh Billings, Nasby, and Mark Twain were close friends. They had themselves photographed in a group, and there was always some pleasantry going on among them. Josh Billings once wrote on "Lekturing," and under the head of "Rule Seven," which treated of unwisdom of inviting a lecturer to a private house, he said:

> Think of asking Mark Twain home with yu, for instance. Yure good wife has put her house in apple-pie order for the ockashun; everything is just in the right place. Yu don't smoke in yure house, *never*. Yu don't put yure feet on the center-table, yu don't skatter the nuzepapers all over the room, in utter confushion: order and ekonemy governs yure premises. But if yu expeckt Mark Twain to be happy, or even kumfortable yu hav got to buy a box of cigars worth at least seventeen dollars and yu hav got to move all the tender things out ov yure parlor. Yu hav got to skatter all the latest papers around the room careless, you hav got to hav a pitcher ov ice-water handy, for Mark is a dry humorist. Yu hav got to ketch and tie all yure yung ones, hed and foot, for Mark luvs babys only in theory; yu hav got to send yure favorite kat over to the nabors and hide yure poodle. These are things that hav to be done, or Mark will pak hiz valise with hiz extry shirt collar and hiz lektur on the Sandwich Islands, and travel around yure streets, smoking and reading the sighns over the store doorways untill lektur time begins.

As we are not likely to touch upon Mark Twain's lecturing, save only lightly, hereafter, it may be as well to say something of his method at this period. At all places visited by lecturers there was a committee, and it was the place of the chairman to introduce the lecturer, a privilege which he valued, because it gave him a momentary association with distinction and fame. Clemens was a great disappointment to these officials. He had learned long ago that he could introduce himself more effectively than any one else. His usual formula was to present himself as the chairman of the committee, introducing the lecturer of the evening; then, with what was in effect a complete change of personality, to begin his lecture. It was always startling and amusing, always a success; but the papers finally printed this formula, which took the freshness out of it, so that he had to invent others. Sometimes he got up with the frank statement that he was introducing himself because he had never met any one who could pay a proper tribute to his talents; but the newspapers printed that too, and he often rose and began with no introduction at all.

Whatever his method of beginning, Mark Twain's procedure probably was the purest exemplification of the platform entertainer's art which this country has ever seen. It was the art that makes you forget the artisanship, the art that made each hearer forget that he was not being personally entertained by a new and marvelous friend, who had traveled a long way for his particular benefit. One listener has written that he sat "simmering with laughter" through what he supposed was the continuation of the introduction, waiting for the traditional lecture to begin, when presently the lecturer, with a bow, disappeared, and it was over. The listener looked at his watch; he had been there more than an hour. He thought it could be no more than ten minutes, at most. Many have tried to set down something of the effect his art produced on them, but one may not clearly convey the story of a vanished presence and a silent voice.

There were other pleasant associations in Boston. Howells was there, and Aldrich; also Bret Harte, who had finished his triumphal progress across the continent to join the *Atlantic* group. Clemens appears not to have met Aldrich before, though their acquaintance had begun a year earlier, when Aldrich, as editor of *Every Saturday*, had commented on a poem entitled, "The Three Aces," which had appeared in the Buffalo *Express*. Aldrich had assumed the poem to be the work of Mark Twain, and had characterized it as "a feeble imitation of Bret Harte's 'Heathen Chinee.'" Clemens, in a letter, had mildly protested as to the charge of authorship, and Aldrich had promptly printed the letter with apologetic explanation. A playful exchange of personal letters followed, and the beginning of a lifelong friendship.

One of the letters has a special interest here. Clemens had followed his protest with an apology for it, asking that no further notice be taken of the matter. Aldrich replied that it was too late to prevent "doing him justice," as his explanation was already on the press, but that if Clemens insisted he would withdraw it in the next issue. Clemens then wrote that he did not want it withdrawn, and explained that he hated to be accused of plagiarizing Bret Harte, to whom he was deeply indebted for literary schooling in the California days. Continuing he said:

Do you know the prettiest fancy and the neatest that ever shot through Harte's brain? It was this. When they were trying to decide upon a vignette cover for the *Overland* a grizzly bear (of the arms of the State of California) was chosen. Nahl Bros. carved him and the page was printed with him in it.

As a bear he was a success. He was a good bear, but then, it was objected, he was an *objectless* bear—a bear that *meant* nothing, signified nothing, simply stood there, snarling over his shoulder at nothing, and was painfully and manifestly a boorish and ill-natured intruder upon the fair page. All hands said that —none were satisfied; they hated badly to give him up, and yet they hated as much to have him there when there was no *point* to him. But presently Harte took a pencil and drew two simple lines under his feet, and behold he was a magnificent success!—the ancient symbol of California savagery, snarling at the approaching type of high and progressive civilization, the first Overland locomotive! I just think that was nothing less than an inspiration.[1]

Among the Boston group was another Californian, Ralph Keeler, an eccentric, gifted, and altogether charming fellow, whom Clemens had known on the Pacific slope. Keeler had been adopted by the Boston writers, and was grateful and happy accordingly. He was poor of purse, but inexhaustibly rich in the happier gifts of fortune. He was unfailingly buoyant, light-hearted, and hopeful. On an infinitesimal capital he had made a tour of many lands, and had written of it for the *Atlantic*. In that charmed circle he was as overflowingly happy as if he had been admitted to the company of the gods. Keeler was affectionately regarded by all who knew him, and he offered a sort of worship in return. He often accompanied Mark Twain on his lecture engagements to the various outlying towns, and Clemens brought him back to his hotel for breakfast, where they had good, enjoyable talks together. Once Keeler came eagerly to the hotel and made his way up to Clemens's room.

"Come with me," he said. "Quick!"

"What is it? What's happened?"

"Don't wait to talk. Come with me."

They tramped briskly through the streets till they reached the public library, entered, Keeler leading the way, not stopping till he faced a row of shelves filled with books. He pointed at one of them, his face radiant with joy.

"Look," he said. "Do you see it?"

[1] The "bear" was that which has always appeared on the *Overland* cover; the "two lines" formed a railway track under his feet. Clemens's original letter contained crude sketches illustrating these things.

Clemens looked carefully now and identified one of the books as a still-born novel which Keeler had published.

"This is a library," said Keeler, eagerly, "and they've got it!"

His whole being was aglow with the wonder of it. He had been investigating; the library records showed that in the two years the book had been there it had been taken out and read three times! It never occurred to Clemens even to smile. Knowing Mark Twain, one would guess that his eyes were likely to be filled with tears.

In his book about Mark Twain, Howells tells of a luncheon which Keeler gave to his more famous associates —Aldrich, Fields, Harte, Clemens, and Howells himself— a merry informal occasion. Says Howells:

> Nothing remains to me of the happy time but a sense of idle and aimless and joyful talk-play, beginning and ending nowhere, of eager laughter, of countless good stories from Fields, of a heat-lightning shimmer of wit from Aldrich, of an occasional concentration of our joint mockeries upon our host, who took it gladly; and amid the discourse, so little improving, but so full of good-fellowship, Bret Harte's fleering dramatization of Clemens's mental attitude toward a symposium of Boston illuminates. "Why, fellows," he spluttered, "this is the dream of Mark's life," and I remember the glance from under Clemens's feathery eyebrows which betrayed his enjoyment of the fun.

Very likely Keeler gave that luncheon in celebration of his book's triumph; it would be like him.

Keeler's end was a mystery. The New York *Tribune* commissioned him to go to Cuba to report the facts of some Spanish outrages. He sailed from New York in the steamer, and was last seen alive the night before the vessel reached Havana. He had made no secret of his mission, but had discussed it in his frank, innocent way. There were some Spanish military men on the ship.

Clemens, commenting on the matter, once said:

"It may be that he was not flung into the sea, still the belief was general that that was what had happened."

In his book Howells refers to the doubt with which Mark Twain was then received by the polite culture of Boston; which, on the other hand, accepted Bret Harte as one of its own, forgiving even social shortcomings.

The reason is not difficult to understand. Harte had made his appeal with legitimate fiction of the kind which, however fresh in flavor and environment, was of a sort to be measured and classified. Harte spoke a language they could understand; his humor, his pathos, his point of view were all recognizable. It was an art already standardized by a master. It is no reflection on the genius of Bret Harte to liken his splendid achievements to those of Charles Dickens. Much of Harte's work is in no way inferior to that of his great English prototype. Dickens never wrote a better short story than "The Outcasts of Poker Flats." He never wrote as good a short story as "The Luck of Roaring Camp." Boston critics promptly realized these things and gave Harte his correct rating. That they failed to do this with Mark Twain, lay chiefly in the fact that he spoke to them in new and startling tongues. His gospels were likely to be heresies; his literary eccentricities were all unclassified. Of the ultra-fastidious set Howells tells us that Charles Eliot Norton and Prof. Francis J. Child were about the only ones who accorded him unqualified approval. The others smiled and enjoyed him, but with that condescension which the courtier is likely to accord to motley and the cap and bells. Only the great, simple-hearted, unbiased multitude, the public, which had no standards but the direct appeal from one human heart to another, could recognize immediately his mightier heritage, could exalt and place him on the throne.

LXXXIV

"ROUGHING IT"

TELEGRAM to Redpath:

How in the name of God does a man find his way from here to Amherst, and when must he start? Give me full particulars, and send a man with me. If I had another engagement I would rot before I would fill it. S. L. CLEMENS.

This was at the end of February, and he believed that he was standing on the platform for the last time. He loathed the drudgery of the work, and he considered there was no further need. He was no longer in debt, and his income he accounted ample. His new book, *Roughing It*,[1] had had a large advance sale, and its earnings promised to rival those of the *Innocents*. He resolved in the future to confine himself to the trade and profits of authorship.

The new book had advantages in its favor. Issued early in the year, it was offered at the best canvassing season; particularly so, as the author's lectures had prepared the public for its reception. Furthermore, it dealt with the most picturesque phases of American life, scenes and episodes vastly interesting at that time, and peculiarly adapted to Mark Twain's literary expression. In a different way *Roughing It* is quite as remarkable as *The*

[1] It was Bliss who had given the new book the title of *Roughing It*. *Innocents at Home* had been its provisional title, certainly a misleading one, though it has been retained in England for the second volume; for what reason it would be difficult to explain.

Innocents Abroad. If it has less charm, it has greater interest, and it is by no means without charm. There is something delicious, for instance, in this bit of pure enjoyment of the first day's overland travel:

> It was now just dawn, and as we stretched our cramped legs full length on the mail-sacks, and gazed out through the windows across the wide wastes of greensward clad in cool, powdery mist to where there was an expectant look in the Eastern horizon, our perfect enjoyment took the form of a tranquil and contented ecstasy. The stage whirled along at a spanking gait, the breeze flapping the curtains and suspended coats in a most exhilarating way; the cradle swayed and swung luxuriously, the pattering of the horses' hoofs, the cracking of the driver's whip, and his "Hi-yi! g'lang!" were music; the spinning ground and the waltzing trees appeared to give us a mute hurrah as we went by, and then slack up and look after us with interest and envy, or something; and as we lay and smoked the pipe of peace, and compared all this luxury with the years of tiresome city life that had gone before it, we felt that there was only one complete and satisfying happiness in the world, and we had found it.

Also, there is that lofty presentation of South Pass, and a picture of the alkali desert, so parching, so withering in its choking realism, that it makes the throat ache and the tongue dry to read it. Just a bit of the desert in passing:

> The sun beats down with a dead, blistering, relentless malignity; the perspiration is welling from every pore in man and beast, but scarcely a sign of it finds its way to the surface—it is absorbed before it gets there; there is not the faintest breath of air stirring; there is not a merciful shred of cloud in all the brilliant firmament; there is not a living creature visible in any direction whither one searches the blank level that stretches its monotonous miles on every hand; there is not a sound, not a sigh, not a whisper, not a buzz, or a whir of wings, or distant pipe of bird; not even a sob from the lost souls that doubtless people that dead air.

As for the humor of the book, it has been chiefly famous for that. "Buck Fanshaw's Funeral" has become a classic, and the purchase of the "Mexican Plug." But it is to no purpose to review the book here in detail. We have already reviewed the life and environment out of which it grew.

Without doubt the story would have contained more of the poetic and contemplative, in which he was always at his best, if the subject itself, as in the *Innocents*, had lent itself oftener to this form of writing. It was the lack of that halo perhaps which caused the new book never quite to rank with its great forerunner in public favor. There could hardly be any other reason. It presented a fresher theme; it abounded in humor; technically, it was better written; seemingly it had all the elements of popularity and of permanence. It did, in fact, possess these qualities, but its sales, except during the earlier months of its canvass, never quite equaled those of *The Innocents Abroad*.

Roughing It was accepted by the public for just what it was and is, a great picture of the Overland Pioneer days —a marvelous picture of frontier aspects at a time when the frontier itself, even with its hardships and its tragedies, was little more than a vast primal joke; when all frontiersmen were obliged to be laughing philosophers in order to survive the stress of its warfares.

A word here about this Western humor: It is a distinct product. It grew out of a distinct condition—the battle with the frontier. The fight was so desperate, to take it seriously was to surrender. Women laughed that they might not weep; men, when they could no longer swear. "Western humor" was the result. It is the freshest, wildest humor in the world, but there is tragedy behind it.

Roughing It presented the picture of those early conditions with the startling vividness and truth of a great novel, which, in effect, it was. It was not accurate history, even of the author's own adventures. It was true in its aspects, rather than in its details. The greater artist disregards the truth of detail to render more strikingly a phase or a condition, to produce an atmosphere, to reconstruct a vanished time. This was what Mark Twain did in *Roughing It.* He told the story of overland travel and the frontier, for his own and future generations, in what is essentially a picaresque novel, a work of unperishing fiction, founded on fact.

The sales of *Roughing It* during the first three months aggregated nearly forty thousand copies, and the author was lavishly elate accordingly. To Orion (who had already closed his career with Bliss, by exercise of those hereditary eccentricities through which he so often came to grief) he gave $1,000 out of the first royalty check, in acknowledgment of the memorandum book and other data which Orion had supplied. Clemens believed the new book would sell one hundred thousand copies within the year; but the sale diminished presently, and at the end of the first year it was considerably behind the *Innocents* for the same period. As already stated, it required ten years for *Roughing It* to reach the one-hundred-thousand mark, which the *Innocents* reached in three.

LXXXV

A BIRTH, A DEATH, AND A VOYAGE

THE year 1872 was an eventful one in Mark Twain's life. At Elmira, on March 19th, his second child, a little girl, whom they named Susan Olivia, was born. On June 2d, in the new home in Hartford, to which they had recently moved, his first child, a little boy, Langdon, died. He had never been strong, his wavering life had often been uncertain, always more of the spirit than the body, and in Elimira he contracted a heavy cold, or perhaps it was diphtheria from the beginning. In later years, whenever Clemens spoke of the little fellow, he never failed to accuse himself of having been the cause of the child's death. It was Mrs. Clemens's custom to drive out each morning with Langdon, and once when she was unable to go Clemens himself went instead.

"I should not have been permitted to do it," he said, remembering. "I was not qualified for any such responsibility as that. Some one should have gone who had at least the rudiments of a mind. Necessarily I would lose myself dreaming. After a while the coachman looked around and noticed that the carriage-robes had dropped away from the little fellow, and that he was exposed to the chilly air. He called my attention to it, but it was too late. Tonsilitis or something of the sort set in, and he did not get any better, so we took him to Hartford. There it was pronounced diphtheria, and of course he died."

So, with or without reason, he added the blame of another tragedy to the heavy burden of remorse which he would go on piling up while he lived.

The blow was a terrible one to Mrs. Clemens; even the comfort of the little new baby on her arm could not ease the ache in her breast. It seemed to her that death was pursuing her. In one of her letters she says:

"I feel so often as if my path is to be lined with graves," and she expresses the wish that she may drop out of life herself before her sister and her husband—a wish which the years would grant.

They did not return to Elmira, for it was thought that the air of the shore would be better for the little girl; so they spent the summer at Saybrook, Connecticut, at Fenwick Hall, leaving Orion and his wife in charge of the house at Hartford.

Beyond a few sketches, Clemens did very little literary work that summer, but he planned a trip to Europe, and he invented what is still known and sold as the "Mark Twain Scrap-Book."

He wrote to Orion of his proposed trip to England, and dilated upon his scrap-book with considerable enthusiasm. The idea had grown out of the inconvenience of finding a paste-jar, and the general mussiness of scrap-book keeping. His new plan was a self-pasting scrap-book with the gum laid on in narrow strips, requring only to be dampened with a sponge or other moist substance to be ready for the clipping. He states that he intends to put the invention into the hands of Slote, Woodman & Co., of whom Dan Slote, his old *Quaker City* room-mate, was the senior partner, and have it manufactured for the trade.

About this time began Mark Twain's long and active interest in copyright. Previously he had not much considered the subject; he had taken it for granted there was no step that he could take, while international piracy was a recognized institution. On both sides of the water books were appropriated, often without profit, sometimes even without credit, to the author. To tell the truth, Clemens had at first regarded it rather in the nature of a compliment that his books should be thought worth pirating in England, but as time passed he realized that he was paying heavily for this recognition. Furthermore, he decided that he was forfeiting a right; rather that he was being deprived of it: something which it was in his nature to resent.

When *Roughing It* had been ready for issue he agreed with Bliss that they should try the experiment of copyrighting it in England, and see how far the law would protect them against the voracious little publisher, who thus far had not only snapped up everything bearing Mark Twain's signature, but had included in a volume of Mark Twain sketches certain examples of very weak humor with which Mark Twain had been previously unfamiliar.

Whatever the English pirate's opinion of the copyright protection of *Roughing It* may have been, he did not attempt to violate it. This was gratifying. Clemens came to regard England as a friendly power. He decided to visit it and spy out the land. He would make the acquaintance of its people and institutions and write a book which would do these things justice.

He gave out no word of his real purpose. He merely said that he was going over to see his English publishers, and perhaps to arrange for a few lectures. He provided himself with some stylographic note-books, by which he could produce two copies of his daily memoranda—one for himself and one to mail to Mrs. Clemens—and sailed on the *Scotia* August 21, 1872.

Arriving in Liverpool he took train for London, and presently the wonderful charm of that old, finished country broke upon him. His "first hour in England was an hour of delight," he records; "of rapture and ecstasy.

These are the best words I can find, but they are not adequate; they are not strong enough to convey the feeling which this first vision of rural England brought me." Then he noticed that the gentleman opposite in his compartment paid no attention to the scenery, but was absorbed in a green-covered volume. He was so absorbed in it that, by and by, Clemens's curiosity was aroused. He shifted his position a little and his eye caught the title. It was the first volume of the English edition of *The Innocents Abroad.* This was gratifying for a moment; then he remembered that the man had never laughed, never even smiled during the hour of his steady reading. Clemens recalled what he had heard of the English lack of humor. He wondered if this was a fair example of it, and if the man could be really taking seriously every word he was reading. Clemens could not look at the scenery any more for watching his fellow-passenger, waiting with a fascinated interest for the paragraph that would break up that iron-clad solemnity. It did not come. During all the rest of the trip to London the atmosphere of the compartment remained heavy with gloom.

He drove to the Langham Hotel, always popular with Americans, established himself, and went to look up his publishers. He found the Routledges about to sit down to luncheon in a private room, up-stairs, in their publishing house. He joined them, and not a soul stirred from that table again until evening. The Routledges had never heard Mark Twain talk before, never heard any one talk who in the least resembled him. Various refreshments were served during the afternoon, came and went, while this marvelous creature talked on and they listened, reveling, and wondering if America had any more of that sort at home. By and by dinner was served; then after a long time, when there was no further excuse for keeping him there, they took him to the Savage Club, where there were yet other refreshments and a gathering of the clans to welcome this new arrival as a being from some remote and unfamiliar star.

Tom Hood, the younger, was there, and Harry Lee, and Stanley the explorer, who had but just returned from finding Livingstone, and Henry Irving, and many another whose name remains, though the owners of those names are all dead now, and their laughter and their good-fellowship are only a part of that intangible fabric which we call the past.[1]

[1] Clemens had first known Stanley as a newspaper man. "I first met him when he reported a lecture of mine in St. Louis," he said once in a conversation where the name of Stanley was mentioned.

LXXXVI

ENGLAND

FROM that night Mark Twain's stay in England could not properly be called a gloomy one.

Routledge, Hood, Lee, and, in fact, all literary London, set themselves the task of giving him a good time. Whatever place of interest they could think of he was taken there; whatever there was to see he saw it. Dinners, receptions, and assemblies were not complete without him. The White Friars' Club and others gave banquets in his honor. He was the sensation of the day. When he rose to speak on these occasions he was greeted with wild cheers. Whatever he said they eagerly applauded—too eagerly sometimes, in the fear that they might be regarded as insensible to American humor. Other speakers delighted in chaffing him in order to provoke his retorts. When a speaker humorously referred to his American habit of carrying a cotton umbrella, his reply that he followed this custom because a cotton umbrella was the only kind of an umbrella that an Englishman wouldn't steal, was all over England next day, and regarded as one of the finest examples of wit since the days of Swift.

The suddenness and completeness of his acceptance by the great ones of London rather overwhelmed and frightened him—made him timid. Joaquin Miller writes:

> He was shy as a girl, although time was already coyly flirting white flowers at his temples, and could hardly be coaxed to meet the learned and great who wanted to take him by the hand.

Many came to call on him at his hotel, among them Charles Reade and Canon Kingsley. Kingsley came twice without finding him; then wrote, asking for an appointment. Reade invited his assistance on a novel. Indeed, it was in England that Mark Twain was first made to feel that he had come into his rightful heritage. Whatever may have been the doubts concerning him in America, there was no question in England. Howells says:

> In England rank, fashion, and culture rejoiced in him. Lord mayors, lord chief justices, and magnates of many kinds were his hosts; he was desired in country houses, and his bold genius captivated the favor of periodicals which spurned the rest of our nation.

After that first visit of Mark Twain's, when Americans in England, referring to their great statesmen, authors, and the like, naturally mentioned the names of Seward, Webster, Lowell, or Holmes, the English comment was likely to be: "Never mind those. We can turn out academic Sewards by the dozen, and cultured humorists like Lowell and Holmes by the score. Tell us of Lincoln, Artemus Ward, and Mark Twain. We cannot match these; they interest us." And it was true. History could not match them, for they were unique.

Clemens would have been more than human if in time he had not realized the fuller meaning of this triumph, and exulted in it a little to the folks at home. There never lived a more modest, less pretentious, less aggressive man than Mark Twain, but there never lived a man who took a more childlike delight in genuine appreciation; and, being childlike, it was only human that he should wish those nearest to him to share his happiness. After one memorable affair he wrote:

> I have been received in a sort of tremendous way to-night by the brains of London, assembled at the annual dinner of the sheriffs of London; mine being (between you and me) a name

which was received with a thundering outburst of spontaneous applause when the long list of guests was called.

I might have perished on the spot but for the friendly support and assistance of my excellent friend, Sir John Bennett.

This letter does not tell all of the incident or the real reason why he might have perished on the spot. During the long roll-call of guests he had lost interest a little, and was conversing in whispers with his "excellent friend," Sir John Bennett, stopping to applaud now and then when the applause of the others indicated that some distinguished name had been pronounced. All at once the applause broke out with great vehemence. This must be some very distinguished person indeed. He joined in it with great enthusiasm. When it was over he whispered to Sir John:

"Whose name was that we were just applauding?"

"Mark Twain's."

Whereupon the support was needed.

Poor little pirate Hotten did not have a happy time during this visit. He had reveled in the prospect at first, for he anticipated a large increase to be derived from his purloined property; but suddenly, one morning, he was aghast to find in the *Spectator* a signed letter from Mark Twain, in which he was repudiated, referred to as "John Camden Hottentot," an unsavory person generally. Hotten also sent a letter to the *Spectator*, in which he attempted to justify himself, but it was a feeble performance. Clemens prepared two other communications, each worse than the other and both more destructive than the first one. But these were only to relieve his mind. He did not print them. In one of them he pursued the fancy of John Camden Hottentot, whom he offers as a specimen to the Zoological Gardens.

It is not a bird. It is not a man. It is not a fish. It does not seem to be in all respects a reptile. It has the body and features of a man, but scarcely any of the instincts that belong to such a structure. . . . I am sure that this singular little creature is the missing link between the man and the hyena.

Hotten had preyed upon explorer Stanley and libeled him in a so-called biography to a degree that had really aroused some feeling against Stanley in England. Only for the moment—the Queen invited Stanley to luncheon, and newspaper criticism ceased. Hotten was in general disrepute, therefore, so it was not worth while throwing a second brick at him.

In fact, now that Clemens had expended his venom, on paper, Hotten seemed to him rather an amusing figure than otherwise. An incident grew out of it all, however, that was not amusing. E. P. Hingston, whom the reader may remember as having been with Artemus Ward in Virginia City, and one of that happy group that wined and dined the year away, had been engaged by Hotten to write the introductory to his edition of *The Innocents Abroad*. It was a well-written, highly complimentary appreciation. Hingston did not dream that he was committing an offense, nor did Clemens himself regard it as such in the beginning.

But Mark Twain's views had undergone a radical change, and with characteristic dismissal of previous conditions he had forgotten that he had ever had any other views than those he now held. Hingston was in London, and one evening, at a gathering, approached Clemens with outstretched hand. But Clemens failed to see Hingston's hand or to recognize him. In after-years his conscience hurt him terribly for this. He remembered it only with remorse and shame. Once, in his old age, he spoke of it with deep sorrow.

LXXXVII

THE BOOK THAT WAS NEVER WRITTEN

THE book on England, which he had prepared for so carefully, was never written. Hundreds of the stylographic pages were filled, and the duplicates sent home for the entertainment of Olivia Clemens, but the notes were not completed, and the actual writing was never begun. There was too much sociability in London for one thing, and then he found that he could not write entertainingly of England without introducing too many personalities, and running the risk of offending those who had taken him into their hearts and homes. In a word, he would have to write too seriously or not at all.

He began his memoranda industriously enough, and the volume might have been as charming and as valuable as any he has left behind. The reader will hardly fail to find a few of the entries interesting. They are offered here as examples of his daily observation during those early weeks of his stay, and to show somewhat of his purpose:

AN EXPATRIATE

There was once an American thief who fled his country and took refuge in England. He dressed himself after the fashion of the Londoners, and taught his tongue the peculiarities of the London pronunciation and did his best in all ways to pass himself for a native. But he did two fatal things: he stopped at the Langham Hotel, and the first trip he took was to visit Stratford-on-Avon and the grave of Shakespeare. These things betrayed his nationality.

STANLEY AND THE QUEEN

See the power a monarch wields! When I arrived here, two weeks ago, the papers and geographers were in a fair way to eat poor Stanley up without salt or sauce. The Queen says, "Come four hundred miles up into Scotland and sit at my luncheon-table fifteen minutes"; which, being translated, means, "Gentlemen, I believe in this man and take him under my protection"; and not another yelp is heard.

AT THE BRITISH MUSEUM

What a place it is!

Mention some very rare curiosity of a peculiar nature—a something which you have *read* about somewhere but never seen—they show you a dozen! They show you all the possible *varieties* of that thing! They show you curiously wrought jeweled necklaces of beaten gold, worn by the ancient Egyptians, Assyrians, Etruscans, Greeks, Britons—every people of the forgotten ages, indeed. They show you the ornaments of all the tribes and peoples that live or ever did live. Then they show you a cast taken from Cromwell's face in death; then the venerable vase that once contained the ashes of Xerxes.

I am wonderfully thankful for the British Museum. Nobody comes bothering around me—nobody elbows me—all the room and all the light I want, under this huge dome—no disturbing noises—and people standing ready to bring me a copy of pretty much any book that ever was printed under the sun—and if I choose to go wandering about the long corridors and galleries of the great building the secrets of all the earth and all the ages are laid open to me. I am not capable of expressing my gratitude for the British Museum—it seems as if I do not know any but little words and weak ones.

WESTMINSTER ABBEY BY NIGHT

It was past eleven o'clock and I was just going to bed. But this friend of mine was as reliable as he was eccentric, and so there was not a doubt in my mind that his "expedition" had merit in it. I put on my coat and boots again, and we drove away.

"Where is it? Where are we going?"

"Don't worry. You'll see."

He was not inclined to talk. So I thought this must be a weighty matter. My curiosity grew with the minutes, but I kept it manfully under the surface. I watched the lamps, the signs, the numbers as we thundered down the long street. I am always lost in London, day or night. It was very chilly, almost bleak. People leaned against the gusty blasts as if it were the dead of winter. The crowds grew thinner and thinner, and the noises waxed faint and seemed far away. The sky was overcast and threatening. We drove on, and still on, till I wondered if we were ever going to stop. At last we passed by a spacious bridge and a vast building, and presently entered a gateway, passed through a sort of tunnel, and stopped in a court surrounded by the black outlines of a great edifice. Then we alighted, walked a dozen steps or so, and waited. In a little while footsteps were heard, a man emerged from the darkness, and we dropped into his wake without saying anything. He led us under an archway of masonry, and from that into a roomy tunnel, through a tall iron gate, which he locked behind us. We followed him down this tunnel, guided more by his footsteps on the stone flagging than by anything we could very distinctly see. At the end of it we came to another iron gate, and our conductor stopped there and lit a bull's-eye lantern. Then he unlocked the gate; and I wished he had oiled it first, it grated so dismally. The gate swung open and we stood on the threshold of what seemed a limitless domed and pillared cavern, carved out of the solid darkness. The conductor and my friend took off their hats reverently, and I did likewise. For the moment that we stood thus there was not a sound, and the stillness seemed to add to the solemnity of the gloom. I looked my inquiry!

"It is the tomb of the great dead of England—Westminster Abbey." . . .

We were among the tombs; on every hand dull shapes of men, sitting, standing, or stooping, inspected us curiously out of the darkness—reached out their hands toward us—some appealing, some beckoning, some warning us away. Effigies they were—statues over the graves; but they looked human and natural in the murky shadows. Now a little half-grown black and white cat squeezed herself through the bars of the iron gate and came purring lovingly about us, unawed by the time or the place, unimpressed by the marble pomp that sepulchers a line of mighty dead that ends with a great author of yesterday and began with a sceptered monarch away back in the dawn of history, more than twelve hundred years ago. . . .

Mr. Wright flashed his lantern first upon this object and then upon that, and kept up a running commentary that showed there was nothing about the venerable Abbey that was trivial in his eyes or void of interest. He is a man in authority, being superintendent, and his daily business keeps him familiar with every nook and corner of the great pile. Casting a luminous ray now here, now yonder, he would say:

"Observe the height of the Abbey—one hundred and three feet to the base of the roof; I measured it myself the other day. Notice the base of this column—old, very old—hundreds and hundreds of years—and how well they knew how to build in those old days! Notice it—every stone is laid horizontally; that is to say, just as nature laid it originally in the quarry—not set up edgewise; in our day some people set them on edge, and then wonder why they split and flake. Architects cannot teach nature anything. Let me remove this matting—it is put here to preserve the pavement; now there is a bit of pavement that is seven hundred years old; you can see by these scattering clusters of colored mosaics how beautiful it was before time and sacrilegious idlers marred it. Now there, in the border, was an inscription, once see, follow the circle—you can trace it by the ornaments that have been pulled out—here is an A and there is an O, and yonder another A—all beautiful Old English capitals; there is no telling what the inscription was — no record left now. Now move along in this direction, if you please. Yonder is where old King Sebert the Saxon lies—his monument is the oldest one in the Abbey; Sebert died in 616,[1] and that's as much as twelve hundred and fifty years ago—think of it! Twelve hundred and fifty years! Now yonder is the last one—Charles Dickens—there on the floor, with the

[1] Clemens probably misunderstood the name. It was Ethelbert who died in 616. The name Sebert does not appear in any Saxon annals accessible to the author.

brass letters on the slab—and to this day the people come and put flowers on it. . . . There is Garrick's monument; and Addison's, and Thackeray's bust—and Macaulay lies there. And close to Dickens and Garrick lie Sheridan and Dr. Johnson—and here is old Parr. . . .

"That stone there covers Campbell the poet. Here are names you know pretty well—Milton, and Gray who wrote the *Elegy*, and Butler who wrote *Hudibras*; and Edmund Spenser, and Ben Jonson—there are three tablets to him scattered about the Abbey, and all got 'O, Rare Ben Jonson' cut on them. You were standing on one of them just now—he is buried standing up. There used to be a tradition here that explains it. The story goes that he did not dare ask to be buried in the Abbey, so he asked King James if he would make him a present of eighteen inches of English ground, and the King said 'yes,' and asked him where he would have it, and he said in Westminster Abbey. Well, the King wouldn't go back on his word, and so there he is, sure enough—stood up on end."

The reader may regret that there are not more of these entries, and that the book itself was never written. Just when he gave up the project is not recorded. He was urged to lecture in London, but declined. To Mrs. Clemens, in September, he wrote:

Everybody says lecture, lecture, lecture, but I have not the least idea of doing it; certainly not at present. Mr. Dolby, who took Dickens to America, is coming to talk business to-morrow, though I have sent him word once before that I can't be hired to talk here; because I have no time to spare. There is too much sociability; I do not get along fast enough with work.

In October he declared that he was very homesick, and proposed that Mrs. Clemens and Susie join him at once in London, unless she would prefer to have him come home for the winter and all of them return to London in the spring. So it is likely that the book was not then abandoned. He felt that his visit was by no means ended;

that it was, in fact, only just begun, but he wanted the ones he loved most to share it with him. To his mother and sister, in November, he wrote:

> I came here to take notes for a book, but I haven't done much but attend dinners and make speeches. I have had a jolly good time, and I do hate to go away from these English folks; they make a stranger feel entirely at home, and they laugh so easily that it is a comfort to make after-dinner speeches here. I have made hundreds of friends; and last night, in the crush at the opening of the new Guild Hall Library and Museum, I was surprised to meet a familiar face every other step.

All his impressions of England had been happy ones. He could deliver a gentle satire now and then at certain British institutions—certain London localities and features—as in his speech at the Savage Club,[1] but taking the snug island as a whole, its people, its institutions, its fair, rural aspects, he had found in it only delight. To Mrs. Crane he wrote:

> If you and Theodore will come over in the spring with Livy and me, and spend the summer, you shall see a country that is so beautiful that you will be obliged to believe in fairy-land. There is nothing like it elsewhere on the globe. You should have a season ticket and travel up and down every day between London and Oxford and worship nature.
>
> And Theodore can browse with me among dusty old dens that look now as they looked five hundred years ago; and puzzle over books in the British Museum that were made before Christ was born; and in the customs of their public dinners, and the ceremonies of every official act, and the dresses of a thousand dignitaries, trace the speech and manners of all the centuries that have dragged their lagging decades over England since the Heptarchy fell asunder. I would a good deal rather live here if I could get the rest of you over.

[1] September 28, 1872. This is probably the most characteristic speech made by Mark Twain during his first London visit; the reader will find it in full in Appendix L, at the end of last volume.

He sailed November 12th, on the *Batavia*, loaded with Christmas presents for everybody; jewelry, furs, laces; also a practical steam-engine for his namesake, Sam Moffett. Half-way across the Atlantic the *Batavia* ran into a hurricane and was badly damaged by heavy seas, and driven far out of her course. It was a lucky event on the whole, for she fell in with a water-logged lumber bark, a complete wreck, with nine surviving sailors clinging to her rigging. In the midst of the wild gale a life-boat was launched and the perishing men were rescued. Clemens prepared a graphic report of the matter for the Royal Humane Society, asking that medals be conferred upon the brave rescuers, a document that was signed by his fellow-passengers and obtained for the men complete recognition and wide celebrity. Closing, the writer said:

> As might have been anticipated, if I have been of any service toward rescuing these nine shipwrecked human beings by standing around the deck in a furious storm, without an umbrella, keeping an eye on things and seeing that they were done right, and yelling whenever a cheer seemed to be the important thing, I am glad and I am satisfied. I ask no reward. I would do it again under the same circumstances. But what I do plead for, earnestly and sincerely, is that the Royal Humane Society will remember our captain and our life-boat crew, and in so remembering them increase the high honor and esteem in which the society is held all over the civilized world.

The *Batavia* reached New York November 26, 1872. Mark Twain had been absent three months, during which he had been brought to at least a partial realization of what his work meant to him and to mankind.

An election had taken place during his absence—an election which gratified him deeply, for it had resulted in the second presidency of General Grant and in the defeat of Horace Greeley, whom he admired perhaps, but not as presidential material. To Thomas Nast, who had aided very effectually in Mr. Greeley's overwhelming defeat, Clemens wrote:

Nast, you more than any other man have won a prodigious victory for Grant—I mean, rather, for civilization and progress. Those pictures were simply marvelous, and if any man in the land has a right to hold his head up and be honestly proud of his share in this year's vast events that man is unquestionably yourself. We all do sincerely honor you, and are proud of you.

Horace Greeley's peculiar abilities and eccentricities won celebrity for him, rather than voters. Mark Twain once said of him:

"He was a great man, an honest man, and served his country well and was an honor to it. Also, he was a good-natured man, but abrupt with strangers if they annoyed him when he was busy. He was profane, but that is nothing; the best of us is that. I did not know him well, but only just casually, and by accident. I never met him but once. I called on him in the *Tribune* office, but I was not intending to. I was looking for Whitelaw Reid, and got into the wrong den. He was alone at his desk, writing, and we conversed—not long, but just a little. I asked him if he was well, and he said, 'What the hell do *you* want?' Well, I couldn't remember what I wanted, so I said I would call again. But I didn't."

Clemens did not always tell the incident just in this way. Sometimes it was John Hay he was looking for instead of Reid, and the conversation with Greeley varied; but perhaps there was a germ of history under it somewhere, and at any rate it could have happened well enough, and not have been out of character with either of the men.

LXXXVIII

"THE GILDED AGE"

MARK TWAIN did not go on the lecture circuit that winter. Redpath had besought him as usual, and even in midsummer had written:

"Will you? Won't you? We have seven thousand to eight thousand dollars in engagements recorded for you," and he named a list of towns ranging geographically from Boston to St. Paul.

But Clemens had no intention then of ever lecturing any more, and again in November, from London, he announced (to Redpath):

"When I yell again for less than $500 I'll be pretty hungry, but I haven't any intention of yelling at any price."

Redpath pursued him, and in January proposed $400 for a single night in Philadelphia, but without result. He did lecture two nights in Steinway Hall for the Mercantile Library Association, on the basis of half profits, netting $1,300 for the two nights as his share; and he lectured one night in Hartford, at a profit of $1,500, for charity. Father Hawley, of Hartford, had announced that his missionary work was suffering for lack of funds. Some of his people were actually without food, he said, their children crying with hunger. No one ever responded to an appeal like that quicker than Samuel Clemens. He offered to deliver a lecture free, and to bear an equal proportion of whatever expenses were incurred by the committee of eight who agreed to join in forwarding the project. He gave the Sandwich Island lecture, and at the close of it a large card was handed him with the figures of the receipts printed upon it. It was held up to view, and the house broke into a storm of cheers.

He did very little writing during the early weeks following his return. Early in the year (January 3 and 6, 1873) he contributed two Sandwich Island letters to the *Tribune*, in which, in his own peculiar fashion, he urged annexation.

"We must annex those people," he declared, and proceeded to specify the blessings we could give them, such as "leather-headed juries, the insanity law, and the Tweed Ring."

> We can confer Woodhull and Claflin on them, and George Francis Train. We can give them lecturers! I will go myself.
>
> We can make that little bunch of sleepy islands the hottest corner on earth, and array it in the moral splendor of our high and holy civilization. Annexation is what the poor islanders need!
>
> "Shall we, to men benighted, the lamp of life deny?"

His success in England became an incentive to certain American institutions to recognize his gifts at home. Early in the year he was dined as the guest of the Lotos Club of New York, and a week or two later elected to its membership. This was but a beginning. Some new membership or honor was offered every little while, and so many banquets that he finally invented a set form for declining them. He was not yet recognized as the foremost American man of letters, but undoubtedly he had become the most popular; and Edwin Whipple, writing at this time, or but little later, said:

"Mark Twain is regarded chiefly as a humorist, but the exercise of his real talents would rank him with the ablest of our authors in the past fifty years." So he was beginning to be "discovered" in high places.

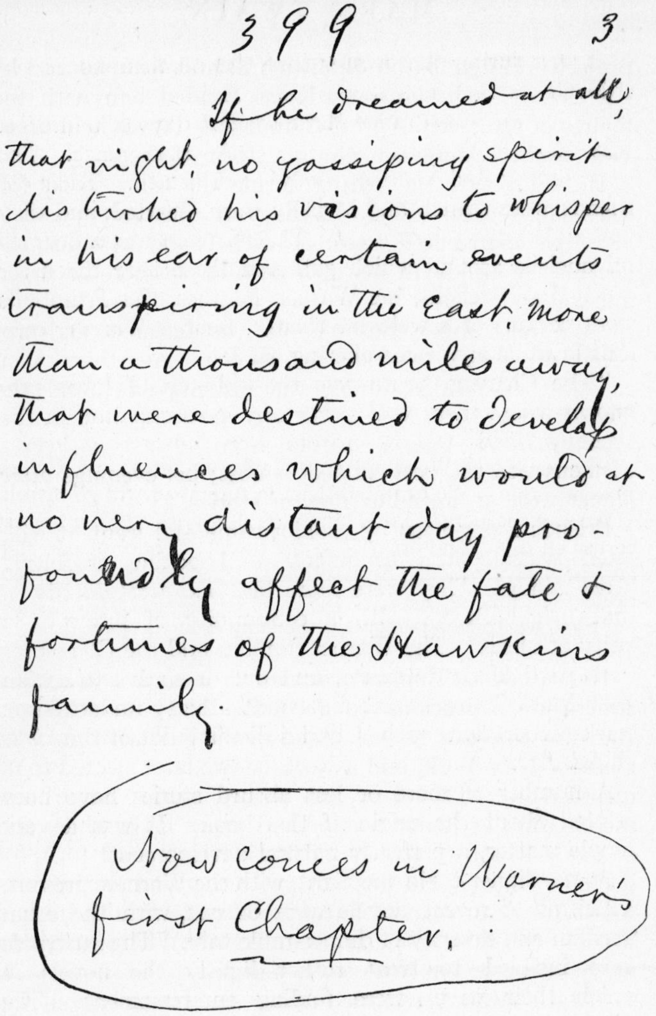
399 3

If he dreamed at all, that night, no gossiping spirit disturbed his visions to whisper in his ear of certain events transpiring in the East, more than a thousand miles away, that were destined to develop influences which would at no very distant day profoundly affect the fate & fortunes of the Hawkins family.

Now comes in Warner's first Chapter.

A PAGE FROM THE MANUSCRIPT OF "THE GILDED AGE"

The end of Mark Twain's first instalment

It was during this winter that the Clemens household enjoyed its first real home life in Hartford, its first real home life anywhere since those earliest days of marriage. The Hooker mansion was a comfortable place. The little family had comparatively good health. Their old friends were stanch and lavishly warm-hearted, and they had added many new ones. Their fireside was a delightful nucleus around which gathered those they cared for most, the Twichells, the Warner families, the Trumbulls—all certain of a welcome there. George Warner, only a little while ago, remembering, said:

"The Clemens house was the only one I have ever known where there was never any *pre*occupation in the evenings, and where visitors were always welcome. Clemens was the best kind of a host; his evenings after dinner were an unending flow of stories."

Friends living near by usually came and went at will, often without the ceremony of knocking or formal leave-taking. They were more like one great family in that neighborhood, with a community of interests, a unity of ideals. The Warner families and the Clemenses were particularly intimate, and out of their association grew Mark Twain's next important literary undertaking, his collaboration with Charles Dudley Warner in *The Gilded Age*.

A number of more or less absurd stories have been printed about the origin of this book. It was a very simple matter, a perfectly natural development.

At the dinner-table one night, with the Warners present, criticisms of recent novels were offered, with the usual freedom and severity of dinner-table talk. The husbands were inclined to treat rather lightly the novels in which their wives were finding entertainment. The wives naturally retorted that the proper thing for the husbands to do was to furnish the American people with better ones. This was regarded in the nature of a challenge, and as such was accepted—mutually accepted: that is to say, in partnership. On the spur of the moment Clemens and Warner agreed that they would do a novel together, that they would begin it immediately. This is the whole story of the book's origin; so far, at least, as the collaboration is concerned. Clemens, in fact, had the beginning of a story in his mind, but had been unwilling to undertake an extended work of fiction alone. He welcomed only too eagerly, therefore, the proposition of joint authorship. His purpose was to write a tale around that lovable character of his youth, his mother's cousin, James Lampton—to let that gentle visionary stand as the central figure against a proper background. The idea appealed to Warner, and there was no delay in the beginning. Clemens immediately set to work and completed 399 pages of the manuscript, the first eleven chapters of the book, before the early flush of enthusiasm waned.

Warner came over then, and Clemens read it aloud to him. Warner had some plans for the story, and took it up at this point, and continued it through the next twelve chapters; and so they worked alternately, "in the superstition," as Mark Twain long afterward declared, "that we were writing one coherent yarn, when I suppose, as a matter of fact, we were writing two *in*coherent ones." [1]

[1] The reader may be interested in the division of labor. Clemens wrote chapters I to XI; also chapters XXIV, XXV, XXVII, XXVIII, XXX, XXXII, XXXIII, XXXIV, XXXVI, XXXVII, XLII, XLIII, XLV, LI, LII, LIII, LVII, LIX, LX, LXI, LXII, and portions of chapters XXXV, XLIX, LVI. Warner wrote chapters XII to XXIII; also chapters XXVI, XXIX, XXXI, XXXVIII, XXXIX, XL, XLI, XLIV, XLVI, XLVII, XLVIII, L, LIV, LV, LVIII, LXIII, and portions of chapters XXXV, XLIX, and LVI. The work was therefore very evenly divided.

There was another co-worker on *The Gilded Age* before the book was finally completed. This was J. Hammond Trumbull, who pre-

The book was begun in February and finished in April, so the work did not lag. The result, if not highly artistic, made astonishingly good reading. Warner had the touch of romance, Clemens, the gift of creating, or at least of portraying, human realities. Most of his characters reflected intimate personalities of his early life. Besides the apotheosis of James Lampton into the immortal Sellers, Orion became Washington Hawkins, Squire Clemens the judge, while Mark Twain's own personality, in a greater or lesser degree, is reflected in most of his creations. As for the Tennessee land, so long a will-o'-the-wisp and a bugbear, it became tangible property at last. Only a year or two before Clemens had written to Orion:

> Oh, here! I don't want to be consulted at all about Tennessee. I don't want it even mentioned to me. When I make a suggestion it is for you to act upon it or throw it aside, but I beseech you never to ask my advice, opinion, or consent about that hated property.

But it came in good play now. It is the important theme of the story.

Mark Twain was well qualified to construct his share of the tale. He knew his characters, their lives, and their atmospheres perfectly. Senator Dilworthy (otherwise Senator Pomeroy, of Kansas, then notorious for attempted vote-buying) was familiar enough. That winter in Washington had acquainted Clemens with the life there,

pared the variegated, marvelous cryptographic chapter headings. Trumbull was the most learned man that ever lived in Hartford. He was familiar with all literary and scientific data, and according to Clemens could swear in twenty-seven languages. It was thought to be a choice idea to get Trumbull to supply a lingual medley of quotations to precede the chapters in the new book, the purpose being to excite interest and possibly to amuse the reader—a purpose which to some extent appears to have miscarried.

its political intrigues, and the disrepute of Congress. Warner was equally well qualified for his share of the undertaking, and the chief criticism that one may offer is the one stated by Clemens himself—that the divisions of the tale remain divisions rather than unity.

As for the story itself—the romance and tragedy of it—the character of Laura in the hands of either author is one not easy to forget. Whether this means that the work is well done, or only strikingly done, the reader himself must judge. Morally, the character is not justified. Laura was a victim of circumstance from the beginning. There could be no poetic justice in her doom. To drag her out of a steamer wreck, only to make her the victim of a scoundrel, later an adventuress, and finally a murderess, all may be good art, but of a very bad kind. Laura is a sort of American Becky Sharp; but there is retributive justice in Becky's fate, whereas Laura's doom is warranted only by the author's whim. As for her end, whatever the virtuous public of that day might have done, a present-day audience would not have pelted her from the stage, destroyed her future, taken away her life.

The authors regarded their work highly when it was finished, but that is nothing. Any author regards his work highly at the moment of its completion. In later years neither of them thought very well of their production; but that also is nothing. The author seldom cares very deeply for his offspring once it is turned over to the public charge. The fact that the story is still popular, still delights thousands of readers, when a myriad of novels that have been written since it was completed have lived their little day and died so utterly that even their names have passed out of memory, is the best verdict as to its worth.

LXXXIX

PLANNING A NEW HOME

CLEMENS and his wife bought a lot for the new home that winter, a fine, sightly piece of land on Farmington Avenue—table-land, sloping down to a pretty stream that wound through the willows and among the trees. They were as delighted as children with their new purchase and the prospect of building. To her sister Mrs. Clemens wrote:

> Mr. Clemens seems to glory in his sense of possession; he goes daily into the lot, has had several falls trying to lay off the land by sliding around on his feet. . . .
>
> For three days the ice has covered the trees, and they have been glorious. We could do nothing but watch the beauty outside; if you looked at the trees as the sun struck them, with your back toward the sun, they were covered with jewels. If you looked toward the sun it was all crystal whiteness, a perfect fairy-land. Then the nights were moonlight, and that was a great beauty, the moon giving us the same prismatic effect.

This was the storm of which Mark Twain wrote his matchless description, given first in his speech on New England weather, and later preserved in *Following the Equator*, in more extended form. In that book he likens an ice-storm to his impressions derived from reading descriptions of the Taj Mahal, that wonderful tomb of a fair East Indian queen. It is a marvelous bit of word-painting—his description of that majestic vision: "When every bough and twig is strung with ice-beads, frozen dewdrops, and the whole tree sparkles cold and white, like the Shah of Persia's diamond plume." It will pay any one to look up that description and read it all, though it has been said, by the fortunate one or two who heard him first give it utterance as an impromptu outburst, that in the subsequent process of writing the bloom of its original magnificence was lost.

The plans for the new house were drawn forthwith by that gentle architect Edward Potter, whose art to-day may be considered open to criticism, but not because of any lack of originality. Hartford houses of that period were mainly of the goods-box form of architecture, perfectly square, typifying the commercial pursuits of many of their owners. Potter agreed to get away from this idea, and a radical and even frenzied departure was the result. Certainly his plans presented beautiful pictures, and all who saw them were filled with wonder and delight. Architecture has lavished itself in many florescent forms since then, but we may imagine that Potter's "English violet" order of design, as he himself designated it, startled, dazzled, and captivated in a day, when most houses were mere habitations, built with a view to economy and the largest possible amount of room.

Workmen were put on the ground without delay, to prepare for the builders, and work was rapidly pushed along. Then in May the whole matter was left in the hands of the architect and the carpenters (with Lawyer Charles E. Perkins to stand between Potter and the violent builder, who roared at Potter and frightened him when he wanted changes), while the Clemens household, with Clara Spaulding, a girlhood friend of Mrs. Clemens, sailed away to England for a half-year holiday.

XC

A LONG ENGLISH HOLIDAY

THEY sailed on the *Batavia*, and with them went a young man named Thompson, a theological student whom Clemens had consented to take as an amanuensis. There is a pathetic incident connected with this young man, and it may as well be set down here. Clemens found, a few weeks after his arrival in England, that so great was the tax upon his time that he could make no use of Thompson's services. He gave Thompson fifty dollars, and upon the possibility of the young man's desiring to return to America, advanced him another fifty dollars, saying that he could return it some day, and never thought of it again. But the young man remembered it, and one day, thirty-six years later, after a life of hardship and struggle, such as the life of a country minister is apt to be, he wrote and inclosed a money-order, a payment on his debt. That letter and its inclosure brought only sorrow to Mark Twain. He felt that it laid upon him the accumulated burden of the weary thirty-six years' struggle with ill-fortune. He returned the money, of course, and in a biographical note commented:

How pale painted heroisms of romance look beside it! Thompson's heroism, which is real, which is colossal, which is sublime, and which is costly beyond all estimate, is achieved in profound obscurity, and its hero walks in rags to the end of his days. I had forgotten Thompson completely, but he flashes before me as vividly as lightning. I can see him now. It was on the deck of the *Batavia*, in the dock. The ship was casting off, with that hubbub and confusion and rushing of sailors, and shouting of orders and shrieking of boatswain whistles, which marked the departure preparations in those days—an impressive contrast with the solemn silence which marks the departure preparations of the giant ships of the present day. Mrs. Clemens, Clara Spaulding, little Susy, and the nurse-maid were all properly garbed for the occasion. We all had on our storm-rig, heavy clothes of somber hue, but new and designed and constructed for the purpose, strictly in accordance with sea-going etiquette; anything wearable on land being distinctly and odiously out of the question.

Very well. On that deck, and gliding placidly among those honorable and properly upholstered groups, appeared Thompson, young, grave, long, slim, with an aged fuzzy plug hat towering high on the upper end of him and followed by a gray duster, which flowed down, without break or wrinkle, to his ankles. He came straight to us, and shook hands and compromised us. Everybody could see that we knew him. A nigger in heaven could not have created a profounder astonishment.

However, Thompson didn't know that anything was happening. He had no prejudices about clothes. I can still see him as he looked when we passed Sandy Hook and the winds of the big ocean smote us. Erect, lofty, and grand he stood facing the blast, holding his plug on with both hands and his generous duster blowing out behind, level with his neck. There were scoffers observing, but he didn't know it; he wasn't disturbed.

In my mind, I see him once afterward, clothed as before, taking me down in shorthand. The Shah of Persia had come to England and Dr. Hosmer, of the *Herald*, had sent me to Ostend, to view his Majesty's progress across the Channel and write an account of it. I can't recall Thompson after that, and I wish *his* memory had been as poor as mine.

They had been a month in London, when the final incident referred to took place—the arrival of the Shah of Persia—and were comfortably quartered at the Langham Hotel. To Twichell Clemens wrote:

We have a luxuriously ample suite of apartments on the third floor, our bedroom looking straight up Portland Place, our parlor having a noble array of great windows looking out upon both streets (Portland Place and the crook that joins it onto Regent Street).

Nine P. M. full twilight, rich sunset tints lingering in the west.

I am not going to write anything; rather tell it when I get back. I love you and Harmony, and that is all the fresh news I've got anyway. And I mean to keep that fresh all the time.

Mrs. Clemens, in a letter to her sister, declared: "It is perfectly discouraging to try to write you. There is so much to write about that it makes me feel as if it was no use to begin."

It was a period of continuous honor and entertainment. If Mark Twain had been a lion on his first visit, he was little less than royalty now. His rooms at the Langham were like a court. Miss Spaulding (now Mrs. John B. Stanchfield) remembers that Robert Browning, Turgenieff, Sir John Millais, Lord Houghton, and Sir Charles Dilke (then at the height of his fame) were among those that called to pay their respects. In a recent letter she says:

I remember a delightful luncheon that Charles Kingsley gave for Mr. Clemens; also an evening when Lord Dunraven brought Mr. Home, the medium, Lord Dunraven telling many of the remarkable things he had seen Mr. Home do. I remember I wanted so much to see him float out of a seven or eight story window, and enter another, which Lord Dunraven said he had seen him do many times. But Mr. Home had been very ill, and said his power had left him. My great regret was that we did not see Carlyle, who was too sad and ill for visits.

Among others they met Lewis Carroll, the author of *Alice in Wonderland*, and found him so shy that it was almost impossible to get him to say a word on any subject.

"The shyest full-grown man, except Uncle Remus, I ever met," Clemens once wrote. "Dr. MacDonald and several other lively talkers were present, and the talk went briskly on for a couple of hours, but Carroll sat still all the while, except now and then when he answered a question."

At a dinner given by George Smalley they met Herbert Spencer, and at a luncheon-party at Lord Houghton's, Sir Arthur Helps, then a world-wide celebrity.

Lord Elcho, a large, vigorous man, sat at some distance down the table. He was talking earnestly about the town of Godalming. It was a deep, flowing, and inarticulate rumble, but I caught the Godalming pretty nearly every time it broke free of the rumbling, and as all the strength was on the first end of the word, it startled me every time, because it sounded so like swearing. In the middle of the luncheon Lady Houghton rose, remarked to the guests on her right and on her left, in a matter-of-fact way, "Excuse me, I have an engagement," and without further ceremony, she went off to meet it. This would have been doubtful etiquette in America. Lord Houghton told a number of delightful stories. He told them in French, and I lost nothing of them but the nubs.

Little Susy and her father thrived on London life, but after a time it wore on Mrs. Clemens. She delighted in the English cordiality and culture, but the demands were heavy, the social forms sometimes trying. Life in London was interesting, and in its way charming, but she did not enter into it with quite her husband's enthusiasm and heartiness. In the end they canceled all London engagements and quietly set out for Scotland. On the way they rested a few days in York, a venerable place such as Mark Twain always loved to describe. In a letter to Mrs. Langdon he wrote:

For the present we shall remain in this queer old walled town, with its crooked, narrow lanes, that tell us of their old day that knew no wheeled vehicles; its plaster-and-timber dwellings, with upper stories far overhanging the street, and thus marking *their* date, say three hundred years ago; the stately city walls, the castellated gates, the ivy-grown, foliage-sheltered, most noble and picturesque ruin of St. Mary's Abbey, suggesting *their* date, say five hundred years ago, in the heart of Crusading times and the glory of English chivalry and romance; the vast Cathedral of York, with its worn carvings and quaintly pictured windows, preaching of still remoter days; the outlandish names of streets and courts and byways that stand as a record and a memorial, all these centuries, of Danish dominion here in still earlier times; the hint here and there of King Arthur and his knights and their bloody fights with Saxon oppressors round about this old city more than thirteen hundred years gone by; and, last of all, the melancholy old stone coffins and sculptured inscriptions, a venerable arch and a hoary tower of stone that still remain and are kissed by the sun and caressed by the shadows every day, just as the sun and the shadows have kissed and caressed them every lagging day since the Roman Emperor's soldiers placed them here in the times when Jesus the Son of Mary walked the streets of Nazareth a youth, with no more name or fame than the Yorkshire boy who is loitering down this street this moment.

They reached Edinburgh at the end of July and secluded themselves in Veitch's family hotel in George Street, intending to see no one. But this plan was not a success; the social stress of London had been too much for Mrs. Clemens, and she collapsed immediately after their arrival. Clemens was unacquainted in Edinburgh, but remembered that Dr. John Brown, who had written *Rab and His Friend*, lived there. He learned his address, and that he was still a practising physician. He walked around to 23 Rutland Street, and made himself known. Dr. Brown came forthwith, and Mrs. Clemens speedily recovered under his able and inspiring treatment.

The association did not end there. For nearly a month Dr. Brown was their daily companion, either at the hotel, or in his own home, or on protracted drives when he made his round of visits, taking these new friends along. Dr. John was beloved by everybody in Edinburgh, everybody in Scotland, for that matter, and his story of Rab had won him a following throughout Christendom. He was an unpretentious sovereign. Clemens once wrote of him:

> His was a sweet and winning face, as beautiful a face as I have ever known. Reposeful, gentle, benignant; the face of a saint at peace with all the world and placidly beaming upon it the sunshine of love that filled his heart.

He was the friend of all dogs, and of all people. It has been told of him that once, when driving, he thrust his head suddenly out of the carriage window, then resumed his place with a disappointed look.

"Who was it?" asked his companion. "Some one you know?"

"No," he said. "A dog I *don't* know."

He became the boon companion and playmate of little Susy, then not quite a year and a half old. He called her Megalopis, a Greek term, suggested by her eyes; those deep, burning eyes that seemed always so full of life's sadder philosophies, and impending tragedy. In a collection of Dr. Brown's letters he refers to this period. In one place he says:

> Had the author of *The Innocents Abroad* not come to Edinburgh at that time we in all human probability might never have met, and what a deprivation that would have been to me during the last quarter of a century!

And in another place:

> I am attending the wife of Mark Twain. His real name is Clemens. She is a quite lovely little woman, modest and clever, and she has a girlie eighteen months old, her ludicrous miniature—and such eyes!

Those playmates, the good doctor and Megalopis, romped together through the hotel rooms with that complete abandon which few grown persons can assume in their play with children, and not all children can assume in their play with grown-ups. They played "bear," and the "bear" (which was a very little one, so little that when it stood up behind the sofa you could just get a glimpse of yellow hair) would lie in wait for her victim, and spring out and surprise him and throw him into frenzies of fear.

Almost every day they made his professional rounds with him. He always carried a basket of grapes for his patients. His guests brought along books to read while they waited. When he stopped for a call he would say:

"Entertain yourselves while I go in and reduce the population."

There was much sight-seeing to do in Edinburgh, and they could not quite escape social affairs. There were teas and luncheons and dinners with the Dunfermlines and the Abercrombies, and the MacDonalds, and with others of those brave clans that no longer slew one another among the grim northern crags and glens, but were as sociable and entertaining lords and ladies as ever the southland could produce. They were very gentle folk indeed, and Mrs. Clemens, in future years, found her heart going back oftener to Edinburgh than to any other haven of those first wanderings. August 24th she wrote to her sister:

> We leave Edinburgh to-morrow with sincere regret; we have had such a delightful stay here—we do so regret leaving Dr. Brown and his sister, thinking that we shall probably never see them again [as indeed they never did].

They spent a day or two at Glasgow and sailed for Ireland, where they put in a fortnight, and early in September were back in England again, at Chester, that queer old city where, from a tower on the wall, Charles I.

read the story of his doom. Reginald Cholmondeley had invited them to visit his country seat, beautiful Condover Hall, near Shrewsbury, and in that lovely retreat they spent some happy, restful days. Then they were in the whirl of London once more, but escaped for a fortnight to Paris, sight-seeing and making purchases for the new home.

Mrs. Clemens was quite ready to return to America by this time.

I am blue and cross and homesick [she wrote]. I suppose what makes me feel the latter is because we are contemplating to stay in London another *month*. There has not one sheet of Mr. Clemens's proof come yet, and if he goes home before the book is published here he will lose his copyright. And then his friends feel that it will be better for him to lecture in London before his book is published, not only that it will give him a larger but a more enviable reputation. I would not hesitate *one moment* if it were simply for the money that his copyright will bring him, but if his reputation will be better for his staying and lecturing, of course he ought to stay. . . . The truth is, I can't bear the thought of postponing going home.

It is rather gratifying to find Olivia Clemens human, like that, now and then. Otherwise, on general testimony, one might well be tempted to regard her as altogether of another race and kind.

XCI

A LONDON LECTURE

CLEMENS concluded to hasten the homeward journey, but to lecture a few nights in London before starting. He would then accompany his little family home, and return at once to continue the lecture series and protect his copyright. This plan was carried out. In a communication to the *Standard*, October 7th, he said:

SIR,—In view of the prevailing frenzy concerning the Sandwich Islands, and the inflamed desire of the public to acquire information concerning them, I have thought it well to tarry yet another week in England and deliver a lecture upon this absorbing subject. And lest it should be thought unbecoming in me, a stranger, to come to the public rescue at such a time, instead of leaving to abler hands a matter of so much moment, I desire to explain that I do it with the best motives and the most honorable intentions. I do it because I am convinced that no one can allay this unwholesome excitement as effectually as I can, and to allay it, and allay it as quickly as possible, is surely one thing that is absolutely necessary at this juncture. I feel and know that I am equal to this task, for I can allay any kind of an excitement by lecturing upon it. I have saved many communities in this way. I have always been able to paralyze the public interest in any topic that I chose to take hold of and elucidate with all my strength.

Hoping that this explanation will show that if I am seeming to intrude I am at least doing it from a high impulse, I am, sir, your obedient servant,

MARK TWAIN.

A day later the following announcement appeared:

QUEEN'S CONCERT ROOMS,

HANOVER SQUARE.

Mr. George Dolby begs to announce that

MR. MARK TWAIN

WILL DELIVER A

LECTURE

OF A

HUMOROUS CHARACTER,

AS ABOVE, ON

MONDAY EVENING NEXT, OCTOBER 13th, 1873,

AND REPEAT IT IN THE SAME PLACE, ON

TUESDAY	EVENING,	OCTOBER	14th,
WEDNESDAY	"	"	15th,
THURSDAY	"	"	16th,
FRIDAY	"	"	17th,

At Eight o'Clock,

AND

SATURDAY AFTERNOON, OCTOBER 18th,

At Three o'Clock.

SUBJECT:

"Our Fellow Savages of the Sandwich Islands."

As Mr. Twain has spent several months in these Islands, and is well acquainted with his subject, the Lecture may be expected to furnish matter of interest.

STALLS, 5s. UNRESERVED SEATS, 3s.

The prospect of a lecture from Mark Twain interested the London public. Those who had not seen him were willing to pay even for that privilege. The papers were encouraging; *Punch* sounded a characteristic note:

WELCOME TO A LECTURER

"'Tis time we Twain did show ourselves." 'Twas said
By Cæsar, when one Mark had lost his head:
By Mark, whose head's quite bright, 'tis said again:
Therefore, "go with me, friends, to bless this Twain."
—*Punch.*

Dolby had managed the Dickens lectures, and he proved his sound business judgment and experience by taking the largest available hall in London for Mark Twain.

On the evening of October 13th, in the spacious Queen's Concert Rooms, Hanover Square, Mark Twain delivered his first public address in England. The subject was "Our Fellow Savages of the Sandwich Islands," the old lecture with which he had made his first great successes. He was not introduced. He appeared on the platform in evening dress, assuming the character of a manager announcing a disappointment.

Mr. Clemens, he said, had fully expected to be present. He paused and loud murmurs arose from the audience. He lifted his hand and they subsided. Then he added, "I am happy to say that Mark Twain is present, and will now give his lecture." Whereupon the audience roared its approval.

It would be hardly an exaggeration to say that his triumph that week was a regal one. For five successive nights and a Saturday matinée the culture and fashion of London thronged to hear him discourse of their "fellow savages." It was a lecture event wholly without precedent. The lectures of Artemus Ward,[1] who had

[1] "Artemus the delicious," as Charles Reade called him, came to London in June, 1866, and gave his "piece" in Egyptian Hall. The refined, delicate, intellectual countenance, the sweet, grave,

quickly become a favorite in London, had prepared the public for American platform humor, while the daily doings of this new American product, as reported by the press, had aroused interest, or curiosity, to a high pitch. On no occasion in his own country had he won such a complete triumph. The papers for a week devoted columns of space to appreciation and editorial comment. The *Daily News* of October 17th published a column-and-a-half editorial on American humor, with Mark Twain's public appearance as the general text. The *Times* referred to the continued popularity of the lectures:

They can't be said to have more than whetted the public appetite, if we are to take the fact which has been imparted to us, that the holding capacity of the Hanover Square Rooms has been inadequate to the demand made upon it every night by Twain's lecturing, as a criterion. The last lecture of this too brief course was delivered yesterday before an audience which crammed to discomfort every part of the principal apartment of the Hanover Square Rooms. . . .

At the close of yesterday's lecture Mark Twain was so loudly applauded that he returned to the stage, and, as soon as the audience gave him a chance of being heard, he said, with much apparent emotion:

"Ladies and Gentlemen,—I won't keep you one single mo-

mouth, from which one might have expected philosophical lectures, retained their seriousness while listeners were convulsed with laughter. There was something magical about it. Every sentence was a surprise. He played on his audience as Liszt did on a piano—most easily when most effectively. Who can ever forget his attempt to stop his Italian pianist—"a count in his own country, but not much account in this"—who went on playing loudly while he was trying to tell us an "affecting incident" that occurred near a small clump of trees shown on his panorama of the Far West. The music stormed on—we could see only lips and arms pathetically moving till the piano suddenly ceased, and we heard—it was all we heard—"and she fainted in Reginald's arms." His tricks have been attempted in many theaters, but Artemus Ward was inimitable. And all the time the man was dying. (Moncure D. Conway, *Autobiography*.)

ment in this suffocating atmosphere. I simply wish to say that this is the last lecture I shall have the honor to deliver in London until I return from America, four weeks from now. I only wish to say (here Mr. Clemens faltered as if too much affected to proceed) I am very grateful. I do not wish to appear pathetic, but it is something magnificent for a stranger to come to the metropolis of the world and be received so handsomely as I have been. I simply thank you."

The *Saturday Review* devoted a page, and *Once a Week*, under the head of "Cracking Jokes," gave three pages, to praise of the literary and lecture methods of the new American humorist. With the promise of speedy return, he left London, gave the lecture once in Liverpool, and with his party (October 21st) set sail for home.

In mid-Atlantic he remembered Dr. Brown, and wrote him:

We have plowed a long way over the sea, and there's twenty-two hundred miles of restless water between us now, besides the railway stretch. And yet you are so present with us, so close to us, that a span and a whisper would bridge the distance.

So it would seem that of all the many memories of that eventful half-year, that of Dr. Brown was the most present, the most tender.

XCII

FURTHER LONDON LECTURE TRIUMPHS

ORION CLEMENS records that he met "Sam and Livy" on their arrival from England, November 2d, and that the president of the Mercantile Library Association sent up his card "*four times,*" in the hope of getting a chance to propose a lecture engagement—an incident which impressed Orion deeply in its evidence of his brother's towering importance. Orion himself was by this time engaged in various projects. He was inventing a flying-machine, for one thing, writing a Jules Verne story, reading proof on a New York daily, and contemplating the lecture field. This great blaze of international appreciation which had come to the little boy who used to set type for him in Hannibal, and wash up the forms and cry over the dirty proof, made him gasp.

> They went to see Booth in *Hamlet* [he says], and Booth sent for Sam to come behind the scenes, and when Sam proposed to add a part to *Hamlet*, the part of a bystander who makes humorous modern comment on the situations in the play, Booth laughed immoderately.

Proposing a sacrilege like that to Booth! To what heights had this printer-pilot, miner-brother not attained![1]

[1] This idea of introducing a new character in *Hamlet* was really attempted later by Mark Twain, with the connivance of Joe Goodman [of all men], sad to relate. So far as is known it is the one stain on Goodman's literary record.

Clemens returned immediately to England—the following Saturday, in fact—and was back in London lecturing again after barely a month's absence. He gave the "Roughing It" address, this time under the title of "Roughing It on the Silver Frontier," and if his audiences were any less enthusiastic, or his houses less crowded than before, the newspapers of that day have left no record of it. It was the height of the season now, and being free to do so, he threw himself into the whirl of it, and for two months, beyond doubt, was the most talked-of figure in London. The Athenæum Club made him a visiting member (an honor considered next to knighthood); *Punch* quoted him; societies banqueted him; his apartments, as before, were besieged by callers. Afternoons one was likely to find him in "Poets' Corner" of the Langham smoking-room, with a group of London and American authors—Reade, Collins, Miller, and the others—frankly rioting in his bold fancies. Charles Warren Stoddard was in London at the time, and acted as his secretary. Stoddard was a gentle poet, a delightful fellow, and Clemens was very fond of him. His only complaint of Stoddard was that he did not laugh enough at his humorous yarns. Clemens once said:

"Dolby and I used to come in after the lecture, or perhaps after being out to some dinner, and we liked to sit down and talk it over and tell yarns, and we expected Stoddard to laugh at them, but Stoddard would lie there on the couch and snore. Otherwise, as a secretary, he was perfect."

The great Tichborne trial was in progress then, and the spectacle of an illiterate impostor trying to establish his claim as the rightful heir to a great estate was highly diverting to Mark Twain.[1] He wanted to preserve the evidence as future literary material, and Stoddard day

[1] In a letter of this period he speaks of having attended one of the Claimant's "Evenings."

after day patiently collected the news reports and neatly pasted them into scrap-books, where they still rest, a complete record of that now forgotten farce. The Tichborne trial recalled to Mark Twain the claimant in the Lampton family, who from time to time wrote him long letters, urging him to join in the effort to establish his rights to the earldom of Durham. This American claimant was a distant cousin, who had "somehow gotten hold of, or had fabricated a full set of documents."

Colonel Henry Watterson, just quoted (also a Lampton connection), adds:

> During the Tichborne trial Mark and I were in London, and one day he said to me: "I have investigated this Durham business down at the Herald's office. There is nothing to it. The Lamptons passed out of the earldom of Durham a hundred years ago. There were never any estates; the title lapsed; the present earldom is a new creation, not in the same family at all. But I'll tell you what: if you'll put up $500, I'll put up $500 more; we'll bring our chap over here and set him in as claimant, and, my word for it, Kenealy's fat boy won't be a marker to him."

It was a characteristic Mark Twain project, one of the sort he never carried out in reality, but loved to follow in fancy, and with the pen sometimes. The "Rightful Earl of Durham" continued to send letters for a long time after that (some of them still exist), but he did not establish his claim. No one but Mark Twain ever really got anything out of it. Like the Tennessee land, it furnished material by and by for a book. Colonel Watterson goes on to say that Clemens was only joking about having looked up the matter in the peerage; that he hadn't really looked it up at all, and that the earldom lies still in the Lampton family.

Another of Clemens's friends in London at this time was Prentice Mulford, of California. In later years

Mulford acquired a wide reputation for his optimistic and practical psychologies. Through them he lifted himself out of the slough of despond, and he sought to extend a helping hand to others. His "White Cross Library" had a wide reading and a wide influence; perhaps has to this day. But in 1873 Mulford had not found the tangibility of thought, the secret of strength; he was only finding it, maybe, in his frank acknowledgment of shortcoming:

Now, Mark, I am down—very much down at present; you are up—where you deserve to be. I can't ask this on the score of any past favors, for there have been none. I have not always spoken of you in terms of extravagant praise; have sometimes criticized you, which was due, I suppose, in part to an envious spirit. I am simply human. Some people in the same profession say they entertain no jealousy of those more successful. I can't. They are divine; I am not.

It was only that he wished Clemens to speak a word for him to Routledge, to get him a hearing for his work. He adds:

I shall be up myself some day, although my line is far apart from yours. Whether you can do anything that I ask of you or not, I shall be happy then, as I would be now, to do you any just and right service. . . . Perhaps I have mistaken my vocation. Certainly, if I was back with my rocker on the Tuolumne, I'd make it rattle livelier than ever I did before. I have occasionally thought of London Bridge, but the Thames is now so d—d cold and dirty, and besides I can swim, and any attempt at drowning would, through the mere instinct of self-preservation, only result in my swimming ashore and ruining my best clothes; wherefore I should be worse off than ever.

Of course Mark Twain granted the favor Mulford asked, and a great deal more, no doubt, for that was his way. Mulford came up, as he had prophesied, but the sea in due time claimed him, though not in the way he had contemplated. Years after he was one day found drifting off the shores of Long Island in an open boat, dead.

Clemens made a number of notable dinner speeches during this second London lecture period. His response to the toast of the "Ladies," delivered at the annual dinner of the Scottish Corporation of London, was the sensational event of the evening.

He was obliged to decline an invitation to the Lord Mayor's dinner, whereupon his Lordship wrote to urge him to be present at least at the *finale*, when the welcome would be "none the less hearty," and bespoke his attendance for any future dinners.

Clemens lectured steadily at the Hanover Square Rooms during the two months of his stay in London, and it was only toward the end of this astonishing engagement that the audience began to show any sign of diminishing. Early in January he wrote to Twichell:

> I am not going to the provinces because I cannot get halls that are large enough. I always felt cramped in the Hanover Square Rooms, but I find that everybody here speaks with awe and respect of that prodigious hall and wonders that I could fill it so long.
>
> I am *hoping* to be back in twenty days, but I have *so much* to go home to and enjoy with a jubilant joy that it hardly seems possible that it can come to pass in so uncertain a world as this.

In the same letter he speaks of attending an exhibition of Landseer's paintings at the Royal Academy:

> Ah, they are wonderfully beautiful! There are such rich moonlights and dusks in the "Challenge" and the "Combat," and in that long flight of birds across a lake in the subdued flush of sunset (or sunrise, for no man can ever tell t'other from which in a picture, except it has the filmy morning mist breathing itself up from the water), and there is such a grave analytical

profundity in the face of the connoisseurs; and such pathos in the picture of a fawn suckling its dead mother on a snowy waste, with only the blood in the footprints to hint that she is not asleep. And the way that he makes animals' flesh and blood, insomuch that if the room were darkened ever so little, and a motionless living animal placed beside the painted one, no man could tell which was which.

I interrupted myself here, to drop a line to Shirley Brooks and suggest a cartoon for *Punch*. It was this: in one of the Academy saloons (in a suite where these pictures are) a fine bust of Landseer stands on a pedestal in the center of the room. I suggested that some of Landseer's best known animals be represented as having come down out of their frames in the moonlight and grouped themselves about the bust in mourning attitudes.

He sailed January 13 (1874), on the *Parthia*, and two weeks later was at home, where all was going well. *The Gilded Age* had been issued a day or two before Christmas, and was already in its third edition. By the end of January 26,000 copies had been sold, a sale that had increased to 40,000 a month later. The new house was progressing, though it was by no means finished. Mrs. Clemens was in good health. Little Susy was full of such American activities as to earn the name of "The Modoc." The promise of the year was bright.

XCIII

THE REAL COLONEL SELLERS—GOLDEN DAYS

THERE are bound to be vexations, flies in the ointment, as we say. It was Warner who conferred the name of Eschol Sellers on the chief figure of the collaborated novel. Warner had known it as the name of an obscure person, or perhaps he had only heard of it. At all events, it seemed a good one for the character and had been adopted. But behold, the book had been issued but a little while when there rose "out of the vasty deeps" a genuine Eschol Sellers, who was a very respectable person. He was a stout, prosperous-looking man, gray and about fifty-five years old. He came into the American Publishing Company offices and asked permission to look at the book. Mr. Bliss was out at the moment, but presently arrived. The visitor rose and introduced himself.

"My name is Eschol Sellers," he said. "You have used it in one of your publications. It has brought upon me a lot of ridicule. My people wish me to sue you for $10,000 damages."

He had documents to prove his identity, and there was only one thing to be done; he must be satisfied. Bliss agreed to recall as many of the offending volumes as possible and change the name on the plates. He consulted the authors, and the name Beriah was substituted for the offending Eschol. It turned out that the real Sellers family was a large one, and that the given name Eschol was not uncommon in its several branches. This particular Eschol Sellers, curiously enough, was an inventor and a promoter, though of a much more substantial sort than his fiction namesake. He was also a painter of considerable merit, a writer and an antiquarian. He was said to have been a grandson of the famous painter, Rembrandt Peale.

Clemens vowed that he would not lecture in America that winter. The irrepressible Redpath besieged him as usual, and at the end of January Clemens telegraphed him, as he thought, finally. Following it with a letter of explanation, he added:

"I said to her, 'There isn't money enough in America to hire me to leave you for one day.'"

But Redpath was a persistent devil. He used arguments and held out inducements which even Mrs. Clemens thought should not be resisted, and Clemens yielded from time to time, and gave a lecture here and there during February. Finally, on the 3d of March (1874) he telegraphed his tormentor:

"Why don't you congratulate me? I never expect to stand on a lecture platform again after Thursday night."

Howells tells delightfully of a visit which he and Aldrich paid to Hartford just at this period. Aldrich went to visit Clemens and Howells to visit Charles Dudley Warner, Clemens coming as far as Springfield to welcome them.

> In the good-fellowship of that cordial neighborhood we had two such days as the aging sun no longer shines on in his round. There was constant running in and out of friendly houses where the lively hosts and guests called one another by their Christian names or nicknames, and no such vain ceremony as knocking or ringing at doors. Clemens was then building the stately mansion in which he satisfied his love of magnificence as if it had been another sealskin coat, and he was at the crest of the prosperity which enabled him to humor every whim or extravagance.

WILLIAM DEAN HOWELLS

THOMAS BAILEY ALDRICH

REV. JOSEPH H. TWICHELL

CHARLES DUDLEY WARNER

FOUR OF MARK TWAIN'S FRIENDS

Howells tells how Clemens dilated on the advantages of subscription sale over the usual methods of publication, and urged the two Boston authors to prepare something which canvassers could handle.

"Why, any other means of bringing out a book is privately printing it," he declared, and added that his subscription books in Bliss's hands sold right along, "just like the Bible."

On the way back to Boston Howells and Aldrich planned a subscription book which would sell straight along, like the Bible. It was to be called "Twelve Memorable Murders." They had dreamed two or three fortunes by the time they had reached Boston, but the project ended there.

"We never killed a single soul," Howells said once to the writer of this memoir.

Clemens was always urging Howells to visit him after that. He offered all sorts of inducements.

> You will find us the most reasonable people in the world. We had thought of precipitating upon you, George Warner and his wife one day, Twichell and his jewel of a wife another day, and Charles Perkins and wife another. Only those—simply members of our family they are. But I'll close the door against them all, which will "fix" all of the lot except Twichell, who will no more hesitate to climb in the back window than *nothing*.
>
> And you shall go to bed when you please, get up when you please, talk when you please, read when you please.

A little later he was urging Howells or Aldrich, or both of them, to come to Hartford to live.

> Mr. Hall, who lives in the house next to Mrs. Stowe's (just where we drive in to go to our new house), will sell for $16,000 or $17,000. You can do your work just as well here as in Cambridge, can't you? Come! Will one of you boys buy that house? Now, say yes.

Certainly those were golden, blessed days, and perhaps, as Howells says, the sun does not shine on their like any more—not in Hartford, at least, for the old group that made them no longer assembles there. Hartford about this time became a sort of shrine for all literary visitors, and for other notables as well, whether of America or from overseas. It was the half-way place between Boston and New York, and pilgrims going in either direction rested there. It is said that travelers arriving in America were apt to remember two things they wished to see: Niagara Falls and Mark Twain. But the Falls had no such recent advertising advantage as that spectacular success in London. Visitors were apt to begin in Hartford.

Howells went with considerable frequency after that, or rather with regularity, twice a year, or oftener, and his coming was always hailed with great rejoicing. They visited and ate around at one place and another among that pleasant circle of friends. But they were happiest afterward together, Clemens smoking continually, "soothing his tense nerves with a mild hot Scotch," says Howells, "while we both talked, and talked, and talked of everything in the heavens and on the earth, and the waters under the earth. After two days of this talk I would come away hollow, realizing myself best in the image of one of those locust-shells which you find sticking to the bark of trees at the end of summer." Sometimes Clemens told the story of his early life, "the inexhaustible, the fairy, the *Arabian Nights* story, which I could never tire of even when it began to be told over again."

XCIV

BEGINNING "TOM SAWYER"

THE Clemens household went to Quarry Farm in April, leaving the new house once more in the hands of the architect and builders. It was costing a vast sum of money, and there was a financial stress upon land. Mrs. Clemens, always prudent, became a little uneasy at times, though without warrant in those days, for her business statement showed that her holdings were only a little less than a quarter of a million in her own right, while her husband's books and lectures had been highly remunerative, and would be more so. They were justified in living in ample, even luxurious comfort, and how free from financial worries they could have lived for the rest of their days!

Clemens, realizing his happiness, wrote Dr. Brown:

> Indeed I *am* thankful for the wifey and the child, and if there is one individual creature on all this footstool who is more thoroughly and uniformly and unceasingly *happy* than I am I defy the world to produce him and *prove* him. In my opinion he don't exist. I was a mighty rough, coarse, unpromising subject when Livy took charge of me, four years ago, and I may *still* be to the rest of the world, but not to her. She has made a very creditable job of me.

Truly fortune not only smiled, but laughed. Every mail brought great bundles of letters that sang his praises. Robert Watt, who had translated his books into Danish, wrote of their wide popularity among his people. Madame

Blanc (Th. Bentzon), who as early as 1872 had translated *The Jumping Frog* into French, and published it, with extended comment on the author and his work, in the *Revue des deux mondes*, was said to be preparing a review of *The Gilded Age*. All the world seemed ready to do him honor.

Of course, one must always pay the price, usually a vexatious one. Bores stopped him on the street to repeat ancient and witless stories. Invented anecdotes, some of them exasperating ones, went the rounds of the press. Impostors in distant localities personated him, or claimed to be near relatives, and obtained favors, sometimes money, in his name. Trivial letters, seeking benefactions of every kind, took the savor from his daily mail. Letters from literary aspirants were so numerous that he prepared a "form" letter of reply:

DEAR SIR OR MADAM,—Experience has not taught me very much, still it has taught me that it is not wise to criticize a piece of literature, except to an *enemy* of the person who wrote it; then if you praise it that enemy admires you for your honest manliness, and if you dispraise it he admires you for your sound judgment.

Yours truly, S. L. C.

Even Orion, now in Keokuk on a chicken farm, pursued him with manuscripts and proposals of schemes. Clemens had bought this farm for Orion, who had counted on large and quick returns, but was planning new enterprises before the first eggs were hatched. Orion Clemens was as delightful a character as was ever created in fiction, but he must have been a trial now and then to Mark Twain. We may gather something of this from a letter written by the latter to his mother and sister at this period:

I *can't* "encourage" Orion. Nobody can do that conscientiously, for the reason that before one's letter has time to reach him he is off on some new wild-goose chase. Would you encourage in literature a man who the older he grows the worse he writes?

I cannot encourage him to try the ministry, because he would change his religion so fast that he would have to keep a traveling agent under wages to go ahead of him to engage pulpits and board for him.

I cannot conscientiously encourage him to do *anything* but potter around his little farm and put in his odd hours contriving new and impossible projects at the rate of 365 a year—which is his customary average. He says he did well in Hannibal! Now there is a man who ought to be entirely satisfied with the grandeurs, emoluments, and activities of a hen farm.

If you ask me to pity Orion I can do that. I can do it every day and all day long. But one can't "encourage" quicksilver, because the instant you put your finger on it, it isn't there. No, I am saying too much. He *does* stick to his literary and legal aspirations, and he naturally would elect the very two things which he is wholly and preposterously unfitted for. If I ever become able, I mean to put Orion on a regular pension without revealing the fact that it is a pension.

He did presently allow the pension, a liberal one, which continued until neither Orion Clemens nor his wife had further earthly need of it.

Mark Twain for some time had contemplated one of the books that will longest preserve his memory, *The Adventures of Tom Sawyer*. The success of *Roughing It* naturally made him cast about for other autobiographical material, and he remembered those days along the river-front in Hannibal—his skylarking with Tom Blankenship, the Bowen boys, John Briggs, and the rest. He had recognized these things as material—inviting material it was—and now in the cool luxury of Quarry Farm he set himself to spin the fabric of youth.

He found summer-time always his best period for literary effort, and on a hillside just by the old quarry, Mrs. Crane had built for him that spring a study—a little room of windows, somewhat suggestive of a pilot-house

—overlooking the long sweep of grass and the dream-like city below. Vines were planted that in the course of time would cover and embower it; there was a tiny fireplace for chilly days. To Twichell, of his new retreat, Clemens wrote:

> It is the loveliest study you ever saw. It is octagonal, with a peaked roof, each face filled with a spacious window, and it sits perched in complete isolation on the top of an elevation that commands leagues of valley and city and retreating ranges of distant blue hills. It is a cozy nest and just room in it for a sofa, table, and three or four chairs, and when the storms sweep down the remote valley and the lightning flashes behind the hills beyond, and the rain beats upon the roof over my head, imagine the luxury of it.

He worked steadily there that summer. He would go up mornings, after breakfast, remaining until nearly dinner-time, say until five o'clock or after, for it was not his habit to eat luncheon. Other members of the family did not venture near the place, and if he was urgently wanted they blew a horn. Each evening he brought down his day's performance to read to the assembled family. He felt the need of audience and approval. Usually he earned the latter, but not always. Once, when for a day he put aside other matters to record a young undertaker's love-affair, and brought down the result in the evening, fairly bubbling with the joy of it, he met with a surprise. The tale was a ghastly burlesque, its humor of the most disheartening, unsavory sort. No one spoke during the reading, nobody laughed. The air was thick with disapproval. His voice lagged and faltered toward the end. When he finished there was heavy silence. Mrs. Clemens was the only one who could speak.

"Youth, let's walk a little," she said.

The "Undertaker's Love Story" is still among the

THE STUDY AT QUARRY FARM

MARK TWAIN IN STUDY AT QUARRY FARM

manuscripts of that period, but it is unlikely that it will ever see the light of print.[1]

The *Tom Sawyer* tale progressed steadily and satisfactorily. Clemens wrote Dr. Brown:

> I have been writing fifty pages of manuscript a day, on an average, for some time now, on a book (a story), and consequently have been so wrapped up in it, and dead to everything else, that I have fallen mighty short in letter-writing. . . .
>
> On hot days I spread the study wide open, anchor my papers down with brickbats, and write in the midst of the hurricane, clothed in the same thin linen we make shirts of.

He incloses some photographs in this letter.

> The group [he says] represents the vine-clad carriageway in front of the farm-house. On the left is Megalopis sitting in the lap of her German nurse-maid. I am sitting behind them. Mrs. Crane is in the center. Mr. Crane next to her. Then Mrs. Clemens and the new baby. Her Irish nurse stands at her back. Then comes the table waitress, a young negro girl, born free. Next to her is Auntie Cord (a fragment of whose history I have just sent to a magazine). She is the cook; was in slavery more than forty years; and the self-satisfied wench, the last of the group, is the little baby's American nurse-maid. In the middle distance my mother-in-law's coachman (up on errand) has taken a position unsolicited to help out the picture. No, that is not true. He was waiting there a minute or two before the photographer came. In the extreme background, under the archway, you glimpse my study.

The "new baby," "Bay," as they came to call her, was another little daughter, born in June, a happy, healthy addition to the household. In a letter written to Twichell we get a sweet summer picture of this

[1] This tale bears no relation to "The Undertaker's Story" in *Sketches New and Old.*

period, particularly of little sunny-haired, two-year-old Susy.

There is nothing selfish about the Modoc. She is fascinated with the new baby. The Modoc rips and tears around outdoors most of the time, and consequently is as hard as a pine-knot and as brown as an Indian. She is bosom friend to all the chickens, ducks, turkeys, and guinea-hens on the place. Yesterday, as she marched along the winding path that leads up the hill through the red-clover beds to the summer-house, there was a long procession of these fowls stringing contentedly after her, led by a stately rooster, who can look over the Modoc's head. The devotion of these vassals has been purchased with daily largess of Indian meal, and so the Modoc, attended by her body-guard, moves in state wherever she goes.

There were days, mainly Sundays, when he did not work at all; peaceful days of lying fallow, dreaming in shady places, drowsily watching little Susy, or reading with Mrs. Clemens. Howells's "Foregone Conclusion" was running in the *Atlantic* that year, and they delighted in it. Clemens wrote the author:

I should think that this must be the daintiest, truest, most admirable workmanship that was ever put on a story. The creatures of God do not act out their natures more unerringly than yours do. If *your* genuine stories can die I wonder by what right old Walter Scott's artificialities shall continue to live.

At other times he found comfort in the society of Theodore Crane. These two were always fond of each other, and often read together the books in which they were mutually interested. They had portable-hammock arrangements, which they placed side by side on the lawn, and read and discussed through summer afternoons. *The Mutineers of the Bounty* was one of the books they liked best, and there was a story of an Iceland farmer, a human document, that had an unfading interest. Also there were certain articles in old numbers of the *Atlantic* that

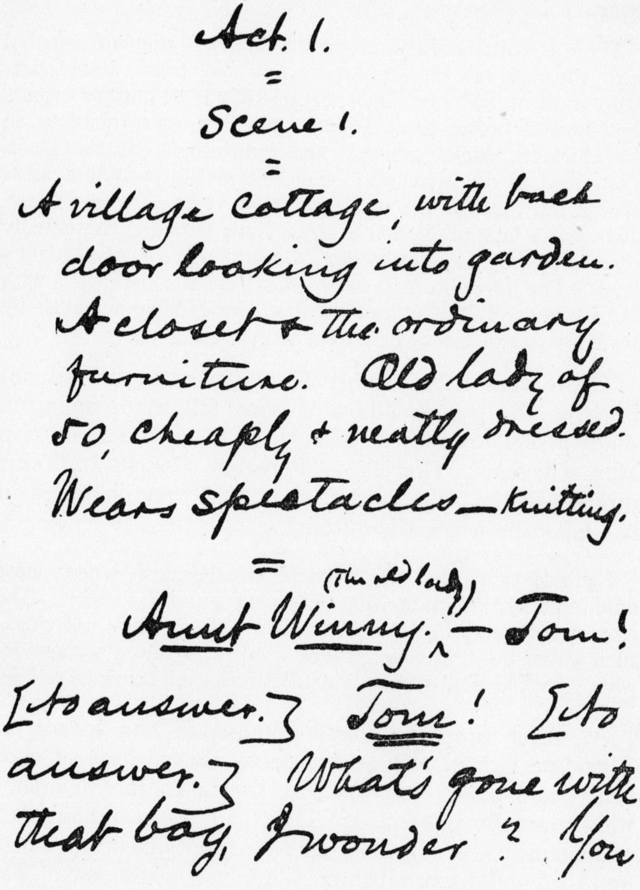

Act 1.

=

Scene 1.

=

A village cottage, with back door looking into garden. A closet & the ordinary furniture. Old lady of 50, cheaply & neatly dressed. Wears spectacles—knitting.

=

Aunt Winny. (the old lady)—Tom! [No answer.] Tom! [No answer.] What's gone with that boy, I wonder? You

FIRST MANUSCRIPT PAGE OF "TOM SAWYER." BEGUN AS A PLAY ABOUT 1872. "AUNT WINNY" LATER BECAME "AUNT POLLY"

they read and reread. *Pepys' Diary*, *Two Years Before the Mast*, and a book on the Andes were reliable favorites. Mark Twain read not so many books, but read a few books often. Those named were among the literature he asked for each year of his return to Quarry Farm. Without them, the farm and the summer would not be the same.

Then there was Lecky's *History of European Morals;* there were periods when they read Lecky avidly and discussed it in original and unorthodox ways. Mark Twain found an echo of his own philosophies in Lecky. He made frequent marginal notes along the pages of the world's moral history—notes not always quotable in the family circle. Mainly, however, they were short, crisp interjections of assent or disapproval. In one place Lecky refers to those who have undertaken to prove that all our morality is a product of experience, holding that a desire to obtain happiness and to avoid pain is the only possible motive to action; the reason, and the only reason, why we should perform virtuous actions being "that on the whole such a course will bring us the greatest amount of happiness." Clemens has indorsed these philosophies by writing on the margin, "Sound and true." It was the philosophy which he himself would always hold (though, apparently, never live by), and in the end would embody a volume of his own.[1] In another place Lecky, himself speaking, says:

> Fortunately we are all dependent for many of our pleasures on others. Co-operation and organization are essential to our happiness, and these are impossible without some restraint being placed upon our appetites. Laws are made to secure this restraint, and being sustained by rewards and punishments they make it the interest of the individual to regard that of the community.

[1] *What Is Man?* Privately printed in 1906.

"Correct!" comments Clemens. "He has proceeded from unreasoned selfishness to reasoned selfishness. All our acts, reasoned and unreasoned, are selfish." It was a conclusion he logically never departed from; not the happiest one, it would seem, at first glance, but one easier to deny than to disprove.

On the back of an old envelope Mark Twain set down his literary declaration of this period.

"I like history, biography, travels, curious facts and strange happenings, and science. And I detest novels, poetry, and theology."

But of course the novels of Howells would be excepted; Lecky was not theology, but the history of it; his taste for poetry would develop later, though it would never become a fixed quantity, as was his devotion to history and science. His interest in these amounted to a passion.

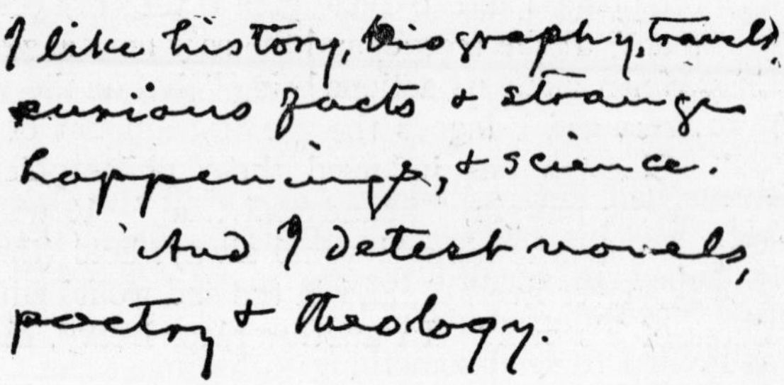
I like history, biography, travels, curious facts & strange happenings, & science.
And I detest novels, poetry & theology.

XCV

AN "ATLANTIC" STORY AND A PLAY

THE reference to "Auntie Cord" in the letter to Dr. Brown brings us to Mark Twain's first contribution to the *Atlantic Monthly*. Howells in his *Recollections* of his *Atlantic* editorship, after referring to certain Western contributors, says:

> Later came Mark Twain, originally of Missouri, but then provisionally of Hartford, and now ultimately of the solar system, not to say the universe. He came first with "A True Story," one of those noble pieces of humanity with which the South has atoned chiefly, if not solely, through him for all its despite to the negro.

Clemens had long aspired to appear in the *Atlantic*, but such was his own rating of his literature that he hardly hoped to qualify for its pages. Twichell remembers his "mingled astonishment and triumph" when he was invited to send something to the magazine.

He was obliged to "send something" once or twice before the acceptance of "A True Story," the narrative of Auntie Cord, and even this acceptance brought with it the return of a fable which had accompanied it, with the explanation that a fable like that would disqualify the magazine for every denominational reader, though Howells hastened to express his own joy in it, having been particularly touched by the author's reference to Sisyphus and Atlas as ancestors of the tumble-bug. The "True Story," he said, with its "realest king of black talk," won him, and a few days later he wrote again: "This little story delights me more and more. I wish you had about forty of 'em."

And so, modestly enough, as became him, for the story was of the simplest, most unpretentious sort, Mark Twain entered into the school of the elect.

In his letter to Howells, accompanying the MS., the author said:

> I inclose also "A True Story," which has no humor in it. You can pay as lightly as you choose for that if you want it, for it is rather out of my line. I have not altered the old colored woman's story, except to begin it at the beginning, instead of the middle, as she did—and traveled both ways.

Howells in his *Recollections* tells of the business anxiety in the *Atlantic* office in the effort to estimate the story's pecuniary value. Clemens and Harte had raised literary rates enormously; the latter was reputed to have received as much as five cents a word from affluent newspapers! But the *Atlantic* was poor, and when sixty dollars was finally decided upon for the three pages (about two and a half cents a word) the rate was regarded as handsome —without precedent in *Atlantic* history. Howells adds that as much as forty times this amount was sometimes offered to Mark Twain in later years. Even in '74 he had received a much higher rate than that offered by the *Atlantic*, but no acceptance, then or later, ever made him happier, or seemed more richly rewarded.

"A True Story, Repeated Word for Word as I Heard It" was precisely what it claimed to be.[1] Auntie Cord, the Auntie Rachel of that tale, cook at Quarry Farm, was a Virginia negress who had been twice sold as a slave, and was proud of the fact; particularly proud that she had brought $1,000 on the block. All her children had

[1] *Atlantic Monthly* for November, 1874; also included in *Sketches New and Old*.

been sold away from her, but it was a long time ago, and now at sixty she was fat and seemingly without care. She had told her story to Mrs. Crane, who had more than once tried to persuade her to tell it to Clemens; but Auntie Cord was reluctant. One evening, however, when the family sat on the front veranda in the moonlight, looking down on the picture city, as was their habit, Auntie Cord came around to say good night, and Clemens engaged her in conversation. He led up to her story, and almost before she knew it she was seated at his feet telling the strange tale in almost the exact words in which it was set down by him next morning. It gave Mark Twain a chance to exercise two of his chief gifts—transcription and portrayal. He was always greater at these things than at invention. Auntie Cord's story is a little masterpiece.

He wished to do more with Auntie Cord and her associates of the farm, for they were extraordinarily interesting. Two other negroes on the place, John Lewis and his wife (we shall hear notably of Lewis later), were not always on terms of amity with Auntie Cord. They disagreed on religion, and there were frequent battles in the kitchen. These depressed the mistress of the house, but they gave only joy to Mark Twain. His Southern raising had given him an understanding of their humors, their native emotions which made these riots a spiritual gratification. He would slip around among the shrubbery and listen to the noise and strife of battle, and hug himself with delight. Sometimes they resorted to missiles—stones, tinware—even dressed poultry which Auntie Cord was preparing for the oven. Lewis was very black, Auntie Cord was a bright mulatto, Lewis's wife several shades lighter. Wherever the discussion began it promptly shaded off toward the color-line and insult. Auntie Cord was a Methodist; Lewis was a Dunkard. Auntie Cord was ignorant and dogmatic; Lewis could read and was intelligent. Theology invariably led to personality, and eventually to epithets, crockery, geology, and victuals. How the greatest joker of the age did enjoy that summer warfare!

The fun was not all one-sided. An incident of that summer probably furnished more enjoyment for the colored members of the household than it did for Mark Twain. Lewis had some fowls, and among them was a particularly pestiferous guinea-hen that used to get up at three in the morning and go around making the kind of a noise that a guinea-hen must like and is willing to get up early to hear. Mark Twain did not care for it. He stood it as long as he could one morning, then crept softly from the house to stop it.

It was a clear, bright night; locating the guinea-hen, he slipped up stealthily with a stout stick. The bird was pouring out its heart, tearing the moonlight to tatters. Stealing up close, Clemens made a vicious swing with his bludgeon, but just then the guinea stepped forward a little, and he missed. The stroke and his explosion frightened the fowl, and it started to run. Clemens, with his mind now on the single purpose of revenge, started after it. Around the trees, along the paths, up and down the lawn, through gates and across the garden, out over the fields, they raced, "pursuer and pursued." The guinea no longer sang, and Clemens was presently too exhausted to swear. Hour after hour the silent, deadly hunt continued, both stopping to rest at intervals; then up again and away. It was like something in a dream. It was nearly breakfast-time when he dragged himself into the house at last, and the guinea was resting and panting under a currant-bush. Later in the day Clemens gave orders to Lewis to "kill and eat that guinea-hen," which Lewis did. Clemens himself had then never eaten a guinea, but some years later, in Paris, when the delicious breast of one of those fowls was served him, he remembered and said:

"And to think, after chasing that creature all night, John Lewis got to eat him instead of me."

The interest in Tom and Huck, or the inspiration for their adventures, gave out at last, or was superseded by a more immediate demand. As early as May, Goodman, in San Francisco, had seen a play announced there, presenting the character of Colonel Sellers, dramatized by Gilbert S. Densmore and played by John T. Raymond. Goodman immediately wrote Clemens; also a letter came from Warner, in Hartford, who had noticed in San Francisco papers announcements of the play. Of course Clemens would take action immediately; he telegraphed, enjoining the performance. Then began a correspondence with the dramatist and actor. This in time resulted in an amicable arrangement, by which the dramatist agreed to dispose of his version to Clemens. Clemens did not wait for it to arrive, but began immediately a version of his own. Just how much or how little of Densmore's work found its way into the completed play, as presented by Raymond later, cannot be known now. Howells conveys the impression that Clemens had no hand in its authorship beyond the character of Sellers as taken from the book. But in a letter still extant, which Clemens wrote to Howells at the time, he says:

> I worked a month on my play, and launched it in New York last Wednesday. I believe it will go. The newspapers have been complimentary. It is simply a *setting* for one character, Colonel Sellers. As a play I guess it will not bear critical assault in force.
>
> The Warners are as charming as ever. They go shortly to the devil for a year—that is, to Egypt.

Raymond, in a letter which he wrote to the *Sun*, November 3, 1874, declared that "not one line" of Densmore's dramatization was used, "except that which was taken bodily from *The Gilded Age*. During the newspaper discussion of the matter, Clemens himself prepared a letter for the Hartford *Post*. This letter was suppressed, but it still exists. In it he says:

> I entirely rewrote the play three separate and distinct times. I had expected to use little of his [Densmore's] language and but little of his plot. I do not think there are now twenty sentences of Mr. Densmore's in the play, but I used so much of his plot that I wrote and told him that I should pay him about as much more as I had already paid him in case the play proved a success. I shall keep my word.

This letter, written while the matter was fresh in his mind, is undoubtedly in accordance with the facts. That Densmore was fully satisfied may be gathered from an acknowledgment, in which he says: "Your letter reached me on the 2d, with check. In this place permit me to thank you for the very handsome manner in which you have acted in this matter."

Warner, meantime, realizing that the play was constructed almost entirely of the Mark Twain chapters of the book, agreed that his collaborator should undertake the work and financial responsibilities of the dramatic venture and reap such rewards as might result. Various stories have been told of this matter, most of them untrue. There was no bitterness between the friends, no semblance of an estrangement of any sort. Warner very generously and promptly admitted that he was not concerned with the play, its authorship, or its profits, whatever the latter might amount to. Moreover, Warner was going to Egypt very soon, and his labors and responsibilities were doubly sufficient as they stood.

Clemens's estimate of the play as a dramatic composition was correct enough, but the public liked it, and it was a financial success from the start. He employed a representative to travel with Raymond, to assist in the management and in the division of spoil. The agent had instructions to mail a card every day, stating the amount of his share in the profits. Howells once arrived in Hartford just when this postal tide of fortune was at its flood:

> One hundred and fifty dollars—two hundred dollars—three hundred dollars—were the gay figures which they bore, and which he flaunted in the air, before he sat down at the table, or rose from it to brandish, and then, flinging his napkin in the chair, walked up and down to exult in.

Once, in later years, referring to the matter, Howells said:

"He was never a man who cared anything about money except as a dream, and he wanted more and more of it to fill out the spaces of this dream." Which was a true word. Mark Twain with money was like a child with a heap of bright pebbles, ready to pile up more and still more, then presently to throw them all away and begin gathering anew.

XCVI

THE NEW HOME

THE Clemenses returned to Hartford to find their new house "ready," though still full of workmen—decorators, plumbers, and such other minions of labor as make life miserable to those with ambitions for new or improved habitations. The carpenters were still on the lower floor, but the family moved in and camped about in rooms up-stairs that were more or less free from the invader. They had stopped in New York ten days to buy carpets and furnishings, and these began to arrive, with no particular place to put them; but the owners were excited and happy with it all, for it was the pleasant season of the year, and all the new features of the house were fascinating, while the daily progress of the decorators furnished a fresh surprise when they roamed through the rooms at evening. Mrs. Clemens wrote home:

We are perfectly delighted with everything here and do so want you all to see it.

Her husband, as he was likely to do, picked up the letter and finished it:

Livy appoints me to finish this; but how can a headless man perform an intelligent function? I have been bullyragged all day by the builder, by his foreman, by the architect, by the tapestry devil who is to upholster the furniture, by the idiot who is putting down the carpets, by the scoundrel who is setting up the billiard-table (and has left the balls in New York), by the wildcat who is sodding the ground and finishing the driveway (after the sun went down), by a book *agent*, whose body is in the back yard and the coroner notified. Just think of this thing going on the whole day long, and I a man who loathes details with all his heart! But I haven't lost my temper, and I've made Livy lie down *most* of the time; could anybody make her lie down *all* the time?

Warner wrote from Egypt expressing sympathy for their unfurnished state of affairs, but added, "I would rather fit out three houses and fill them with furniture than to fit out one dahabiyeh." Warner was at that moment undertaking his charmingly remembered trip up the Nile.

The new home was not entirely done for a long time. One never knows when a big house like that—or a little house, for that matter—*is* done. But they were settled at last, with all their beautiful things in place; and perhaps there have been richer homes, possibly more artistic ones, but there has never been a more charming home, within or without, than that one.

So many frequenters have tried to express the charm of that household. None of them has quite succeeded, for it lay not so much in its arrangement of rooms or their decorations or their outlook, though these were all beautiful enough, but rather in the personality, the atmosphere; and these are elusive things to convey in words. We can only see and feel and recognize; we cannot translate them. Even Howells, with his subtle touch, can present only an aspect here and there; an essence, as it were, from a happy garden, rather than the fullness of its bloom.

As Mark Twain was unlike any other man that ever lived, so his house was unlike any other house ever built. People asked him why he built the kitchen toward the street, and he said:

"So the servants can see the circus go by without running out into the front yard."

But this was probably an after-thought. The kitchen end of the house extended toward Farmington Avenue, but it was by no means unbeautiful. It was a pleasing detail of the general scheme. The main entrance faced at right angles with the street and opened to a spacious hall. In turn, the hall opened to a parlor, where there was a grand piano, and to the dining-room and library, and the library opened to a little conservatory, semicircular in form, of a design invented by Harriet Beecher Stowe. Says Howells:

> The plants were set in the ground, and the flowering vines climbed up the sides and overhung the roof above the silent spray of the fountain companied by callas and other water-loving lilies. There, while we breakfasted, Patrick came in from the barn and sprinkled the pretty bower, which poured out its responsive perfume in the delicate accents of its varied blossoms.

In the library was an old carved mantel which Clemens and his wife had bought in Scotland, salvage from a dismantled castle, and across the top of the fireplace a plate of brass with the motto, "The ornament of a house is the friends that frequent it," surely never more appropriately inscribed.

There was the mahogany room, a large bedroom on the ground floor, and up-stairs were other spacious bedrooms and many baths, while everywhere were Oriental rugs and draperies, and statuary and paintings. There was a fireplace under a window, after the English pattern, so that in winter-time one could at the same moment watch the blaze and the falling snow. The library windows looked out over the valley with the little stream in it, and through and across the tree-tops. At the top of the house was what became Clemens's favorite retreat, the billiard-room, and here and there were unexpected little balconies, which one could step out upon for the view.

THE NEW HOUSE IN HARTFORD

ON THE "OMBRA," HARTFORD. MR. AND MRS. CLEMENS AND SUSY
Also Dr. and Mrs. Jackson. (Dr. Jackson was "The Doctor" of *Innocents Abroad*)

Below was a wide, covered veranda, the "ombra," as they called it, secluded from the public eye—a favorite family gathering-place on pleasant days.

But a house might easily have all these things without being more than usually attractive, and a house with a great deal less might have been as full of charm; only it seemed just the proper setting for that particular household, and undoubtedly it acquired the personality of its occupants.

Howells assures us that there never was another home like it, and we may accept his statement. It was unique. It was the home of one of the most unusual and unaccountable personalities in the world, yet was perfectly and serenely ordered. Mark Twain was not responsible for this blissful condition. He was its beacon-light; it was around Mrs. Clemens that its affairs steadily revolved.

If in the four years and more of marriage Clemens had made advancement in culture and capabilities, Olivia Clemens also had become something more than the half-timid, inexperienced girl he had first known. In a way her education had been no less notable than his. She had worked and studied, and her half-year of travel and entertainment abroad had given her opportunity for acquiring knowledge and confidence. Her vision of life had vastly enlarged; her intellect had flowered; her grasp of practicalities had become firm and sure.

In spite of her delicate physical structure, her continued uncertainty of health, she capably undertook the management of their large new house, and supervised its economies. Any one of her undertakings was sufficient for one woman, but she compassed them all. No children had more careful direction than hers. No husband had more devoted attendance and companionship. No household was ever directed with a sweeter and gentler grace, or with greater perfection of detail. When the great ones of the world came to visit America's most picturesque literary figure she gave welcome to them all, and filled her place at his side with such sweet and capable dignity that those who came to pay their duties to him often returned to pay even greater devotion to his companion. Says Howells:

> She was, in a way, the loveliest person I have ever seen—the gentlest, the kindest, without a touch of weakness; she united wonderful tact with wonderful truth; and Clemens not only accepted her rule implicitly, but he rejoiced, he gloried in it.

And once, in an interview with the writer of these chapters, Howells declared: "She was not only a beautiful soul, but a woman of singular intellectual power. I never knew any one quite like her." Then he added: "Words cannot express Mrs. Clemens—her fineness, her delicate, her wonderful tact with a man who was in some respects, and wished to be, the most outrageous creature that ever breathed."

Howells meant a good many things by that, no doubt: Clemens's violent methods, for one thing, his sudden, savage impulses, which sometimes worked injustice and hardship for others, though he was first to discover the wrong and to repair it only too fully. Then, too, Howells may have meant his boyish teasing tendency to disturb Mrs. Clemens's exquisite sense of decorum.

> Once I remember seeing him come into his drawing-room at Hartford in a pair of white cowskin slippers with the hair out, and do a crippled colored uncle, to the joy of all beholders. I must not say all, for I remember also the dismay of Mrs. Clemens, and her low, despairing cry of "Oh, Youth!"

He was continually doing such things as the "crippled colored uncle"; partly for the very joy of the performance, but partly, too, to disturb her serenity, to incur her reproof, to shiver her a little—"shock" would be too strong a word. And he liked to fancy her in a spirit and attitude of belligerence, to present that fancy to those who knew the measure of her gentle nature. Writing to Mrs. Howells of a picture of herself in a group, he said:

You look exactly as Mrs. Clemens does after she has said: "Indeed, I do not *wonder* that you can frame no reply; for you know only too well that your conduct admits of no excuse, palliation, or argument—*none!*"

Clemens would pretend to a visitor that she had been violently indignant over some offense of his; perhaps he would say:

"Well I contradicted her just now, and the crockery will begin to fly pretty soon."

She could never quite get used to this pleasantry, and a faint glow would steal over her face. He liked to produce that glow. Yet always his manner toward her was tenderness itself. He regarded her as some dainty bit of porcelain, and it was said that he was always following her about with a chair. Their union has been regarded as ideal. That is Twichell's opinion and Howells's. The latter sums up:

Marriages are what the parties to them alone really know them to be, but from the outside I should say that this marriage was one of the most perfect.

XCVII

THE WALK TO BOSTON

THE new home became more beautiful to them as things found their places, as the year deepened, and the wonder of autumn foliage lit up their landscape. Sitting on one of the little upper balconies Mrs. Clemens wrote:

The atmosphere is very hazy, and it makes the autumn tints even more soft and beautiful than usual. Mr. Twichell came for Mr. Clemens to go walking with him; they returned at dinner-time, heavily laden with autumn leaves.

And as usual Clemens, finding the letter unfinished, took up the story.

Twichell came up here with me to luncheon after services, and I went back home with him and took Susy along in her little carriage. We have just got home again, middle of afternoon, and Livy has gone to rest and left the west balcony to me. There is a shining and most marvelous miracle of cloud-effects mirrored in the brook; a picture which began with perfection, and has momently surpassed it ever since, until at last it is almost unendurably beautiful. . . .

There is a cloud-picture in the stream now whose hues are as manifold as those in an opal and as delicate as the tintings of a sea-shell. But now a muskrat is swimming through it and obliterating it with the turmoil of wavelets he casts abroad from his shoulders.

The customary Sunday assemblage of strangers is gathered together in the grounds discussing the house.

Twichell and Clemens took a good many walks these days; long walks, for Twichell was an athlete and Clemens had not then outgrown the Nevada habit of pedestrian wandering. Talcott's Tower, a wooden structure about five miles from Hartford, was one of their favorite objective points; and often they walked out and back, talking so continuously, and so absorbed in the themes of their discussions, that time and distance slipped away almost unnoticed. How many things they talked of in those long walks! They discussed philosophies and religions and creeds, and all the range of human possibility and shortcoming, and all the phases of literature and history and politics. Unorthodox discussions they were, illuminating, marvelously enchanting, and vanished now forever. Sometimes they took the train as far as Bloomfield, a little station on the way, and walked the rest of the distance, or they took the train from Bloomfield home. It seems a strange association, perhaps, the fellowship of that violent dissenter with that fervent soul dedicated to church and creed, but the root of their friendship lay in the frankness with which each man delivered his dogmas and respected those of his companion.

It was during one of their walks to the tower that they planned a far more extraordinary undertaking—nothing less, in fact, than a walk from Hartford to Boston. This was early in November. They did not delay the matter, for the weather was getting too uncertain.

Clemens wrote Redpath:

DEAR REDPATH,—Rev. J. H. Twichell and I expect to start at 8 o'clock Thursday morning to walk to Boston in twenty-four hours—or more. We shall telegraph Young's Hotel for rooms Saturday night, in order to allow for a low average of pedestrianism.

It was half past eight on Thursday morning, November 12, 1874, that they left Twichell's house in a carriage, drove to the East Hartford bridge, and there took to the road, Twichell carrying a little bag and Clemens a basket of lunch.

The papers had got hold of it by this time, and were watching the result. They did well enough that first day, following the old Boston stage road, arriving at Westford about seven o'clock in the evening, twenty-eight miles from the starting-point. There was no real hotel at Westford, only a sort of tavern, but it afforded the luxury of rest. "Also," says Twichell, in a memoranda of the trip, "a sublimely profane hostler whom you couldn't jostle with any sort of mild remark without bringing down upon yourself a perfect avalanche of oaths."

This was a joy to Clemens, who sat behind the stove, rubbing his lame knees and fairly reveling in Twichell's discomfiture in his efforts to divert the hostler's blasphemy. There was also a mellow inebriate there who recommended kerosene for Clemens's lameness, and offered as testimony the fact that he himself had frequently used it for stiffness in his joints after lying out all night in cold weather, drunk: altogether it was a notable evening.

Westford was about as far as they continued the journey afoot. Clemens was exceedingly lame next morning, and had had a rather bad night; but he swore and limped along six miles farther, to North Ashford, then gave it up. They drove from North Ashford to the railway, where Clemens telegraphed Redpath and Howells of their approach. To Redpath:

We have made thirty-five miles in less than five days. This demonstrates that the thing can be done. Shall now finish by rail. Did you have any bets on us?

To Howells:

Arrive by rail at seven o'clock, the first of a series of grand annual pedestrian tours from Hartford to Boston to be performed by us. The next will take place *next year*.

Redpath read his despatch to a lecture audience, with effect. Howells made immediate preparation for receiving two wayworn, hungry men. He telegraphed to Young's Hotel: "You and Twichell come right up to 37 Concord Avenue, Cambridge, near observatory. Party waiting for you."

They got to Howells's about nine o'clock, and the refreshments were waiting. Miss Longfellow was there, Rose Hawthorne, John Fiske, Larkin B. Meade, the sculptor, and others of their kind. Howells tells in his book how Clemens, with Twichell, "suddenly stormed in," and immediately began to eat and drink:

> I can see him now as he stood up in the midst of our friends, with his head thrown back, and in his hand a dish of those escalloped oysters without which no party in Cambridge was really a party, exulting in the tale of his adventure, which had abounded in the most original characters and amusing incidents at every mile of their progress.

Clemens gave a dinner, next night, to Howells, Aldrich, Osgood, and the rest. The papers were full of jokes concerning the Boston expedition; some even had illustrations, and it was all amusing enough at the time.

Next morning, sitting in the writing-room of Young's Hotel, he wrote a curious letter to Mrs. Clemens, though intended as much for Howells and Aldrich as for her. It was dated sixty-one years ahead, and was a sort of *Looking Backwards*, though that notable book had not yet been written. It presupposed a monarchy in which the name of Boston has been changed to "Limerick," and Hartford to "Dublin." In it, Twichell has become the "Archbishop of Dublin," Howells "Duke of Cambridge," Aldrich "Marquis of Ponkapog," Clemens the "Earl of Hartford." It was too whimsical and delightful a fancy to be forgotten.[1]

[1] This remarkable and amusing document will be found under Appendix M, at the end of last volume.

A long time afterward, thirty-four years, he came across this letter. He said:

"It seems curious now that I should have been dreaming dreams of a future monarchy and never suspect that the monarchy was already present and the Republic a thing of the past."

What he meant, was the political succession that had fostered those commercial trusts which, in turn, had established party dominion.

To Howells, on his return, Clemens wrote his acknowledgments, and added:

Mrs. Clemens gets upon the verge of swearing, and goes tearing around in an unseemly fury when I enlarge upon the delightful time we had in Boston, and she not there to have her share. I have tried hard to reproduce Mrs. Howells to her, and have probably not made a shining success of it.

XCVIII

"OLD TIMES ON THE MISSISSIPPI"

HOWELLS had been urging Clemens to do something more for the *Atlantic*, specifically something for the January number. Clemens cudgeled his brains, but finally declared he must give it up:

Mrs. Clemens has diligently persecuted me day by day with urgings to go to work and do that something, but it's no use. I find I can't. We are in such a state of worry and endless confusion that my head won't go.

Two hours later he sent another hasty line:

I take back the remark that I can't write for the January number, for Twichell and I have had a long walk in the woods, and I got to telling him about old Mississippi days of steamboating glory and grandeur as I saw them (during four years) *from the pilot-house*. He said, "What a virgin subject to hurl into a magazine!" I hadn't thought of that before. Would you like a series of papers to run through three months or six or nine—or about four months, say?

Howells welcomed this offer as an echo of his own thought. He had come from a piloting family himself, and knew the interest that Mark Twain could put into such a series.

Acting promptly under the new inspiration, Clemens forthwith sent the first chapter of that monumental, that absolutely unique, series of papers on Mississippi River life, which to-day constitutes one of his chief claims to immortality.

His first number was in the nature of an experiment. Perhaps, after all, the idea would not suit the *Atlantic* readers.

"Cut it, scarify it, reject it, handle it with entire freedom," he wrote, and awaited the result.

The "result" was that Howells expressed his delight:

The piece about the Mississippi is capital. It almost made the water in our ice-pitcher muddy as I read it. I don't think I shall meddle much with it, even in the way of suggestion. The sketch of the low-lived little town was so good that I could have wished there was more of it. I want the sketches, if you can make them, *every month.*

Mark Twain was now really interested in this new literary venture. He was fairly saturated with memories. He was writing on the theme that lay nearest to his heart. Within ten days he reported that he had finished three of the papers, and had begun the fourth.

And yet I have spoken of nothing but piloting as a science so far, and I doubt if I ever get beyond that portion of my subject. And I don't care to. Any Muggins can write about old days on the Mississippi of five hundred different kinds, but I am the only man alive that can scribble about the piloting of that day, and no man has ever tried to scribble about it yet. Its newness pleases me all the time, and it is about the only new subject I know of.

He became so enthusiastic presently that he wanted to take Howells with him on a trip down the Mississippi, with their wives for company, to go over the old ground again and obtain added material enough for a book. Howells was willing enough—agreed to go, in fact—but found it hard to get away. He began to temporize and finally backed out. Clemens tried to inveigle Osgood into the trip, but without success; also John Hay, but Hay had a new baby at his house just then—"three days old, and with a voice beyond price," he said, offering it as an excuse for non-acceptance. So the plan for revisiting the river and the conclusion of the book were held in abeyance for nearly seven years.

Those early piloting chapters, as they appeared in the *Atlantic*, constituted Mark Twain's best literary exhibit up to that time. In some respects they are his best literature of any time. As pictures of an intensely interesting phase of life, they are so convincing, so real, and at the same time of such extraordinary charm and interest, that if the English language should survive a thousand years, or ten times as long, they would be as fresh and vivid at the end of that period as the day they were penned. In them the atmosphere of the river and its environment—its pictures, its thousand aspects of life—are reproduced with what is no less than literary necromancy. Not only does he make you smell the river you can fairly hear it breathe. On the appearance of the first number John Hay wrote:

"It is perfect; no more nor less. I don't see how you do it," and added, "you know what my opinion is of time not spent with you."

Howells wrote:

> You are doing the science of piloting splendidly. Every word interesting, and don't you drop the series till you've got every bit of anecdote and reminiscence into it.

He let Clemens write the articles to suit himself. Once he said:

> If I might put in my jaw at this point I should say, stick to actual fact and character in the thing and give things in *detail*. *All* that belongs to the old river life is novel, and is now mostly historical. Don't write *at* any supposed *Atlantic* audience, but yarn it off as if into my sympathetic ear.

Clemens replied that he had no dread of the *Atlantic* audience; he declared it was the only audience that did not require a humorist to "paint himself striped and stand on his head to amuse it."

The "Old Times" papers ran through seven numbers of the *Atlantic*. They were reprinted everywhere by the newspapers, who in that day had little respect for magazine copyrights, and were promptly pirated in book form in Canada. They added vastly to Mark Twain's literary capital, though Howells informs us that the *Atlantic* circulation did not thrive proportionately, for the reason that the newspapers gave the articles to their readers from advanced sheets of the magazine, even before the latter could be placed on sale. It so happened that in the January *Atlantic*, which contained the first of the Mississippi papers, there appeared Robert Dale Owen's article on "Spiritualism," which brought such humility both to author and publisher because of the exposure of the medium Katie King, which came along while the magazine was in press. Clemens has written this marginal note on the opening page of the copy at Quarry Farm:

While this number of the *Atlantic* was being printed the Katie King manifestations were discovered to be the cheapest, wretchedest shams and frauds, and were exposed in the newspapers. The awful humiliation of it unseated Robert Dale Owen's reason, and he died in the madhouse.

XCIX

A TYPEWRITER, AND A JOKE ON ALDRICH

IT was during the trip to Boston with Twichell that Mark Twain saw for the first time what was then a brand-new invention, a typewriter; or it may have been during a subsequent visit, a week or two later. At all events, he had the machine and was practising on it December 9, 1874, for he wrote two letters on it that day, one to Howells and the other to Orion Clemens. In the latter he says:

> I am trying to get the hang of this new-fangled writing-machine, but am not making a shining success of it. However, this is the first attempt I ever have made, and yet I perceive that I shall soon easily acquire a fine facility in its use. I saw the thing in Boston the other day and was greatly taken with it.

He goes on to explain the new wonder, and on the whole his first attempt is a very creditable performance. With his usual enthusiasm over an innovation, he believes it is going to be a great help to him, and proclaims its advantages.

This is the letter to Howells, with the errors preserved:

> You neednt a!swer this; I am only practicing to get three; *anothe slip-up there;* only practici?ng ti get the hang of the thing. I notice I miss fire & get in a good many unnecessary letters & punctuation marks. I am simply using you for a target to bang at. Blame my cats, but this thing requires genius in order to work it just right.

In an article written long after he tells how he was with Nasby when he first saw the machine in Boston through a window, and how they went in to see it perform. In the same article he states that he was the first person in the world to apply the type-machine to literature, and that he thinks the story of *Tom Sawyer* was the first type-copied manuscript.[1]

The new enthusiasm ran its course and died. Three months later, when the Remington makers wrote him for a recommendation of the machine, he replied that he had entirely stopped using it. The typewriter was not perfect in those days, and the keys did not always respond readily. He declared it was ruining his morals—that it made him "*want* to swear." He offered it to Howells because, he said, Howells had no morals anyway. Howells hesitated, so Clemens traded the machine to Bliss for a side-saddle. But perhaps Bliss also became afraid of its influence, for in due time he brought it back. Howells, again tempted, hesitated, and this time was lost. What eventually became of the machine is not history.

One of those happy *Atlantic* dinners which Howells tells of came about the end of that year. It was at the Parker House, and Emerson was there, and Aldrich, and the rest of that group.

"Don't you dare to refuse the invitation," said Howells, and naturally Clemens didn't, and wrote back:

> I want you to ask Mrs. Howells to let you stay all night at the Parker House and tell lies and have an improving time, and take breakfast with me in the morning. I will have a good room for you and a fire. Can't you tell her it always makes you sick to go home late at night or something like that? That sort of thing arouses Mrs. Clemens's sympathies easily.

[1] *Tom Sawyer* was not then complete, and had been laid aside. The first type-copied manuscript was probably early chapters of the Mississippi story, two discarded typewritten pages of which still exist.

BJUYT KIOP M LKJHGFDSA:QWERTYUIOP:_-98V86432QW RT
HA

HARTFORD, DEC. 9.

DEAR BROTHER:

I AM TRYING T TO GET THE HANG OF THIS NEW F FANGLED WRITING MACHINE, BUT AM NOT MAKING A SHINING SUCCESS OF IT. HOWEVER THIS IS THE FIRST ATTEMPT I EVER HAVE MADE, & YET I PERCEIVETHAT I SHALL SOON & EASILY ACQUIRE A FINE FACILITY IN ITS USE. I SAW THE THING IN BOSTON THE OTHER DAY & WAS GREATLY TAKEN WI:TH IT. SUSIE HAS STRUCK THE KEYS ONCE OR TWICE, & NO DOUBT HAS PRINTED SOME LETTERS WHICH DO NOT BELONG WHERE SHE PUT THEM.

THE HAVING BEEN A COMPOSITOR IS LIKELY TO BE A GREAT HELP TO ME, SINCE O NE CHIEFLY NEEDS SWIFTNESS IN BANGING THE KEYS. THE MACHINE COSTS 125 DOLLARS. THE MACHINE HAS SEVERAL VIRTUES I BELIEVE IT WILL PRINT FASTER THAN I CAN WRITE. ONE MAY LEAN BACK IN HIS CHAIR & WORK IT. IT PILES AN AWFUL STACK OF WORDS ON ONE PAGE. IT DONT MUSS THINGS OR SCATTER INK BLOTS AROUND. OF COURSE IT SAVES PAPER.

SUSIE IS GONE, NOW, & I FANCY I SHALL MAKE BETTER PROGRESS. WORKING THIS TYPE-WRITER REMINDS ME OF OLD ROBERT BUCHANAN, WHO, YOU REMEMBER, USED TO SET UP ARTICLES AT THE CASE WITHOUT PREVIOUSLY PUTTING THEM IN THE FORM OF MANUSCRIPT. I WAS LOST IN ADMIRATION OF SUOH MARVELOUS INTELLECTUAL CAPACITY.

LOVE TO MOLLIE.

YOUR-BROTHER,

SAM.

MARK TWAIN'S FIRST ATTEMPT AT TYPEWRITING

Two memories of that old dinner remain to-day. Aldrich and Howells were not satisfied with the kind of neckties that Mark Twain wore (the old-fashioned black "string" tie, a Western survival), so they made him a present of two cravats when he set out on his return for Hartford. Next day he wrote:

> You and Aldrich have made one woman deeply and sincerely grateful—Mrs. Clemens. For months—I may even say years—she has shown an unaccountable animosity toward my necktie, even getting up in the night to take it with the tongs and blackguard it, sometimes also getting so far as to threaten it.
>
> When I said you and Aldrich had given me two new neckties, and that they were in a paper in my overcoat pocket, she was in a fever of happiness until she found I was going to frame them; then all the venom in her nature gathered itself together, insomuch that I, being near to a door, went without, perceiving danger.

It is recorded that eventually he wore the neckties, and returned no more to the earlier mode.

Another memory of that dinner is linked to a demand that Aldrich made of Clemens that night, for his photograph. Clemens, returning to Hartford, put up fifty-two different specimens in as many envelopes, with the idea of sending one a week for a year. Then he concluded that this was too slow a process, and for a week sent one every morning to "His Grace of Ponkapog."

Aldrich stood it for a few days, then protested. "The police," he said, "are in the habit of swooping down upon a publication of that sort."

On New-Year's no less than twenty pictures came at once—photographs and prints of Mark Twain, his house, his family, his various belongings. Aldrich sent a warning then that the perpetrator of this outrage was known to the police as Mark Twain, *alias* "The Jumping Frog," a well-known California desperado, who would be speedily arrested and brought to Ponkapog to face his victim. This letter was signed "T. Bayleigh, Chief of Police," and on the outside of the envelope there was a statement that it would be useless for tha person to send any more mail-matter, as the post-office had been blown up. The jolly farce closed there. It was the sort of thing that both men enjoyed.

Aldrich was writing a story at this time which contained some Western mining incident and environment. He sent the manuscript to Clemens for "expert" consideration and advice. Clemens wrote him at great length and in careful detail. He was fond of Aldrich, regarding him as one of the most brilliant of men. Once, to Robert Louis Stevenson, he said:

"Aldrich has never had his peer for prompt and pithy and witty and humorous sayings. None has equaled him, certainly none has surpassed him, in the felicity of phrasing with which he clothed these children of his fancy. Aldrich is always brilliant; he can't help it; he is a fire-opal set round with rose diamonds; when he is not speaking you know that his dainty fancies are twinkling and glimmering around in him; when he speaks the diamonds flash. Yes, he is always brilliant, he will always be brilliant; he will be brilliant in hell—you will see."

Stevenson, smiling a chuckly smile, said, "I hope not."

"Well, you will, and he will dim even those ruddy fires and look like a transfigured Adonis backed against a pink sunset." [1]

[1] *North American Review*, September, 1906.

C

RAYMOND, MENTAL TELEGRAPHY, ETC.

THE Sellers play was given in Hartford, in January (1875), to as many people as could crowd into the Opera House. Raymond had reached the perfection of his art by that time, and the townsmen of Mark Twain saw the play and the actor at their best. Kate Field played the part of Laura Hawkins, and there was a Hartford girl in the company; also a Hartford young man, who would one day be about as well known to playgoers as any playwright or actor that America has produced. His name was William Gillette, and it was largely due to Mark Twain that the author of *Secret Service* and of the dramatic "Sherlock Holmes" got a fair public start. Clemens and his wife loaned Gillette the three thousand dollars which tided him through his period of dramatic education. Their faith in his ability was justified.

Hartford would naturally be enthusiastic on a first "Sellers-Raymond" night. At the end of the fourth act there was an urgent demand for the author of the play, who was supposed to be present. He was not there in person, but had sent a letter, which Raymond read:

MY DEAR RAYMOND,—I am aware that you are going to be welcomed to our town by great audiences on both nights of your stay there, and I beg to add my hearty welcome also, through this note. I cannot come to the theater on either evening, Raymond, because there is something so touching about your acting that I can't stand it.

(I do not mention a couple of colds in my head, because I

hardly mind them as much as I would the erysipelas, but between you and me I *would* prefer it if they were rights and lefts.)

And then there is another thing. I have always taken a pride in earning my living in outside places and spending it in Hartford; I have said that no good citizen would live on his own people, but go forth and make it sultry for other communities and fetch home the result; and now at this late day I find myself in the crushed and bleeding position of fattening myself upon the spoils of my brethren! Can I support such grief as this? (This is literary emotion, you understand. Take the money at the door just the same.)

Once more I welcome you to Hartford, Raymond, but as for me let me stay at home and blush.

Yours truly, MARK.

The play was equally successful wherever it went. It made what in that day was regarded as a fortune. One hundred thousand dollars is hardly too large an estimate of the amount divided between author and actor. Raymond was a great actor in that part, as he interpreted it, though he did not interpret it fully, or always in its best way. The finer side, the subtle, tender side of Colonel Sellers, he was likely to overlook. Yet, with a natural human self-estimate, Raymond believed he had created a much greater part than Mark Twain had written. Doubtless from the point of view of a number of people this was so, though the idea was naturally obnoxious to Clemens. In course of time their personal relations ceased.

Clemens that winter gave another benefit for Father Hawley. In reply to an invitation to appear in behalf of the poor, he wrote that he had quit the lecture field, and would not return to the platform unless driven there by lack of bread. But he added:

By the spirit of that remark I am debarred from delivering this proposed lecture, and so I fall back upon the letter of it, and emerge upon the platform for this last and final time because I am confronted by a lack of bread—among Father Hawley's flock.

He made an introductory speech at an old-fashioned spelling-bee, given at the Asylum Hill Church; a breezy, charming talk of which the following is a sample:

I don't see any use in spelling a word right—and never did. I mean I don't see any use in having a uniform and arbitrary way of spelling words. We might as well make all clothes alike and cook all dishes alike. Sameness is tiresome; variety is pleasing. I have a correspondent whose letters are always a refreshment to me; there is such a breezy, unfettered originality about his orthography. He always spells "kow" with a large "K." Now that is just as good as to spell it with a small one. It is better. It gives the imagination a broader field, a wider scope. It suggests to the mind a grand, vague, impressive new kind of a cow.

He took part in the contest, and in spite of his early reputation, was spelled down on the word "chaldron," which he spelled "cauldron," as he had been taught, while the dictionary used as authority gave that form as second choice.

Another time that winter, Clemens read before the Monday Evening Club a paper on "Universal Suffrage," which is still remembered by the surviving members of that time. A paragraph or two will convey its purport:

Our marvelous latter-day statesmanship has invented universal suffrage. That is the finest feather in our cap. All that we require of a voter is that he shall be forked, wear pantaloons instead of petticoats, and bear a more or less humorous resemblance to the reported image of God. He need not know anything whatever; he may be wholly useless and a cumberer of the earth; he may even be known to be a consummate scoundrel. No matter. While he can steer clear of the penitentiary his vote is as weighty as the vote of a president, a bishop, a college professor, a merchant prince. We brag of our universal, unrestricted suffrage; but we are shams after all, for we restrict when we come to the women.

The Monday Evening Club was an organization which included the best minds of Hartford. Dr. Horace Bushnell, Prof. Calvin E. Stowe, and J. Hammond Trumbull founded it back in the sixties, and it included such men as Rev. Dr. Parker, Rev. Dr. Burton, Charles H. Clark, of the *Courant*, Warner, and Twichell, with others of their kind. Clemens had been elected after his first sojourn in England (February, 1873), and had then read a paper on the "License of the Press." The club met alternate Mondays, from October to May. There was one paper for each evening, and, after the usual fashion of such clubs, the reading was followed by discussion. Members of that time agree that Mark Twain's association with the club had a tendency to give it a life, or at least an exhilaration, which it had not previously known. His papers were serious in their purpose—he always preferred to be serious—but they evidenced the magic gift which made whatever he touched turn to literary jewelry.

Psychic theories and phenomena always attracted Mark Twain. In thought-transference, especially, he had a frank interest—an interest awakened and kept alive by certain phenomena—psychic manifestations we call them now. In his association with Mrs. Clemens it not infrequently happened that one spoke the other's thought, or perhaps a long, procrastinated letter to a friend would bring an answer as quickly as mailed; but these are things familiar to us all. A more startling example of thought-communication developed at the time of which we are writing, an example which raised to a fever-point whatever interest he may have had in the subject before. (He was always having these vehement interests—rages we may call them, for it would be inadequate to speak of them as fads, inasmuch as they tended in the direction of human enlightenment, or progress, or reform.)

Clemens one morning was lying in bed when, as he says, "suddenly a red-hot new idea came whistling down into my camp." The idea was that the time was ripe for a book that would tell the story of the Comstock—of the Nevada silver mines. It seemed to him that the person best qualified for the work was his old friend William Wright—Dan de Quille. He had not heard from Dan, or *of* him, for a long time, but decided to write and urge him to take up the idea. He prepared the letter, going fully into the details of his plan, as was natural for him to do, then laid it aside until he could see Bliss and secure his approval of the scheme from a publishing standpoint. Just a week later, it was the 9th of March, a letter came—a thick letter bearing a Nevada postmark, and addressed in a handwriting which he presently recognized as De Quille's. To a visitor who was present he said:

"Now I will do a miracle. I will tell you everything this letter contains—date, signature, and all—without breaking the seal."

He stated what he believed was in the letter. Then he opened it and showed that he had correctly given its contents, which were the same in all essential details as those of his own letter, not yet mailed.

In an article on "Mental Telegraphy" (he invented the name) he relates this instance, with others, and in *Following the Equator* and elsewhere he records other such happenings. It was one of the "mysteries" in which he never lost interest, though his concern in it in time became a passive one.

The result of the De Quille manifestation, however, he has not recorded. Clemens immediately wrote, urging Dan to come to Hartford for an extended visit. De Quille came, and put in a happy spring in his old comrade's luxurious home, writing *The Big Bonanza*, which Bliss successfully published a year later.

Mark Twain was continually inviting old friends to share his success with him. Any comrade of former days found welcome in his home as often as he would come, and for as long as he would stay. Clemens dropped his own affairs to advise in their undertakings; and if their undertakings were literary he found them a publisher. He did this for Joaquin Miller and for Bret Harte, and he was always urging Goodman to make his house a home.

The Beecher-Tilton trial was the sensation of the spring of 1875, and Clemens, in common with many others, was greatly worked up over it. The printed testimony had left him decidedly in doubt as to Beecher's innocence, though his blame would seem to have been less for the possible offense than because of the great leader's attitude in the matter. To Twichell he said:

"His quibbling was fatal. Innocent or guilty, he should have made an unqualified statement in the beginning."

Together they attended one of the sessions, on a day when Beecher himself was on the witness-stand. The tension was very great; the excitement was painful. Twichell thought that Beecher appeared well under the stress of examination and was deeply sorry for him; Clemens was far from convinced.

The feeling was especially strong in Hartford, where Henry Ward Beecher's relatives were prominent, and animosities grew out of it. They are all forgotten now; most of those who cherished bitterness are dead. Any feeling that Clemens had in the matter lasted but a little while. Howells tells us that when he met him some months after the trial ended, and was tempted to mention it, Clemens discouraged any discussion of the event. Says Howells:

> He would only say the man had suffered enough; as if the man had expiated his wrong, and he was not going to do any-

thing to renew his penalty. I found that very curious, very delicate. His continued blame could not come to the sufferer's knowledge, but he felt it his duty to forbear it.

It was one hundred years, that 19th of April, since the battles of Lexington and Concord, and there was to be a great celebration. The Howellses had visited Hartford in March, and the Clemenses were invited to Cambridge for the celebration. Only Clemens could go, which in the event proved a good thing perhaps; for when Clemens and Howells set out for Concord they did not go over to Boston to take the train, but decided to wait for it at Cambridge. Apparently it did not occur to them that the train would be jammed the moment the doors were opened at the Boston station; but when it came along they saw how hopeless was their chance. They had special invitations and passage from Boston, but these were only mockeries now. It was cold and chilly, and they forlornly set out in search of some sort of a conveyance. They tramped around in the mud and raw wind, but vehicles were either filled or engaged, and drivers and occupants were inclined to jeer at them. Clemens was taken with an acute attack of indigestion, which made him rather dismal and savage. Their effort finally ended with his trying to run down a tally-ho which was empty inside and had a party of Harvard students riding atop. The students, who did not recognize their would-be fare, enjoyed the race. They encouraged their pursuer, and perhaps their driver, with merriment and cheers. Clemens was handicapped by having to run in the slippery mud, and soon "dropped by the wayside."

"I am glad," says Howells, "I cannot recall what he said when he came back to me."

They hung about a little longer, then dragged themselves home, slipped into the house, and built up a fine, cheerful fire on the hearth. They proposed to practise a deception on Mrs. Howells by pretending they had been to Concord and returned. But it was no use. Their statements were flimsy, and guilt was plainly written on their faces. Howells recalls this incident delightfully, and expresses the belief that the humor of the situation was finally a greater pleasure to Clemens than the actual visit to Concord would have been.

Twichell did not have any such trouble in attending the celebration. He had adventures (he was always having adventures), but they were of a more successful kind. Clemens heard the tale of them when he returned to Hartford. He wrote it to Howells:

Joe Twichell preached morning and evening here last Sunday; took midnight train for Boston; got an early breakfast and started by rail at 7.30 A.M. for Concord; swelled around there until 1 P.M., seeing everything; then traveled on top of a train to Lexington; saw everything there; traveled on top of a train to Boston (with hundreds in company), deluged with dust, smoke, and cinders; yelled and hurrahed all the way like a school-boy; lay flat down, to dodge numerous bridges, and sailed into the depot howling with excitement and as black as a chimney-sweep; got to Young's Hotel at 7 P.M.; sat down in the reading-room and immediately fell asleep; was promptly awakened by a porter, who supposed he was drunk; wandered around an hour and a half; then took 9 P.M. train, sat down in a smoking-car, and remembered nothing more until awakened by conductor as the train came into Hartford at 1.30 A.M. Thinks he had simply a glorious time, and wouldn't have missed the Centennial for the world. He would have run out to see us a moment at Cambridge but he was too dirty. I wouldn't have wanted him there; his appalling energy would have been an insufferable reproach to mild adventurers like you and me.

CI

CONCLUDING "TOM SAWYER"—MARK TWAIN'S "EDITORS"

MEANTIME the "inspiration tank," as Clemens sometimes called it, had filled up again. He had received from somewhere new afflatus for the story of Tom and Huck, and was working on it steadily. The family remained in Hartford, and early in July, under full head of steam, he brought the story to a close. On the 5th he wrote Howells:

> I have finished the story and didn't take the chap beyond boyhood. I believe it would be fatal to do it in any shape but autobiographically, like *Gil Blas*. I perhaps made a mistake in not writing it in the first person. If I went on now, and took him into manhood, he would just lie, like all the one-horse men in literature, and the reader would conceive a hearty contempt for him. It is not a boy's book at all. It will only be read by adults. It is only written for adults.

He would like to see the story in the *Atlantic*, he said, but doubted the wisdom of serialization.

"By and by I shall take a boy of twelve and run him through life (in the first person), but not Tom Sawyer, he would not make a good character for it." From which we get the first glimpse of Huck's later adventures.

Of course he wanted Howells to look at the story. It was a tremendous favor to ask, he said, and added, "But I know of no other person whose judgment I could venture to take, fully and entirely. Don't hesitate to say no, for I know how your time is taxed, and I would have honest need to blush if you said yes."

"Send on your MS.," wrote Howells. "You've no idea what I may ask you to do for *me* some day."

But Clemens, conscience-stricken, "blushed and weakened," as he said. When Howells insisted, he wrote:

> But I will gladly send it to you if you will do as follows: dramatize it, if you perceive that you can, and take, for your remuneration, half of the first $6,000 which I receive for its representation on the stage. You could alter the plot entirely if you chose. I could help in the work most cheerfully after you had arranged the plot. I have my eye upon two young girls who can play Tom and Huck.

Howells in his reply urged Clemens to do the playwriting himself. He could never find time, he said, and he doubted whether he could enter into the spirit of another man's story. Clemens did begin a dramatization then or a little later, but it was not completed. Mrs. Clemens, to whom he had read the story as it proceeded, was as anxious as her husband for Howells's opinion, for it was the first extended piece of fiction Mark Twain had undertaken alone. He carried the manuscript over to Boston himself, and whatever their doubts may have been, Howells's subsequent letter set them at rest. He wrote that he had sat up till one in the morning to get to the end of it, simply because it was impossible to leave off.

> It is altogether the best boy story I ever read. It will be an immense success, but I think you ought to treat it explicitly *as* a boy's story; grown-ups will enjoy it just as much if you do, and if you should put it forth as a story of boys' character from the grown-up point of view you give the wrong key to it.

Viewed in the light of later events, there has never been any better literary opinion than that—none that has been more fully justified.

Clemens was delighted. He wrote concerning a point

here and there, one inquiry referring to the use of a certain strong word. Howells's reply left no doubt:

> I'd have that swearing out in an instant. I suppose I didn't notice it because the location was so familiar to my Western sense, and so exactly the thing Huck would say, but it won't do for children.

It was in the last chapter, where Huck relates to Tom the sorrows of reform and tells how they comb him "all to thunder." In the original, "They comb me all to hell," says Huck; which statement, one must agree, is more effective, more the thing Huck would be likely to say.

Clemens's acknowledgment of the correction was characteristic:

> Mrs. Clemens received the mail this morning, and the next minute she lit into the study with danger in her eye and this demand on her tongue, "Where is the profanity Mr. Howells speaks of?" Then I had to miserably confess that I had left it out when reading the MS. to her. Nothing but almost inspired lying got me out of this scrape with my scalp. Does your wife give you rats, like that, when you go a little one-sided?

The Clemens family did not go to Elmira that year. The children's health seemed to require the sea-shore, and in August they went to Bateman's Point, Rhode Island, where Clemens most of the time played tenpins in an alley that had gone to ruin. The balls would not stay on the track; the pins stood at inebriate angles. It reminded him of the old billiard-tables of Western mining-camps, and furnished the same uncertainty of play. It was his delight, after he had become accustomed to the eccentricities of the alley, to invite in a stranger and watch his suffering and his frantic effort to score.

CII

"SKETCHES NEW AND OLD"

THE long-delayed book of *Sketches*, contracted for five years before, was issued that autumn. "The Jumping Frog," which he had bought from Webb, was included in the volume, also the French translation which Madame Blanc (Th. Bentzon) had made for the *Revue des deux mondes*, with Mark Twain's retranslation back into English, a most astonishing performance in its literal rendition of the French idiom. One example will suffice here. It is where the stranger says to Smiley, "I don't see no p'ints about that frog that's any better'n any other frog."

Says the French, retranslated:

> "*Eh bien!* I no saw not that that frog had nothing of better than each frog" (*Je ne vois pas que cette grenouille ait mieux qu'aucune grenouille*). (If that isn't grammar gone to seed then I count myself no judge.—M. T.)
>
> "Possible that you not it saw not," said Smiley; "possible that you—you comprehend frogs; possible that you not you there comprehend nothing; possible that you had of the experience, and possible that you not be but an amateur. Of all manner (*de toute manière*) I bet forty dollars that she batter in jumping, no matter which frog of the county of Calaveras."

He included a number of sketches originally published with the Frog, also a selection from the "Memoranda" and Buffalo *Express* contributions, and he put in the story of Auntie Cord, with some matter which had never hitherto appeared. True Williams illustrated the book, but either it furnished him no inspiration or he was allowed too much of another sort, for the pictures do not compare with his earlier work.

Among the new matter in the book were "Some Fables for Good Old Boys and Girls," in which certain wood creatures are supposed to make a scientific excursion into a place at some time occupied by men. It is the most pretentious feature of the book, and in its way about as good as any. Like *Gulliver's Travels*, its object was satire, but its result is also interest.

Clemens was very anxious that Howells should be first to review this volume. He had a superstition that Howells's verdicts were echoed by the lesser reviewers, and that a book was made or damned accordingly; a belief hardly warranted, for the review has seldom been written that meant to any book the difference between success and failure. Howells's review of *Sketches* may be offered as a case in point. It was highly commendatory, much more so than the notice of the *Innocents* had been, or even that of *Roughing It*, also more extensive than the latter. Yet after the initial sale of some twenty thousand copies, mainly on the strength of the author's reputation, the book made a comparatively poor showing, and soon lagged far behind its predecessors.

We cannot judge, of course, the taste of that day, but it appears now an unattractive, incoherent volume. The pictures were absurdly bad, the sketches were of unequal merit. Many of them are amusing, some of them delightful, but most of them seem ephemeral. If we except "The Jumping Frog," and possibly "A True Story" (and the latter was altogether out of place in the collection), there is no reason to suppose that any of its contents will escape oblivion. The greater number of the sketches, as Mark Twain himself presently realized and declared, would better have been allowed to die.

Howells did, however, take occasion to point out in his review, or at least to suggest, the more serious side of Mark Twain. He particularly called attention to "A True Story," which the reviewers, at the time of its publication in the *Atlantic*, had treated lightly, fearing a lurking joke in it; or it may be they had not read it, for reviewers are busy people. Howells spoke of it as the choicest piece of work in the volume, and of its "perfect fidelity to the tragic fact." He urged the reader to turn to it again, and to read it as a "simple dramatic report of reality," such as had been equaled by no other American writer.

It was in this volume of sketches that Mark Twain first spoke in print concerning copyright, showing the absurd injustice of discriminating against literary ownership by statute of limitation. He did this in the form of an open petition to Congress, asking that all property, real and personal, should be put on the copyright basis, its period of ownership limited to a "beneficent term of forty-two years." Generally this was regarded as a joke, as in a sense it was; but like most of Mark Twain's jokes it was founded on reason and justice.

The approval with which it was received by his literary associates led him to still further flights. He began a determined crusade for international copyright laws. It was a transcendental beginning, but it contained the germ of what, in the course of time, he would be largely instrumental in bringing to a ripe and magnificent conclusion. In this first effort he framed a petition to enact laws by which the United States would declare itself to be for right and justice, regardless of other nations, and become a good example to the world by refusing to pirate the books of any foreign author. He wrote to Howells, urging him to get Lowell, Longfellow, Holmes, Whittier, and others to sign this petition.

I will then put a gentlemanly chap under wages, and send him personally to every author of distinction in the country and corral the rest of the signatures. Then I'll have the whole thing lithographed (about one thousand copies), and move upon the President and Congress *in person*, but in the subordinate capacity of the party who is merely the agent of better and wiser men, or men whom the country cannot venture to laugh at.

I will ask the President to recommend the thing in his message (and if he should ask me to sit down and frame the paragraph for him I should blush, but still I would frame it). And *then* if Europe chooses to go on stealing from us we would say, with noble enthusiasm, "American lawmakers *do steal*, but not from foreign authors—*not from foreign authors!*" . . . If we only had some God in the country's laws, instead of being in such a sweat to get Him into the Constitution, it would be better all around.

The petition never reached Congress. Holmes agreed to sign it—with a smile, and the comment that governments were not in the habit of setting themselves up as high moral examples, except for revenue. Longfellow also pledged himself, as did a few others; but if there was any general concurrence in the effort there is no memory of it now. Clemens abandoned the original idea, but remained one of the most persistent and influential advocates of copyright betterment, and lived to see most of his dream fulfilled.[1]

[1] For the petition concerning copyright term in the United States, see *Sketches New and Old*. For the petition concerning international copyright and related matters, see Appendix N, at the end of last volume.

CIII

"ATLANTIC" DAYS

IT was about this period that Mark Twain began to exhibit openly his more serious side; that is to say his advocacy of public reforms. His paper on "Universal Suffrage" had sounded a first note, and his copyright petitions were of the same spirit. In later years he used to say that he had always felt it was his mission to teach, to carry the banner of moral reconstruction, and here at forty we find him furnishing evidences of this inclination. In the *Atlantic* for October, 1875, there was published an unsigned three-page article entitled, "The Curious Republic of Gondour." In this article was developed the idea that the voting privilege should be estimated not by the individuals, but by their intellectual qualifications. The republic of Gondour was a Utopia, where this plan had been established:

> It was an odd idea and ingenious. You must understand the constitution gave every man a vote; therefore that vote was a vested right, and could not be taken away. But the constitution did not say that certain individuals might not be given two votes or ten. So an amendatory clause was inserted in a quiet way, a clause which authorized the enlargement of the suffrage in certain cases to be specified by statute. . . .
>
> The victory was complete. The new law was framed and passed. Under it every citizen, howsoever poor or ignorant, possessed one vote, so universal suffrage still reigned; but if a man possessed a good common-school education and no money he had two votes, a high-school education gave him four; if he

had property, likewise, to the value of three thousand *sacos* he wielded one more vote; for every fifty thousand *sacos* a man added to his property he was entitled to another vote; a university education entitled a man to nine votes, even though he owned no property.

The author goes on to show the beneficent results of this enaction; how the country was benefited and glorified by this stimulus toward enlightenment and industry. No one ever suspected that Mark Twain was the author of this fable. It contained almost no trace of his usual literary manner. Nevertheless he wrote it, and only withheld his name, as he did in a few other instances, in the fear that the world might refuse to take him seriously over his own signature or *nom de plume*.

Howells urged him to follow up the "Gondour" paper; to send some more reports from that model land. But Clemens was engaged in other things by that time, and was not pledged altogether to national reforms.

He was writing a skit about a bit of doggerel which was then making nights and days unhappy for many undeserving persons who in an evil moment had fallen upon it in some stray newspaper corner. A certain car line had recently adopted the "punch system," and posted in its cars, for the information of passengers and conductor, this placard:

A Blue Trip Slip for an 8 Cents Fare,
A Buff Trip Slip for a 6 Cents Fare,
A Pink Trip Slip for a 3 Cents Fare,
For Coupon And Transfer, Punch The Tickets.

Noah Brooks and Isaac Bromley were riding down-town one evening on the Fourth Avenue line, when Bromley said:

"Brooks, it's poetry. By George, it's poetry!"

Brooks followed the direction of Bromley's finger and

read the card of instructions. They began perfecting the poetic character of the notice, giving it still more of a rhythmic twist and jingle; arrived at the *Tribune* office, W. C. Wyckoff, scientific editor, and Moses P. Handy lent intellectual and poetic assistance, with this result:

Conductor, when you receive a fare,
Punch in the presence of the passenjare!
A blue trip slip for an eight-cent fare,
A buff trip slip for a six-cent fare,
A pink trip slip for a three-cent fare.
Punch in the presence of the passenjare!

CHORUS

Punch, brothers! Punch with care!
Punch in the presence of the passenjare!

It was printed, and street-car poetry became popular. Different papers had a turn at it, and each usually preceded its own effort with all other examples, as far as perpetrated. Clemens discovered the lines, and on one of their walks recited them to Twichell. "A Literary Nightmare" was written a few days later. In it the author tells how the jingle took instant and entire possession of him and went waltzing through his brain; how, when he had finished his breakfast, he couldn't tell whether he had eaten anything or not; and how, when he went to finish the novel he was writing, and took up his pen, he could only get it to say:

Punch in the presence of the passenjare.

He found relief at last in telling it to his reverend friend, that is, Twichell, upon whom he unloaded it with sad results.

It was an amusing and timely skit, and is worth reading to-day. Its publication in the *Atlantic* had the effect of waking up horse-car poetry all over the world. Howells, going to dine at Ernest Longfellow's the day following its appearance, heard his host and Tom Appleton urging each other to "Punch with care." The Longfellow ladies had it by heart. Boston was devastated by it. At home, Howells's children recited it to him in chorus. The streets were full of it; in Harvard it became an epidemic.

It was transformed into other tongues. Even Swinburne, the musical, is said to have done a French version for the *Revue des deux mondes*.[1] A St. Louis magazine, *The Western*, found relief in a Latin anthem with this chorus:

Pungite, fratres, pungite,
Pungite cum amore,
Pungite pro vectore,
Diligentissime pungite.

[1] LE CHANT DU CONDUCTEUR

Ayant été payé, le conducteur
Percera en pleine vue du voyageur,
Quand il reçoit trois sous un coupon vert,
Un coupon jaune pour six sous c'est l'affaire,
Et pour huit sous c'est un coupon couleur
De rose, en pleine vue du voyageur.

CHŒUR

Donc, percez soigneusement, mes frères
Tout en pleine vue des voyageurs, etc.

CIV

MARK TWAIN AND HIS WIFE

CLEMENS and his wife traveled to Boston for one of those happy foregatherings with the Howellses, which continued, at one end of the journey or another, for so many years. There was a luncheon with Longfellow at Craigie House, and, on the return to Hartford, Clemens reported to Howells how Mrs. Clemens had thrived on the happiness of the visit. Also he confesses his punishment for the usual crimes:

I "caught it" for letting Mrs. Howells bother and bother about her coffee, when it was a "good deal better than we get at home." I "caught it" for interrupting Mrs. C. at the last moment and losing her the opportunity to urge you not to forget to send her that MS. when the printers are done with it. I "caught it" once more for personating that drunken Colonel James. I "caught it" for mentioning that Mr. Longfellow's picture was slightly damaged; and when, after a lull in the storm, I confessed, shamefacedly, that I had privately suggested to you that we hadn't any *frames*, and that if you wouldn't mind hinting to Mr. Houghton, etc., etc., etc., the madam was simply speechless for the space of a minute. Then she said:

"How *could* you, Youth! The idea of sending Mr. Howells, with his sensitive nature, upon such a repulsive er—"

"Oh, Howells won't mind it! You don't know Howells. Howells is a man who—"

She was gone. But George was the first person she stumbled on in the hall, so she took it out of George. I am glad of that, because it saved the babies.

Clemens used to admit, at a later day, that his education did not advance by leaps and bounds, but gradually, very gradually; and it used to give him a pathetic relief in those after-years, when that sweet presence had gone out of his life, to tell the way of it, to confess over-fully, perhaps, what a responsibility he had been to her.

He used to tell how, for a long time, he concealed his profanity from her; how one morning, when he thought the door was shut between their bedroom and the bath-room, he was in there dressing and shaving, accompanying these trying things with language intended only for the strictest privacy; how presently, when he discovered a button off the shirt he intended to put on, he hurled it through the window into the yard with appropriate remarks, followed it with another shirt that was in the same condition, and added certain collars and neckties and bath-room requisites, decorating the shrubbery outside, where the people were going by to church; how in this extreme moment he heard a slight cough, and turned to find that the door was open! There was only one door to the bath-room, and he knew he had to pass her. He felt pale and sick, and sat down for a few moments to consider. He decided to assume that she was asleep, and to walk out and through the room, head up, as if he had nothing on his conscience. He attempted it, but without success. Half-way across the room he heard a voice suddenly repeat his last terrific remark. He turned to see her sitting up in bed, regarding him with a look as withering as she could find in her gentle soul. The humor of it struck him.

"Livy," he said, "did it sound like that?"

"Of course it did," she said, "only worse. I wanted you to hear just how it sounded."

"Livy," he said, "it would pain me to think that when I swear it sounds like that. You got the words right, Livy, but you don't know the tune."

Yet he never willingly gave her pain, and he adored her and gloried in her dominion, his life long. Howells speaks of his beautiful and tender loyalty to her as the "most moving quality of his most faithful soul."

> It was a greater part of him than the love of most men for their wives, and she merited all the worship he could give her, all the devotion, all the implicit obedience, by her surpassing force and beauty of character.

She guarded his work sacredly; and reviewing the manuscripts which he was induced to discard, and certain edited manuscripts, one gets a partial idea of what the reading world owes to Olivia Clemens. Of the discarded manuscripts (he seems seldom to have destroyed them) there are a multitude, and among them all scarcely one that is not a proof of her sanity and high regard for his literary honor. They are amusing—some of them; they are interesting—some of them; they are strong and virile—some of them; but they are unworthy—most of them, though a number remain unfinished because theme or interest failed.

Mark Twain was likely to write not wisely but too much, piling up hundreds of manuscript pages only because his brain was thronging as with a myriad of fireflies, a swarm of darting, flashing ideas demanding release. As often as not he began writing with only a nebulous idea of what he proposed to do. He would start with a few characters and situations, trusting in Providence to supply material as needed. So he was likely to run ashore any time. As for those other attempts—stories "unavailable" for one reason or another—he was just as apt to begin those as the better sort, for somehow he could never tell the difference. That is one of the hall-marks of genius—the thing which sharply differentiates genius from talent. Genius is likely to rate a literary disaster as its best work. Talent rarely makes that mistake.

MRS. SAMUEL L. CLEMENS, 1873

Among the abandoned literary undertakings of these early years of authorship there is the beginning of what was doubtless intended to become a book, "The Second Advent," a story which opens with a very doubtful miraculous conception in Arkansas, and leads only to grotesquery and literary disorder. There is another, "The Autobiography of a Damn Fool," a burlesque on family history, hopelessly impossible; yet he began it with vast enthusiasm and, until he allowed her to see the manuscript, thought it especially good. "Livy wouldn't have it," he said, "so I gave it up." There is another, "The Mysterious Chamber," strong and fine in conception, vividly and intensely interesting; the story of a young lover who is accidentally locked behind a secret door in an old castle and cannot announce himself. He wanders at last down into subterranean passages beneath the castle, and he lives in this isolation for twenty years. The question of sustenance was the weak point in the story. Clemens could invent no way of providing it, except by means of a waste or conduit from the kitchen into which scraps of meat, bread, and other items of garbage were thrown. This he thought sufficient, but Mrs. Clemens did not highly regard such a literary device. Clemens could think of no good way to improve upon it, so this effort too was consigned to the penal colony, a set of pigeonholes kept in his study. To Howells and others, when they came along, he would read the discarded yarns, and they were delightful enough for such a purpose, as delightful as the sketches which every artist has, turned face to the wall.

"Captain Stormfield" lay under the ban for many a year, though never entirely abandoned. This manuscript was even recommended for publication by Howells, who has since admitted that it would not have done then; and indeed, in its original, primitive nakedness it would hardly have done even in this day of wider toleration.

It should be said here that there is not the least evidence (and the manuscripts are full of evidence) that Mrs. Clemens was ever supersensitive, or narrow, or unliterary in her restraints. She became his public, as it were, and no man ever had a more open-minded, clear-headed public than that. For Mark Twain's reputation it would have been better had she exercised her editorial prerogative even more actively—if, in her love for him and her jealousy of his reputation, she had been even more severe. She did all that lay in her strength, from the beginning to the end, and if we dwell upon this phase of their life together it is because it is so large a part of Mark Twain's literary story. On her birthday in the year we are now closing (1875) he wrote her a letter which conveys an acknowledgment of his debt.

Livy Darling,—Six years have gone by since I made my first great success in life and won you, and thirty years have passed since Providence made preparation for that happy success by sending you into the world. Every day we live together adds to the security of my confidence that we can never any more wish to be separated than we can imagine a regret that we were ever joined. You are dearer to me to-day, my child, than you were upon the last anniversary of this birthday; you were dearer then than you were a year before; you have grown more and more dear from the first of those anniversaries, and I do not doubt that this precious progression will continue on to the end.

Let us look forward to the coming anniversaries, with their age and their gray hairs, without fear and without depression, trusting and believing that the love we bear each other will be sufficient to make them blessed.

So, with abounding affection for you and our babies I hail this day that brings you the matronly grace and dignity of three decades!

CV

MARK TWAIN AT FORTY

IN conversation with John Hay, Hay said to Clemens: "A man reaches the zenith at forty, the top of the hill. From that time forward he begins to descend. If you have any great undertaking ahead, begin it now. You will never be so capable again."

Of course this was only a theory of Hay's, a rule where rules do not apply, where in the end the problem resolves itself into a question of individualities. John Hay did as great work after forty as ever before, so did Mark Twain, and both of them gained in intellectual strength and public honor to the very end.

Yet it must have seemed to many who knew him, and to himself, like enough, that Mark Twain at forty had reached the pinnacle of his fame and achievement. His name was on every lip; in whatever environment observation and argument were likely to be pointed with some saying or anecdote attributed, rightly or otherwise, to Mark Twain. "As Mark Twain says," or, "You know that story of Mark Twain's," were universal and daily commonplaces. It was dazzling, towering fame, not of the best or most enduring kind as yet, but holding somewhere within it the structure of immortality.

He was in a constant state of siege, besought by all varieties and conditions of humanity for favors such as only human need and abnormal ingenuity can invent. His ever-increasing mail presented a marvelous exhibition of the human species on undress parade. True, there were hundreds of appreciative tributes from readers who spoke only out of a heart's gratitude; but there were nearly as great a number who came with a compliment, and added a petition, or a demand, or a suggestion, usually unwarranted, often impertinent. Politicians, public speakers, aspiring writers, actors, elocutionists, singers, inventors (most of them he had never seen or heard of) cheerfully asked him for a recommendation as to their abilities and projects.

Young men wrote requesting verses or sentiments to be inscribed in young ladies' autograph albums; young girls wrote asking him to write the story of his life, to be used as a school composition; men starting obscure papers coolly invited him to lend them his name as editor, assuring him that he would be put to no trouble, and that it would help advertise his books; a fruitful humorist wrote that he had invented some five thousand puns, and invited Mark Twain to father this terrific progeny in book form for a share of the returns. But the list is endless. He said once:

"The symbol of the race ought to be a human being carrying an ax, for every human being has one concealed about him somewhere, and is always seeking the opportunity to grind it."

Even P. T. Barnum had an ax, the large ax of advertising, and he was perpetually trying to grind it on Mark Twain's reputation; in other words, trying to get him to write something that would help to popularize "The Greatest Show on Earth."

There were a good many curious letters—letters from humorists, would-be and genuine. A bright man in Duluth sent him an old Allen "pepper-box" revolver with the statement that it had been found among a pile of bones under a tree, from the limb of which was suspended a lasso and a buffalo skull; this as evidence that the weapon was the genuine Allen which Bemis had lost on that memorable Overland buffalo-hunt. Mark Twain enjoyed that, and kept the old pepper-box as long as he lived. There were letters from people with fads; letters from cranks of every description; curious letters even from friends. Reginald Cholmondeley, that lovely eccentric of Condover Hall, where Mr. and Mrs. Clemens had spent some halcyon days in 1873, wrote him invitations to be at his castle on a certain day, naming the hour, and adding that he had asked friends to meet him. Cholmondeley had a fancy for birds, and spared nothing to improve his collection. Once he wrote Clemens asking him to collect for him two hundred and five American specimens, naming the varieties and the amount which he was to pay for each. Clemens was to catch these birds and bring them over to England, arriving at Condover on a certain day, when there would be friends to meet him, of course.

Then there was a report which came now and then from another English castle—the minutes of a certain "Mark Twain Club," all neatly and elaborately written out, with the speech of each member and the discussions which had followed—the work, he found out later, of another eccentric; for there was no Mark Twain Club, the reports being just the mental diversion of a rich young man, with nothing else to do.[1]

Letters came queerly addressed. There is one envelope still in existence which bears Clemens's name in elaborate design and a very good silhouette likeness, the work of some talented artist. "Mark Twain, United States," was a common address; "Mark Twain, The World," was also used; "Mark Twain, Somewhere," mailed in a foreign country, reached him promptly, and "Mark Twain, Anywhere," found its way to Hartford in due season. Then there was a letter (though this was

[1] In *Following the Equator* Clemens combined these two pleasant characters in one story, with elaborations.

later; he was abroad at the time), mailed by Brander Matthews and Francis Wilson, addressed, "Mark Twain, God Knows Where." It found him after traveling half around the world on its errand, and in his answer he said, "He *did*." Then some one sent a letter addressed, "The Devil Knows Where." Which also reached him, and he answered, "*He* did, too."

Surely this was the farthest horizon of fame.

Countless Mark Twain anecdotes are told of this period, of every period, and will be told and personally vouched for so long as the last soul of his generation remains alive. For seventy years longer, perhaps, there will be those who will relate "personal recollections" of Mark Twain. Many of them will be interesting; some of them will be true; most of them will become history at last. It is too soon to make history of much of this drift now. It is only safe to admit a few authenticated examples.

It happens that one of the oftenest-told anecdotes has been the least elaborated. It is the one about his call on Mrs. Stowe. Twichell's journal entry, set down at the time, verifies it:

Mrs. Stowe was leaving for Florida one morning, and Clemens ran over early to say good-by. On his return Mrs. Clemens regarded him disapprovingly:

"Why, Youth," she said, "you haven't on any collar and tie."

He said nothing, but went up to his room, did up these items in a neat package, and sent it over by a servant, with a line:

"Herewith receive a call from the rest of me."

Mrs. Stowe returned a witty note, in which she said that he had discovered a new principle, the principle of making calls by instalments, and asked whether, in extreme cases, a man might not send his hat, coat, and boots and be otherwise excused.

Col. Henry Watterson tells the story of an after-theater

supper at the Brevoort House, where Murat Halstead, Mark Twain, and himself were present. A reporter sent in a card for Colonel Watterson, who was about to deny himself when Clemens said:

"Give it to me; I'll fix it." And left the table. He came back in a moment and beckoned to Watterson.

"He is young and as innocent as a lamb," he said. "I represented myself as your secretary. I said that you were not here, but if Mr. Halstead would do as well I would fetch him out. I'll introduce you as Halstead, and we'll have some fun."

Now, while Watterson and Halstead were always good friends, they were political enemies. It was a political season and the reporter wanted that kind of an interview. Watterson gave it to him, repudiating every principle that Halstead stood for, reversing him in every expressed opinion. Halstead was for hard money and given to flying the "bloody shirt" of sectional prejudice; Watterson lowered the bloody shirt and declared for greenbacks in Halstead's name. Then he and Clemens returned to the table and told frankly what they had done. Of course, nobody believed it. The report passed the *World* night-editor, and appeared next morning. Halstead woke up, then, and wrote a note to the *World*, denying the interview throughout. The *World* printed his note with the added line:

"When Mr. Halstead saw our reporter he had dined."

It required John Hay (then on the *Tribune*) to place the joke where it belonged.

There is a Lotos Club anecdote of Mark Twain that carries the internal evidence of truth. Saturday evening at the Lotos always brought a gathering of the "wits," and on certain evenings—"Hens and chickens" nights—each man had to tell a story, make a speech, or sing a song. On one evening a young man, an invited guest, was called upon and recited a very long poem.

One by one those who sat within easy reach of the various exits melted away, until no one remained but Mark Twain. Perhaps he saw the earnestness of the young man, and sympathized with it. He may have remembered a time when he would have been grateful for one such attentive auditor. At all events, he sat perfectly still, never taking his eyes from the reader, never showing the least inclination toward discomfort or impatience, but listening, as with rapt attention, to the very last line. Douglas Taylor, one of the faithful Saturday-night members, said to him later:

"Mark, how did you manage to sit through that dreary, interminable poem?"

"Well," he said, "that young man thought he had a divine message to deliver, and I thought he was entitled to at least one auditor, so I stayed with him."

We may believe that for that one auditor the young author was willing to sacrifice all the others.

One might continue these anecdotes for as long as the young man's poem lasted, and perhaps hold as large an audience. But anecdotes are not all of history. These are set down because they reflect a phase of the man and an aspect of his life at this period. For at the most we can only present an angle here and there, and tell a little of the story, letting each reader from his fancy construct the rest.

CVI

HIS FIRST STAGE APPEARANCE

ONCE that winter the Monday Evening Club met at Mark Twain's home, and instead of the usual essay he read them a story: "The Facts Concerning the Recent Carnival of Crime in Connecticut." It was the story of a man's warfare with a personified conscience—a sort of "William Wilson" idea, though less weird, less somber, and with more actuality, more verisimilitude. It was, in fact, autobiographical, a setting-down of the author's daily self-chidings. The climax, where conscience is slain, is a startling picture which appeals to most of humanity. So vivid is it all, that it is difficult in places not to believe in the reality of the tale, though the allegory is always present.

The club was deeply impressed by the little fictional sermon. One of its ministerial members offered his pulpit for the next Sunday if Mark Twain would deliver it to his congregation. Howells welcomed it for the *Atlantic*, and published it in June. It was immensely successful at the time, though for some reason it seems to be little known or remembered to-day. Now and then a reader mentions it, always with enthusiasm. Howells referred to it repeatedly in his letters, and finally persuaded Clemens to let Osgood bring it out, with "A True Story," in dainty, booklet form. If the reader does not already know the tale, it will pay him to look it up and read it, and then to read it again.

Meantime *Tom Sawyer* remained unpublished.

"Get Bliss to hurry it up!" wrote Howells. "That boy is going to make a prodigious hit."

But Clemens delayed the book, to find some means to outwit the Canadian pirates, who thus far had laid hands on everything, and now were clamoring at the *Atlantic* because there was no more to steal.

Moncure D. Conway was in America, and agreed to take the manuscript of *Sawyer* to London and arrange for its publication and copyright. In Conway's *Memoirs* he speaks of Mark Twain's beautiful home, comparing it and its surroundings with the homes of Surrey, England. He tells of an entertainment given to Harriet Beecher Stowe, a sort of animated Jarley wax-works. Clemens and Conway went over as if to pay a call, when presently the old lady was rather startled by an invasion of costumed figures. Clemens rose and began introducing them in his gay, fanciful fashion. He began with a knight in full armor, saying, as if in an aside, "Bring along that tinshop," and went on to tell the romance of the knight's achievements.

Conway read *Tom Sawyer* on the ship and was greatly excited over it. Later, in London, he lectured on it, arranging meantime for its publication with Chatto & Windus, thus establishing a friendly business relation with that firm which Mark Twain continued during his lifetime.

Clemens lent himself to a number of institutional amusements that year, and on the 26th of April, 1876, made his first public appearance on the dramatic stage.

It was an amateur performance, but not of the usual kind. There was genuine dramatic talent in Hartford, and the old play of the "Loan of the Lover," with Mark Twain as Peter Spuyk and Miss Helen Smith[1] as Gertrude, with a support sufficient for their needs, gave a performance that probably furnished as much entertainment as that

[1] Now Mrs. William W. Ellsworth.

pleasant old play is capable of providing. Mark Twain had in him the making of a great actor. Henry Irving once said to him:

"You made a mistake by not adopting the stage as a profession. You would have made even a greater actor than a writer."

Yet it is unlikely that he would ever have been satisfied with the stage. He had too many original literary ideas. He would never have been satisfied to repeat the same part over and over again, night after night from week to month, and from month to year. He could not stick to the author's lines even for one night. In his performance of the easy-going, thick-headed Peter Spuyk his impromptu additions to the lines made it hard on the company, who found their cues all at sixes and sevens, but it delighted the audience beyond measure. No such impersonation of that character was ever given before, or ever will be given again. It was repeated with new and astonishing variations on the part of Peter, and it could have been put on for a long run. Augustin Daly wrote immediately, offering the Fifth Avenue Theater for a "benefit" performance, and again, a few days later, urging acceptance. "Not for one night, but for many."

Clemens was tempted, no doubt. Perhaps, if he had yielded, he would to-day have had one more claim on immortality.

CVII

HOWELLS, CLEMENS, AND "GEORGE"

HOWELLS and Clemens were visiting back and forth rather oftener just then. Clemens was particularly fond of the Boston crowd—Aldrich, Fields, Osgood, and the rest—delighting in those luncheons or dinners which Osgood, that hospitable publisher, was always giving on one pretext or another. No man ever loved company more than Osgood, or to play the part of host and pay for the enjoyment of others. His dinners were elaborate affairs, where the sages and poets and wits of that day (and sometimes their wives) gathered. They were happy reunions, those foregatherings, though perhaps a more intimate enjoyment was found at the luncheons, where only two or three were invited, usually Aldrich, Howells, and Clemens, and the talk continued through the afternoon and into the deepening twilight, such company and such twilight as somehow one seems never to find any more.

On one of the visits which Howells made to Hartford that year he took his son John, then a small boy, with him. John was about six years old at the time, with his head full of stories of Aladdin, and of other Arabian fancies. On the way over his father said to him:

"Now, John, you will see a perfect palace."

They arrived, and John was awed into silence by the magnificence and splendors of his surroundings until they went to the bath-room to wash off the dust of travel. There he happened to notice a cake of pink soap.

"Why," he said, "they've even got their soap painted!"

Next morning he woke early—they were occupying the mahogany room on the ground floor—and slipping out through the library, and to the door of the dining-room, he saw the colored butler, George—the immortal George—setting the breakfast-table. He hurriedly tiptoed back and whispered to his father:

"Come quick! The slave is setting the table!"

This being the second mention of George, it seems proper here that he should be formally presented. Clemens used to say that George came one day to wash windows and remained eighteen years. He was precisely the sort of character that Mark Twain loved. He had formerly been the body-servant of an army general and was typically racially Southern, with those delightful attributes of wit and policy and gentleness which go with the best type of negro character. The children loved him no less than did their father. Mrs. Clemens likewise had a weakness for George, though she did not approve of him. George's morals were defective. He was an inveterate gambler. He would bet on anything, though prudently and with knowledge. He would investigate before he invested. If he placed his money on a horse, he knew the horse's pedigree and the pedigree of the horses against it, also of their riders. If he invested in an election, he knew all about the candidates. He had agents among his own race, and among the whites as well, to supply him with information. He kept them faithful to him by lending them money—at ruinous interest. He buttonholed Mark Twain's callers while he was removing their coats concerning the political situation, much to the chagrin of Mrs. Clemens, who protested, though vainly, for the men liked George and his ways, and upheld him in his iniquities.

Mrs. Clemens's disapproval of George reached the point, now and then, where she declared he could not remain.

She even discharged him once, but next morning George was at the breakfast-table, in attendance, as usual. Mrs. Clemens looked at him gravely:

"George," she said, "didn't I discharge you yesterday?"

"Yes, Mis' Clemens, but I knew you couldn't get along without me, so I thought I'd better stay a while."

In one of the letters to Howells Clemens wrote:

> When George first came he was one of the most religious of men. He had but one fault—young George Washington's. But I have trained him; and now it fairly breaks Mrs. Clemens's heart to hear him stand at that front door and lie to an unwelcome visitor.

George was a fine diplomat. He would come up to the billiard-room with a card or message from some one waiting below, and Clemens would fling his soul into a sultry denial which became a soothing and balmy subterfuge before it reached the front door.

The "slave" must have been setting the table in good season, for the Clemens breakfasts were likely to be late. They usually came along about nine o'clock, by which time Howells and John were fairly clawing with hunger.

Clemens did not have an early appetite, but when it came it was a good one. Breakfast and dinner were his important meals. He seldom ate at all during the middle of the day, though if guests were present he would join them at luncheon-time and walk up and down while they were eating, talking and gesticulating in his fervent, fascinating way. Sometimes Mrs. Clemens would say:

"Oh, Youth, do come and sit down with us. We can listen so much better."

But he seldom did. At dinner, too, it was his habit, between the courses, to rise from the table and walk up and down the room, waving his napkin and talking—talking in a strain and with a charm that he could never quite equal with his pen. It is the opinion of most people who knew Mark Twain personally that his impromptu utterances, delivered with that ineffable quality of speech, manifested the culmination of his genius.

When Clemens came to Boston the Howells household was regulated, or rather unregulated, without regard to former routine. Mark Twain's personality was of a sort that unconsciously compelled the general attendance of any household. The reader may recall Josh Billings's remark on the subject. Howells tells how they kept their guest to themselves when he visited their home in Cambridge, permitting him to indulge in as many unconventions as he chose; how Clemens would take a room at the Parker House, leaving the gas burning day and night, and perhaps arrive at Cambridge, after a dinner or a reading, in evening dress and slippers, and joyously remain with them for a day or more in that guise, slipping on an overcoat and a pair of rubbers when they went for a walk. Also, how he smoked continuously in every room of the house, smoked during every waking moment, and how Howells, mindful of his insurance, sometimes slipped in and removed the still-burning cigar after he was asleep.

Clemens had difficulty in getting to sleep in that earlier day, and for a time found it soothing to drink a little champagne on retiring. Once, when he arrived in Boston, Howells said:

"Clemens, we've laid in a bottle of champagne for you."

But he answered:

"Oh, that's no good any more. Beer's the thing."

So Howells provided the beer, and always afterward had a vision of his guest going up-stairs that night with a pint bottle under each arm.

He invented other methods of inducing slumber as the years went by, and at one time found that this precious boon came more easily when he stretched himself on the bath-room floor.

He was a perpetual joy to the Howells family when he was there, even though the household required a general reorganization when he was gone.

Mildred Howells remembers how, as a very little girl, her mother cautioned her not to ask for anything she wanted at the table when company was present, but to speak privately of it to her. Miss Howells declares that while Mark Twain was their guest she nearly starved because it was impossible to get her mother's attention; and Mrs. Howells, after one of those visits of hilarity and disorder, said:

"Well, it 'most kills me, but it pays," a remark which Clemens vastly enjoyed. Howells himself once wrote:

> Your visit was a perfect ovation for us; we *never* enjoy anything so much as those visits of yours. The smoke and the Scotch and the late hours almost kill us; but we look each other in the eyes when you are gone, and say what a glorious time it was, and air the library, and begin sleeping and longing to have you back again.

CVIII

SUMMER LABORS AT QUARRY FARM

THEY went to Elmira, that summer of '76, to be "hermits and eschew caves and live in the sun," as Clemens wrote in a letter to Dr. Brown. They returned to the place as to Paradise: Clemens to his study and the books which he always called for, Mrs. Clemens to a blessed relief from social obligations, the children to the shady play-places, the green, sloping hill, where they could race and tumble, and to all their animal friends.

Susy was really growing up. She had had several birthdays, quite grand affairs, when she had been brought down in the morning, decked, and with proper ceremonies, with subsequent celebration. She was a strange, thoughtful child, much given to reflecting on the power and presence of infinity, for she was religiously taught. Down in the city, one night, there was a grand display of fireworks, and the hilltop was a good place from which to enjoy it; but it grew late after a little, and Susy was ordered to bed. She said, thoughtfully:

"I wish I could sit up all night, as God does."

The baby, whom they still called "Bay," was a tiny, brown creature who liked to romp in the sun and be rocked to sleep at night with a song. Clemens often took them for extended walks, pushing Bay in her carriage. Once, in a preoccupied moment, he let go of the little vehicle and it started downhill, gaining speed rapidly. He awoke then, and set off in wild pursuit. Before he could overtake the runaway carriage it had turned to the roadside and upset. Bay was lying among the stones and her head was bleeding. Hastily binding the wound with a handkerchief he started full speed with her up the hill toward the house, calling for restoratives as he came. It was no serious matter. The little girl was strong and did not readily give way to affliction.

The children were unlike: Susy was all contemplation and nerves; Bay serene and practical. It was said, when a pet cat died—this was some years later—that Susy deeply reflected as to its life here and hereafter, while Bay was concerned only as to the style of its funeral. Susy showed early her father's quaintness of remark. Once they bought her a heavier pair of shoes than she approved of. She was not in the best of humors during the day, and that night, when at prayer-time her mother said, "Now, Susy, put your thoughts on God," she answered, "Mama, I can't with those shoes."

Clemens worked steadily that summer and did a variety of things. He had given up a novel, begun with much enthusiasm, but he had undertaken another long manuscript. By the middle of August he had written several hundred pages of a story which was to be a continuation of *Tom Sawyer—The Adventures of Huckleberry Finn*. Now, here is a curious phase of genius. The novel which for a time had filled him with enthusiasm and faith had no important literary value, whereas, concerning this new tale, he says:

"I like it only tolerably well, as far as I have gone, and may possibly pigeonhole or burn the manuscript when it is done"—this of the story which, of his books of pure fiction, will perhaps longest survive. He did, in fact, give the story up, and without much regret, when it was about half completed, and let it lie unfinished for years.

He wrote one short tale, "The Canvasser's Story," a burlesque of no special distinction, and he projected for

QUARRY FARM, ELIMRA, N. Y.

GROUP AT FARM ABOUT 1874

the *Atlantic* a scheme of "blindfold novelettes," a series of stories to be written by well-known authors and others, each to be constructed on the same plot. One can easily imagine Clemens's enthusiasm over a banal project like that; his impulses were always rainbow-hued, whether valuable or not; but it is curious that Howells should welcome and even encourage an enterprise so far removed from all the traditions of art. It fell to pieces, at last, of inherent misconstruction. The title was to be, "A Murder and a Marriage." Clemens could not arrive at a logical climax that did not bring the marriage and the hanging on the same day.

The *Atlantic* started its "Contributors' Club," and Howells wrote to Clemens for a paragraph or more of personal opinion on any subject, assuring him that he could "spit his spite" out at somebody or something as if it were a passage from a letter. That was a fairly large permission to give Mark Twain. The paragraph he sent was the sort of thing he would write with glee, and hug himself over in the thought of Howells's necessity of rejecting it. In the accompanying note he said:

> Say, Boss, do you want this to lighten up your old freight-train with? I suppose you won't, but then it won't take long to say so.

He was always sending impossible offerings to the magazines; innocently enough sometimes, but often out of pure mischievousness. Yet they were constantly after him, for they knew they were likely to get a first-water gem. Mary Mapes Dodge, of *St. Nicholas*, wrote time and again, and finally said:

"I know a man who was persecuted by an editor till he went distracted."

In his reading that year at the farm he gave more than customary attention to one of his favorite books, *Pepys'*

Diary, that captivating old record which no one can follow continuously without catching the infection of its manner and the desire of imitation. He had been reading diligently one day, when he determined to try his hand on an imaginary record of conversation and court manners of a bygone day, written in the phrase of the period. The result was *Fireside Conversation in the Time of Queen Elizabeth*, or, as he later called it, *1601*. The "conversation," recorded by a supposed Pepys of that period, was written with all the outspoken coarseness and nakedness of that rank day, when fireside sociabilities were limited only by the range of loosened fancy, vocabulary, and physical performance, and not by any bounds of convention. Howells has spoken of Mark Twain's "Elizabethan breadth of parlance," and how he, Howells, was always hiding away in discreet holes and corners the letters in which Clemens had "loosed his bold fancy to stoop on rank suggestion." "I could not bear to burn them," he declares, "and I could not, after the first reading, quite bear to look at them."

In the *1601* Mark Twain outdid himself in the Elizabethan field. It was written as a letter to that robust divine, Rev. Joseph Twichell, who had no special scruples concerning Shakespearian parlance and customs. Before it was mailed it was shown to David Gray, who was spending a Sunday at Elmira. Gray said:

"Print it and put your name to it, Mark. You have never done a greater piece of work than that."

John Hay, whom it also reached in due time, pronounced it a classic—a "most exquisite bit of old English morality." Hay surreptitiously permitted some proofs to be made of it, and it has been circulated privately, though sparingly, ever since. At one time a special font of antique type was made for it and one hundred copies were taken on hand-made paper. They would easily bring a hundred dollars each to-day.

1601 is a genuine classic, as classics of that sort go. It is better than the gross obscenities of Rabelais, and perhaps, in some day to come, the taste that justified *Gargantua* and the *Decameron* will give this literary refugee shelter and setting among the more conventional writings of Mark Twain. Human taste is a curious thing; delicacy is purely a matter of environment and point of view.[1]

Eighteen hundred and seventy-six was a Presidential year—the year of the Hayes-Tilden campaign. Clemens and Howells were both warm Republicans and actively interested in the outcome, Clemens, as he confessed, for the first time in his life. Before his return to Hartford he announced himself publicly as a Hayes man, made so by Governor Hayes's letter of acceptance, which, he said, "expresses my own political convictions." His politics had not been generally known up to that time, and a Tilden and Hendricks club in Jersey City had invited him to be present and give them some political counsel, at a flag-raising. He wrote, declining pleasantly enough, then added:

"You have asked me for some political counsel or advice: In view of Mr. Tilden's Civil War record my advice is not to raise the flag."

[1] In a note-book of a later period Clemens himself wrote:

"It depends on who writes a thing whether it is coarse or not. I once wrote a conversation between Elizabeth, Shakespeare, Ben Jonson, Beaumont, Sir W. Raleigh, Lord Bacon, Sir Nicholas Throckmorton, and a stupid old nobleman—this latter being cup-bearer to the queen and ostensible reporter of the talk.

"There were four maids of honor present and a sweet young girl two years younger than the boy Beaumont. I built a conversation which *could* have happened—I used words such as *were* used at that time—1601. I sent it anonymously to a magazine, and how the editor abused it and the sender! But that man was a praiser of Rabelais, and had been saying, 'O that we had a Rabelais!' I judged that I could furnish him one."

He wrote Howells: "If Tilden is elected I think the entire country will go pretty straight to—Mrs. Howells's bad place."

Howells was writing a campaign biography of Hayes, which he hoped would have a large sale, and Clemens urged him to get it out quickly and save the country. Howells, working like a beaver, in turn urged Clemens to take the field in the cause. Returning to Hartford, Clemens presided at a political rally and made a speech, the most widely quoted of the campaign. All papers, without distinction as to party, quoted it, and all readers, regardless of politics, read it with joy.

Yet conditions did not improve. When Howells's book had been out a reasonable length of time he wrote that it had sold only two thousand copies.

"There's success for you," he said. "It makes me despair of the Republic, I can tell you."

Clemens, however, did not lose faith, and went on shouting for Hayes and damning Tilden till the final vote was cast. In later life he changed his mind about Tilden (as did many others) through sympathy. Sympathy could make Mark Twain change his mind any time. He stood for the right, but, above all, for justice. He stood for the wronged, regardless of all other things.

CIX

THE PUBLIC APPEARANCE OF "TOM SAWYER"

CLEMENS gave a few readings in Boston and Philadelphia, but when urged to go elsewhere made the excuse that he was having his portrait painted and could not leave home.

As a matter of fact, he was enjoying himself with Frank Millet, who had been invited to the house to do the portrait and had captured the fervent admiration of the whole family. Millet was young, handsome, and lively; Clemens couldn't see enough of him, the children adored him and added his name to the prayer which included each member of the household—the "Holy Family," Clemens called it.

Millet had brought with him but one piece of canvas for the portrait, and when the first sketch was finished Mrs. Clemens was so delighted with it that she did not wish him to touch it again. She was afraid of losing some particular feeling in it which she valued. Millet went to the city for another canvas and Clemens accompanied him. While Millet was doing his shopping it happened to occur to Clemens that it would be well to fill in the time by having his hair cut. He left word with a clerk to tell Millet that he had gone across the street. By and by the artist came over, and nearly wept with despair when he saw his subject sheared of the auburn, gray-sprinkled aureola that had made his first sketch a success. He tried it again, and the result was an excellent likeness, but it never satisfied Millet.

The Adventures of Tom Sawyer appeared late in December (1876), and immediately took its place as foremost of American stories of boy life, a place which it unquestionably holds to this day. We have already considered the personal details of this story, for they were essentially nothing more than the various aspects of Mark Twain's own boyhood. It is only necessary to add a word concerning the elaboration of this period in literary form.

From every point it is a masterpiece, this picture of boy life in a little lazy, drowsy town, with all the irresponsibility and general disreputability of boy character coupled with that indefinable, formless, elusive something we call boy conscience, which is more likely to be boy terror and a latent instinct of manliness. These things are so truly portrayed that every boy and man reader finds the tale fitting into his own remembered years, as if it had grown there. Every boy has played off sick to escape school; every boy has reflected in his heart Tom's picture of himself being brought home dead, and gloated over the stricken consciences of those who had blighted his young life; every boy—of that day, at least—every normal, respectable boy, grew up to "fear God and dread the Sunday-school," as Howells puts it in his review.

As for the story itself, the narrative of it, it is pure delight. The pirate camp on the island is simply boy heaven. What boy, for instance, would not change any other glory or boon that the world holds for this:

They built a fire against the side of a great log twenty or thirty steps within the somber depths of the forest, and then cooked some bacon in the frying-pan for supper, and used up half of the corn "pone" stock they had brought. It seemed glorious sport to be feasting in that wild, free way in the virgin forest of an unexplored and uninhabited island, far from the haunts of men, and they said they never would return to civilization. The climbing fire lit up their faces and threw its ruddy glare upon the pillared tree-trunks of their forest-temple, and upon the varnished foliage and the festooning vines.

There is a magic in it. Mark Twain, when he wrote it, felt renewed in him all the old fascination of those days and nights with Tom Blankenship, John Briggs, and the Bowen boys on Glasscock's Island. Everywhere in *Tom Sawyer* there is a quality, entirely apart from the humor and the narrative, which the younger reader is likely to overlook. No one forgets the whitewashing scene, but not many of us, from our early reading, recall this delicious bit of description which introduces it:

> The locust-trees were in bloom, and the fragrance of the blossoms filled the air. Cardiff Hill, beyond the village and above it, was green with vegetation, and it lay just far enough away to seem a delectable land, dreamy, reposeful, and inviting.

Tom's night visit home; the graveyard scene, with the murder of Dr. Robinson; the adventures of Tom and Becky in the cave—these are all marvelously invented. Literary thrill touches the ultimate in one incident of the cave episode. Brander Matthews has written:

> Nor is there any situation quite as thrilling as that awful moment in the cave when the boy and girl are lost in the darkness, and when Tom suddenly sees a human hand bearing a light, and then finds that the hand is the hand of Indian Joe, his one mortal enemy. I have always thought that the vision of the hand in the cave in *Tom Sawyer* was one of the very finest things in the literature of adventure since Robinson Crusoe first saw a single footprint in the sand of the sea-shore.

Mark Twain's invention was not always a reliable quantity, but with that eccentricity which goes with any attribute of genius, it was likely at any moment to rise supreme. If to the critical, hardened reader the tale seems a shade overdone here and there, a trifle extravagant in its delineations, let him go back to his first long-ago reading of it and see if he recalls anything but his pure delight in it then. As a boy's story it has not been equaled.

Tom Sawyer has ranked in popularity with *Roughing It.* Its sales go steadily on from year to year, and are likely to continue so long as boys and girls do not change, and men and women remember.[1]

[1] Col. Henry Watterson, when he finished *Tom Sawyer*, wrote:

"I have just laid down *Tom Sawyer*, and cannot resist the pressure. It is immense! I read every word of it, didn't skip a line, and nearly disgraced myself several times in the presence of a sleeping-car full of honorable and pious people. Once I had to get to one side and have a cry, and as for an internal compound of laughter and tears there was no end to it. . . . The 'funeral' of the boys, the cave business, and the hunt for the hidden treasure are as dramatic as anything I know of in fiction, while the pathos—particularly everything relating to Huck and Aunt Polly—makes a cross between Dickens's skill and Thackeray's nature, which, resembling neither, is thoroughly impressive and original."

CX

MARK TWAIN AND BRET HARTE WRITE A PLAY

IT was the fall and winter of '76 that Bret Harte came to Hartford and collaborated with Mark Twain on the play "Ah Sin," a comedy-drama, or melodrama, written for Charles T. Parsloe, the great impersonator of Chinese character. Harte had written a successful play which unfortunately he had sold outright for no great sum, and was eager for another venture. Harte had the dramatic sense and constructive invention. He also had humor, but he felt the need of the sort of humor that Mark Twain could furnish. Furthermore, he believed that a play backed by both their reputations must start with great advantages. Clemens also realized these things, and the arrangement was made. Speaking of their method of working, Clemens once said:

"Well, Bret came down to Hartford and we talked it over, and then Bret wrote it while I played billiards, but of course I had to go over it to get the dialect right. Bret never did know anything about dialect." Which is hardly a fair statement of the case. They both worked on the play, and worked hard.

During the period of its construction Harte had an order for a story which he said he must finish at once, as he needed the money. It must be delivered by the following night, and he insisted that he must be getting at it without a moment's delay. Still he seemed in no haste to begin. The evening passed; bedtime came. Then he asked that an open fire might be made in his room and a bottle of whisky sent up, in case he needed something to keep him awake. George attended to these matters, and nothing more was heard of Harte until very early next morning, when he rang for George and asked for a fresh fire and an additional supply of whisky. At breakfast-time he appeared, fresh, rosy, and elate, with the announcement that his story was complete.

That forenoon the Saturday Morning Club met at the Clemens home. It was a young women's club, of which Mark Twain was a sort of honorary member—a club for the purpose of intellectual advancement, somewhat on the order of the Monday Evening Club of men, except that the papers read before it were not prepared by members, but by men and women prominent in some field of intellectual progress. Bret Harte had agreed to read to them on this particular occasion, and he gaily appeared and gave them the story just finished, "Thankful Blossom," a tale which Mark Twain always regarded as one of Harte's very best.

The new play, "Ah Sin," by Mark Twain and Bret Harte, was put on at Washington, at the National Theater, on the evening of May 7, 1877. It had been widely exploited in the newspapers, and the fame of the authors insured a crowded opening. Clemens was unable to go over on account of a sudden attack of bronchitis. Parsloe was nervous accordingly, and the presence of Harte does not seem to have added to his happiness.

"I am not very well myself," he wrote to Clemens. "The excitement of the first night is bad enough, but to have the annoyance with Harte that I have is too much for a new beginner."

Nevertheless, the play seems to have gone well, with Parsloe as Ah Sin—a Chinese laundryman who was also a great number of other diverting things—with a fair support and a happy-go-lucky presentation of frontier life, which included a supposed murder, a false accusation, and a general clearing-up of mystery by the pleasant and wily and useful and entertaining Ah Sin. It was not a great play. It was neither very coherent nor convincing, but it had a lot of good fun in it, with character parts which, if not faithful to life, were faithful enough to the public conception of it to be amusing and exciting. At the end of each act not only Parsloe, but also the principal members of the company, were called before the curtain for special acknowledgments. When it was over there was a general call for Ah Sin, who came before the curtain and read a telegram.

> CHARLES T. PARSLOE,—I am on the sick-list, and therefore cannot come to Washington; but I have prepared two speeches —one to deliver in event of failure of the play, and the other if successful. Please tell me which I shall send. May be better to put it to vote.
>
> MARK TWAIN.

The house cheered the letter, and when it was put to vote decided unanimously that the play had been a success—a verdict more kindly than true.

J. I. Ford, of the theater management, wrote to Clemens, next morning after the first performance, urging him to come to Washington in person and "wet nurse" the play until "it could do for itself."

Ford expressed satisfaction with the play and its prospects, and concludes:

> I inclose notices. Come if you can. "Your presence will be worth ten thousand men. The king's name is a tower of strength." I have urged the President to come to-night.

The play made no money in Washington, but Augustin Daly decided to put it on in New York at the Fifth

Avenue Theater, with a company which included, besides Parsloe, Edmund Collier, P. A. Anderson, Dora Goldthwaite, Henry Crisp, and Mrs. Wells, a very worthy group of players indeed. Clemens was present at the opening, dressed in white, which he affected only for warm-weather use in those days, and made a speech at the end of the third act.

"Ah Sin" did not excite much enthusiasm among New York dramatic critics. The houses were promising for a time, but for some reason the performance as a whole did not contain the elements of prosperity. It set out on its provincial travels with no particular prestige beyond the reputation of its authors; and it would seem that this was not enough, for it failed to pay, and all parties concerned presently abandoned it to its fate and it was heard of no more. Just why "Ah Sin" did not prosper it would not become us to decide at this far remove of time and taste. Poorer plays have succeeded and better plays have failed since then, and no one has ever been able to demonstrate the mystery. A touch somewhere, a pulling-about and a readjustment, might have saved "Ah Sin," but the pullings and haulings which they gave it did not. Perhaps it still lies in some managerial vault, and some day may be dragged to light and reconstructed and recast, and come into its reward. Who knows? Or it may have drifted to that harbor of forgotten plays, whence there is no returning.

As between Harte and Clemens, the whole matter was unfortunate. In the course of their association there arose a friction and the long-time friendship disappeared.

CXI

A BERMUDA HOLIDAY

ON the 16th of May, 1877, Mark Twain set out on what, in his note-book, he declared to be "the first actual pleasure-trip" he had ever taken, meaning that on every previous trip he had started with a purpose other than that of mere enjoyment. He took with him his friend and pastor, the Rev. Joseph H. Twichell, and they sailed for Bermuda, an island resort not so well known or so fashionable as to-day.

They did not go to a hotel. Under assumed names they took up quarters in a boarding-house, with a Mrs. Kirkham, and were unmolested and altogether happy in their wanderings through four golden days. Mark Twain could not resist keeping a note-book, setting down bits of scenery and character and incident, just as he had always done. He was impressed with the cheapness of property and living in the Bermuda of that period. He makes special mention of some cottages constructed of coral blocks: "All as beautiful and as neat as a pin, at the cost of four hundred and eighty dollars each." To Twichell he remarked:

"Joe, this place is like Heaven, and I'm going to make the most of it."

"Mark," said Twichell, "that's right; make the most of a place that is *like* Heaven while you have a chance."

In one of the entries—the final one—Clemens says:

"Bermuda is free (at present) from the triple curse of

railways, telegraphs, and newspapers, but this will not last the year. I propose to spend next year here and no more."

When they were ready to leave, and started for the steamer, Twichell made an excuse to go back, his purpose being to tell their landlady and her daughter that, without knowing it, they had been entertaining Mark Twain.

"Did you ever hear of Mark Twain?" asked Twichell.

The daughter answered.

"Yes," she said, "until I'm tired of the name. I know a young man who never talks of anything else."

"Well," said Twichell, "that gentleman with me is Mark Twain."

The Kirkhams declined to believe it at first, and then were in deep sorrow that they had not known it earlier. Twichell promised that he and Clemens would come back the next year; and they meant to go back—we always mean to go back to places—but it was thirty years before they returned at last, and then their pleasant landlady was dead.

On the home trip they sighted a wandering vessel, manned by blacks, trying to get to New York. She had no cargo and was pretty helpless. Later, when she was reported again, Clemens wrote about it in a Hartford paper, telling the story as he knew it. The vessel had shipped the crew, on a basis of passage to New York, in exchange for labor. So it was a "pleasure-excursion!" Clemens dwelt on this fancy:

> I have heard of a good many pleasure-excursions, but this heads the list. It is monumental, and if ever the tired old tramp is found I should like to be there and see him in his sorrowful rags and his venerable head of grass and seaweed, and hear the ancient mariners tell the story of their mysterious wanderings through the solemn solitudes of the ocean.

Long afterward this vagrant craft was reported again, still drifting with the relentless Gulf Stream. Perhaps she reached New York in time; one would like to know, but there seems no good way to find out.

That first Bermuda voyage was always a happy memory to Mark Twain. To Twichell he wrote that it was the "joyousest trip" he had ever made:

> Not a heartache anywhere, not a twinge of conscience. I often come to myself out of a reverie and detect an undertone of thought that had been thinking itself without volition of mind—*viz.*, that if we had only had ten days of those walks and talks instead of four.

There was but one regret: Howells had not been with them. Clemens denounced him for his absence:

> If you had gone with us and let me pay the fifty dollars, which the trip and the board and the various knick-knacks and mementos would cost, I would have picked up enough droppings from your conversation to pay me five hundred per cent. profit in the way of the *several* magazine articles which I could have written; whereas I can now write only one or two, and am therefore largely out of pocket by your proud ways.

Clemens would not fail to write about his trip. He could not help doing that, and he began "Some Rambling Notes of an Idle Excursion" as soon as he landed in Hartford. They were quite what the name would signify—leisurely, pleasant commentaries on a loafing, peaceful vacation. They are not startling in their humor or description, but are gently amusing and summery, reflecting, bubble-like, evanescent fancies of Bermuda. Howells, shut up in a Boston editorial office, found them delightful enough, and very likely his *Atlantic* readers agreed with him. The story of "Isaac and the Prophets of Baal" was one that Capt. Ned Wakeman had told to Twichell during a voyage which the latter had made to Aspinwall with that vigorous old seafarer; so in the "Rambling Notes" Wakeman appears as Captain Hurricane Jones, probably a step in the evolution of the later name of Stormfield. The best feature of the series (there were four papers in all) is a story of a rescue in mid-ocean; but surely the brightest ripple of humor is the reference to Bermuda's mahogany-tree:

> There was exactly one mahogany-tree on the island. I know this to be reliable because I saw a man who said he had counted it many a time and could not be mistaken. He was a man with a hare lip and a pure heart, and everybody said he was as true as steel. Such men are all too few.

Clemens cared less for these papers than did Howells. He had serious doubts about the first two and suggested their destruction, but with Howells's appreciation his own confidence in them returned and he let them all go in. They did not especially advance his reputation, but perhaps they did it no harm.

CXII

A NEW PLAY AND A NEW TALE

HE wrote a short story that year which is notable mainly for the fact that in it the telephone becomes a literary property, probably for the first time. "The Loves of Alonzo Fitz-Clarence and Rosannah Ethelton" employed in the consummation what was then a prospect, rather than a reality—long-distance communication.

His work that summer consisted mainly of two extensive undertakings, one of which he completed without delay. He still had the dramatic ambition, and he believed that he was capable now of constructing a play entirely from his own resources.

To Howells, in June, he wrote:

> To-day I am deep in a comedy which I began this morning—principal character an old detective. I skeletoned the first act and *wrote* the second to-day, and am dog-tired now. Fifty-four pages of MS. in seven hours.

Seven days later, the Fourth of July, he said:

> I have piled up one hundred and fifty-one pages on my comedy. The first, second and fourth acts are done, and done to my satisfaction, too. To-morrow and next day will finish the third act, and the play. Never had so much fun over anything in my life—never such consuming interest and delight. And just think! I had Sol Smith Russell in my mind's eye for the old detective's part, and hang it! he has gone off pottering with Oliver Optic, or else the papers lie.

He was working with enthusiasm, you see, believing in it with a faith which, alas, was no warrant for its quality. Even Howells caught his enthusiasm and became eager to see the play, and to have the story it contained told for the *Atlantic*.

But in the end it proved a mistake. Dion Boucicault, when he read the manuscript, pronounced it better than "Ah Sin," but that was only qualified praise. Actors who considered the play, anxious enough to have Mark Twain's name on their posters and small bills, were obliged to admit that, while it contained marvelous lines, it wouldn't "go." John Brougham wrote:

> There is an absolute "embarrassment of riches" in your "Detective" most assuredly, but the difficulty is to put it into profitable form. The quartz is there in abundance, only requiring the necessary manipulation to extract the gold.
>
> In narrative structure the story would be full of life, character, and the most exuberant fun, but it is altogether too diffuse in its present condition for dramatic representation, and I confess I do not feel sufficient confidence in my own experience (even if I had the time, which on reflection I find I have not) to undertake what, under different circumstances, would be a "labor of love."
>
> Yours sincerely,
>
> John Brougham.

That was frank, manly, and to the point; it covered the ground exactly. "Simon Wheeler, the Amateur Detective," had plenty of good material in it—plenty of dialogue and situations; but the dialogue wouldn't play and the situations wouldn't act. Clemens realized that perhaps the drama was not, after all, his forte; he dropped "Simon Wheeler," lost his interest in "Ah Sin," even leased "Colonel Sellers" for the coming season, and so, in a sort of fury, put theatrical matters out of his mind.

He had entered upon what, for him, was a truer domain. One day he picked up from among the books at the farm a little juvenile volume, an English story of the thirteenth century by Charlotte M. Yonge, entitled, *The Prince and the Page*. It was a story of Edward I. and his cousins, Richard and Henry de Montfort; in part it told of the submerged personality of the latter, picturing him as having dwelt in disguise as a blind beggar for a period of years. It was a story of a sort and with a setting that Mark Twain loved, and as he read there came a correlative idea. Not only would he disguise a prince as a beggar, but a beggar a a prince. He would have them change places in the world, and each learn the burdens of the other's life.[1]

The plot presented physical difficulties. He still had some lurking thought of stage performance, and saw in his mind a spectacular presentation, with all the costumery of an early period as background for a young and beautiful creature who would play the part of prince. The old device of changelings in the cradle (later used in *Pudd'nhead Wilson*) presented itself to him, but it could not provide the situations he had in mind. Finally came the thought of a playful interchange of raiment and state (with startling and unlooked-for consequence)—the guise and personality of Tom Canty, of Offal Court, for those of the son of Henry VIII., little Edward Tudor, more lately sixth English king of that name. This little prince was not his first selection for the part. His original idea had been to use the late King Edward VII. (then Prince of Wales) at about fifteen, but he found that it would never answer to lose a prince among the slums of modern London, and have his proud estate denied and jeered at by a modern mob. He felt that he could not make it seem real; so he followed back through history, looking along

[1] There is no point of resemblance between the *Prince and the Pauper* and the tale that inspired it. No one would ever guess that the one had grown out of the readings of the other, and no comparison of any sort is possible between them.

for the proper time and prince, till he came to little Edward, who was too young—but no matter, he would do.

He decided to begin his new venture in story form. He could dramatize it later. The situation appealed to him immensely. The idea seemed a brand-new one; it was delightful, it was fascinating, and he was saturated with the atmosphere and literature and history—the data and detail of that delightful old time. He put away all thought of cheap, modern play-acting and writing, to begin one of the loveliest and most entertaining and instructive tales of old English life. He decided to be quite accurate in his picture of the period, and he posted himself on old London very carefully. He bought a pocket-map which he studied in the minutest detail.

He wrote about four hundred manuscript pages of the tale that summer; then, as the inspiration seemed to lag a little, put it aside, as was his habit, to wait until the ambition for it should be renewed. It was a long wait, as usual. He did not touch it again for more than three years.

CXIII

TWO DOMESTIC DRAMAS

SOME unusual happenings took place that summer of 1877. John T. Lewis (colored), already referred to as the religious antagonist of Auntie Cord, by great presence of mind and bravery saved the lives of Mrs. Clemens's sister-in-law, Mrs. Charles ("Charley") Langdon, her little daughter Julia, and her nurse-maid. They were in a buggy, and their runaway horse was flying down East Hill toward Elmira to certain destruction, when Lewis, laboring slowly homeward with a loaded wagon, saw them coming and turned his team across the road, after which he leaped out and with extraordinary strength and quickness grabbed the horse's bridle and brought him to a standstill. The Clemens and Crane families, who had seen the runaway start at the farm gate, arrived half wild with fear, only to find the supposed victims entirely safe.

Everybody contributed in rewarding Lewis. He received money ($1,500) and various other presents, including inscribed books and trinkets, also, what he perhaps valued more than anything, a marvelous stem-winding gold watch. Clemens, writing a full account to Dr. Brown of the watch, says:

> And if any scoffer shall say, "behold this thing is out of character," there is an inscription within which will silence him; for it will teach him that this wearer aggrandizes the watch, not the watch the wearer.

In another paragraph he says:

> When Lewis arrived the other evening, after having saved those lives by a feat which I think is the most marvelous I can call to mind, when he arrived hunched up on his manure-wagon and as grotesquely picturesque as usual, everybody wanted to go and see how he looked. They came back and said he was beautiful. It was *so*, too, and yet he would have *photographed* exactly as he would have done any day these past seven years that he has occupied this farm.

Lewis acknowledged his gifts in a letter which closed with a paragraph of rare native loftiness:

> But I beg to say, humbly, that inasmuch as divine Providence saw fit to use me as an instrument for the saving of those preshious lives, the honner conferd upon me was greater than the feat performed.

Lewis lived to enjoy his prosperity, and the honor of the Clemens and Langdon households, for twenty-nine years. When he was too old to work there was a pension, to which Clemens contributed; also Henry H. Rogers. So the simple-hearted, noble old negro closed his days in peace.

Mrs. Crane, in a letter, late in July, 1906, told of his death:

> He was always cheerful, and seemed not to suffer much pain, told stories, and was able to eat almost everything.
>
> Three days ago a new difficulty appeared, on account of which his doctor said he must go to the hospital for care such as it was quite impossible to give in his home.
>
> He died on his way there.

Thus it happened that he died on the road where he had performed his great deed.

A second unusual incident of that summer occurred in Hartford. There had been a report of a strange man seen about the Clemens place, thought to be a prospecting burglar, and Clemens went over to investigate. A little searching inquiry revealed that the man was not a burglar, but a mechanic out of employment, a lover of one of the house-maids, who had given him food and shelter on the premises, intending no real harm. When the girl found that her secret was discovered, she protested that he was her *fiancé*, though she said he appeared lately to have changed his mind and no longer wished to marry her.

The girl seemed heartbroken, and sympathy for her was naturally the first and about the only feeling which Clemens developed, for the time being. He reasoned with the young man, but without making much headway. Finally his dramatic instinct prompted him to a plan of a sort which would have satisfied even Tom Sawyer. He asked Twichell to procure a license for the couple, and to conceal himself in a ground floor bath-room. He arranged with the chief of police to be on hand in another room; with the rest of the servants quietly to prepare a wedding-feast, and finally with Lizzie herself to be dressed for the ceremony. He had already made an appointment with the young man to come to see him at a certain hour on a "matter of business," and the young man arrived in the belief, no doubt, that it was something which would lead to profitable employment. When he came in Clemens gently and quietly reviewed the situation, told him of the young girl's love for him; how he had been sheltered and fed by her; how through her kindness to him she had compromised her reputation for honesty and brought upon her all the suspicion of having sheltered a burglar; how she was ready and willing to marry him, and how he (Clemens) was ready to assist them to obtain work and a start in life.

But the young man was not enthusiastic. He was a Swede and slow of action. He resolutely declared that he was not ready to marry yet, and in the end refused to do so. Then came the dramatic moment. Clemens quietly but firmly informed him that the wedding ceremony must take place; that by infesting his premises he had broken the law, not only against trespass, but most likely against house-breaking. There was a brief discussion of this point. Finally Clemens gave him five minutes to make up his mind, with the statement that he had an officer in waiting, and unless he would consent to the wedding he would be taken in charge. The young man began to temporize, saying that it would be necessary for him to get a license and a preacher. But Clemens stepped to the door of the bath-room, opened it, and let out Twichell, who had been sweltering there in that fearful place for more than an hour, it being August. The delinquent lover found himself confronted with all the requisites of matrimony except the bride, and just then this detail appeared on the scene, dressed for the occasion. Behind her ranged the rest of the servants and a few invited guests. Before the young man knew it he had a wife, and on the whole did not seem displeased. It ended with a gay supper and festivities. Then Clemens started them handsomely by giving each of them a check for one hundred dollars; and in truth (which in this case, at least, is stranger than fiction) they lived happily and prosperously ever after.

Some years later Mark Twain based a story on this episode, but it was never entirely satisfactory and remains unpublished.

CXIV

THE WHITTIER BIRTHDAY SPEECH

IT was the night of December 17, 1877, that Mark Twain made his unfortunate speech at the dinner given by the *Atlantic* staff to John G. Whittier on his seventieth birthday. Clemens had attended a number of the dinners which the *Atlantic* gave on one occasion or another, and had provided a part of the entertainment. It is only fair to say that his after-dinner speeches at such times had been regarded as very special events, genuine triumphs of humor and delivery. But on this particular occasion he determined to outdo himself, to prepare something unusual, startling, something altogether unheard of.

When Mark Twain had an impulse like that it was possible for it to result in something dangerous, especially in those earlier days. This time it produced a bombshell; not just an ordinary bombshell, or even a twelve-inch projectile, but a shell of planetary size. It was a sort of hoax—always a doubtful plaything—and in this case it brought even quicker and more terrible retribution than usual. It was an imaginary presentation of three disreputable frontier tramps who at some time had imposed themselves on a lonely miner as Longfellow, Emerson, and Holmes, quoting apposite selections from their verses to the accompaniment of cards and drink, and altogether conducting themselves in a most unsavory fashion. At the end came the enlightenment that these were not what they pretended to be, but only impostors—disgusting frauds. A feature like that would be a doubtful thing to try in any cultured atmosphere. The thought of associating, ever so remotely, those three old bummers which he had conjured up with the venerable and venerated Emerson, Longfellow, and Holmes, the Olympian trinity, seems ghastly enough to-day, and must have seemed even more so then. But Clemens, dazzled by the rainbow splendor of his conception, saw in it only a rare colossal humor, which would fairly lift and bear his hearers along on a tide of mirth. He did not show his effort to any one beforehand. He wanted its full beauty to burst upon the entire company as a surprise.

It did that. Howells was toastmaster, and when he came to present Clemens he took particular pains to introduce him as one of his foremost contributors and dearest friends. Here, he said, was "a humorist who never left you hanging you head for having enjoyed his joke."

Thirty years later Clemens himself wrote of his impressions as he rose to deliver his speech.

> I vaguely remember some of the details of that gathering: dimly I can see a hundred people—no, perhaps fifty—shadowy figures, sitting at tables feeding, ghosts now to me, and nameless forevermore. I don't know who they were, but I can very distinctly see, seated at the grand table and facing the rest of us, Mr. Emerson, supernaturally grave, unsmiling; Mr. Whittier, grave, lovely, his beautiful spirit shining out of his face; Mr. Longfellow, with his silken-white hair and his benignant face; Dr. Oliver Wendell Holmes, flashing smiles and affection and all good-fellowship everywhere, like a rose-diamond whose facets are being turned toward the light, first one way and then another—a charming man, and always fascinating, whether he was talking or whether he was sitting still (what he would call still, but what would be more or less motion to other people). I can see those figures with entire distinctiness across this abyss of time.

William Winter, the poet, had just preceded him, and it seemed a moment aptly chosen for his so-different theme. "And then," to quote Howells, "the amazing mistake, the bewildering blunder, the cruel catastrophe was upon us."

After the first two or three hundred words, when the general plan and purpose of the burlesque had developed, when the names of Longfellow, Emerson, and Holmes began to be flung about by those bleary outcasts, and their verses given that sorry association, those *Atlantic* diners became petrified with amazement and horror. Too late, then, the speaker realized his mistake. He could not stop, he must go on to the ghastly end. And somehow he did it, while "there fell a silence weighing many tons to the square inch, which deepened from moment to moment, and was broken only by the hysterical and blood-curdling laughter of a single guest, whose name shall not be handed down to infamy."

Howells can remember little more than that, but Clemens recalls that one speaker made an effort to follow him—Bishop, the novelist, and that Bishop didn't last long.

> It was not many sentences after his first before he began to hesitate and break, and lose his grip, and totter and wobble, and at last he slumped down in a limp and mushy pile.

The next man had not strength to rise, and somehow the company broke up.

Howells's next recollection is of being in a room of the hotel, and of hearing Charles Dudley Warner saying in the gloom:

"Well, Mark, *you're* a funny fellow."

He remembers how, after a sleepless night, Clemens went out to buy some bric-à-brac, with a soul far from bric-à-brac, and returned to Hartford in a writhing agony of spirit. He believed that he was ruined forever, so far as his Boston associations were concerned; and when he confessed all the tragedy to Mrs. Clemens it seemed to her also that the mistake could never be wholly repaired. The fact that certain papers quoted the speech and spoke well of it, and certain readers who had not listened to it thought it enormously funny, gave very little comfort. But perhaps his chief concern was the ruin which he believed he had brought upon Howells. He put his heart into a brief letter:

My dear Howells,—My sense of disgrace does not abate. It grows. I see that it is going to add itself to my list of permanencies, a list of humiliations that extends back to when I was seven years old, and which keep on persecuting me regardless of my repentances.

I feel that my misfortune has injured me all over the country; therefore it will be best that I retire from before the public at present. It will hurt the *Atlantic* for me to appear in its pages now. So it is my opinion, and my wife's, that the telephone story had better be suppressed. Will you return those proofs or revises to me, so that I can use the same on some future occasion?

It seems as if I must have been insane when I wrote that speech and saw no harm in it, no disrespect toward those men whom I reverenced so much. And what shame I brought upon *you*, after what you said in introducing me! It burns me like fire to think of it.

The whole matter is a dreadful subject. Let me drop it here—at least on paper.

Penitently yours, Mark.

So, all in a moment, his world had come to an end—as it seemed. But Howells's letter, which came rushing back by first mail, brought hope.

"It was a fatality," Howells said. "One of those sorrows into which a man walks with his eyes wide open, no one knows why."

Howells assured him that Longfellow, Emerson, and Holmes would so consider it, beyond doubt; that Charles Eliot Norton had already expressed himself exactly in the right spirit concerning it. Howells declared that there was no intention of dropping Mark Twain's work from the *Atlantic*.

You are not going to be floored by it; there is more justice than that even in *this* world. Especially as regards *me*, just call the sore spot well. I can say more, and with better heart, in praise of your good feeling (which was what I always liked in you), since this thing happened than I could before.

It was agreed that he should at once write a letter to Longfellow, Emerson, and Holmes, and he did write, laying his heart bare to them. Longfellow and Holmes answered in a fine spirit of kindliness, and Miss Emerson wrote for her father in the same tone. Emerson had not been offended, for he had not heard the speech, having arrived even then at that stage of semi-oblivion as to immediate things which eventually so completely shut him away. Longfellow's letter made light of the whole matter. The newspapers, he said, had caused all the mischief.

A bit of humor at a dinner-table talk is one thing; a report of it in the morning papers is another. One needs the lamplight and the scenery. These failing, what was meant in jest assumes a serious aspect.

I do not believe that anybody was much hurt. Certainly I was not, and Holmes tells me that he was not. So I think you may dismiss the matter from your mind, without further remorse.

It was a very pleasant dinner, and I think Whittier enjoyed it very much.

Holmes likewise referred to it as a trifle.

It never occurred to me for a moment to take offense, or to feel wounded by your playful use of my name. I have heard some mild questioning as to whether, even in fun, it was good taste to associate the names of the authors with the absurdly unlike personalities attributed to them, but it seems to be an open question. Two of my friends, gentlemen of education and the highest social standing, were infinitely amused by your speech, and stoutly defended it against the charge of impropriety. More than this, one of the cleverest and best-known ladies we have among us was highly delighted with it.

Miss Emerson's letter was to Mrs. Clemens and its homelike New England fashion did much to lift the gloom.

DEAR MRS. CLEMENS,—At New Year's our family always meets, to spend two days together. To-day my father came last, and brought with him Mr. Clemens's letter, so that I read it to the assembled family, and I have come right up-stairs to write to you about it. My sister said, "Oh, let father write!" but my mother said, "No, don't wait for him. Go now; don't stop to pick that up. Go this minute and write. I think that is a noble letter. Tell them so." First let me say that no shadow of indignation has ever been in any of our minds. The night of the dinner, my father says, he did not hear Mr. Clemens's speech. He was too far off, and my mother says that when she read it to him the next day it amused him. But what you will want is to know, without any softening, how we did feel. We were disappointed. We have liked almost everything we have ever seen over Mark Twain's signature. It has made us like the man, and we have delighted in the fun. Father has often asked us to repeat certain passages of *The Innocents Abroad*, and of a speech at a London dinner in 1872, and we all expect both to approve and to enjoy when we see his name. Therefore, when we read this speech it was a real disappointment. I said to my brother that it didn't seem good or funny, and he said, "No, it was unfortunate. Still some of those quotations were very good"; and he gave them with relish and my father laughed, though never having seen a card in his life, he couldn't understand them like his children. My mother read it lightly and had hardly any second thoughts about it. To my father it is as if it had not been; he never quite heard, never quite understood it, and he forgets easily and entirely. I think it doubtful whether he writes to Mr. Clemens, for he is old and long ago gave up answering letters. I think you can see just *how* bad, and how little bad, it was as far as we are concerned, and this lovely heartbreaking letter makes up for our diasppointment in our much-liked author, and restores our former feeling about him.

ELLEN T. EMERSON.

The sorrow dulled a little as the days passed. Just after Christmas Clemens wrote to Howells:

I haven't done a stroke of work since the *Atlantic* dinner. But I'm going to try to-morrow. How could I ever—

Ah, well, I am a great and sublime fool. But then I am God's fool, and all his work must be contemplated with respect.

So long as that unfortunate speech is remembered there will be differences of opinion as to its merits and propriety. Clemens himself, reading it for the first time in nearly thirty years, said:

"I find it gross, coarse—well, I needn't go on with particulars. I don't like any part of it, from the beginning to the end. I find it always offensive and detestable. How do I account for this change of view? I don't know."

But almost immediately afterward he gave it another consideration and reversed his opinion completely. All the spirit and delight of his old first conception returned, and preparing it for publication[1] he wrote:

I have read it twice, and unless I am an idiot it hasn't a single defect in it, from the first word to the last. It is just as good as good can be. It is smart; it is saturated with humor. There isn't a suggestion of coarseness or vulgarity in it anywhere.

It was altogether like Mark Twain to have those two absolutely opposing opinions in that brief time; for, after all, it was only a question of the human point of view, and Mark Twain's points of view were likely to be as extremely human as they were varied.

[1] *North American Review*, December, 1907, now with comment included in the volume of "Speeches." Also see Appendix O, at the end of last volume.

Of course the first of these impressions, the verdict of the fresh mind uninfluenced by the old conception, was the more correct one. The speech was decidedly out of place in that company. The skit was harmless enough, but it was of the Comstock grain. It lacked refinement, and, what was still worse, it lacked humor, at least the humor of a kind suited to that long-ago company of listeners. It was another of those grievous mistakes which genius (and not talent) can make, for genius is a sort of possession. The individual is pervaded, dominated for a time by an angel or an imp, and he seldom, of himself, is able to discriminate between his controls. A literary imp was always lying in wait for Mark Twain; the imp of the burlesque, tempting him to do the *outré*, the outlandish, the shocking thing. It was this that Olivia Clemens had to labor hardest against: the cheapening of his own high purpose with an extravagant false note, at which sincerity, conviction, and artistic harmony took wings and fled away. Notably he did a good burlesque now and then, but his fame would not have suffered if he had been delivered altogether from his besetting temptation.

CXV

HARTFORD AND BILLIARDS

CLEMENS was never much inclined to work, away from his Elmira study. "Magnanimous Incident Literature" (for the *Atlantic*) was about his only completed work of the winter of 1877-78. He was always tinkering with the "Visit to Heaven," and after one reconstruction Howells suggested that he bring it out as a book, in England, with Dean Stanley's indorsement, though this may have been only semi-serious counsel. The story continued to lie in seclusion.

Clemens had one new book in the field—a small book, but profitable. Dan Slote's firm issued for him the Mark Twain Scrap-book, and at the end of the first royalty period rendered a statement of twenty-five thousand copies sold, which was well enough for a book that did not contain a single word that critics could praise or condemn. Slote issued another little book for him soon after—*Punch, Brothers, Punch!*—which, besides that lively sketch, contained the "Random Notes" and seven other selections.

Mark Twain was tempted to go into the lecture field that winter, not by any of the offers, though these were numerous enough, but by the idea of a combination which he thought might be not only profitable but pleasant. Thomas Nast had made a great success of his caricature lectures, and Clemens, recalling Nast's long-ago proposal, found it newly attractive. He wrote characteristically:

My dear Nast,—I did not think I should ever stand on a platform again until the time was come for me to say, "I die innocent." But the same old offers keep arriving. I have declined them all, just as usual, though sorely tempted, as usual.

Now, I do not decline because I mind talking to an audience, but because (1) traveling alone is so heartbreakingly dreary, and (2) shouldering the whole show is such a cheer-killing responsibility.

Therefore, I now propose to you what you proposed to me in 1867, ten years ago (when I was unknown)—*viz.*, that you stand on the platform and make pictures, and I stand by you and blackguard the audience. I should enormously enjoy meandering around (to big towns—don't want to go to the little ones), with you for company.

My idea is not to fatten the lecture agents and lyceums on the spoils, but to put all the ducats religiously into two equal piles, and say to the artist and lecturer, "absorb these."

For instance, [here follows a plan and a possible list of the cities to be visited]. The letter continues:

Call the gross receipts $100,000 for four months and a half, and the profit from $60,000 to $75,000 (I try to make the figures large enough, and leave it to the public to reduce them).

I did not put in Philadelphia because Pugh owns that town, and last winter, when I made a little reading-trip, he only paid me $300, and pretended his concert (I read fifteen minutes in the midst of a concert) cost him a vast sum, and so he couldn't afford any more. I could get up a better concert with a barrel of cats.

I have imagined two or three pictures and concocted the accompanying remarks, to see how the thing would go. I was charmed.

Well, you think it over, Nast, and drop me a line. We should have some fun.

Undoubtedly this would have been a profitable combination, but Nast had a distaste for platforming—had given it up, as he thought, for life. So Clemens settled down to the fireside days, that afforded him always the larger comfort. The children were at an age to be entertaining, and to be entertained. In either case they furnished him plenty of diversion when he did not care to write. They had learned his gift as a romancer, and with this audience he might be as extravagant as he liked. They sometimes assisted by furnishing subjects. They would bring him a picture, requiring him to invent a story for it without a moment's delay. Sometimes they suggested the names of certain animals or objects, and demanded that these be made into a fairy tale. If they heard the name of any new creature or occupation they were likely to offer them as impromptu inspiration. Once he was suddenly required to make a story out of a plumber and a "bawgunstrictor," but he was equal to it. On one side of the library, along the book-shelves that joined the mantelpiece, were numerous ornaments and pictures. At one end was the head of a girl, that they called "Emeline," and at the other was an oil-painting of a cat. When other subjects failed, the romancer was obliged to build a story impromptu, and without preparation, beginning with the cat, working along through the bric-à-brac, and ending with "Emeline." This was the unvarying program. He was not allowed to begin with "Emeline" and end with the cat, and he was not permitted to introduce an ornament from any other portion of the room. He could vary the story as much as he liked. In fact, he was required to do that. The trend of its chapters, from the cat to "Emeline," was a well-trodden and ever-entertaining way.

He gave up his luxurious study to the children as a sort of nursery and playroom, and took up his writing-quarters, first in a room over the stables, then in the billiard-room, which, on the whole, he preferred to any other place, for it was a third-story remoteness, and he could knock the balls about for inspiration.

The billiard-room became his headquarters. He received his callers there and impressed them into the game. If they could play, well and good; if they could not play, so much the better—he could beat them extravagantly, and he took a huge delight in such conquests. Every Friday evening, or oftener, a small party of billiard-lovers gathered, and played until a late hour, told stories, and smoked till the room was blue, comforting themselves with hot Scotch and general good-fellowship. Mark Twain always had a genuine passion for billiards. He was never tired of the game. He could play all night. He would stay till the last man gave out from sheer weariness; then he would go on knocking the balls about alone. He liked to invent new games and new rules for old games, often inventing a rule on the spur of the moment to fit some particular shot or position on the table. It amused him highly to do this, to make the rule advantage his own play, and to pretend a deep indignation when his opponents disqualified his rulings and rode him down. S. C. Dunham was among those who belonged to the "Friday Evening Club," as they called it, and Henry C. Robinson, long dead, and rare Ned Bunce, and F. G. Whitmore; and the old room there at the top of the house, with its little outside balcony, rang with their voices and their laughter in that day when life and the world for them was young. Clemens quoted to them sometimes:

> Come, fill the cup, and in the fire of spring
> Your winter garment of repentance fling;
>   The bird of time has but a little way
> To flutter, and the bird is on the wing.

Omar was new then on this side of the Atlantic, and to his serene "eat, drink, and be merry" philosophy, in Fitzgerald's rhyme, these were early converts. Mark Twain had an impressive, musical delivery of verse; the players were willing at any moment to listen as he recited:

> For some we loved, the loveliest and best
> That from his vintage rolling time has prest,

Have drunk their cup a round or two before,
And one by one crept silently to rest.

Ah, make the most of what we yet may spend,
Before we too into the dust descend;
Dust unto dust, and under dust to lie,
Sans wine, sans song, sans singer, and—sans End.[1]

[1] The *Rubaiyat* had made its first appearance, in Hartford, a little before in a column of extracts published in the *Courant*. Twichell immediately wrote Clemens a card:

"Read (if you haven't) the extracts from Omar Khayyam, on the first page of this morning's *Courant*. I think we'll have to get the book. I never yet came across anything that uttered certain thoughts of mine so adequately. And it's only a translation. Read it, and we'll talk it over. There is something in it very like the passage of Emerson you read me last night, in fact identical with it in thought.

"Surely this Omar was a great poet. Anyhow, he has given me an immense revelation this morning.

"Hoping that you are better, J. H. T."

Twichell's "only a translation" has acquired a certain humor with time.

CXVI

OFF FOR GERMANY

THE German language became one of the interests of the Clemens home during the early months of 1878. The Clemenses had long looked forward to a sojourn in Europe, and the demand for another Mark Twain book of travel furnished an added reason for their going. They planned for the spring sailing, and to spend a year or more on the Continent, making their headquarters in Germany. So they entered into the study of the language with an enthusiasm and perseverance that insured progress. There was a German nurse for the children, and the whole atmosphere of the household presently became lingually Teutonic. It amused Mark Twain, as everything amused him, but he was a good student; he acquired a working knowledge of the language in an extraordinarily brief time, just as in an earlier day he had picked up piloting. He would never become a German scholar, but his vocabulary and use of picturesque phrases, particularly those that combined English and German words, were often really startling, not only for their humor, but for their expressiveness.

Necessarily the new study would infect his literature. He conceived a plan for making Captain Wakeman (Stormfield) come across a copy of Ollendorf in Heaven, and proceed to learn the language of a near-lying district.

They arranged to sail early in April, and, as on their former trip, persuaded Miss Clara Spaulding, of Elmira, to accompany them. They wrote to the Howellses, breaking the news of the journey, urging them to come to Hartford for a good-by visit. Howells and his wife came. The Twichells, Warners, and other Hartford friends paid repeated farewell calls. The furniture was packed, the rooms desolated, the beautiful home made ready for closing.

They were to have pleasant company on the ship. Bayard Taylor, then recently appointed Minister to Germany, wrote that he had planned to sail on the same vessel; Murat Halstead's wife and daughter were listed among the passengers. Clemens made a brief speech at Taylor's "farewell dinner."

The "Mark Twain" party, consisting of Mr. and Mrs. Clemens, Miss Spaulding, little Susy and Clara ("Bay"), and a nurse-maid, Rosa, sailed on the *Holsatia*, April 11, 1878. Bayard Taylor and the Halstead ladies also sailed, as per program; likewise Murat Halstead himself, for whom no program had been made. There was a storm outside, and the *Holsatia* anchored down the bay to wait until the worst was over. As the weather began to moderate Halstead and others came down in a tug for a final word of good-by. When the tug left, Halstead somehow managed to get overlooked, and was presently on his way across the ocean with only such wardrobe as he had on, and what Bayard Taylor, a large man like himself, was willing to lend him. Halstead was accused of having intentionally allowed himself to be left behind, and his case did have a suspicious look; but in any event they were glad to have him along.

In a written word of good-by to Howells, Clemens remembered a debt of gratitude, and paid it in the full measure that was his habit.

And that reminds me, ungrateful dog that I am, that I owe as much to your training as the rude country job-printer owes to the city boss who takes him in hand and teaches him the right way to handle his art. I was talking to Mrs. Clemens about this the other day, and grieving because I never mentioned it to you, thereby seeming to ignore it or to be unaware of it. Nothing that has passed under your eye needs any revision before going into a volume, while all my other stuff does need so *much.*

In that ancient day, before the wireless telegraph, the voyager, when the land fell away behind him, felt a mighty sense of relief and rest, which to some extent has gone now forever. He cannot entirely escape the world in this new day; but *then* he had a complete sense of dismissal from all encumbering cares of life. Among the first note-book entries Mark Twain wrote:

> To go abroad has something of the same sense that death brings—"I am no longer of ye; what ye say of me is now of no consequence—but of how much consequence when I am with ye and of ye. I know you will refrain from saying harsh things *because* they cannot hurt me, since I am out of reach and cannot hear them. This is why we say no harsh things of the dead."

It was a rough voyage outside, but the company made it pleasant within. Halstead and Taylor were good smoking-room companions. Taylor had a large capacity for languages and a memory that was always a marvel. He would repeat for them Arabian, Hungarian, and Russian poetry, and show them the music and construction of it. He sang German folk-lore songs for them, and the "Lorelei," then comparatively unknown in America. Such was his knowledge of the language that even educated Germans on board submitted questions of construction to him and accepted his decisions. He was wisely chosen for the mission he had to fill, but unfortunately he did not fill it long. Both Halstead and Taylor were said to have heart trouble. Halstead, however, survived many years. Taylor died December 19, 1878.

CXVII

GERMANY AND GERMAN

FROM the note-book:

It is a marvel that never loses its surprise by repetition, this aiming a ship at a mark three thousand miles away and hitting the bull's-eye in a fog—as we did. When the fog fell on us the captain said we ought to be at such and such a spot (it had been eighteen hours since an observation was had), with the Scilly islands bearing so and so, and about so many miles away. Hove the lead and got forty-eight fathoms; looked on the chart, and sure enough this depth of water showed that we were right where the captain said we were.

Another idea. For ages man probably did not know why God carpeted the ocean bottom with sand in one place, shells in another, and so on. But we see now; the kind of bottom the lead brings up shows where a ship is when the soundings don't, and also it confirms the soundings.

They reached Hamburg after two weeks' stormy sailing. They rested a few days there, then went to Hanover and Frankfort, arriving at Heidelberg early in May.

They had no lodgings selected in Heidelberg, and leaving the others at an inn, Clemens set out immediately to find apartments. Chance or direction, or both, led him to the beautiful Schloss Hotel, on a hill overlooking the city, and as fair a view as one may find in all Germany. He did not go back after his party. He sent a message telling them to take carriage and drive at once to the Schloss, then he sat down to enjoy the view.

Coming up the hill they saw him standing on the

veranda, waving his hat in welcome. He led them to their rooms—spacious apartments—and pointed to the view. They were looking down on beautiful Heidelberg Castle, densely wooded hills, the far-flowing Neckar, and the haze-empurpled valley of the Rhine. By and by, pointing to a small cottage on the hilltop, he said:

"I have been picking out my little house to work in; there it is over there; the one with the gable in the roof. Mine is the middle room on the third floor."

Mrs. Clemens thought the occupants of the house might be surprised if he should suddenly knock and tell them he had come to take possession of his room. Nevertheless, they often looked over in that direction and referred to it as his office. They amused themselves by watching his "people" and trying to make out what they were like. One day he went over there, and sure enough there was a sign out, "Möblirte Wohnung zu Vermiethen." A day or two later he was established in the very room he had selected, it being the only room but one vacant.

In *A Tramp Abroad* Mark Twain tells of the beauty of their Heidelberg environment. To Howells he wrote:

> Our bedroom has two great glass bird-cages (inclosed balconies), one looking toward the Rhine Valley and sunset, the other looking up the Neckar *cul-de-sac*, and naturally we spend nearly all our time in these. We have tables and chairs in them; we do our reading, writing, studying, smoking, and suppering in them. . . . It must have been a noble genius who devised this hotel. Lord, how blessed is the repose, the tranquillity of this place! Only two sounds: the happy clamor of the birds in the groves and the muffled music of the Neckar tumbling over the opposing dikes. It is no hardship to lie awake awhile nights, for this subdued roar has exactly the sound of a steady rain beating upon a roof. It is so healing to the spirit; and it bears up the thread of one's imaginings as the accompaniment bears up a song. . . .
>
> I have waited for a "call" to go to work—I knew it would come. Well, it began to come a week ago; my note-book comes out more and more frequently every day since; three days ago

I concluded to move my manuscripts over to my den. *Now* the call is loud and decided at last. So to-morrow I shall begin regular, steady work, and stick to it till the middle of July or August 1st, when I look for Twichell; we will then walk about Germany two or three weeks, and then I'll go to work again (perhaps in Munich).

The walking tour with Twichell had been contemplated in the scheme for gathering book material, but the plan for it had not been completed when he left Hartford. Now he was anxious that they should start as soon as possible. Twichell, receiving the news in Hartford, wrote that it was a great day for him: that his third son had been happily born early that morning, and now the arrival of this glorious gift of a tramp through Germany and Switzerland completed his blessings.

I am almost too joyful for pleasure [he wrote]. I labor with my felicities. How I shall get to sleep to-night I don't know, though I have had a good start, in not having slept much last night. Oh, my! *do* you realize, Mark, what a symposium it is to be? I do. To begin with, I am thoroughly tired and the rest will be worth everything. To walk with you and talk with you for weeks together—why, it's my dream of luxury. Harmony, who at sunrise this morning deemed herself the happiest woman on the Continent when I read your letter to her, widened her smile perceptibly, and revived another degree of strength in a minute. She refused to consider her being left alone, but only the great chance opened to me.

SHOES—Mark, remember that ever so much of our pleasure depends upon your shoes. Don't fail to have adequate preparation made in that department.

Meantime, the struggle with the "awful German language" went on. It was a general hand-to-hand contest. From the head of the household down to little Clara not one was exempt. To Clemens it became a sort of nightmare. Once in his note-book he says:

"Dreamed all bad foreigners went to German heaven;

couldn't talk, and wished they had gone to the other place"; and a little farther along, "I wish I could hear myself talk German."

To Mrs. Crane, in Elmira, he reported their troubles:

Clara Spaulding is working herself to death with her German; never loses an instant while she is awake—or asleep, either, for that matter; dreams of enormous serpents, who poke their heads up under her arms and glare upon her with red-hot eyes, and inquire about the genitive case and the declensions of the definite article. Livy is bullyragging herself about as hard; pesters over her grammar and her reader and her dictionary all day; then in the evening these two students stretch themselves out on sofas and sigh and say, "Oh, there's no use! We never can learn it in the world!" Then Livy takes a sentence to go to bed on: goes gaping and stretching to her pillow murmuring, "Ich bin Ihnen sehr verbunden—Ich bin Ihnen sehr verbunden—Ich bin Ihnen sehr verbunden—I wonder if I *can* get that packed away so it will stay till morning"—and about an hour after midnight she wakes me up and says, "I do so hate to disturb you, but is it 'Ich Ben Jonson sehr befinden'?"

And Mrs. Clemens wrote:

Oh, Sue dear, strive to enter in at the straight gate, for many shall seek to enter it and shall not be able. I am not striving these days. I am just interested in German.

Rosa, the maid, was required to speak to the children only in German, though Bay at first would have none of it. The nurse and governess tried to blandish her, in vain. She maintained a calm and persistent attitude of scorn. Little Susy tried, and really made progress; but one day she said, pathetically:

"Mama, I wish Rosa was made in English."

Yet a little later Susy herself wrote her Aunt Sue:

I know a lot of German; everybody says I know a lot. I give you a million dollars to see you, and you would give two hundred dollars to see the lovely woods that we see.

Even Howells, in far-off America, caught the infection and began a letter in German, though he hastened to add, "Or do you prefer English by this time? Really I could imagine the German going hard with you, for you always seemed to me a man who liked to be understood with the least possible personal inconvenience."

Clemens declared more than once that he scorned the "outrageous and impossible German grammar," and abandoned it altogether. In his note-book he records how two Germans, strangers in Heidelberg, asked him a direction, and that when he gave it, in the most elaborate and correct German he could muster, one of them only lifted his eyes and murmured:

"Gott im Himmel!"

He was daily impressed with the lingual attainments of foreigners and his own lack of them. In the notes he comments:

> Am addressed in German, and when I can't speak it immediately the person tackles me in French, and plainly shows astonishment when I stop him. They naturally despise such an ignoramus. Our doctor here speaks as pure English as I.

On the Fourth of July he addressed the American students in Heidelberg in one of those mixtures of tongues for which he had a peculiar gift.

The room he had rented for a study was let by a typical German family, and he was a great delight to them. He practised his German on them, and interested himself in their daily affairs.

Howells wrote insistently for some assurance of contributions to the *Atlantic*.

"I must begin printing your private letters to satisfy the popular demand," he said. "People are constantly asking when you are going to begin."

Clemens replied that he would be only too glad to write for the *Atlantic* if his contributions could be copyrighted in Canada, where pirates were persistently enterprising.

I do not know that I have any printable stuff just now—separatable stuff, that is—but I shall have by and by. It is very gratifying to hear that it is wanted by anybody. I stand always prepared to hear the reverse, and am constantly surprised that it is delayed so long. Consequently it is not going to astonish me when it comes.

The Clemens party enjoyed Heidelberg, though in different ways. The children romped and picnicked in the castle grounds, which adjoined the hotel; Mrs. Clemens and Miss Spaulding were devoted to bric-à-brac hunting, picture-galleries, and music. Clemens took long walks, or made excursions by rail and diligence to farther points. Art and opera did not appeal to him. The note-book says:

I have attended operas, whenever I could not help it, for fourteen years now; I am sure I know of no agony comparable to the listening to an unfamiliar opera. I am enchanted with the airs of "Trovatore" and other old operas which the hand-organ and the music-box have made entirely familiar to my ear. I am carried away with delighted enthusiasm when they are sung at the opera. But oh, how far between they are! And what long, arid, heartbreaking and headaching "between-times" of that sort of intense but incoherent noise which always so reminds me of the time the orphan asylum burned down.

Sunday night, 11th. Huge crowd out to-night to hear the band play the "Fremersberg." I suppose it is very low-grade music—I know it *must* be low-grade music—because it so delighted me, it so warmed me, moved me, stirred me, uplifted me, enraptured me, that at times I could have cried, and at others split my throat with shouting. The great crowd was another evidence that it was low-grade music, for only the few are educated up to a point where high-class music gives pleasure. I have never heard enough classic music to be able to enjoy it, and the simple truth is I detest it. Not mildly, but with all my heart.

What a poor lot we human beings are anyway! If base music gives me wings, why should I want any other? But I do. I want to like the higher music because the higher and better like it. But you see I want to like it without taking the necessary trouble, and giving the thing the necessary amount of time and attention. The natural suggestion is, to get into that upper tier, that dress-circle, by a lie—we will *pretend* we like it. This lie, this pretense, gives to opera what support it has in America.

And then there is painting. What a red rag is to a bull Turner's "Slave Ship" is to me. Mr. Ruskin is educated in art up to a point where that picture throws him into as mad an ecstasy of pleasure as it throws me into one of rage. His cultivation enables him to see water in that yellow mud; his cultivation reconciles the floating of unfloatable things to him—chains etc.; it reconciles him to fishes swimming on top of the water. The most of the picture is a manifest impossibility, that is to say, a lie; and only rigid cultivation can enable a man to find truth in a lie. A Boston critic said the "Slave Ship" reminded him of a cat having a fit in a platter of tomatoes. That went home to my non-cultivation, and I thought, here is a man with an unobstructed eye.

Mark Twain has dwelt somewhat upon these matters in *A Tramp Abroad*. He confesses in that book that later he became a great admirer of Turner, though perhaps never of the "Slave Ship" picture. In fact, Mark Twain was never artistic, in the common acceptance of that term; neither his art nor his tastes were of an "artistic" kind.

CXVIII

TRAMPING WITH TWICHELL

TWICHELL arrived on time, August 1st. Clemens met him at Baden-Baden, and they immediately set out on a tramp through the Black Forest, excursioning as pleased them, and having an idyllic good time. They did not always walk, but they often did. At least they did sometimes, when the weather was just right and Clemens's rheumatism did not trouble him. But they were likely to take a carriage, or a donkey-cart, or a train, or any convenient thing that happened along. They did not hurry, but idled and talked and gathered flowers, or gossiped with wayside natives and tourists, though always preferring to wander along together, beguiling the way with discussion and speculation and entertaining tales. They crossed over into Switzerland in due time and considered the conquest of the Alps. The family followed by rail or diligence, and greeted them here and there when they rested from their wanderings. Mark Twain found an immunity from attention in Switzerland, which for years he had not known elsewhere. His face was not so well known and his pen-name was carefully concealed.

It was a large relief to be no longer an object of public curiosity; but Twichell, as in the Bermuda trip, did not feel quite honest, perhaps, in altogether preserving the mask of unrecognition. In one of his letters home he tells how, when a young man at their table was especially delighted with Mark Twain's conversation, he could not resist taking the young man aside and divulging to him the speaker's identity.

"I could not forbear telling him who Mark was," he says, "and the mingled surprise and pleasure his face exhibited made me glad I had done so."

They climbed the Rigi, after which Clemens was not in good walking trim for some time; so Twichell went on a trip on his own account, to give his comrade a chance to rest. Then away again to Interlaken, where the Jungfrau rises, cold and white; on over the loneliness of Gemmi Pass, with glaciers for neighbors and the unfading white peaks against the blue; to Visp and to Zermatt, where the Matterhorn points like a finger that directs mankind to God. This was true Alpine wandering—sweet vagabondage.

The association of the wanderers was a very intimate one. Their minds were closely attuned, and there were numerous instances of thought-echo—mind answering to mind without the employment of words. Clemens records in his notes:

Sunday A.M., *August* 11th. Been reading *Romola* yesterday afternoon, last night, and this morning; at last I came upon the only passage which has thus far *hit me with force*—Tito compromising with his conscience, and resolving to do, not a bad thing, but not the *best* thing. Joe entered the room five minutes—no, three minutes later—and without prelude said, "I read that book you've got there six years ago, and got a mighty good text for a sermon out of it—the passage where the young fellow compromises with his conscience, and resolves to do, not a bad thing, but not the *best* thing." This is Joe's first reference to this book since he saw me buy it twenty-four hours ago. So my mind operated on his in this instance. He said he was sitting yonder in the reading-room, three minutes ago (I have not got up yet), thinking of nothing in particular, and didn't know what brought *Romola* into his head; but into his head it came and that particular passage. Now I, forty feet away, in another room, was reading that particular passage at that particular moment.

Couldn't suggest *Romola* to him earlier, because nothing in the book had taken hold of me till I came to that one passage on page 112, Tauchnitz edition.

And again:

The instances of mind-telegraphing are simply innumerable. This evening Joe and I sat long at the edge of the village looking at the Matterhorn. Then Joe said, "We ought to go to the Cervin Hotel and inquire for Livy's telegram." If he had been but one instant later I should have said those words instead of him.

Such entries are frequent, and one day there came along a kind of object-lesson. They were toiling up a mountain-side, when Twichell began telling a very interesting story which had happened in connection with a friend still living, though Twichell had no knowledge of his whereabouts at this time. The story finished just as they rounded a turn in the cliff, and Twichell, looking up, ended his last sentence, "And *there's the man!*" Which was true, for they were face to face with the very man of whom he had been telling.

Another subject that entered into their discussion was the law of accidents. Clemens held that there was no such thing as an accident: that it was all forewritten in the day of the beginning; that every event, however slight, was embryonic in that first instant of created life, and immutably timed to its appearance in the web of destiny. Once on their travels, when they were on a high bank above a brawling stream, a little girl, who started to run toward them, slipped and rolled under the bottom rail of the protecting fence, her feet momentarily hanging out over the precipice and the tearing torrent below. It seemed a miraculous escape from death, and furnished an illustration for their discussion. The condition of the ground, the force of her fall, the nearness of the fatal edge, all these had grown inevitably out of the first great projection of thought, and the child's fall and its escape had been invested in life's primal atom.

The author of *A Tramp Abroad* tells us of the rushing stream that flows out of the Arcadian sky valley, the Gasternthal, and goes plunging down to Kandersteg, and how he took exercise by making "Harris" (Twichell) set stranded logs adrift while he lounged comfortably on a boulder, and watched them go tearing by; also how he made Harris run a race with one of those logs. But that is literature. Twichell, in a letter home, has preserved a likelier and lovelier story:

Mark is a queer fellow. There is nothing that he so delights in as a swift, strong stream. You can hardly get him to leave one when once he is within the influence of its fascinations. To throw in stones and sticks seems to afford him rapture. To-night, as we were on our way back to the hotel, seeing a lot of driftwood caught by the torrent side below the path, I climbed down and threw it in. When I got back to the path Mark was running down-stream after it as hard as he could go, throwing up his hands and shouting in the wildest ecstasy, and when a piece went over a fall and emerged to view in the foam below he would jump up and down and yell. He said afterward that he hadn't been so excited in three months. He acted just like a boy; another feature of his extreme sensitiveness in certain directions.

Then generalizing, Twichell adds:

He has coarse spots in him. But I never knew a person so finely regardful of the feelings of others in some ways. He hates to pass another person walking, and will practise some subterfuge to take off what he feels is the discourtesy of it. And he is exceedingly timid, tremblingly timid, about approaching strangers; hates to ask a question. His sensitive regard for others extends to animals. When we are driving his concern is all about the horse. He can't bear to see the whip used, or to see a horse pull hard. To-day, when the driver clucked up his horse and quickened his pace a little, Mark said, "The fellow's got the notion that we are in a hurry." He is exceedingly considerate toward me in regard of everything—or most things.

The days were not all sunshine. Sometimes it rained and they took shelter by the wayside, or, if there was no shelter, they plodded along under their umbrellas, still talking away, and if something occurred that Clemens wanted to put down they would stand stock still in the rain, and Twichell would hold the umbrella while Clemens wrote—a good while sometimes—oblivious to storm and discomfort and the long way yet ahead.

After the day on Gemmi Pass Twichell wrote home:

Mark, to-day, was immensely absorbed in the flowers. He scrambled around and gathered a great variety, and manifested the intensest pleasure in them. He crowded a pocket of his note-book with his specimens and wanted more room. So I stopped the guide and got out my needle and thread, and out of a stiff paper, a hotel advertisement, I had about me made a paper bag, a cornucopia like, and tied it to his vest in front, and it answered the purpose admirably. He filled it full with a beautiful collection, and as soon as we got here to-night he transferred it to a cardboard box and sent it by mail to Livy. A strange Mark he is, full of contradictions. I spoke last night of his sensitiveness to others' feelings. To-day the guide got behind, and came up as if he would like to go by, yet hesitated to do so. Mark paused, went aside and busied himself a minute picking a flower. In the halt the guide got by and resumed his place in front. Mark threw the flower away, saying, "I didn't want that. I only wanted to give the old man a chance to go on without seeming to pass us." Mark is splendid to walk with amid such grand scenery, for he talks so well about it, has such a power of strong, picturesque expression. I wish you might have heard him to-day. His vigorous speech nearly did justice to the things we saw.

In an address which Twichell gave many years later he recalls another pretty incident of their travels. They had been toiling up the Gorner Grat.

As we paused for a rest, a lamb from a flock of sheep near by ventured inquisitively toward us, whereupon Mark seated himself on a rock, and with beckoning hand and soft words tried to get it to come to him.

On the lamb's part it was a struggle between curiosity and timidity, but in a succession of advances and retreats it gained confidence, though at a very gradual rate. It was a scene for a painter: the great American humorist on one side of the game and that silly little creature on the other, with the Matterhorn for a background. Mark was reminded that the time he was consuming was valuable—but to no purpose. The Gorner Grat could wait. He held on with undiscouraged perseverance till he carried his point: the lamb finally put its nose in his hand, and he was happy over it all the rest of the day.

The matter of religion came up now and again in the drift of their discussions. It was Twichell's habit to have prayers in their room every night at the hotels, and Clemens was willing to join in the observances. Once Twichell, finding him in a responsive mood—a remorseful mood—gave his sympathy, and spoke of the larger sympathy of divinity. Clemens listened and seemed soothed and impressed, but his philosophies were too wide and too deep for creeds and doctrines. A day or two later, as they were tramping along in the hot sun, his honesty had to speak out.

"Joe," he said, "I'm going to make a confession. I don't believe in your religion at all. I've been living a lie right straight along whenever I pretended to. For a moment, sometimes, I have been almost a believer, but it immediately drifts away from me again. I don't believe one word of your Bible was inspired by God any more than any other book. I believe it is entirely the work of man from beginning to end—atonement and all. The problem of life and death and eternity and the true conception of God is a bigger thing than is contained in that book."

So the personal side of religious discussion closed between them, and was never afterward reopened.

They joined Mrs. Clemens and the others at Lausanne at last, and their Swiss holiday was over. Twichell set out for home by way of England, and Clemens gave himself up to reflection and rest after his wanderings. Then, as the days of their companionship passed in review, quickly and characteristically he sent a letter after his comrade:

DEAR OLD JOE,—It is actually all over! I was so low-spirited at the station yesterday, and this morning, when I woke, I couldn't seem to accept the dismal truth that you were really gone, and the pleasant tramping and talking at an end. Ah, my boy! it has been such a rich holiday to me, and I feel under such deep and honest obligations to you for coming. I am putting out of my mind all memory of the times when I misbehaved toward you and hurt you; I am resolved to consider it forgiven, and to store up and remember only the charming hours of the journeys and the times when I was not unworthy to be with you and share a companionship which to me stands first after Livy's. It is justifiable to do this; for why should I let my small infirmities of disposition live and grovel among my mental pictures of the eternal sublimities of the Alps?

Livy can't accept or endure the fact that you are gone. But you *are*, and we cannot get around it. So take our love with you, and bear it also over the sea to Harmony, and God bless you both.

MARK.

CXIX

ITALIAN DAYS

THE Clemens party wandered down into Italy—to the lakes, Venice, Florence, Rome—loitering through the galleries, gathering here and there beautiful furnishings—pictures, marbles, and the like—for the Hartford home.

In Venice they bought an old carven bed, a massive regal affair with serpentine columns surmounted by singularly graceful cupids, and with other cupids sporting on the headboard: the work of some artist who had been dust three centuries maybe, for this bed had come out of an old Venetian palace, dismantled and abandoned. It was a furniture with a long story, and the years would add mightily to its memories. It would become a stately institution in the Clemens household. The cupids on the posts were removable, and one of the highest privileges of childhood would be to occupy that bed and have down one of the cupids to play with. It was necessary to be ill to acquire that privilege—not violently and dangerously ill, but interestingly so—ill enough to be propped up with pillows and have one's meals served on a tray, with dolls and picture-books handy, and among them a beautiful rosewood cupid who had kept dimpled and dainty for so many, many years.

They spent three weeks in Venice: a dreamlike experience, especially for the children, who were on the water most of the time, and became fast friends with their gondolier, who taught them some Italian words; then a week in Florence and a fortnight in Rome.[1] Clemens discovered that in twelve years his attitude had changed somewhat concerning the old masters. He no longer found the bright, new copies an improvement on the originals, though the originals still failed to wake his enthusiasm. Mrs. Clemens and Miss Spaulding spent long hours wandering down avenues of art, accompanied by him on occasion, though not always willingly. He wrote his sorrow to Twichell:

> I do wish you were in Rome to do my sight-seeing for me. Rome interests me as much as East Hartford could, and no more; that is, the Rome which the average tourist feels an interest in. There are other things here which stir me enough to make life worth living. Livy and Clara are having a royal time worshiping the old masters, and I as good a time gritting my ineffectual teeth over them.

Once when Sarah Orne Jewett was with the party he remarked that if the old masters had labeled their fruit one wouldn't be so likely to mistake pears for turnips.

"Youth," said Mrs. Clemens, gravely, "if you do not care for these masterpieces yourself, you might at least consider the feelings of others"; and Miss Jewett, regarding him severely, added, in her quaint Yankee fashion:

"Now, you've been spoke to!"

He felt duly reprimanded, but his taste did not materially reform. He realized that he was no longer in a proper frame of mind to write of general sight-seeing. One

[1] From the note-book:

"Bay—When the waiter brought my breakfast this morning I spoke to him in Italian.

"Mama—What did you say?

"B.—I said, 'Polly-vo fransay.'

"M.—What does it mean?

"B.—I don't know. What *does* it mean, Susy?

"S.—It means, 'Polly wants a cracker.'"

must be eager, verdant, to write happily the story of travel. Replying to a letter from Howells on the subject he said:

> I wish I *could* give those sharp satires on European life which you mention, but of course a man can't write successful satire except he be in a calm, judicial good-humor; whereas I *hate* travel, and I *hate* hotels, and I *hate* the opera, and I *hate* the old masters. In truth I don't ever seem to be in a good enough humor with anything to satirize it. No, I want to stand up before it and curse it and foam at the mouth, or take a club and pound it to rags and pulp. I have got in two or three chapters about Wagner's operas, and managed to do it without showing temper, but the strain of another such effort would burst me.

Clemens became his own courier for a time in Italy, and would seem to have made more of a success of it than he did a good many years afterward, if we may believe the story he has left us of his later attempt.

"Am a shining success as a courier," he records, "by the use of francs. Have learned how to handle the railway guide intelligently and with confidence."

He declares that he will have no more couriers; but possibly he could have employed one to advantage on the trip out of Italy, for it was a desperately hard one, with bad connections and delayed telegrams. When, after thirty-six hours' weary, continuous traveling, they arrived at last in Munich in a drizzle and fog, and were domiciled in their winter quarters, at No. 1a, Karlstrasse, they felt that they had reached the home of desolation itself, the very throne of human misery.

> And the rooms were *so* small, the conveniences so meager, and the porcelain stove was grim, ghastly, dismal, intolerable! So Livy and Clara Spaulding sat down forlorn and cried, and I retired to a private place to pray. By and by we all retired to our narrow German beds, and when Livy and I had finished talking across the room it was all decided that we should rest

twenty-four hours, then pay whatever damages were required and straightway fly to the south of France.

The rooms had been engaged by letter, months before, of their proprietress, Fräulein Dahlweiner, who had met them at the door with a lantern in her hand, full of joy in their arrival and faith in her ability to make them happy. It was a faith that was justified. Next morning, when they all woke, rested, the weather had cleared, there were bright fires in the rooms, the world had taken on a new aspect. Fräulein Dahlweiner, the pathetic, hard-working little figure, became almost beautiful in their eyes in her efforts for their comfort. She arranged larger rooms and better conveniences for them. Their location was central and there was a near-by park. They had no wish to change. Clemens, in his letter to Howells, boasts that he brought the party through from Rome himself, and that they never had so little trouble before; but in looking over this letter, thirty years later, he commented, "Probably a lie."

He secured a room some distance away for his work, but then could not find his Swiss note-book. He wrote Twichell that he had lost it, and that after all he might not be obliged to write a volume of travels. But the note-book turned up and the work on the new book proceeded. For a time it went badly. He wrote many chapters, only to throw them aside. He had the feeling that he had somehow lost the knack of descriptive narrative. He had become, as it seemed, too didactic. He thought his description was inclined to be too literal, his humor manufactured. These impressions passed, by and by; interest developed, and with it enthusiasm and confidence. In a letter to Twichell he reported his progress:

I was about to write to my publisher and propose some other book, when the confounded thing [the note-book] turned up, and down went my heart into my boots. But there was now no excuse, so I went solidly to work, tore up a great part of the MS. written in Heidelberg—wrote and tore up, continued to write and tear up—and at last, reward of patient and noble persistence, my pen got the old swing again! Since then I'm glad that Providence knew better what to do with the Swiss notebook than I did.

Further along in the same letter there breaks forth a true heart-answer to that voice of the Alps which, once heard, is never wholly silent:

O Switzerland! The further it recedes into the enriching haze of time, the more intolerably delicious the charm of it and the cheer of it and the glory and majesty, and solemnity and pathos of it grow. Those mountains had a soul: they thought, they spoke. And what a voice it was! And how real! Deep down in my memory it is sounding yet. Alp calleth unto Alp! That stately old Scriptural wording is the right one for God's Alps and God's ocean. How puny we were in that awful Presence, and how painless it was to be so! How fitting and right it seemed, and how stingless was the sense of our unspeakable insignificance! And Lord, how pervading were the repose and peace and blessedness that poured out of the heart of the invisible Great Spirit of the mountains!

Now what *is* it? There are mountains and mountains and mountains in this world, but only these take you by the heartstrings. I wonder what the secret of it is. Well, time and time again it has seemed to me that I *must* drop everything and flee to Switzerland once more. It is a *longing*—a deep, strong, tugging *longing*. That is the word. We must go again, Joe.

CXX

IN MUNICH

THAT winter in Munich was not recalled as an unpleasant one in after-years. His work went well enough—always a chief source of gratification. Mrs. Clemens and Miss Spaulding found interest in the galleries, in quaint shops, in the music and picturesque life of that beautiful old Bavarian town. The children also liked Munich. It was easy for them to adopt any new environment or custom. The German Christmas, with its lavish tree and toys and cakes, was an especial delight. The German language they seemed fairly to absorb. Writing to his mother Clemens said:

> I cannot see but that the children speak German as well as they do English. Susy often translates Livy's orders to the servants. I cannot work and study German at the same time; so I have dropped the latter and do not even read the language, except in the morning paper to get the news.

In Munich—as was the case wherever they were known—there were many callers. Most Americans and many foreigners felt it proper to call on Mark Twain. It was complimentary, but it was wearying sometimes. Mrs. Clemens, in a letter written from Venice, where they had received even more than usual attention, declared there were moments when she almost wished she might never see a visitor again.

Originally there was a good deal about Munich in the new book, and some of the discarded chapters might have been retained with advantage. They were ruled out in the final weeding as being too serious, along with the French chapters. Only a few Italian memories were left to follow the Switzerland wanderings.

The book does record one Munich event, though transferring it to Heilsbronn. It is the incident of the finding of the lost sock in the vast bedroom. It may interest the reader to compare what really happened, as set down in a letter to Twichell, with the story as written for publication:

Last night I awoke at three this morning, and after raging to myself for two interminable hours I gave it up. I rose, assumed a catlike stealthiness, to keep from waking Livy, and proceeded to dress in the pitch-dark. Slowly but surely I got on garment after garment—all down to one sock; I had one slipper on and the other in my hand. Well, on my hands and knees I crept softly around, pawing and feeling and scooping along the carpet, and among chair-legs, for that missing sock, I kept that up, and still kept it up, and *kept* it up. At first I only said to myself, "Blame that sock," but that soon ceased to answer. My expletives grew steadily stronger and stronger, and at last, when I found I was *lost*, I had to sit flat down on the floor and take hold of something to keep from lifting the roof off with the profane explosion that was trying to get out of me. I could see the dim blur of the window, but of course it was in the wrong place and could give me no information as to where I was. But I had one comfort—I had not waked Livy; I believed I could find that sock in silence if the night lasted long enough. So I started again and softly pawed all over the place, and sure enough, at the end of half an hour I laid my hand on the missing article. I rose joyfully up and butted the wash-bowl and pitcher off the stand, and simply raised —— so to speak. Livy screamed, then said, "Who is it? What *is* the matter?" I said, "There ain't anything the matter. I'm hunting for my sock." She said, "Are you hunting for it with a club?"

I went in the parlor and lit the lamp, and gradually the fury subsided and the ridiculous features of the thing began to suggest themselves. So I lay on the sofa with note-book and pencil, and transferred the adventure to our big room in the hotel at Heilsbronn, and got it on paper a good deal to my satisfaction.

He wrote with frequency to Howells, and sent him something for the magazine now and then: the "Gambetta Duel" burlesque, which would make a chapter in the book later, and the story of "The Great Revolution in Pitcairn."[1]

Howells's novel, *The Lady of the Aroostook*, was then running through the *Atlantic*, and in one of his letters Clemens expresses the general deep satisfaction of his household in that tale:

> If your literature has not struck perfection now we are not able to see what is lacking. It is all such truth—truth to the life; everywhere your pen falls it leaves a photograph. . . . Possibly you will not be a fully accepted classic until you have been dead one hundred years—it is the fate of the Shakespeares of all genuine professions—but then your books will be as common as Bibles, I believe. In that day I shall be in the encyclopedias too, thus: "Mark Twain, history and occupation unknown; but he was personally acquainted with Howells."

Though in humorous form, this was a sincere tribute. Clemens always regarded with awe William Dean Howells's ability to dissect and photograph with such delicacy the minutiæ of human nature; just as Howells always stood in awe of Mark Twain's ability to light, with a single flashing sentence, the whole human horizon.

[1] Included in *The Stolen White Elephant* volume. The "Pitcairn" and "Elephant" tales were originally chapters in *A Tramp Abroad;* also the unpleasant "Coffin-box" yarn, which Howells rejected for the *Atlantic* and generally condemned, though for a time it remained a favorite with its author.

CXXI

PARIS, ENGLAND, AND HOMEWARD BOUND

THEY decided to spend the spring months in Paris, so they gave up their pleasant quarters with Fräulein Dahlweiner, and journeyed across Europe, arriving at the French capital February 28, 1879. Here they met another discouraging prospect, for the weather was cold and damp, the cabmen seemed brutally ill-mannered, their first hotel was chilly, dingy, uninviting. Clemens, in his note-book, set down his impressions of their rooms. A paragraph will serve:

> Ten squatty, ugly arm-chairs, upholstered in the ugliest and coarsest conceivable scarlet plush; two hideous sofas of the same—uncounted armless chairs ditto. Five ornamental chairs, seats covered with a coarse rag, embroidered in flat expanse with a confusion of leaves such as no tree ever bore, six or seven a dirty white and the rest a faded red. How those hideous chairs do swear at the hideous sofa near them! This is the very hatefulest room I have seen in Europe.
>
> Oh, how *cold* and raw and unwarmable it is!

It was better than that when the sun came out, and they found happier quarters presently at the Hotel Normandy, rue de l'Échelle.

But, alas, the sun did not come out often enough. It was one of those French springs and summers when it rains nearly every day, and is distressingly foggy and chill between times. Clemens received a bad impression of France and the French during that Parisian sojourn, from which he never entirely recovered. In his note-book he wrote: "France has neither winter, nor summer, nor morals. Apart from these drawbacks it is a fine country."

The weather may not have been entirely accountable for his prejudice, but from whatever cause Mark Twain, to the day of his death, had no great love for the French as a nation. Conversely, the French as a nation did not care greatly for Mark Twain. There were many individual Frenchmen that Mark Twain admired, as there were many Frenchmen who admired the work and personality of Mark Twain; but on neither side was there the warm, fond, general affection which elsewhere throughout Europe he invited and returned.

His book was not yet finished. In Paris he worked on it daily, but without enthusiasm. The city was too noisy, the weather too dismal. His note-book says:

> *May* 7th. I wish this terrible winter would come to an end. Have had rain almost without intermission for two months and one week.
>
> *May* 28th. This is one of the coldest days of this most damnable and interminable winter.

It was not all gloom and discomfort. There was congenial company in Paris, and dinner-parties, and a world of callers. Aldrich the scintillating[1] was there, also Gedney Bunce, of Hartford, Frank Millet and his wife,

[1] Of Aldrich Clemens used to say: "When Aldrich speaks it seems to me he is the bright face of the moon, and I feel like the other side."

Aldrich, unlike Clemens, was not given to swearing. The Parisian note-book has this memorandum:

"Aldrich gives his seat in the horse-car to a crutched cripple, and discovers that what he took for a crutch is only a length of walnut beading and the man not lame; whereupon Aldrich uses the only profanity that ever escaped his lips: 'Damn a dam'd man who would carry a dam'd piece of beading under his dam'd arm!'"

Hjalmar Hjorth Boyesen and his wife, and a Mr. and Mrs. Chamberlain, artist people whom the Clemenses had met pleasantly in Italy. Turgenieff, as in London, came to call; also Baron Tauchnitz, that nobly born philanthropist of German publishers, who devoted his life, often at his personal cost, to making the literature of other nations familiar to his own. Tauchnitz had early published the *Innocents*, following it with other Mark Twain volumes as they appeared, paying always, of his own will and accord, all that he could afford to pay for this privilege; which was not really a privilege, for the law did not require him to pay at all. He traveled down to Paris now to see the author, and to pay his respects to him. "A mighty nice old gentleman," Clemens found him. Richard Whiteing was in Paris that winter, and there were always plenty of young American painters whom it was good to know.

They had what they called the Stomach Club, a jolly organization, whose purpose was indicated by its name. Mark Twain occasionally attended its sessions, and on one memorable evening, when Edwin A. Abbey was there, speeches were made which never appeared in any printed proceedings. Mark Twain's address that night has obtained a wide celebrity among the clubs of the world, though no line of it, or even its title. has ever found its way into published literature.

Clemens had a better time in Paris than the rest of his party. He could go and come, and mingle with the sociabilities when the abnormal weather kept the others housed in. He did a good deal of sight-seeing of his own kind, and once went up in a captive balloon. They were all studying French, more or less, and they read histories and other books relating to France. Clemens renewed his old interest in Joan of Arc, and for the first time appears to have conceived the notion of writing the story of that lovely character.

The Reign of Terror interested him. He reread Carlisle's *Revolution*, a book which he was never long without reading, and they all read *A Tale of Two Cities*. When the weather permitted they visited the scenes of that grim period.[1]

[1] In his note-book he comments:

"The Reign of Terror shows that, without distinction or rank, the people were savages. Marquises, dukes, lawyers, blacksmiths, they each figure in due proportion to their crafts."

And again:

"For 1,000 years this savage nation indulged itself in massacre; every now and then a big massacre or a little one. The spirit is peculiar to France—I mean in Christendom—no other state has had it. In this France has always walked abreast, kept her end up with her brethren, the Turks and the Burmese. Their chief traits—love of glory and massacre."

Yet it was his sense of fairness that made him write, as a sort of quittance:

"You perceive I generalize with intrepidity from single instances. It is the tourists' custom. When I see a man jump from the Vendome Column I say, 'They like to do that in Paris.'"

Following this implied atonement, he records a few conclusions, drawn doubtless from Parisian reading and observation:

"Childish race and great."

"I'm for cremation."

"I disfavor capital punishment."

"Samson was a Jew, therefore not a fool. The Jews have the best average brain of any people in the world. The Jews are the only race in the world who work wholly with their brains, and never with their hands. There are no Jew beggars, no Jew tramps, no Jew ditchers, hod-carriers, day-laborers, or followers of toilsome mechanical trade.

"They are peculiarly and conspicuously the world's intellectual aristocracy."

"Communism is idiocy. They want to divide up the property. Suppose they did it. It requires brains to keep money as well as to make it. In a precious little while the money would be back in the former owner's hands and the communist would be poor again. The division would have to be remade every three years or it would do the communist no good."

A curious thing happened one day in Paris. Boyesen, in great excitement, came to the Normandy and was shown to the Clemens apartments. He was pale and could hardly speak, for his emotion. He asked immediately if his wife had come to their rooms. On learning that she had not, he declared that she was lost or had met with an accident. She had been gone several hours, he said, and had sent no word, a thing which she had never done before. He besought Clemens to aid him in his search for her, to do something to help him find her. Clemens, without showing the least emotion or special concentration of interest, said quietly:

"I will."

"Where will you go first," Boyesen demanded.

Still in the same even voice Clemens said:

"To the elevator."

He passed out of the room, with Boyesen behind him, into the hall. The elevator was just coming up, and as they reached it, it stopped at their landing, and Mrs. Boyesen stepped out. She had been delayed by a breakdown and a blockade. Clemens said afterward that he had a positive conviction that she would be on the elevator when they reached it. It was one of those curious psychic evidences which we find all along during his life; or, if the skeptics prefer to call them coincidences, they are privileged to do so.

PARIS, *June* 1, 1879. Still this vindictive winter continues. Had a raw, cold rain to-day. To-night we sit around a rousing wood fire.

They stood it for another month, and then on the 10th of July, when it was still chilly and disagreeable, they gave it up and left for Brussels, which he calls "a dirty, beautiful (architecturally), interesting town."

Two days in Brussels, then to Antwerp, where they dined on the *Trenton* with Admiral Roan, then to Rotterdam, Dresden, Amsterdam, and London, arriving there the 29th of July, which was rainy and cold, in keeping with all Europe that year.

Had to keep a rousing big cannel-coal fire blazing in the grate all day. A remarkable summer, truly!

London meant a throng of dinners, as always: brilliant, notable affairs, too far away to recall. A letter written by Mrs. Clemens at the time preserves one charming, fresh bit of that departed bloom.

Clara [Spaulding] went in to dinner with Mr. Henry James; she enjoyed him very much. I had a little chat with him before dinner, and he was exceedingly pleasant and easy to talk with. I had expected just the reverse, thinking one would feel looked over by him and criticized. Mr. Whistler, the artist, was at the dinner, but he did not attract me. Then there was a lady, over eighty years old, a Mrs. Stuart, who was Washington Irving's love, and she is said to have been his only love, and because of her he went unmarried to his grave.[1] She was also an intimate friend of Madame Bonaparte. You would judge Mrs. Stuart to be about fifty, and she was the life of the drawing-room after dinner, while the ladies were alone, before the gentlemen came up. It was lovely to see such a sweet old age; every one was so fond of her, every one deferred to her, yet every one was joking her, making fun of her, but she was always equal to the occasion, giving back as bright replies as possible; you had not the least sense that she was aged. She quoted French in her stories with perfect ease and fluency, and had all the time such a kindly, lovely way. When she entered the room, before dinner, Mr. James, who was then talking with me, shook hands with her and said, "Good evening, you wonderful lady." After she had passed . . . he said, "She is the youngest person in London. She has the youngest feelings and the youngest interests. . . . She is always interested."

It was a perfect delight to hear her and see her.

For more than two years they had had an invitation from Reginald Cholmondeley to pay him another visit.

[1] Mrs. Clemens was misinformed. Irving's only "love" was a Miss Hoffman.

CONDOVER HALL

So they went for a week to Condover, where many friends were gathered, including Millais, the painter, and his wife (who had been the wife of Ruskin), numerous relatives, and other delightful company. It was one of the happiest chapters of their foreign sojourn.[1]

From the note-book:

Sunday, August 17, '79. Raw and cold, and a drenching rain. Went to hear Mr. Spurgeon. House three-quarters full—say three thousand people. First hour, lacking one minute, taken up with two prayers, two ugly hymns, and Scripture-reading. Sermon three-quarters of an hour long. A fluent talker, good, sonorous voice. Topic treated in the unpleasant, old fashion: Man a mighty bad child, God working at him in forty ways and having a world of trouble with him.

A wooden-faced congregation; just the sort to see no incongruity in the majesty of Heaven stooping to plead and sentimentalize over such, and see in their salvation an important matter.

Tuesday, August 19th. Went up Windermere Lake in the steamer. Talked with the great Darwin.

They had planned to visit Dr. Brown in Scotland. Mrs. Clemens, in particular, longed to go, for his health had not been of the best, and she felt that they would never have a chance to see him again. Clemens in after-

[1] Moncure D. Conway, who was in London at the time, recalls, in his *Autobiography*, a visit which he made with Mr. and Mrs. Clemens to Stratford-on-Avon.

"Mrs. Clemens was an ardent Shakespearian, and Mark Twain determined to give her a surprise. He told her that we were going on a journey to Epworth, and persuaded me to connive with the joke by writing to Charles Flower not to meet us himself, but send his carriage. On arrival at the station we directed the driver to take us straight to the church. When we entered, and Mrs. Clemens read on Shakespeare's grave, 'Good friend, for Jesus' sake, forbear,' she started back, exclaiming, 'Where am I?' Mark received her reproaches with an affluence of guilt, but never did lady enjoy a visit more than that to Avonbank. Mrs. Charles Flower (*née* Martineau) took Mrs. Clemens to her heart, and contrived that every social or other attraction of that region should surround her."

years blamed himself harshly for not making the trip, declaring that their whole reason for not going was an irritable reluctance on his part to take the troublesome journey and a perversity of spirit for which there was no real excuse. There is documentary evidence against this harsh conclusion. They were, in fact, delayed here and there by misconnections and the continued terrific weather, barely reaching Liverpool in time for their sailing date, August 23d. Unquestionably he was weary of railway travel, for he always detested it. Time would magnify his remembered reluctance, until, in the end, he would load his conscience with the entire burden of blame.

Their ship was the *Gallia*, and one night, when they were nearing the opposite side of the Atlantic, Mark Twain, standing on deck, saw for the third time in his experience a magnificent lunar rainbow: a complete arch, the colors part of the time very brilliant, but little different from a day rainbow. It is not given to many persons in this world to see even one of these phenomena. After each previous vision there had come to him a period of good-fortune. Perhaps this also boded well for him.

CXXII

AN INTERLUDE

THE *Gallia* reached New York September 3, 1879. A report of his arrival, in the New York *Sun*, stated that Mark Twain had changed in his absence; that only his drawl seemed natural.

His hat, as he stood on the deck of the incoming Cunarder, *Gallia*, was of the pattern that English officers wear in India, and his suit of clothes was such as a merchant might wear in his store. He looked older than when he went to Germany, and his hair has turned quite gray.

It was a late hour when they were finally up to the dock, and Clemens, anxious to get through the Custom House, urged the inspector to accept his carefully prepared list of dutiable articles, without opening the baggage. But the official was dubious. Clemens argued eloquently, and a higher authority was consulted. Again Clemens stated his case and presented his arguments. A still higher chief of inspection was summoned, evidently from his bed. He listened sleepily to the preamble, then suddenly said: "Oh, chalk his baggage, of course! Don't you know it's Mark Twain and that he'll talk all night?"

They went directly to the farm, for whose high sunlit loveliness they had been longing through all their days of absence. Mrs. Clemens, in her letters, had never failed to dwell on her hunger for that fair hilltop. From his accustomed study-table Clemens wrote to Twichell:

"You have run about a good deal, Joe, but you have never seen any place that was so divine as the farm. Why don't you come here and take a foretaste of Heaven?" Clemens declared he would roam no more forever, and settled down to the happy farm routine. He took up his work, which had not gone well in Paris, and found his interest in it renewed. In the letter to Twichell he said:

I am revising my MS. I did not expect to like it, but I do. I have been knocking out early chapters for more than a year now, not because they had not merit, but merely because they hindered the flow of the narrative; it was a dredging process. Day before yesterday my shovel fetched up three more chapters and laid them, reeking, on the festering shore-pile of their predecessors, and now I think the yarn swims right along, without hitch or halt. I believe it will be a readable book of travels. I cannot see that it lacks anything but information.

Mrs. Clemens was no less weary of travel than her husband. Yet she had enjoyed their roaming, and her gain from it had been greater than his. Her knowledge of art and literature, and of the personal geography of nations, had vastly increased; her philosophy of life had grown beyond all counting.

She had lost something, too; she had outstripped her traditions. One day, when she and her sister had walked across the fields, and had stopped to rest in a little grove by a pretty pond, she confessed, timidly enough and not without sorrow, how she had drifted away from her orthodox views. She had ceased to believe, she said, in the orthodox Bible God, who exercised a personal supervision over every human soul. The hordes of people she had seen in many lands, the philosophies she had listened to from her husband and those wise ones about him, the life away from the restricted round of home, all had contributed to this change. Her God had become a larger God; the greater mind which exerts its care of the individual through immutable laws of time and change and environment—the Supreme Good which comprehends the individual flower, dumb creature, or human being only as a unit in the larger scheme of life and love. Her sister was not shocked or grieved; she too had grown with the years, and though perhaps less positively directed, had by a path of her own reached a wider prospect of conclusions. It was a sweet day there in the little grove by the water, and would linger in the memory of both so long as life lasted. Certainly it was the larger faith; though the moment must always come when the narrower, nearer, more humanly protecting arm of orthodoxy lends closer comfort. Long afterward, in the years that followed the sorrow of heavy bereavement, Clemens once said to his wife, "Livy, if it comforts you to lean on the Christian faith do so," and she answered, "I can't, Youth. I haven't any."

And the thought that he had destroyed her illusion, without affording a compensating solace, was one that would come back to him, now and then, all his days.

CXXIII

THE GRANT SPEECH OF 1879

IF the lunar rainbow had any fortuitous significance, perhaps we may find it in the two speeches which Mark Twain made in November and December of that year. The first of these was delivered at Chicago, on the occasion of the reception of General Grant by the Army of the Tennessee, on the evening of November 13, 1879. Grant had just returned from his splendid tour of the world. His progress from San Francisco eastward had been such an ovation as is only accorded to sovereignty. Clemens received an invitation to the reunion, but, dreading the long railway journey, was at first moved to decline. He prepared a letter in which he made "business" his excuse, and expressed his regret that he would not be present to see and hear the veterans of the Army of the Tennessee at the moment when their old commander entered the room and rose in his place to speak.

"Besides," he said, "I wanted to see the General again anyway and renew the acquaintance. He would remember me, because I was the person who did not ask him for an office."

He did not send the letter. Reconsidering, it seemed to him that there was something strikingly picturesque in the idea of a Confederate soldier who had been chased for a fortnight in the rain through Ralls and Monroe counties, Missouri, now being invited to come and give welcome home to his old imaginary pursuer. It was in the nature of an imperative command, which he could not refuse to obey.

He accepted and agreed to speak. They had asked him to respond to the toast of "The Ladies," but for him the subject was worn out. He had already responded to that toast at least twice. He telegraphed that there was one class of the community that had always been overlooked upon such occasions, and that if they would allow him to do so he would take that class for a toast: *the babies*. Necessarily they agreed, and he prepared himself accordingly.

He arrived in Chicago in time for the prodigious procession of welcome. Grant was to witness the march from a grand reviewing stand, which had been built out from the second story of the Palmer House. Clemens had not seen the General since the "embarrassing" introduction in Washington, twelve years before. Their meeting was characteristic enough. Carter Harrison, Mayor of Chicago, arriving with Grant, stepped over to Clemens, and asked him if he wouldn't like to be presented. Grant also came forward, and a moment later Harrison was saying:

"General, let me present Mr. Clemens, a man almost as great as yourself." They shook hands; there was a pause of a moment, then Grant said, looking at him gravely:

"Mr. Clemens, *I* am not embarrassed, are *you?*"

So he remembered that first, long-ago meeting. It was a conspicuous performance. The crowd could not hear the words, but they saw the greeting and the laugh, and cheered both men.

Following the procession, there were certain imposing ceremonies of welcome at Haverly's Theater where long, laudatory eloquence was poured out upon the returning hero, who sat unmoved while the storm of music and cheers and oratory swept about him. Clemens, writing of it that evening to Mrs. Clemens, said:

I never sat elbow to elbow with so many historic names before. Grant, Sherman, Sheridan, Schofield, Pope, Logan, and so on.

What an iron man Grant is! He sat facing the house, with his right leg crossed over his left, his right boot sole tilted up at an angle, and his left hand and arm reposing on the arm of his chair. You note that position? Well, when glowing references were made to *other* grandees on the stage, those grandees always showed a trifle of nervous consciousness, and as these references came frequently the nervous changes of position and attitude were also frequent. *But* Grant! He was under a tremendous and ceaseless bombardment of praise and congratulation; but as true as I'm sitting here he never moved a muscle of his body for a single instant during thirty minutes! You could have played him on a stranger for an effigy. Perhaps he never *would* have moved, but at last a speaker made such a particularly ripping and blood-stirring remark about him that the audience rose and roared and yelled and stamped and clapped an entire minute—Grant sitting as serene as ever—when General Sherman stepped up to him, laid his hand affectionately on his shoulder, bent respectfully down, and whispered in his ear. Then Grant got up and bowed, and the storm of applause swelled into a hurricane.

But it was the next evening that the celebration rose to a climax. This was at the grand banquet at the Palmer House, where six hundred guests sat down to dinner and Grant himself spoke, and Logan and Hurlbut, and Vilas and Woodford and Pope, fifteen in all, including Robert G. Ingersoll and Mark Twain. Chicago has never known a greater event than that dinner, for there has never been a time since when those great soldiers and citizens could have been gathered there.

To Howells Clemens wrote:

Imagine what it was like to see a bullet-shredded old battle-flag reverently unfolded to the gaze of a thousand middle-aged soldiers, most of whom hadn't seen it since they saw it advancing over victorious fields when they were in their prime. And imagine what it was like when Grant, their first commander, stepped into view while they were still going mad over the flag, and then right in the midst of it all somebody struck up "When we were marching through Georgia." Well, you should have heard the thousand voices lift that chorus and seen the tears stream down. If I live a hundred years I sha'n't ever forget these things, nor be able to talk about them. I sha'n't ever forget that I saw Phil Sheridan, with martial cloak and plumed chapeau, riding his big black horse in the midst of his own cannon; by all odds the superbest figure of a soldier *I* ever looked upon!

Grand times, my boy, grand times!

Mark Twain declared afterward that he listened to four speeches that night which he would remember as long as he lived. One of them was by Emory Storrs, another by General Vilas, another by Logan, and the last and greatest by Robert Ingersoll, whose eloquence swept the house like a flame. The Howells letter continues:

I doubt if America has ever seen anything quite equal to it; I am well satisfied I shall not live to see its equal again. How pale those speeches are in print, but how radiant, how full of color, how blinding they were in the delivery! Bob Ingersoll's music will sing through my memory always as the divinest that ever enchanted my ears. And I shall always see him, as he stood that night on a dinner-table, under the flash of lights and banners, in the midst of seven hundred frantic shouters, the most beautiful human creature that ever lived. "They fought, that a mother might own her child." The words look like any other print, but, Lord bless me! he borrowed the very accent of the angel of mercy to say them in, and you should have seen that vast house rise to its feet; and you should have heard the hurricane that followed. That's the *only* test! People may shout, clap their hands, stamp, wave their napkins, but none but the master can make them *get up on their feet.*

Clemens's own speech came last. He had been placed at the end to hold the house. He was preceded by a dull speaker, and his heart sank, for it was two o'clock and the diners were weary and sleepy, and the dreary speech had made them unresponsive.

They gave him a round of applause when he stepped

up upon the table in front of him—a tribute to his name. Then he began the opening words of that memorable, delightful fancy.

"We haven't all had the good-fortune to be ladies; we haven't all been generals, or poets, or statesmen; but when the toast works down to the *babies*—we *stand on common ground*—"

The tired audience had listened in respectful silence through the first half of the sentence. He made one of his effective pauses on the word "*babies*," and when he added, in that slow, rich measure of his, "*we stand on common ground*," they let go a storm of applause. There was no weariness and inattention after that. At the end of each sentence, he had to stop to let the tornado roar itself out and sweep by. When he reached the beginning of the final paragraph, "Among the three or four million cradles now rocking in the land are some which this nation would preserve for ages as sacred things if we could know which ones they are," the vast audience waited breathless for his conclusion. Step by step he led toward some unseen climax—some surprise, of course, for that would be his way. Then steadily, and almost without emphasis, he delivered the opening of his final sentence:

"And now in his cradle, somewhere under the flag, the future illustrious commander-in-chief of the American armies is so little burdened with his approaching grandeurs and responsibilities as to be giving his whole strategic mind, at this moment, to trying to find out some way to get his own big toe into his mouth, an achievement which (meaning no disrespect) the illustrious guest of this evening also turned his attention to some fifty-six years ago."

He paused, and the vast crowd had a chill of fear. After all, he seemed likely to overdo it—to spoil everything with a cheap joke at the end.

No one ever knew better than Mark Twain the value of

a pause. He waited now long enough to let the silence become absolute, until the tension was painful, then wheeling to Grant himself he said, with all the dramatic power of which he was master:

"And if the child is but the father of the man, there are mighty few who will *doubt that he succeeded!*"

The house came down with a crash. The linking of their hero's great military triumphs with that earliest of all conquests seemed to them so grand a figure that they went mad with the joy of it. Even Grant's iron serenity broke; he rocked and laughed while the tears streamed down his cheeks.

They swept around the speaker with their congratulations, in their efforts to seize his hand. He was borne up and down the great dining-hall. Grant himself pressed up to make acknowledgments.

"It tore me all to pieces," he said; and Sherman exclaimed, "Lord bless you, my boy! I don't know how you do it!"

The little speech has been in "cold type" so many years since then that the reader of it to-day may find it hard to understand the flame of response it kindled so long ago. But that was another day—and another nation—and Mark Twain, like Robert Ingersoll, knew always his period and his people.

CXXIV

ANOTHER "ATLANTIC" SPEECH

THE December good-fortune was an opportunity Clemens had to redeem himself with the *Atlantic* contingent, at a breakfast given to Dr. Holmes.

Howells had written concerning it as early as October, and the first impulse had been to decline. It would be something of an ordeal; for though two years had passed since the fatal Whittier dinner, Clemens had not been in that company since, and the lapse of time did not signify. Both Howells and Warner urged him to accept, and he agreed to do so on condition that he be allowed to speak.

> If anybody talks there I shall claim the right to say a word myself, and be heard among the very *earliest*, else it would be confoundedly awkward for me—and for the rest, too. But you may read what I say beforehand, and strike out whatever you choose.

Howells advised against any sort of explanation. Clemens accepted this as wise counsel, and prepared an address relevant only to the guest of honor.

It was a noble gathering. Most of the guests of the Whittier dinner were present, and this time there were ladies. Emerson, Longfellow, and Whittier were there, Harriet Beecher Stowe and Julia Ward Howe; also the knightly Colonel Waring, and Stedman, and Parkman, and grand old John Bigelow, old even then.[1]

Howells was conservative in his introduction this time. It was better taste to be so. He said simply:

[1] He died in 1911 in his 94th year.

ANOTHER "ATLANTIC" SPEECH

"We will now listen to a few words of truth and soberness from Mark Twain."

Clemens is said to have risen diffidently, but that was his natural manner. It probably did not indicate anything of the inner tumult he really felt.

Outwardly he was calm enough, and what he said was delicate and beautiful, the kind of thing that he could say so well. It seems fitting that it should be included here, the more so that it tells a story not elsewhere recorded. This is the speech in full:

MR. CHAIRMAN, LADIES, AND GENTLEMEN,—I would have traveled a much greater distance than I have come to witness the paying of honors to Dr. Holmes, for my feeling toward him has always been one of peculiar warmth. When one receives a letter from a great man for the first time in his life it is a large event to him, as all of you know by your own experience. You never can receive letters enough from famous men afterward to obliterate that one or dim the memory of the pleasant surprise it was and the gratification it gave you. Lapse of time cannot make it commonplace or cheap. Well, the first great man who ever wrote me a letter was our guest, Oliver Wendell Holmes. He was also the first great literary man I ever stole anything from, and that is how I came to write to him and he to me. When my first book was new a friend of mine said, "The dedication is very neat." Yes, I said, I thought it was. My friend said, "I always admired it, even before I saw it in *The Innocents Abroad*." I naturally said, "What do you mean? Where did you ever see it before?" "Well, I saw it first, some years ago, as Dr. Holmes's dedication to his *Songs in Many Keys*." Of course my first impulse was to prepare this man's remains for burial, but upon reflection I said I would reprieve him for a moment or two, and give him a chance to prove his assertion if he could. We stepped into a book-store and he did prove it. I had stolen that dedication almost word for word. I could not imagine how this curious thing happened; for I knew one thing, for a dead certainty—that a certain amount of pride always goes along with a teaspoonful of brains, and that this pride protects a man from deliberately stealing other people's ideas.

That is what a *teaspoonful* of brains will do for a man, and admirers had often told me I had nearly a basketful, though they were rather reserved as to the size of the basket. However, I thought the thing out and solved the mystery. Some years before I had been laid up a couple of weeks in the Sandwich Islands, and had read and reread Dr. Holmes's poems till my mental reservoir was filled with them to the brim. The dedication lay on top and handy, so by and by I unconsciously took it. Well, of course, I wrote to Dr. Holmes and told him I hadn't meant to steal, and he wrote back and said, in the kindest way, that it was all right, and no harm done, and added that he believed we all unconsciously worked over ideas gathered in reading and hearing, imagining they were original with ourselves. He stated a truth and did it in such a pleasant way, and salved over my sore spot so gently and so healingly, that I was rather glad I had committed the crime, for the sake of the letter. I afterward called on him and told him to make perfectly free with any ideas of mine that struck him as good protoplasm for poetry. He could see by that time that there wasn't anything mean about me; so we got along, right from the start.[1]

I have met Dr. Holmes many times since; and lately he said—However, I am wandering wildly away from the one thing which I got on my feet to do; that is, to make my compliments to you, my fellow-teachers of the great public, and likewise to say I am right glad to see that Dr. Holmes is still in his prime and full of generous life, and as age is not determined by years but by trouble, and by infirmities of mind and body, I hope it may be a very long time yet before any can truthfully say, "He is growing old."

Whatever Mark Twain may have lost on that former occasion, came back to him multiplied when he had finished this happy tribute. So the year for him closed prosperously. The rainbow of promise was justified.

[1] Holmes in his letter had said: "I rather think *The Innocents Abroad* will have many more readers than *Songs in Many Keys*. . . . You will be stolen from a great deal oftener than you will borrow from other people."

CXXV

THE QUIETER THINGS OF HOME

UPSET and disturbed as Mark Twain often was, he seldom permitted his distractions to interfere with the program of his fireside. His days and his nights might be fevered, but the evenings belonged to another world. The long European wandering left him more than ever enamoured of his home; to him it had never been so sweet before, so beautiful, so full of peace. Company came: distinguished guests and the old neighborhood circles. Dinner-parties were more frequent than ever, and they were likely to be brilliant affairs. The best minds, the brightest wits, gathered around Mark Twain's table. Booth, Barrett, Irving, Sheridan, Sherman, Howells, Aldrich: they all assembled, and many more. There was always some one on the way to Boston or New York who addressed himself for the day or the night, or for a brief call, to the Mark Twain fireside.

Certain visitors from foreign lands were surprised at his environment, possibly expecting to find him among less substantial, more bohemian surroundings. Henry Drummond, the author of *Natural Law in the Spiritual World*, in a letter of this time, said:

> I had a delightful day at Hartford last Wednesday. . . . Called on Mark Twain, Mrs. Harriet Beecher Stowe, and the widow of Horace Bushnell. I was wishing A—— had been at the Mark Twain interview. He is funnier than any of his books, and to my surprise a most respected citizen, devoted to things esthetic, and the friend of the poor and struggling.[1]

[1] *Life of Henry Drummond*, by George Adam Smith.

The quieter evenings were no less delightful. Clemens did not often go out. He loved his own home best. The children were old enough now to take part in a form of entertainment that gave him and them especial pleasure —acting charades. These he invented for them, and costumed the little performers, and joined in the acting as enthusiastically and as unrestrainedly as if he were back in that frolicsome boyhood on John Quarles's farm. The Warner and Twichell children were often there and took part in the gay amusements. The children of that neighborhood played their impromptu parts well and naturally. They were in a dramatic atmosphere, and had been from infancy. There was never any preparation for the charades. A word was selected and the parts of it were whispered to the little actors. Then they withdrew to the hall, where all sorts of costumes had been laid out for the evening, dressed their parts, and each detachment marched into the library, performed its syllable and retired, leaving the audience, mainly composed of parents, to guess the answer. Often they invented their own words, did their own costuming, and conducted the entire performance independent of grown-up assistance or interference. Now and then, even at this early period, they conceived and produced little plays, and of course their father could not resist joining in these. At other times, evenings, after dinner, he would sit at the piano and recall the old darky songs—spirituals and jubilee choruses—singing them with fine spirit, if not with perfect technic, the children joining in these moving melodies.

He loved to read aloud to them. It was his habit to read his manuscript to Mrs. Clemens, and, now that the children were older, he was likely to include them in his critical audience.

It would seem to have been the winter after their return from Europe that this custom was inaugurated, for *The Prince and the Pauper* manuscript was the first one so read, and it was just then he was resuming work on this tale. Each afternoon or evening, when he had finished his chapter, he assembled his little audience and read them the result. The children were old enough to delight in that half real, half fairy tale of the wandering prince and the royal pauper: and the charm and simplicity of the story are measurably due to those two small listeners, to whom it was adapted in that early day of its creation.

Clemens found the *Prince* a blessed relief from *A Tramp Abroad*, which had become a veritable nightmare. He had thought it finished when he left the farm, but discovered that he must add several hundred pages to complete its bulk. It seemed to him that he had been given a life-sentence. He wrote six hundred pages and tore up all but two hundred and eighty-eight. He was about to destroy these and begin again, when Mrs. Clemens's health became poor and he was advised to take her to Elmira, though it was then midwinter. To Howells he wrote:

I said, "if there is one death that is painfuler than another, may I get it if I don't do that thing."

So I took the 288 pages to Bliss and told him that was the very last line I should ever write on this book (a book which required 2,600 pages of MS., and I have written nearly four thousand, first and last).

I am as soary (and flighty) as a rocket to-day, with the unutterable joy of getting that Old Man of the Sea off my back, where he has been roosting more than a year and a half.

They remained a month at Elmira, and on their return Clemens renewed work on *The Prince and the Pauper*. He reported to Howells that if he never sold a copy his jubilant delight in writing it would suffer no diminution. A week later his enthusiasm had still further increased:

I take so much pleasure in my story that I am loath to hurry, not wanting to get it done. Did I ever tell you the plot of it? It begins at 9 A.M., January 27, 1547.

He follows with a detailed synopsis of his plot, which in this instance he had worked out with unusual completeness—a fact which largely accounts for the unity of the tale. Then he adds:

My idea is to afford a realizing sense of the exceeding severity of the laws of that day by inflicting some of their penalties upon the king himself, and allowing him a chance to see the rest of them applied to others; all of which is to account for certain mildnesses which distinguished Edward VI.'s reign from those that precede it and follow it.

Imagine this fact: I have even fascinated Mrs. Clemens with this yarn for youth. My stuff generally gets considerable damning with faint praise out of her, but this time it is all the other way. She is become the horse-leech's daughter, and my mill doesn't grind fast enough to suit her. This is no mean triumph, my dear sir.

He forgot, perhaps, to mention his smaller auditors, but we may believe they were no less eager in their demands for the tale's continuance.

CXXVI

"A TRAMP ABROAD"

A *TRAMP ABROAD* came from the presses on the 13th of March, 1880. It had been widely heralded, and there was an advance sale of twenty-five thousand copies. It was of the same general size and outward character as the *Innocents*, numerously illustrated, and was regarded by its publishers as a satisfactory book.

It bore no very striking resemblance to the *Innocents* on close examination. Its pictures—drawn, for the most part, by a young art student named Brown, whom Clemens had met in Paris—were extraordinarily bad, while the crude engraving process by which they had been reproduced, tended to bring them still further into disrepute. A few drawings by True Williams were better, and those drawn by Clemens himself had a value of their own. The book would have profited had there been more of what the author calls his "works of art."

Mark Twain himself had dubious anticipations as to the book's reception. But Howells wrote:

> Well, you are a blessing. You ought to believe in God's goodness, since he has bestowed upon the world such a delightful genius as yours to lighten its troubles.

Clemens replied:

> Your praises have been the greatest uplift I ever had. When a body is not even remotely expecting such things, how the surprise takes the breath away! We had been interpreting your stillness to melancholy and depression, caused by that book.

This is honest. Why, everything looks brighter now. A check for untold cash could not have made our hearts sing as your letter has done.

•

A letter from Tauchnitz, proposing to issue an illustrated edition in Germany, besides putting it into his regular series, was an added satisfaction. To be in a Tauchnitz series was of itself a recognition of the book's merit.

To Twichell, Clemens presented a special copy of the *Tramp* with a personal inscription, which must not be omitted here:

MY DEAR "HARRIS"—NO, I MEAN MY DEAR JOE,—Just imagine it for a moment: I was collecting material in Europe during fourteen months for a book, and now that the thing is printed I find that you, who were with me only a month and a half of the fourteen, are in *actual* presence (not imaginary) in 440 of the 531 pages the book contains! Hang it, if you had stayed at home it would have taken me fourteen *years* to get the material. You have saved me an intolerable whole world of hated labor, and I'll not forget it, my boy.

You'll find reminders of things, all along, that happened to us, and of others that didn't happen; but you'll remember the spot where they were invented. You will see how the imaginary perilous trip up the Riffelberg is preposterously expanded. That horse-student is on page 192. The "Fremersberg" is neighboring. The Black Forest novel is on page 211. I remember when and where we projected that: in the leafy glades with the mountain sublimities dozing in the blue haze beyond the gorge of Allerheiligen. There's the "new member," page 213; the dentist yarn, 223; the true Chamois, 242; at page 248 is a pretty long yarn, spun from a mighty brief text—meeting, for a moment, that pretty girl who knew me and whom I had forgotten; at 281 is "Harris," and should have been so entitled, but Bliss has made a mistake and turned you into some other character; 305 brings back the whole Rigi tramp to me at a glance; at 185 and 186 are specimens of my art; and the frontispiece is the combination which I made by pasting one familiar picture over the lower half of an equally familiar one. This fine work being worthy of Titian, I have shed the credit of it upon him. Well, you'll find more reminders of things scattered through here than are printed, or could have been printed, in many books.

All the "legends of the Neckar," which I invented for that unstoried region, are here; one is in the Appendix. The steel portrait of me is just about perfect.

We had a mighty good time, Joe, and the six weeks I would dearly like to repeat *any* time; but the rest of the fourteen months—*never*. With love,

Yours, MARK.

Hartford, March 16, 1880.

Possibly Twichell had vague doubts concerning a book of which he was so large a part, and its favorable reception by the critics and the public generally was a great comfort. When the Howells letter was read to him he is reported as having sat with his hands on his knees, his head bent forward—a favorite attitude—repeating at intervals:

"Howells said that, did he? Old Howells said that!"

There have been many and varying opinions since then as to the literary merits of *A Tramp Abroad*. Human tastes differ, and a "mixed" book of this kind invites as many opinions as it has chapters. The word "uneven" pretty safely describes any book of size, but it has a special application to this one. Written under great stress and uncertainty of mind, it could hardly be uniform. It presents Mark Twain at his best, and at his worst. Almost any American writer was better than Mark Twain at his worst: Mark Twain at his best was unapproachable.

It is inevitable that *A Tramp Abroad* and *The Innocents Abroad* should be compared, though with hardly the warrant of similarity. The books are as different as was their author at the periods when they were written. *A Tramp Abroad* is the work of a man who was traveling and observing for the purpose of writing a book, and for no other reason. *The Innocents Abroad* was written by a man who was reveling in every scene and experience, every new phase and prospect; whose soul was alive to every historic association, and to every humor that a gay party of young sight-seers could find along the way. The note-books of that trip fairly glow with the inspiration of it; those of the later wanderings are mainly filled with brief, terse records, interspersed with satire and denunciation. In the *Innocents* the writer is the enthusiast with a sense of humor. In the *Tramp* he has still the sense of humor, but he has become a cynic; restrained, but a cynic none the less. In the *Innocents* he laughs at delusions and fallacies—and enjoys them. In the *Tramp* he laughs at human foibles and affectations—and wants to smash them. Very often he does not laugh heartily and sincerely at all, but finds his humor in extravagant burlesque. In later life his gentler laughter, his old, untroubled enjoyment of human weakness, would return, but just now he was in that middle period, when the "damned human race" amused him indeed, though less tenderly. (It seems proper to explain that in applying this term to mankind he did not mean that the race was foredoomed, but rather that it ought to be.)

Reading the *Innocents*, the conviction grows that, with all its faults, it is literature from beginning to end. Reading the *Tramp*, the suspicion arises that, regardless of technical improvement, its percentage of literature is not large. Yet, as noted in an earlier volume, so eminent a critic as Brander Matthews has pronounced in its favor, and he undoubtedly had a numerous following; Howells expressed his delight in the book at the time of its issue, though one wonders how far the personal element entered into his enjoyment, and what would be his final decision if he read the two books side by side to-day. He reviewed *A Tramp Abroad* adequately and finely in the

Atlantic, and justly; for on the whole it is a vastly entertaining book, and he did not overpraise it.

A Tramp Abroad had an "Introduction" in the manuscript, a pleasant word to the reader but not a necessary one, and eventually it was omitted. Fortunately the appendix remained. Beyond question it contains some of the very best things in the book. The descriptions of the German *Portier* and the German newspaper are happy enough, and the essay on the awful German language is one of Mark Twain's supreme bits of humor. It is Mark Twain at his best; Mark Twain in a field where he had no rival, the field of good-natured, sincere fun-making—ridicule of the manifest absurdities of some national custom or institution which the nation itself could enjoy, while the individual suffered no wound. The present Emperor of Germany is said to find comfort in this essay on his national speech when all other amusements fail. It is delicious beyond words to express; it is unique.

In the body of the book there are also many delights. The description of the ant might rank next to the German language almost in its humor, and the meeting with the unrecognized girl at Lucerne has a lively charm.

Of the serious matter, some of the word-pictures are flawless in their beauty; this, for instance, suggested by the view of the Jungfrau from Interlaken:

> There was something subduing in the influence of that silent and solemn and awful presence; one seemed to meet the immutable, the indestructible, the eternal, face to face, and to feel the trivial and fleeting nature of his own existence the more sharply by the contrast. One had the sense of being under the brooding contemplation of a spirit, not an inert mass of rocks and ice—a spirit which had looked down, through the slow drift of ages, upon a million vanished races of men and judged them; and would judge a million more—and still be there, watching unchanged and unchangeable, after all life should be gone and the earth have become a vacant desolation.

While I was feeling these things, I was groping, without knowing it, toward an understanding of what the spell is which people find in the Alps, and in no other mountains; that strange, deep, nameless influence which, once felt, cannot be forgotten; once felt, leaves always behind it a restless longing to feel it again—a longing which is like homesickness; a grieving, haunting yearning, which will plead, implore, and persecute till it has its will. I met dozens of people, imaginative and unimaginative, cultivated and uncultivated, who had come from far countries and roamed through the Swiss Alps year after year—they could not explain why. They had come first, they said, out of idle curiosity, because everybody talked about it; they had come since because they could not help it, and they should keep on coming, while they lived, for the same reason; they had tried to break their chains and stay away, but it was futile; now they had no desire to break them. Others came nearer formulating what they felt; they said they could find perfect rest and peace nowhere else when they were troubled: all frets and worries and chafings sank to sleep in the presence of the benignant serenity of the Alps; the Great Spirit of the mountain breathed his own peace upon their hurt minds and sore hearts, and healed them; they could not think base thoughts or do mean and sordid things here, before the visible throne of God.

Indeed, all the serious matter in the book is good. The reader's chief regret is likely to be that there is not more of it. The main difficulty with the humor is that it seems overdone. It is likely to be carried too far and continued too long. The ascent of Riffelberg is an example. Though spotted with delights it seems, to one reader at least, less admirable than other of the book's important features, striking, as it does, more emphatically the chief note of the book's humor—that is to say, exaggeration.

Without doubt there must be many—very many—who agree in finding a fuller enjoyment in *A Tramp Abroad* than in the *Innocents*; only, the burden of the world's opinion lies the other way. The world has a weakness for its illusions: the splendor that falls on castle walls, the glory of the hills at evening, the pathos of the days that are no more. It answers to tenderness, even on the page of humor, and to genuine enthusiasm, sharply sensing the lack of these things; instinctively resenting, even when most amused by it, extravagance and burlesque. *The Innocents Abroad* is more soul-satisfying than its successor, more poetic; more sentimental, if you will. The *Tramp* contains better English usage, without doubt, but it is less full of happiness and bloom and the halo of romance. The heart of the world has felt this, and has demanded the book in fewer numbers.[1]

[1] The sales of the *Innocents* during the earlier years more than doubled those of the *Tramp* during a similar period. The later ratio of popularity is more nearly three to one. It has been repeatedly stated that in England the *Tramp* has the greater popularity, an assertion not sustained by the publisher's accountings.

CXXVII

LETTERS, TALES, AND PLANS

THE reader has not failed to remark the great number of letters which Samuel Clemens wrote to his friend William Dean Howells; yet comparatively few can even be mentioned. He was always writing to Howells, on every subject under the sun; whatever came into his mind—business, literature, personal affairs—he must write about it to Howells. Once, when nothing better occurred, he sent him a series of telegrams, each a stanza from an old hymn, possibly thinking they might carry comfort.[1] Whatever of picturesque happened in the household he immediately set it down for Howells's entertainment. Some of these domestic incidents carry the flavor of his best humor. Once he wrote:

Last night, when I went to bed, Mrs. Clemens said, "George didn't take the cat down to the cellar; Rosa says he has left it shut up in the conservatory." So I went down to attend to Abner (the cat). About three in the morning Mrs. C. woke me and said, "I do believe I hear that cat in the drawing-room. What did you do with him?" I answered with the confidence of a man who has managed to do the right thing for once, and said,

[1] "Clemens had then and for many years the habit of writing to me about what he was doing, and still more of what he was experiencing. Nothing struck his imagination, in or out of the daily routine, but he wished to write me of it, and he wrote with the greatest fullness and a lavish dramatization, sometimes to the length of twenty or forty pages." (*My Mark Twain*, by W. D. Howells.)

"I opened the conservatory doors, took the library off the alarm, and spread everything open, so that there wasn't any obstruction between him and the cellar." Language wasn't capable of conveying this woman's disgust. But the sense of what she said was, "He couldn't have done any harm in the conservatory; so you must go and make the entire house free to him and the burglars, imagining that he will prefer the coal-bins to the drawing-room. If you had had Mr. Howells to help you I should have admired, but not have been astonished, because I should know that *together* you would be equal to it; but how you managed to contrive such a stately blunder all by yourself is what I cannot understand."

So, you see, even *she* knows how to apprecaite our gifts. . . .

I knocked off during these stirring hours, and don't intend to go to work again till we go away for the summer, four or six weeks hence. So I am writing to you, not because I have anything to say, but because you don't have to answer and I need something to do this afternoon.

The rightful earl has—

Friday, 7th.

Well, never mind about the rightful earl; he merely wanted to borrow money. I never knew an American earl that didn't.

After a trip to Boston, during which Mrs. Clemens did some bric-à-brac shopping, he wrote:

Mrs. Clemens has two imperishable topics now: the museum of andirons which she collected and your dinner. It is hard to tell which she admires the most. Sometimes she leans one way and sometimes the other; but I lean pretty steadily toward the dinner because I can appreciate that, whereas I am no prophet in andirons. There has been a procession of Adams Express wagons filing before the door all day delivering andirons.

In a more serious vein he refers to the aged violinist Ole Bull and his wife, whom they had met during their visit, and their enjoyment of that gentle-hearted pair.

Clemens did some shorter work that spring, most of which found its way into the *Atlantic*. "Edward Mills and George Benton," one of the contributions of this time, is a moral sermon in its presentation of a pitiful human spectacle and misdirected human zeal.

It brought a pack of letters of approval, not only from laity, but the church, and in some measure may have helped to destroy the silly sentimentalism which manifested itself in making heroes of spectacular criminals. That fashion has gone out, largely. Mark Twain wrote frequently on the subject, though never more effectively than in this particular instance. "Mrs. McWilliams and the Lightning" was another *Atlantic* story, a companion piece to "Mrs. McWilliams's Experience with the Membranous Croup," and in the same delightful vein—a vein in which Mark Twain was likely to be at his best—the transcription of a scene not so far removed in character from that in the "cat" letter just quoted; something which may or may not have happened, but might have happened, approximately as set down. Rose Terry Cooke wrote:

> Horrid man, how did you know the way I behave in a thunder-storm? Have you been secreted in the closet or lurking on the shed roof? I hope you got thoroughly rained on; and worst of all is that you made me laugh at myself; my real terrors turned round and grimaced at me: they were sublime, and you have made them ridiculous. Just come out here another year and have four houses within a few rods of you struck and then see if you write an article of such exasperating levity. I really hate you, but you are funny.

In addition to his own work, he conceived a plan for Orion. Clemens himself had been attempting, from time to time, an absolutely faithful autobiography; a document in which his deeds and misdeeds, even his moods and inmost thoughts, should be truly set down. He had found it an impossible task. He confessed freely that he lacked the courage, even the actual ability, to pen the words that would lay his soul bare, but he believed Orion equal to the task. He knew how rigidly honest he was, how ready to confess his shortcomings, how eager to be employed at some literary occupation. It was Mark Twain's belief that if Orion would record in detail his long, weary struggle, his succession of attempts and failures, his past dreams and disappointments, along with his sins of omission and commission, it would make one of those priceless human documents such as have been left by Benvenuto Cellini, Cazenova, and Rousseau.

"Simply tell your story to yourself," he wrote, "laying all hideousness utterly bare, reserving nothing. Banish the idea of the audience and all hampering things."

Orion, out in Keokuk, had long since abandoned the chicken farm and a variety of other enterprises. He had prospected insurance, mining, journalism, his old trade of printing, and had taken down and hung up his law shingle between each of these seizures. Aside from business, too, he had been having a rather spectacular experience. He had changed his politics three times (twice in one day), and his religion as many more. Once when he was delivering a political harangue in the street, at night, a parade of the opposition (he had but just abandoned them) marched by carrying certain flaming transparencies, which he himself had made for them the day before. Finally, after delivering a series of infidel lectures, he had been excommunicated and condemned to eternal flames by the Presbyterian Church. He was therefore ripe for any new diversion, and the *Autobiography* appealed to him. He set about it with splendid enthusiasm, wrote a hundred pages or so of his childhood with a startling minutiæ of detail and frankness, and mailed them to his brother for inspection.

They were all that Mark Twain had expected; more than he had expected. He forwarded them to Howells with great satisfaction, suggesting, with certain excisions, they be offered anonymously to the *Atlantic* readers.

But Howells's taste for realism had its limitations. He found the story interesting—indeed, torturingly, heart-wringingly so—and, advising strongly against its publication, returned it.

Orion was steaming along at the rate of ten to twenty pages a day now, forwarding them as fast as written, while his courage was good and the fires warm. Clemens, receiving a package by every morning mail, soon lost interest, then developed a hunted feeling, becoming finally desperate. He wrote wildly to shut Orion off, urging him to let his manuscript accumulate, and to send it in one large consignment at the end. This Orion did, and it is fair to say that in this instance at least he stuck to his work faithfully to the bitter, disheartening end. And it would have been all that Mark Twain had dreamed it would be, had Orion maintained the simple narrative spirit of its early pages. But he drifted off into theological byways; into discussions of his excommunication and infidelities, which were frank enough, but lacked human interest.

In old age Mark Twain once referred to Orion's autobiography in print and his own disappointment in it, which he attributed to Orion's having departed from the idea of frank and unrestricted confession to exalt himself as a hero—a statement altogether unwarranted, and due to one of those curious confusions of memory and imagination that more than once resulted in a complete reversal of the facts. A quantity of Orion's manuscript has been lost and destroyed, but enough fragments of it remain to show its fidelity to the original plan. It is just one long record of fleeting hope, futile effort, and humiliation. It is the story of a life of disappointment; of a man who has been defeated and beaten down and crushed by the world until he has nothing but confession left to surrender.[1]

Whatever may have been Mark Twain's later impression of his brother's manuscript, its story of failure and disappointment moved him to definite action at the time. Several years before, in Hartford, Orion had urged him to make his publishing contracts on a basis of half profits, instead of on the royalty plan. Clemens, remembering this, had insisted on such an arrangement for the publication of *A Tramp Abroad*, and when his first statement came in he realized that the new contract was very largely to his advantage. He remembered Orion's anxiety in the matter, and made it now a valid excuse for placing his brother on a firm financial footing.

Out of the suspicions which you bred in me years ago has grown this result, to wit: that I shall within the twelve months get $40,000 out of this *Tramp*, instead of $20,000. $20,000, after taxes and other expenses are stripped away, is worth to the investor about $75 a month, so I shall tell Mr. Perkins [his lawyer and financial agent] to make your check that amount per month hereafter. . . . This ends the loan business, and hereafter you can reflect that you are living not on borrowed money, but on money which you have squarely earned, and which has no taint or savor of charity about it, and you can also reflect that the money which you have been receiving of me is charged against the heavy bill which the next publisher will have to stand who gets a book of mine.

From that time forward Orion Clemens was worth substantially twenty thousand dollars till the day of his death, and, after him, his widow. Far better was it for him that the endowment be conferred in the form of an income, than had the capital amount been placed in his hands.

[1] Howells, in his letter concerning the opening chapters, said that they would some day make good material. Fortunately the earliest of these chapters were preserved, and, as the reader may remember, furnished much of the childhood details for this biography.

CXXVIII

MARK TWAIN'S ABSENT-MINDEDNESS

A NUMBER of amusing incidents have been more or less accurately reported concerning Mark Twain's dim perception of certain physical surroundings, and his vague resulting memories—his absent-mindedness, as we say.

It was not that he was inattentive—no man was ever less so if the subject interested him—but only that the casual, incidental thing seemed not to find a fixed place in his deeper consciousness.

By no means was Mark Twain's absent-mindedness a development of old age. On the two occasions following he was in the very heyday of his mental strength. Especially was it, when he was engaged upon some absorbing or difficult piece of literature, that his mind seemed to fold up and shut most of the world away. Soon after his return from Europe, when he was still struggling with *A Tramp Abroad*, he wearily put the manuscript aside, one day, and set out to invite F. G. Whitmore over for a game of billiards. Whitmore lived only a little way down the street, and Clemens had been there time and again. It was such a brief distance that he started out in his slippers and with no hat. But when he reached the corner where the house, a stone's-throw away, was in plain view he stopped. He did not recognize it. It was unchanged, but its outlines had left no impress upon his mind. He stood there uncertainly a little while, then returned and got the coachman, Patrick McAleer, to show him the way.

The second, and still more picturesque instance, belongs also to this period. One day, when he was playing billiards with Whitmore, George, the butler, came up with a card.

"Who is he, George?" Clemens asked, without looking at the card.

"I don't know, suh, but he's a gentleman, Mr. Clemens."

"Now, George, how many times have I told you I don't want to see strangers when I'm playing billiards! This is just some book agent, or insurance man, or somebody with something to sell. I don't want to see him, and I'm not going to."

"Oh, but this is a gentleman, I'm sure, Mr. Clemens. Just look at his card, suh."

"Yes, of course, I see—nice engraved card—but I don't know him, and if it was St. Peter himself I wouldn't buy the key of salvation! You tell him so—tell him—*oh, well*, I suppose I've got to go and get rid of him myself. I'll be back in a minute, Whitmore."

He ran down the stairs, and as he got near the parlor door, which stood open, he saw a man sitting on a couch with what seemed to be some framed water-color pictures on the floor near his feet.

"Ah, ha!" he thought, "I see. A picture agent. I'll soon get rid of him."

He went in with his best, "Well, what can I do for you?" air, which he, as well as any man living, knew how to assume; a friendly air enough, but not encouraging. The gentleman rose and extended his hand.

"How are you, Mr. Clemens?" he said.

Of course this was the usual thing with men who had axes to grind or goods to sell. Clemens did not extend a very cordial hand. He merely raised a loose, indifferent hand—a discouraging hand.

"And how is Mrs. Clemens?" asked the uninvited guest.

So this was his game. He would show an interest in the family and ingratiate himself in that way; he would be asking after the children next.

"Well—Mrs. Clemens is about as usual—I believe."

"And the children—Miss Susie and little Clara?"

This was a bit startling. He knew their names! Still, that was easy to find out. He was a smart agent, wonderfully smart. He must be got rid of.

"The children are well, quite well, and" (pointing down at the pictures)—"We've got plenty like these. We don't want any more. No, we don't care for any more," skilfully working his visitor toward the door as he talked.

The man, looking nonplussed—a good deal puzzled—allowed himself to be talked into the hall and toward the front door. Here he paused a moment:

"Mr. Clemens, will you tell me where Mr. Charles Dudley Warner lives?"

This was the chance! He would work him off on Charlie Warner. Perhaps Warner needed pictures.

"Oh, certainly, *certainly!* Right across the yard. I'll show you. There's a walk right through. You don't need to go around the front way at all. You'll find him at home, too, I'm pretty sure"; all the time working his caller out and down the step and in the right direction.

The visitor again extended his hand.

"Please remember me to Mrs. Clemens and the children."

"Oh, certainly, certainly, with pleasure. Good day. Yes, that's the house. Good-by."

On the way back to the billiard-room Mrs. Clemens called to him. She was ill that day.

"Youth!"

"Yes, Livy." He went in for a word.

"George brought me Mr. B——'s card. I hope you were very nice to him; the B——s were so nice to us, once last year, when you were gone."

"The B——s— Why, Livy—"

"Yes, of course, and I asked him to be sure to call when he came to Hartford."

He gazed at her helplessly.

"Well, he's been here."

"Oh, Youth, have you done anything?"

"Yes, of course I have. He seemed to have some pictures to sell, so I sent him over to Warner's. I noticed he didn't take them with him. Land sakes, Livy, what can I do?"

"Which way did he go, Youth?"

"Why, I sent him to Charlie Warner's. I thought—"

"Go right after him. Go quick! Tell him what you have done."

He went without further delay, bareheaded and in his slippers, as usual. Warner and B—— were in cheerful and friendly converse. They had met before. Clemens entered gaily:

"Oh yes, I see! You found him all right. Charlie, we met Mr. B—— and his wife in Europe last summer and they made things pleasant for us. I wanted to come over here *with* him, but was a good deal occupied just then. Livy isn't very well, but she seems a good deal better, so I just followed along to have a good talk, all together."

He stayed an hour, and whatever bad impression had formed in B——'s mind faded long before the hour ended. Returning home Clemens noticed the pictures still on the parlor floor.

"George," he said, "what pictures are those that gentleman left?"

"Why, Mr. Clemens, those are our *own* pictures. I've been straightening up the room a little, and Mrs. Clemens had me set them around to see how they would look in new places. The gentleman was looking at them while he was waiting for you to come down."

CXXIX

FURTHER AFFAIRS AT THE FARM

IT was at Elmira, in July (1880), that the third little girl came—Jane Lampton, for her grandmother, but always called Jean. She was a large, lovely baby, robust and happy. When she had been with them a little more than a month Clemens, writing to Twichell, said:

DEAR OLD JOE,—Concerning Jean Clemens, if anybody said he "didn't see no p'ints about that frog that's any better'n any other frog," I should think he was convicting himself of being a pretty poor sort of observer. She is the comeliest and daintiest and perfectest little creature the continents and archipelagos have seen since the Bay and Susy were her size. I will not go into details; it is not necessary; you will soon be in Hartford, where I have already hired a hall; the admission fee will be but a trifle.

It is curious to note the change in the stock-quotations of the Affection Board brought about by throwing this new security on the market. Four weeks ago the children still put Mama at the head of the list right along, where she had always been. But now:

Jean
Mama
Motley } cats
Fräulein }
Papa

That is the way it stands now. Mama is become No. 2; I have dropped from No. 4, and am become No. 5. Some time ago it used to be nip and tuck between me and the cats, but after the cats "developed" I didn't stand any more show.

Been reading *Daniel Webster's Private Correspondence.* Have read a hundred of his diffuse, conceited, "eloquent," bathotic (or bathostic) letters, written in that dim (no, vanished) past, when he was a student. And Lord! to think that this boy, who is so real to me now, and so booming with fresh young blood and bountiful life, and sappy cynicisms about girls, has since climbed the Alps of fame and stood against the sun one brief, tremendous moment with the world's eyes on him, and then—*fzt!* where is he? Why, the only *long* thing, the only real thing about the whole shadowy business, is the sense of the lagging dull and hoary lapse of time that has drifted by since then; a vast, empty level, it seems, with a formless specter glimpsed fitfully through the smoke and mist that lie along its remote verge.

Well, we are all getting along here first-rate. Livy gains strength daily and sits up a deal; the baby is five weeks old and— But no more of this. Somebody may be reading *this* letter eighty years hence. And so, my friend (you pitying snob, I mean, who are holding this yellow paper in your hand in 1960), save yourself the trouble of looking further. I know how pathetically trivial our small concerns would seem to you, and I will not let your eye profane them. No, I keep my news; you keep your compassion. Suffice it you to know, scoffer and ribald, that the little child is old and blind now, and once more toothless; and the rest of us are shadows these many, many years. Yes, and *your* time cometh!

MARK.

It is the ageless story. He too had written his youthful letters, and later had climbed the Alps of fame and was still outlined against the sun. Happily, the little child was to evade that harsher penalty—the unwarranted bitterness and affront of a lingering, palsied age.

Mrs. Clemens, in a letter somewhat later, set down a thought similar to his:

"We are all going so fast. Pretty soon we shall have been dead a hundred years."

Clemens varied his work that summer, writing alternately on *The Prince and the Pauper* and on the story about Huck Finn, which he had begun four years earlier.

He read the latter over and found in it a new interest. It did not fascinate him, as did the story of the wandering prince. He persevered only as the spirit moved him, piling up pages on both the tales.

He always took a boy's pride in the number of pages he could complete at a sitting, and if the day had gone well he would count them triumphantly, and, lighting a fresh cigar, would come tripping down the long stair that led to the level of the farm-house, and, gathering his audience, would read to them the result of his industry; that is to say, he proceeded with the story of the *Prince.* Apparently he had not yet acquired confidence or pride enough in poor Huck to exhibit him, even to friends.

The reference (in the letter to Twichell) to the cats at the farm introduces one of the most important features of that idyllic resort. There were always cats at the farm. Mark Twain himself dearly loved cats, and the children inherited this passion. Susy once said:

"The difference between papa and mama is, that mama loves morals and papa loves cats."

The cats did not always remain the same, but some of the same ones remained a good while, and were there from season to season, always welcomed and adored. They were commendable cats, with such names as Fräulein, Blatherskite, Sour Mash, Stray Kit, Sin, and Satan, and when, as happened now and then, a vacancy occurred in the cat census there followed deep sorrow and elaborate ceremonies.

Naturally, there would be stories about cats: impromptu bedtime stories, which began anywhere and ended nowhere, and continued indefinitely through a land inhabited only by cats and dreams. One of these stories, as remembered and set down later, began:

Once upon a time there was a noble, big cat whose christian name was Catasaqua, because she lived in that region; but she didn't have any surname, because she was a short-tailed cat, being a manx, and didn't need one. It is very just and becoming in a long-tailed cat to have a surname, but it would be very ostentatious, and even dishonorable, in a manx. Well, Catasaqua had a beautiful family of catlings; and they were of different colors, to harmonize with their characters. Cattaraugus, the eldest, was white, and he had high impulses and a pure heart; Catiline, the youngest, was black, and he had a self-seeking nature, his motives were nearly always base, he was truculent and insincere. He was vain and foolish, and often said that he would rather be what he was, and live like a bandit, yet have none above him, than be a cat-o'-nine-tails and eat with the king.

And so on without end, for the audience was asleep presently and the end could wait.

There was less enthusiasm over dogs at Quarry Farm. Mark Twain himself had no great love for the canine breed. To a woman who wrote, asking for his opinion on dogs, he said, in part:

By what right has the dog come to be regarded as a "noble" animal? The more brutal and cruel and unjust you are to him the more your fawning and adoring slave he becomes; whereas, if you shamefully misuse a cat once she will always maintain a dignified reserve toward you afterward—you can never get her full confidence again.

He was not harsh to dogs; occasionally he made friends with them. There was once at the farm a gentle hound, named Bones, that for some reason even won his way into his affections. Bones was always a welcome companion, and when the end of summer came, and Clemens, as was his habit, started down the drive ahead of the carriage, Bones, half-way to the entrance, was waiting for him. Clemens stooped down, put his arms around him, and bade him an affectionate good-by. He always recalled Bones tenderly, and mentioned him in letters to the farm.

CXXX

COPYRIGHT AND OTHER FANCIES

THE continued assault of Canadian pirates on his books kept Mark Twain's interest sharply alive on the subject of copyright reform. He invented one scheme after another, but the public mind was hazy on the subject, and legislators were concerned with purposes that interested a larger number of voters. There were too few authors to be of much value at the polls, and even of those few only a small percentage were vitally concerned. For the others, foreign publishers rarely paid them the compliment of piracy, while at home the copyright limit of forty-two years was about forty-two times as long as they needed protection. Bliss suggested a law making the selling of pirated books a penal offense, a plan with a promising look, but which came to nothing.

Clemens wrote to his old friend Rollin M. Daggett, who by this time was a Congressman. Daggett replied that he would be glad to introduce any bill that the authors might agree upon, and Clemens made at least one trip to Washington to discuss the matter, but it came to nothing in the end. It was a Presidential year, and it would do just as well to keep the authors quiet by promising to do something next year. Any legislative stir is never a good thing for a campaign.

Clemens's idea for copyright betterment was not a fixed one. Somewhat later, when an international treaty which would include protection for authors was being discussed, his views had undergone a change. He wrote, asking Howells:

> Will the proposed treaty protect us (and effectually) against Canadian piracy? Because, if it doesn't, there is not a single argument in favor of international copyright which a rational American Senate could entertain for a moment. My notions have mightily changed lately. I can buy *Macaulay's History*, three vols., bound, for $1.25; *Chambers's Cyclopædia*, ten vols., cloth, for $7.25 (we paid $60), and other English copyrights in proportion; I can buy a lot of the great copyright classics, in paper, at from three cents to thirty cents apiece. These things must find their way into the very kitchens and hovels of the country. A generation of this sort of thing ought to make this the most intelligent and the best-read nation in the world. International copyright must becloud this sun and bring on the former darkness and dime-novel reading.
>
> Morally this is all wrong; governmentally it is all right. For it is the duty of governments and families to be selfish, and look out simply for their own. International copyright would benefit a few English authors and a lot of American publishers, and be a profound detriment to twenty million Americans; it would benefit a dozen American authors a few dollars a year, and there an end. The *real* advantages all go to English authors and American publishers.
>
> And even if the treaty *will* kill Canadian piracy, and thus save me an average of $5,000 a year, I'm down on it anyway, and I'd like cussed well to write an article opposing the treaty.

It is a characteristic expression. Mark Twain might be first to grab for the life-preserver, but he would also be first to hand it to a humanity in greater need. He could damn the human race competently, but in the final reckoning it was the interest of that race that lay closest to his heart.

Mention has been made in an earlier chapter of Clemens's enthusiasms or "rages" for this thing and that which should benefit humankind. He was seldom entirely without them. Whether it was copyright legislation, the latest invention, or a new empiric practice, he rarely failed to have a burning interest in some anodyne that would provide physical or mental easement for his species. Howells tells how once he was going to save the human race with accordion letter-files—the system of order which would grow out of this useful device being of such nerve and labor saving proportions as to insure long life and happiness to all. The fountain-pen, in its first imperfect form, must have come along about the same time, and Clemens was one of the very earliest authors to own one. For a while it seemed that the world had known no greater boon since the invention of printing; but when it clogged and balked, or suddenly deluged his paper and spilled in his pocket, he flung it to the outer darkness. After which, the stylographic pen. He tried one, and wrote severally to Dr. Brown, to Howells, and to Twichell, urging its adoption. Even in a letter to Mrs. Howells he could not forget his new possession:

And speaking of Howells, he ought to use the stylographic pen, the best fountain-pen yet invented; he *ought* to, but of course he won't—a blamed old sodden-headed conservative—but you see yourself what a nice, clean, uniform MS. it makes.

And at the same time to Twichell:

I am writing with a stylographic pen. It takes a royal amount of cussing to make the thing go the first few days or a week, but by that time the dullest ass gets the hang of the thing, and after that no enrichments of expression are required, and said ass finds the stylographic a geniune God's blessing. I carry one in each breeches pocket, and both loaded. I'd give you one of them if I had you where I could teach you how to use it—not otherwise. For the average ass flings the thing out of the window in disgust the second day, believing it hath no virtue, no merit of any sort; whereas the lack lieth in himself, God of his mercy damn him.

SAMUEL LANGHORNE CLEMENS ABOUT 1880

It was not easy to withstand Mark Twain's enthusiasm. Howells, Twichell, and Dr. Brown were all presently struggling and swearing (figuratively) over their stylographic pens, trying to believe that salvation lay in their conquest. But in the midst of one letter, at last, Howells broke down, seized his old steel weapon, and wrote savagely: "No white man ought to use a stylographic pen, anyhow!" Then, with the more ancient implement, continued in a calmer spirit.

It was only a little later that Clemens himself wrote:

> You see I am trying a new pen. I stood the stylograph as long as I could, and then retired to the pencil. The thing I am trying now is that fountain-pen which is advertised to employ and accommodate itself to any kind of pen. So I selected an ordinary gold pen—a limber one—and sent it to New York and had it cut and fitted to this thing. It goes very well indeed—thus far; but doubtless the devil will be in it by to-morrow.

Mark Twain's schemes were not all in the line of human advancement; some of them were projected, primarily at least, for diversion. He was likely at any moment to organize a club, a sort of private club, and at the time of which we are writing he proposed what was called the "Modest" Club. He wrote to Howells about it:

> At present I am the only member, and as the modesty required must be of a quite aggravated type the enterprise did seem for a time doomed to stop dead still with myself, for lack of further material; but on reflection I have come to the conclusion that you are eligible. Therefore, I have held a meeting and voted to offer you the distinction of membership. I do not know that we can find any others, though I have had some thought of Hay, Warner, Twichell, Aldrich, Osgood, Fields, Higginson, and a few more, together with Mrs. Howells, Mrs. Clemens, and certain others of the sex. I have long felt there ought to be an organized gang of our kind.

He appends the by-laws, the main ones being:

The object of the club shall be to eat and talk.

Qualification for membership shall be aggravated modesty, unobtrusiveness, native humility, learning, talent, intelligence, unassailable character.

There shall be no officers except a president, and any member who has anything to eat and talk about may constitute himself president for the time being.

Any brother or sister of the order finding a brother or a sister in imminently deadly peril shall forsake his own concerns, no matter at what cost, and call the police.

Any member knowing anything scandalous about himself shall immediately inform the club, so that they shall call a meeting and have the first chance to talk about it.

It was one of his whimsical fancies, and Howells replied that he would like to join it, only that he was too modest—that is, too modest to confess that he was modest enough for membership.

He added that he had sent a letter, with the rules, to Hay, but doubted his modesty. He said:

"He will think he has a right to belong as much as you or I."

Howells agreed that his own name might be put down, but the idea seems never to have gone any further. Perhaps the requirements of membership were too severe.

CXXXI

WORKING FOR GARFIELD

EIGHTEEN hundred and eighty was a Presidential year. General Garfield was nominated on the Republican ticket (against General Hancock), and Clemens found him satisfactory.

> Garfield suits me thoroughly and exactly [he wrote Howells]. I prefer him to Grant('s friends). The Presidency can't add anything to Grant; he will shine on without it. It is ephemeral; he is eternal.

That was the year when the Republican party became panicky over the disaffection in its ranks, due to the defeat of Grant in the convention, and at last, by pleadings and promises, conciliated Platt and Conkling and brought them into the field. General Grant also was induced to save the party from defeat, and made a personal tour of oratory for that purpose. He arrived in Hartford with his family on the 16th of October, and while his reception was more or less partizan, it was a momentous event. A vast procession passed in review before him, and everywhere houses and grounds were decorated. To Mrs. Clemens, still in Elmira, Clemens wrote:

> I found Mr. Beals hard at work in the rain with his decorations. With a ladder he had strung flags around our bedroom balcony, and thence around to the porte-cochère, which was elaborately flagged; thence the flags of all nations were suspended from a line which stretched past the greenhouse to the

limit of our grounds. Against each of the two trees on the mound, half-way down to our gate, stands a knight in complete armor. Piles of still-bundled flags clutter up the ombra (to be put up), also gaudy shields of various shapes (arms of this and other countries), also some huge glittering arches and things done in gold and silver paper, containing mottoes in big letters. I broke Mr. Beals's heart by persistently and inflexibly annulling and forbidding the biggest and gorgeousest of the arches—it had on it, in all the fires of the rainbow, "The Home of Mark Twain," in letters as big as your head. Oh, we're going to be decorated sufficient, don't you worry about that, madam.

Clemens was one of those delegated to receive Grant and to make a speech of welcome. It was a short speech but an effective one, for it made Grant laugh. He began:

"I am among those deputed to welcome you to the sincere and cordial hospitalities of Hartford, the city of the historic and revered Charter Oak, of which most of the town is built." He seemed to be at loss what to say next, and, leaning over, pretended to whisper to Grant; then, as if he had obtained the information he wanted, he suddenly straightened up and poured out the old-fashioned eulogy on Grant's achievements, adding, in an aside, as he finished:

"I nearly forgot that part of my speech," which evoked roars of laughter from the assembly and a grim smile from Grant. He spoke of Grant as being out of public employment, with private opportunities closed against him, and added, "But your country will reward you, never fear."

Then he closed:

When Wellington won Waterloo, a battle about on a level with any one of a *dozen* of *your* victories, sordid England tried to pay him for that service with wealth and grandeurs. She made him a duke and gave him $4,000,000. If you had done and suffered for any other country what you have done and suffered for your own you would have been affronted in the same sordid way. But, thank God! this vast and rich and mighty republic is imbued to the core with a delicacy which will forever preserve her from so degrading you.

Your country *loves* you—your country's *proud* of you—your country is *grateful* to you. Her applauses, which have been many, thundering in your ears all these weeks and months, will never cease while the flag you saved continues to wave.

Your country stands ready from this day forth to testify her measureless love and pride and gratitude toward you in every conceivable—*inexpensive* way. Welcome to Hartford, great soldier, honored statesman, unselfish citizen.

Grant's grim smile showed itself more than once during the speech, and when Clemens reached the sentence that spoke of his country rewarding him in "every conceivable—*inexpensive* way" his composure broke up completely and he "nearly laughed his entire head off," according to later testimony, while the spectators shouted their approval.

Grant's son, Col. Fred Grant,[1] dined at the Clemens home that night, and Rev. Joseph Twichell and Henry C. Robinson. Twichell's invitation was in the form of a telegram. It said:

I want you to dine with us Saturday half past five and meet Col. Fred Grant. No ceremony. Wear the same shirt you always wear.

The campaign was at its height now, and on the evening of October 26th there was a grand Republican rally at the opera-house with addresses by Charles Dudley Warner, Henry C. Robinson, and Mark Twain. It was an unpleasant, drizzly evening, but the weather had no effect on their audience. The place was jammed and packed, the aisles, the windows, and the gallery railings full. Hundreds who came as late as the hour announced for

[1] Maj.-Gen'l, U. S. Army, 1906. Died April, 1912.

the opening were obliged to turn back, for the building had been thronged long before. Mark Twain's speech that night is still remembered in Hartford as the greatest effort of his life. It was hardly that, except to those who were caught in the psychology of the moment, the tumult and the shouting of patriotism, the surge and sweep of the political tide. The roaring delight of the audience showed that to them at least it was convincing. Howells wrote that he had read it twice, and that he could not put it out of his mind. Whatever its general effect was need not now be considered. Garfield was elected, and perhaps Grant's visit to Hartford and the great mass-meeting that followed contributed their mite to that result.

Clemens saw General Grant again that year, but not on political business. The Educational Mission, which China had established in Hartford—a thriving institution for eight years or more—was threatened now by certain Chinese authorities with abolishment. Yung Wing (a Yale graduate), the official by whom it had been projected and under whose management it had prospered, was deeply concerned, as was the Rev. Joseph Twichell, whose interest in the mission was a large and personal one. Yung Wing declared that if influence could be brought upon Li Hung Chang, then the most influential of Chinese counselors, the mission might be saved. Twichell, remembering the great honors which Li Hung Chang had paid to General Grant in China, also Grant's admiration of Mark Twain, went to the latter without delay. Necessarily Clemens would be enthusiastic, and act promptly. He wrote to Grant, and Grant replied by telegraph, naming a day when he would see them in New York.

They met at the Fifth Avenue Hotel. Grant was in fine spirits, and by no means the "silent man" of his repute.

He launched at once into as free and flowing talk as I have ever heard [says Twichell], marked by broad and intelligent views on the subject of China, her wants, disadvantages, etc. Now and then he asked a question, but kept the lead of the conversation. At last he proposed, of his own accord, to write a letter to Li Hung Chang, advising the continuance of the Mission, asking only that I would prepare him some notes, giving him points to go by. Thus we succeeded easily beyond our expectations, thanks, very largely, to Clemens's assistance.

Clemens wrote Howells of the interview, detailing at some length Twichell's comical mixture of delight and chagrin at not being given time to air the fund of prepared statistics with which he had come loaded. "It was as if he had come to borrow a dollar and had been offered a thousand before he could unfold his case."

CXXXII

A NEW PUBLISHER

IT was near the end of the year that Clemens wrote to his mother:

I have two stories, and by the verbal agreement they are both going into the same book; but Livy says they're not, and by George I. she ought to know. She says they're going into separate books, and that one of them is going to be elegantly gotten up, even if the elegance of it eats up the publisher's profits and mine too.

I anticipate that publisher's melancholy surprise when he calls here Tuesday. However, let him suffer; it is his own fault. People who fix up agreements with me without first finding out what Livy's plans are take their fate into their own hands.

I said *two* stories, but one of them is only half done; two or three months' work on it yet. I shall tackle it Wednesday or Thursday; that is, if Livy yields and allows both stories to go in one book, which I hope she won't.

The reader may surmise that the finished story—the highly regarded story—was *The Prince and the Pauper*. The other tale—the unfinished and less considered one —was *The Adventures of Huckleberry Finn.* Nobody appears to have been especially concerned about Huck, except, possibly, the publisher.

The publisher was not the American Company. Elisha Bliss, after long ill health, had died that fall, and this fact, in connection with a growing dissatisfaction over the earlier contracts, had induced Clemens to listen to offers from other makers of books. The revelation made by the "half-profit" returns from *A Tramp Abroad* meant to him, simply that the profits had not been fairly apportioned, and he was accordingly hostile. To Orion he wrote that, had Bliss lived, he would have remained with the company and made it reimburse him for his losses, but that as matters stood he would sever the long connection. It seemed a pity, later, that he did this, but the break was bound to come. Clemens was not a business man, and Bliss was not a philanthropist. He was, in fact, a shrewd, capable publisher, who made as good a contract as he could; yet he was square in his dealings, and the contract which Clemens held most bitterly against him —that of *Roughing It*—had been made in good faith and in accordance with the conditions of that period. In most of the later contracts Clemens himself had named his royalties, and it was not in human nature—*business* human nature—for Bliss to encourage the size of these percentages. If one wished to draw a strictly moral conclusion from the situation, one might say that it would have been better for the American Publishing Company, knowing Mark Twain, voluntarily to have allowed him half profits, which was the spirit of his old understanding even if not the letter of it, rather than to have waited till he demanded it and then to lose him by the result. Perhaps that would be also a proper business deduction; only, as a rule, business morals are regulated by the contract, and the contract is regulated by the necessities and the urgency of demand.

Never mind. Mark Twain revised *The Prince and the Pauper*, sent it to Howells, who approved of it mightily (though with reservations as to certain chapters), and gave it to James R. Osgood, who was grateful and agreed to make it into a book upon which no expense for illustration or manufacture should be spared. It was to be a sort of partnership arrangement as between author and publisher, and large returns were anticipated.

Among the many letters which Clemens was just then writing to Howells one was dated "Xmas Eve." It closes with the customary pleasantries and the final line:

"But it is growing dark. Merry Christmas to all of you!"

That last was a line of large significance. It meant that the air was filled with the whisper of hovering events and that he must mingle with the mystery of preparation. Christmas was an important season in the Clemens home. Almost the entire day before, Patrick was out with the sleigh, delivering food and other gifts in baskets to the poor, and the home preparations were no less busy. There was always a tree—a large one—and when all the gifts had been gathered in—when Elmira and Fredonia had delivered their contributions, and Orion and his wife in Keokuk had sent the annual sack of hickory-nuts (the big river-bottom nuts, big as a silver dollar almost, such nuts as few children of this later generation ever see)—when all this happy revenue had been gathered, and the dusk of Christmas Eve had hurried the children off to bed, it was Mrs. Clemens who superintended the dressing of the tree, her husband assisting, with a willingness that was greater than his skill, and with a boy's anticipation in the surprise of it next morning.

Then followed the holidays, with parties and dances and charades, and little plays, with the Warner and Twichell children. To the Clemens home the Christmas season brought all the old round of juvenile happiness—the spirit of kindly giving, the brightness and the merry-making, the gladness and tenderness and mystery that belong to no other season, and have been handed down through all the ages since shepherds watched on the plains of Bethlehem.

ONE VIEW OF THE HARTFORD HOUSE

CXXXIII

THE THREE FIRES—SOME BENEFACTIONS

THE tradition that fires occur in groups of three was justified in the Clemens household that winter. On each of three successive days flames started that might have led to ghastly results.

The children were croupy, and one morning an alcohol lamp near little Clara's bed, blown by the draught, set fire to the canopy. Rosa, the nurse, entered just as the blaze was well started. She did not lose her presence of mind,[1] but snatched the little girl out of danger, then opened the window and threw the burning bedding on the lawn. The child was only slightly scorched, but the escape was narrow enough.

Next day little Jean was lying asleep in her crib, in front of an open wood fire, carefully protected by a fire-screen, when a spark, by some ingenuity, managed to get through the mesh of the screen and land on the crib's lace covering. Jean's nurse, Julia, arrived to find the lace a gust of flame and the fire spreading. She grabbed the sleeping Jean and screamed. Rosa, again at hand, heard the scream, and rushing in once more opened a window and flung out the blazing bedclothes. Clemens himself also arrived, and together they stamped out the fire.

On the third morning, just before breakfast-time, Susy

[1] Rosa was not the kind to lose her head. Once, in Europe, when Bay had crept between the uprights of a high balustrade, and was hanging out over destruction, Rosa, discovering her, did not scream but spoke to her playfully and lifted her over into safety.

was practising at the piano in the school-room, which adjoined the nursery. At one end of the room a fire of large logs was burning. Susy was at the other end of the room, her back to the fire. A log burned in two and fell, scattering coals around the woodwork which supported the mantel. Just as the blaze was getting fairly started a barber, waiting to trim Mr. Clemens's hair, chanced to look in and saw what was going on. He stepped into the nursery bath-room, brought a pitcher of water and extinguished the flames. This period was always referred to in the Clemens household as the "three days of fire."

Clemens would naturally make philosophical deductions from these coincidental dangers and the manner in which they had been averted. He said that all these things were comprehended in the first act of the first atom; that, but for some particular impulse given in that remote time, the alcohol flame would not have blown against the canopy, the spark would not have found its way through the screen, the log would not have broken apart in that dangerous way, and that Rosa and Julia and the barber would not have been at hand to save precious life and property. He did not go further and draw moral conclusions as to the purpose of these things: he never drew conclusions as to purpose. He was willing to rest with the event. Logically he did not believe in reasons for things, but only that things *were*.

Nevertheless, he was always trying to change them; to have a hand in their improvement. Had you asked him, he would have said that this, too, was all in the primal atom; that his nature, such as it was, had been minutely embodied there.

In that charming volume, *My Mark Twain*, Howells tells us of Clemens's consideration, and even tenderness, for the negro race and his effort to repair the wrong done by his nation. Mark Twain's writings are full of similar evidence, and in his daily life he never missed an opportunity to pay tribute to the humbler race. He would go across the street to speak to an old negro, and to take his hand. He would read for a negro church when he would have refused a cathedral. Howells mentions the colored student whose way through college Clemens paid as a partial reparation "due from every white man to every black man."[1] This incident belongs just to the period of which we are now writing, and there is another which, though different enough, indicates the same tendency.

Garfield was about to be inaugurated, and it was rumored that Frederick Douglass might lose his position as Marshal of the District of Columbia. Clemens was continually besought by one and another to use his influence with the Administration, and in every case had refused. Douglass had made no such application. Clemens, learning that the old negro's place was in danger, interceded for him of his own accord. He closed his letter to General Garfield:

> A simple citizen may express a desire, with all propriety, in the matter of recommendation to office, and so I beg permission to hope that you will retain Mr. Douglass in his present office of Marshal of the District of Columbia, if such a course will not clash with your own preferences or with the expediencies and interests of your Administration. I offer this petition with peculiar pleasure and strong desire, because I so honor this man's high and blemishless character, and so admire his brave, long crusade for the liberties and elevation of his race.
>
> He is a personal friend of mine, but that is nothing to the point; his history would move me to say these things without that, and I feel them, too.

[1] Mark Twain paid two colored students through college. One of them, educated in a Southern institution, became a minister of the gospel. The other graduated from the Yale Law School.

Douglass wrote to Clemens, thanking him for his interest; at the end he said:

I think if a man is mean enough to want an office he ought to be noble enough to ask for it, and use all honorable means of getting it. I mean to ask, and I will use your letter as a part of my petition. It will put the President-elect in a good humor, in any case, and that is very important.

With great respect,

Gratefully yours,

FREDERICK DOUGLASS.

Mark Twain's benefactions were not all for the colored race. One morning in February of this same year, while the family were at late breakfast, George came in to announce "a lady waiting to see Mr. Clemens in the drawing-room." Clemens growled.

"George," he said, "it's a book agent. I won't see her. I'll die in my tracks first."

He went, fuming and raging inwardly, and began at once to ask the nature of the intruder's business. Then he saw that she was very young and modest, with none of the assurance of a canvasser, so he gave her a chance to speak. She told him that a young man employed in Pratt & Whitney's machine-shops had made a statue in clay, and would like to have Mark Twain come and look at it and see if it showed any promise of future achievement. His name, she said, was Karl Gerhardt, and he was her husband. Clemens protested that he knew nothing about art, but the young woman's manner and appearance (she seemed scarcely more than a child) won him. He wavered, and finally promised that he would come the first chance he had; that in fact he would come some time during the next week. On her suggestion he agreed to come early in the week; he specified Monday, "without fail."

When she was gone, and the door shut behind her, his usual remorse came upon him. He said to himself:

"Why didn't I go *now?* Why didn't I *go* with her *now?*"

She went from Clemens's over to Warner's. Warner also resisted, but, tempted beyond his strength by her charm, laid down his work and went at once. When he returned he urged Clemens to go without fail, and, true to promise, Clemens took Patrick, the coachman, and hunted up the place. Clemens saw the statue, a semi-nude, for which the young wife had posed, and was struck by its evident merit. Mrs. Gerhardt told him the story of her husband's struggles between his daily work and the effort to develop his talent. He had never had a lesson, she said; if he could only have lessons what might he not accomplish?

Mrs. Clemens and Miss Spaulding called next day, and were equally carried away with Karl Gerhardt, his young wife, and his effort to win his way in art. Clemens and Warner made up their minds to interest themselves personally in the matter, and finally persuaded the painter J. Wells Champney to come over from New York and go with them to the Gerhardts' humble habitation, to see his work. Champney approved of it. He thought it well worth while, he said, for the people of Hartford to go to the expense of Gerhardt's art education. He added that it would be better to get the judgment of a sculptor. So they brought over John Quincy Adams Ward, who, like all the others, came away bewitched with these young people and their struggles for the sake of art. Ward said:

"If any stranger had told me that this 'prentice did not model that thing from plaster-casts I should not have believed it. It's full of crudities, but it's full of genius, too. Hartford must send him to Paris for two years; then, if the promise holds good, keep him there three more."

When he was gone Mrs. Clemens said:

"Youth, we won't wait for Hartford to do it. It would take too long. Let us send the Gerhardts to Paris ourselves, and say nothing about it to any one else."

So the Gerhardts, provided with funds and an arrangement that would enable them to live for five years in Paris if necessary, were started across the sea without further delay.

Clemens and his wife were often doing something of this sort. There was seldom a time that they were not paying the way of some young man or woman through college, or providing means and opportunity for development in some special field of industry.

CXXXIV

LITERARY PROJECTS AND A MONUMENT TO ADAM

MARK TWAIN'S literary work languished during this period. He had a world of plans, as usual, and wrote plentifully, but without direction or conclusion. "A Curious Experience," which relates a circumstance told to him by an army officer, is about the most notable of the few completed manuscripts of this period.

Of the books projected (there were several), a burlesque manual of etiquette would seem to have been the most promising. Howells had faith in it, and of the still remaining fragments a few seem worth quoting:

AT BILLIARDS

If your ball glides along in the intense and immediate vicinity of the object-ball, and a count seems exquisitely imminent, lift one leg; then one shoulder; then squirm your body around in sympathy with the direction of the moving ball; and at the instant when the ball seems on the point of colliding throw up both of your arms violently. Your cue will probably break a chandelier, but no matter; you have done what you could to help the count.

AT THE DOG-FIGHT

If it occur in your block, courteously give way to strangers desiring a view, particularly ladies.

Avoid showing partiality toward the one dog, lest you hurt the feelings of the other one.

Let your secret sympathies and your compassion be always with the under dog in the fight—this is magnanimity; but bet on the other one—this is business.

AT POKER

If you draw to a flush and fail to fill, do not continue the conflict.

If you hold a pair of trays, and your opponent is blind, and it costs you fifty to see him, let him remain unperceived.

If you hold nothing but ace high, and by some means you know that the other man holds the rest of the aces, and he calls, excuse yourself; let him call again another time.

WALL STREET

If you live in the country, buy at 80, sell at 40. Avoid all forms of eccentricity.

IN THE RESTAURANT

When you wish to get the waiter's attention, do not sing out "*Say!*" Simply say "*Szt!*"

His old abandoned notion of "Hamlet" with an added burlesque character came back to him and stirred his enthusiasm anew, until even Howells manifested deep interest in the matter. One reflects how young Howells must have been in those days; how full of the joy of existence; also how mournfully he would consider such a sacrilege now.

Clemens proposed almost as many things to Howells as his brother Orion proposed to him. There was scarcely a letter that didn't contain some new idea, with a request for advice or co-operation. Now it was some book that he meant to write some day, and again it would be a something that he wanted Howells to write.

Once he urged Howells to make a play, or at least a novel, out of Orion. At another time he suggested as material the "Rightful Earl of Durham."

He is a perfectly stunning literary bonanza, and *must* be dug up and put on the market. You must get his entire biography out of him and have it ready for Osgood's magazine. Even if it isn't worth printing, you must have it anyway, and use it one of these days in one of your stories or in a play.

It was this notion about *The American Claimant* which somewhat later would lead to a collaboration with Howells on a drama, and eventually to a story of that title.

But Clemens's chief interest at this time lay in publishing, rather than in writing. His association with Osgood inspired him to devise new ventures of profit. He planned a *Library of American Humor*, which Howells (soon to leave the *Atlantic*) and "Charley" Clark[1] were to edit, and which Osgood would publish, for subscription sale. Without realizing it, Clemens was taking his first step toward becoming his own publisher. His contract with Osgood for *The Prince and the Pauper* made him essentially that, for by the terms of it he agreed to supply all the money for the making of the book, and to pay Osgood a royalty of seven and one-half per cent. for selling it, reversing the usual conditions. The contract for the *Library of Humor* was to be a similar one, though in this case Osgood was to have a larger royalty return, and to share proportionately in the expense and risk. Mark Twain was entering into a field where he did not belong; where in the end he would harvest only disaster and regret.

One curious project came to an end in 1881—the plan for a monument to Adam. In a sketch written a great many years later Mark Twain tells of the memorial which the Rev. Thomas K. Beecher and himself once proposed to erect to our great common ancestor. The story is

[1] Charles Hopkins Clark, managing editor of the Hartford *Courant*.

based on a real incident. Clemens, in Elmira one day (it was October, 1879), heard of a jesting proposal made by F. G. Hall to erect a monument in Elmira to Adam. The idea promptly caught Mark Twain's fancy. He observed to Beecher that the human race really showed a pretty poor regard for its great progenitor, who was about to be deposed by Darwin's simian, not to pay him the tribute of a single monument. Mankind, he said, would probably accept the monkey ancestor, and in time the very name of Adam would be forgotten. He declared Mr. Hall's suggestion to be a sound idea.

Beecher agreed that there were many reasons why a monument should be erected to Adam, and suggested that a subscription be started for the purpose. Certain business men, seeing an opportunity for advertising the city, took the matter semi-seriously, and offered to contribute large sums in the interest of the enterprise. Then it was agreed that Congress should be petitioned to sanction the idea exclusively to Elmira, prohibiting the erection of any such memorial elsewhere. A document to this effect was prepared, headed by F. G. Hall, and signed by other leading citizens of Elmira, including Beecher himself. General Joe Hawley came along just then on a political speech-making tour. Clemens introduced him, and Hawley, in turn, agreed to father the petition in Congress. What had begun merely as pleasantry began to have a formidable look.

But alas! in the end Hawley's courage had failed him. He began to hate his undertaking. He was afraid of the national laugh it would arouse, the jeers of the newspapers. It was certain to leak out that Mark Twain was behind it, in spite of the fact that his name nowhere appeared; that it was one of his colossal jokes. Now and then, in the privacy of his own room at night, Hawley would hunt up the Adam petition and read it and feel the cold sweat breaking out. He postponed the matter from one session to another till the summer of 1881, when he was about to sail for Europe. Then he gave the document to his wife, to turn over to Clemens, and ignominiously fled.[1]

[1] For text of the petition in full, etc., see Appendix P, at the end of last volume.

Mark Twain's introduction of Hawley at Elmira contained this pleasantry:

"General Hawley was president of the Centennial Commission. Was a gallant soldier in the war. He has been Governor of Connecticut, member of Congress, and was president of the convention that nominated Abraham Lincoln."

General Hawley: "That nominated Grant."

Twain: "He says it was Grant, but I know better. He is a member of my church at Hartford, and the author of 'Beautiful Snow.' Maybe he will deny that. But I am only here to give him a character from his last place. As a pure citizen, I respect him; as a personal friend of years, I have the warmest regard for him; as a neighbor whose vegetable garden joins mine, why—why, I watch him. That's nothing; we all do that with any neighbor. General Hawley keeps his promises, not only in private, but in public. He is an editor who believes what he writes in his own paper. As the author of 'Beautiful Snow' he added a new pang to winter. He is broad-souled, generous, noble, liberal, alive to his moral and religious responsibilities. Whenever the contribution-box was passed I never knew him to take out a cent."

CXXXV

A TRIP WITH SHERMAN AND AN INTERVIEW WITH GRANT

THE Army of the Potomac gave a dinner in Hartford on the 8th of June, 1881. But little memory remains of it now beyond Mark Twain's speech and a bill of fare containing original comments, ascribed to various revered authors, such as Johnson, Milton, and Carlyle. A pleasant incident followed, however, which Clemens himself used to relate. General Sherman attended the banquet, and Secretary of War, Robert Lincoln. Next morning Clemens and Twichell were leaving for West Point, where they were to address the military students, guests on the same special train on which Lincoln and Sherman had their private car. This car was at the end of the train, and when the two passengers reached the station, Sherman and Lincoln were out on the rear platform addressing the multitude. Clemens and Twichell went in and, taking seats, waited for them.

As the speakers finished the train started, but they still remained outside, bowing and waving to the assembled citizens, so that it was under good headway before they came in. Sherman came up to Clemens, who sat smoking unconcernedly.

"Well," he said, "who told you you could go in this car?"

"Nobody," said Clemens.

"Do you expect to pay extra fare?" asked Sherman.

"No," said Clemens. "I don't expect to pay *any* fare."

"Oh, you don't. Then you'll work your way."

Sherman took off his coat and military hat and made Clemens put them on.

"Now," said he, "whenever the train stops you go out on the platform and represent me and make a speech."

It was not long before the train stopped, and Clemens, according to orders, stepped out on the rear platform and bowed to the crowd. There was a cheer at the sight of his military uniform. Then the cheer waned, became a murmur of uncertainty, followed by an undertone of discussion. Presently somebody said:

"Say, that ain't Sherman, that's Mark Twain," which brought another cheer.

Then Sherman had to come out too, and the result was that both spoke. They kept this up at the different stations, and sometimes Lincoln came out with them. When there was time all three spoke, much to the satisfaction of their audiences.

President Garfield was shot that summer—July 2, 1881.[1] He died September 19th, and Arthur came into power. There was a great feeling of uncertainty as to what he would do. He was regarded as "an excellent gentleman with a weakness for his friends." Incumbents holding appointive offices were in a state of dread.

Howells's father was consul at Toronto, and, believing his place to be in danger, he appealed to his son. In his book Howells tells how, in turn, he appealed to Clemens,

[1] On the day that President Garfield was shot Mrs. Clemens received from their friend Reginald Cholmondeley a letter of condolence on the death of her husband in Australia; startling enough, though in reality rather comforting than otherwise, for the reason that the "Mark Twain" who had died in Australia was a very persistent impostor. Clemens wrote Cholmondeley: "Being dead I might be excused from writing letters, but I am not that kind of a corpse. May I never be so dead as to neglect the hail of a friend from a far land." Out of this incident grew a feature of an anecdote related in *Following the Equator* the joke played by the man from Bendigo.

remembering his friendship with Grant and Grant's friendship with Arthur. He asked Clemens to write to Grant, but Clemens would hear of nothing less than a call on the General, during which the matter would be presented to him in person. Howells relates how the three of them lunched together, in a little room just out of the office, on baked beans and coffee, brought in from some near-by restaurant:

> The baked beans and coffee were of about the railroad-refreshment quality; but eating them with Grant was like sitting down to baked beans and coffee with Julius Cæsar, or Alexander, or some other great Plutarchan captain.

Clemens, also recalling the interview, once added some interesting details:

"I asked Grant if he wouldn't write a word on a card which Howells could carry to Washington and hand to the President. But, as usual, General Grant was his natural self—that is to say, ready and determined to do a great deal more for you than you could possibly ask him to do. He said he was going to Washington in a couple of days to dine with the President, and he would speak to him himself on the subject and make it a personal matter. Grant was in the humor to talk—he was always in a humor to talk when no strangers were present—he forced us to stay and take luncheon in a private room, and continued to talk all the time. It was baked beans, but how 'he sits and towers,' Howells said, quoting Dante. Grant remembered 'Squibob' Derby (John Phœnix) at West Point very well. He said that Derby was always drawing caricatures of the professors and playing jokes on everybody. He told a thing which I had heard before but had never seen in print. A professor questioning a class concerning certain particulars of a possible siege said, 'Suppose a thousand men are besieging a fortress whose equipment of provisions is so-and-so; it is a military axiom that at the end of forty-five days the fort will surrender. Now, young men, if any of you were in command of such a fortress, how would you proceed?'

"Derby held up his hand in token that he had an answer for that question. He said, 'I would march out, let the enemy in, and at the end of forty-five days I would change places with him.'

"I tried hard, during that interview, to get General Grant to agree to write his personal memoirs for publication, but he wouldn't listen to the suggestion. His inborn diffidence made him shrink from voluntarily coming before the public and placing himself under criticism as an author. He had no confidence in his ability to write well; whereas we all know now that he possessed an admirable literary gift and style. He was also sure that the book would have no sale, and of course that would be a humility too. I argued that the book would have an enormous sale, and that out of my experience I could save him from making unwise contracts with publishers, and would have the contract arranged in such a way that they could not swindle him, but he said he had no necessity for any addition to his income. Of course he could not foresee that he was camping on a volcano; that as Ward's partner he was a ruined man even then, and of course I had no suspicion that in four years from that time I would become his publisher. He would not agree to write his memoirs. He only said that some day he would make very full notes and leave them behind him, and then if his children chose to make them into a book they could do so. We came away then. He fulfilled his promise entirely concerning Howells's father, who held his office until he resigned of his own accord."

CXXXVI

"THE PRINCE AND THE PAUPER"

DURING the summer absence alterations were made in the Hartford home, with extensive decorations by Tiffany. The work was not completed when the family returned. Clemens wrote to Charles Warren Stoddard, then in the Sandwich Islands, that the place was full of carpenters and decorators, whereas what they really needed was "an incendiary."

> If the house would only burn down we would pack up the cubs and fly to the isles of the blest, and shut ourselves up in the healing solitudes of the crater of Haleakala and get a good rest, for the mails do not intrude there, nor yet the telephone and the telegraph; and after resting we would come down the mountain a piece and board with a godly, breech-clouted native, and eat poi and dirt, and give thanks to whom all thanks belong for these privileges, and never housekeep any more.

They had acquired more ground. One morning in the spring Mark Twain had looked out of his window just in time to see a man lift an ax to cut down a tree on the lot which lay between his own and that of his neighbor. He had heard that a house was to be built there; altogether too close to him for comfort and privacy. Leaning out of the window he called sonorously, "Woodman, spare that tree!" Then he hurried down, obtained a stay of proceedings, and without delay purchased the lot from the next-door neighbor who owned it, acquiring thereby one hundred feet of extra ground and a greenhouse which occupied it. It was a costly purchase; the owner knew he could demand his own price; he asked and received twelve thousand dollars for the strip.

In November, Clemens found that he must make another trip to Canada. *The Prince and the Pauper* was ready for issue, and to insure Canadian copyright the author must cross the line in person. He did not enjoy the prospect of a cold-weather trip to the north, and tried to tempt Howells to go with him, but only succeeded in persuading Osgood, who would do anything or go anywhere that offered the opportunity for pleasant company and junket.

It was by no means an unhappy fortnight. Clemens took a note-book, and there are plenty of items that give reality to that long-ago excursion. He found the Canadian girls so pretty that he records it as a relief now and then to see a plain one. On another page he tells how one night in the hotel a mouse gnawed and kept him awake, and how he got up and hunted for it, hoping to destroy it. He made a rebus picture for the children of this incident in a letter home.

We get a glimpse just here of how he was constantly viewing himself as literary material—human material—an example from which some literary aspect or lesson may be drawn. Following the mouse adventure we find it thus dramatized:

Trace Father Brebeuf all through this trip, and when I am in a rage and can't endure the mouse be reading of Brebeuf's marvelous endurances and be shamed.

And finally, after chasing the bright-eyed rascal several days, and throwing things and trying to jump on him when in my overshoes, he darts away with those same bright eyes, then straightway I read Brebeuf's magnificent martyrdom, and turn in, subdued and wondering. By and by the thought occurs to me, Brebeuf, with his good, great heart would spare even that poor humble mousie—and for his sake so will I—I will throw the trap in the fire—jump out of bed, reach under, fetch out the trap, and find him throttled there and not two minutes dead.

They gave him a dinner in Montreal. Louis Frechette, the Canadian poet, was there and Clemens addressed him handsomely in the response he made to the speech of welcome. From that moment Frechette never ceased to adore Mark Twain, and visited him soon after the return to Hartford.

The Prince and the Pauper was published in England, Canada, Germany, and America early in December, 1881. There had been no stint of money, and it was an extremely handsome book. The pen-and-ink drawings were really charming, and they were lavish as to number. It was an attractive volume from every standpoint, and it was properly dedicated "To those good-mannered and agreeable children, Susy and Clara Clemens."

The story itself was totally unlike anything that Mark Twain had done before. Enough of its plan and purpose has been given in former chapters to make a synopsis of it unnecessary here. The story of the wandering prince and the pauper king—an impressive picture of ancient legal and regal cruelty—is as fine and consistent a tale as exists in the realm of pure romance. Unlike its great successor, the *Yankee at King Arthur's Court*, it never sacrifices the illusion to the burlesque, while through it all there runs a delicate vein of humor. Only here and there is there the slightest disillusion, and this mainly in the use of some ultra-modern phrase or word.

Mark Twain never did any better writing than some of the splendid scenes in *The Prince and the Pauper*. The picture of Old London Bridge; the scene in the vagabond's retreat, with its presentation to the little king of the wrongs inflicted by the laws of his realm; the episode of the jail where his revelation reaches a climax—these are but a few of the splendid pictures which the chapters portray, while the spectacle of England acquiring mercy at the hands of two children, a king and a beggar, is one which only genius could create. One might quote here, but to do so without the context would be to sacrifice atmosphere, half the story's charm. How breathlessly interesting is the tale of it! We may imagine that first little audience at Mark Twain's fireside hanging expectant on every paragraph, hungry always for more. Of all Mark Twain's longer works of fiction it is perhaps the most coherent as to plot, the most carefully thought out, the most perfect as to workmanship. This is not to say that it is his greatest story. Probably time will not give it that rank, but it comes near to being a perfectly constructed story, and it has an imperishable charm.

It was well received, though not always understood by the public. The reviewer was so accustomed to looking for the joke in Mark Twain's work, that he found it hard to estimate this new product. Some even went so far as to refer to it as one of Mark Twain's big jokes, meaning probably that he had created a chapter in English history with no foundation beyond his fancy. Of course these things pained the author of the book. At one time, he had been inclined to publish it anonymously, to avert this sort of misunderstanding, and sometimes now he regretted not having done so.

Yet there were many gratifying notices. The New York *Herald* reviewer gave the new book two columns of finely intelligent appreciation. In part he said:

> To those who have followed the career of Mark Twain, his appearance as the author of a charming and noble romance is really no more of a surprise than to see a stately structure risen upon sightly ground owned by an architect of genius, with the resources of abundant building material and ample training at command. Of his capacity they have had no doubt, and they rejoice in his taking a step which they felt he was able to take. Through all his publications may be traced the marks of the path

which has led up to this happy height. His humor has often been the cloak, but not the mask, of a sturdy purpose. His work has been characterized by a manly love of truth, a hatred of humbug, and a scorn for cant. A genial warmth and whole-souledness, a beautiful fancy, a fertile imagination, and a native feeling for the picturesque and a fine eye for color have afforded the basis of a style which has become more and more plastic and finished.

And in closing:

The characters of these two boys, twins in spirit, will rank with the purest and loveliest creations of child-life in the realm of fiction.

CXXXVII

CERTAIN ATTACKS AND REPRISALS

BEYOND the publication of *The Prince and the Pauper* Clemens was sparingly represented in print in '81. A chapter originally intended for the book, the "Whipping Boy's Story," he gave to the *Bazaar Budget*, a little special-edition sheet printed in Hartford. It was the story of the Bull and the Bees which he later adapted for use in *Joan of Arc*, the episode in which Joan's father rides a bull to a funeral. Howells found that it interfered with the action in the story of the *Prince*, and we might have spared it from the story of *Joan*, though hardly without regret.

The military story "A Curious Episode" was published in the *Century Magazine* for November. The fact that Clemens had heard, and not invented, the story was set forth quite definitely and fully in his opening paragraphs. Nevertheless, a "Captious Reader" thought it necessary to write to a New York publication concerning its origin:

> I am an admirer of the writings of Mr. Mark Twain, and consequently, when I saw the table of contents of the November number of the *Century*, I bought it and turned at once to the article bearing his name, and entitled, "A Curious Episode." When I began to read it, it struck me as strangely familiar, and I soon recognized the story as a true one, told me in the summer of 1878 by an officer of the United States artillery. Query: Did Mr. Twain expect the public to credit this narrative to his clever brain?

The editor, seeing a chance for Mark Twain "copy," forwarded a clipping to Clemens and asked him if he had anything to say in the matter. Clemens happened to know the editor very well, and he did have something to say, not for print, but for the editor's private ear.

The newspaper custom of shooting a man in the back and then calling upon him to come out in a card and prove that he was not engaged in any infamy at the time is a good enough custom for those who think it justifiable. Your correspondent is not stupid, I judge, but purely and simply malicious. He knew there was not the shadow of a suggestion, from the beginning to the end of "A Curious Episode," that the story was an *invention;* he knew he had no warrant for trying to persuade the public that I had stolen the narrative and was endeavoring to palm it off as a piece of literary invention; he also knew that he was asking his closing question with a base motive, else he would have asked it of me by letter, not spread it before the public.

I have never wronged you in any way, and I think you had no right to print that communication; no right, neither any excuse. As to publicly answering that correspondent, I would as soon think of bandying words in public with any *other* prostitute.

The editor replied in a manly, frank acknowledgment of error. He had not looked up the article itself in the *Century* before printing the communication.

"Your letter has taught me a lesson," he said. "The blame belongs to me for not hunting up the proofs. Please accept my apology."

Mark Twain was likely to be peculiarly sensitive to printed innuendos. Not always. Sometimes he would only laugh at them or be wholly indifferent. Indeed, in his later years, he seldom cared to read anything about himself, one way or the other, but at the time of which we are now writing—the period of the early eighties—he was alive to any comment of the press. His strong sense of humor, and still stronger sense of human weakness, caused him to overlook many things which another might regard as an affront; but if the thing printed were merely an uncalled-for slur, an inexcusable imputation, he was inclined to rage and plan violence. Sometimes he conceived retribution in the form of libel suits with heavy damages. Sometimes he wrote blasting answers, which Mrs. Clemens would not let him print.

At one time he planned a biography of a certain editor who seemed to be making a deliberate personal campaign against his happiness. Clemens had heard that offending items were being printed in this man's paper; friends, reporting with customary exaggeration, declared that these sneers and brutalities appeared almost daily, so often as to cause general remark.

This was enough. He promptly began to collect data —damaging data—relating to that editor's past history. He even set a man to work in England collecting information concerning his victim. One of his notebooks contains the memoranda; a few items will show how terrific was to be the onslaught.

> When the naturalist finds a new kind of animal, he writes him up in the interest of science. No matter if it is an unpleasant animal. This is a new kind of animal, and in the cause of society must be written up. He is the polecat of our species. . . . He is purely and simply a Guiteau with the courage left out. . . .
>
> Steel portraits of him as a sort of idiot, from infancy up—a dozen scattered through the book—all should resemble him.

But never mind the rest. When he had got thoroughly interested in his project Mrs. Clemens, who had allowed the cyclone to wear itself out a little with its own vehemence, suggested that perhaps it would be well to have some one make an examination of the files of the paper and see just what had been said of him. So he subscribed for the paper himself and set a man to work on the back numbers. We will let him tell the conclusion of the matter himself, in his report of it to Howells:

The result arrived from my New York man this morning. Oh, what a pitiable wreck of high hopes! The "almost daily" assaults for two months consist of (1) adverse criticism of P. & P. from an enraged idiot in the London *Athenæum*, (2) paragraphs from some indignant Englishman in the *Pall Mall Gazette*, who pays me the vast compliment of gravely rebuking some imaginary ass who has set me up in the neighborhood of Rabelais, (3) a remark about the Montreal dinner, touched with an almost invisible satire, and, (4) a remark about refusal of Canadian copyright, not complimentary, but not necessarily malicious; and of course adverse criticism which is not malicious is a thing which none but fools irritate themselves about.

There, that is the prodigious bugaboo in its entirety! Can you conceive of a man's getting himself into a sweat over so diminutive a provocation? I am sure I can't. What the devil can those friends of mine have been thinking about to spread those three or four harmless things out into two months of daily sneers and affronts?

Boiled down, this vast outpouring of malice amounts to simply this: *one* jest (one can make nothing more serious than that out of it). One jest, and that is all; for foreign criticisms do not count, they being matters of news, and proper for publication in anybody's newspaper. . . .

Well, my mountain has brought forth its mouse, and a sufficiently small mouse it is, God knows. And my three weeks' hard work has got to go into the ignominious pigeonhole. Confound it, I could have earned ten thousand dollars with infinitely less trouble.

Howells refers to this episode, and concludes:

So the paper was acquitted and the editor's life was spared. The wretch never, never knew how near he was to losing it, with incredible preliminaries of obloquy, and a subsequent devotion to lasting infamy.

CXXXVIII

MANY UNDERTAKINGS

TO write a detailed biography of Mark Twain at this period would be to defy perusal. Even to set down all the interesting matters, interesting to the public of his time, would mean not only to exhaust the subject, but the reader. He lived at the top of his bent, and almost anything relating to him was regarded as news. Daily and hourly he mingled with important matters or spoke concerning them. A bare list of the interesting events of Mark Twain's life would fill a large volume.

He was so busy, so deeply interested himself, so vitally alive to every human aspect. He read the papers through, and there was always enough to arouse his indignation—the doings of the human race at large could be relied upon to do that—and he would write, and write, to relieve himself. His mental Niagara was always pouring away, turning out articles, essays, communications on every conceivable subject, mainly with the idea of reform. There were many public and private abuses, and he wanted to correct them all. He covered reams of paper with lurid heresies—political, religious, civic—for most of which there was no hope of publication.

Now and then he was allowed to speak out: An order from the Post-office Department at Washington concerning the superscription of envelopes seemed to him unwarranted. He assailed it, and directly the nation was being entertained by a controversy between Mark Twain and the Postmaster-General's private secretary, who subsequently receded from the field.

At another time, on the matter of postage rates he wrote a paper which began: "Reader, suppose you were an idiot. And suppose you were a member of Congress. But I repeat myself."

It is hardly necessary to add that the paper did not appear.

On the whole, Clemens wrote his strictures more for relief than to print, and such of these papers as are preserved to-day form a curious collection of human documents. Many of them could be printed to-day, without distress to any one. The conditions that invited them are changed; the heresies are not heresies any more. He may have had some thought of their publication in later years, for once he wrote:

> Sometimes my feelings are so hot that I have to take the pen and put them out on paper to keep them from setting me afire inside; then all that ink and labor are wasted because I can't print the result. I have just finished an article of this kind, and it satisfies me entirely. It does my weather-beaten soul good to read it, and admire the trouble it would make for me and the family. I will leave it behind and utter it from the grave. There is a free speech there, and no harm to the family.

It is too late and too soon to print most of these things; too late to print them for their salutary influence, too soon to print them as literature.

He was interested in everything: in music, as little as he knew of it. He had an ear for melody, a dramatic vision, and the poetic conception of sound. Reading some lilting lyric, he could fancy the words marching to melody, and would cast about among his friends for some one who could supply a tuneful setting. Once he wrote to his friend the Rev. Dr. Parker, who was a skilled musician, urging him to write a score for Tennyson's

"Bugle Song," outlining an attractive scheme for it which the order of his fancy had formulated. Dr. Parker replied that the "Bugle Song," often attempted, had been the despair of many musicians.

He was interested in business affairs. Already, before the European trip, he had embarked in, and disembarked from, a number of pecuniary ventures. He had not been satisfied with a strictly literary income. The old tendency to speculative investment, acquired during those restless mining days, always possessed him. There were no silver mines in the East, no holes in the ground into which to empty money and effort; but there were plenty of equivalents—inventions, stock companies, and the like. He had begun by putting five thousand dollars into the American Publishing Company; but that was a sound and profitable venture, and deserves to be remembered for that reason.

Then a man came along with a patent steam generator which would save ninety per cent. of the fuel energy, or some such amount, and Mark Twain was early persuaded that it would revolutionize the steam manufactures of the world; so he put in whatever bank surplus he had and bade it a permanent good-by.

Following the steam generator came a steam pulley, a rather small contrivance, but it succeeded in extracting thirty-two thousand dollars from his bank account in a period of sixteen months.

By the time he had accumulated a fresh balance, a new method of marine telegraphy was shown him, so he used it up on that, twenty-five thousand dollars being the price of this adventure.

A watch company in western New York was ready to sell him a block of shares by the time he was prepared to experiment again, but it did not quite live to declare the first dividend on his investment.

Senator John P. Jones invited him to join in the organization of an accident insurance company, and such was Jones's confidence in the venture that he guaranteed Clemens against loss. Mark Twain's only profit from this source was in the delivery of a delicious speech, which he made at a dinner given to Cornelius Walford, of London, an insurance author of repute. Jones was paying back the money presently, and about that time came a young inventor named Graham Bell, offering stock in a contrivance for carrying the human voice on an electric wire. At almost any other time Clemens would eagerly have welcomed this opportunity; but he was so gratified at having got his money out of the insurance venture that he refused to respond to the happy "hello" call of fortune. In some memoranda made thirty years later he said:

I declined. I said I didn't want anything more to do with wildcat speculation. Then he [Bell] offered the stock to me at twenty-five. I said I didn't want it at any price. He became eager; insisted that I take five hundred dollars' worth. He said he would sell me as much as I wanted for five hundred dollars; offered to let me gather it up in my hands and measure it in a plug hat; said I could have a whole hatful for five hundred dollars. But I was the burnt child, and I resisted all these temptations—resisted them easily; went off with my check intact, and next day lent five thousand of it, on an unindorsed note, to a friend who was going to go bankrupt three days later.

About the end of the year I put up a telephone wire from my house down to the *Courant* office, the only telephone wire in town, and the *first* one that was ever used in a private house in the world.

That had been only a little while before he sailed for Europe. When he returned he would have been willing to accept a very trifling interest in the telephone industry for the amount of his insurance salvage.

He had a fresh interest in patents now, and when his old friend Dan Slote got hold of a new process for engraving—the kaolatype or "chalk-plate" process—which was going to revolutionize the world of illustration, he promptly acquired a third interest, and eventually was satisfied with nothing short of control. It was an ingenious process: a sheet of perfectly smooth steel was coated with a preparation of kaolin (or china clay), and a picture was engraved *through* the coating down to the steel surface. This formed the matrix into which the molten metal was poured to make the stereotype plate, or die, for printing. It was Clemens's notion that he could utilize this process for the casting of brass dies for stamping book covers—that, so applied, the fortunes to be made out of it would be larger and more numerous. Howells tells how, at one time, Clemens thought the "damned human race" was almost to be redeemed by a process of founding brass without air-bubbles in it. This was the time referred to and the race had to go unredeemed; for, after long, worried, costly experimenting, the brass refused to accommodate its nature to the new idea, while the chalk plate itself, with all its subsidiary and auxiliary possibilities, was infringed upon right and left, and the protecting patent failed to hold. The process was doomed, in any case. It was barely established before the photographic etching processes, superior in all ways, were developed and came quickly into use. The kaolatype enterprise struggled nobly for a considerable period. Clemens brought his niece's husband, young Charles L. Webster, from Fredonia to manage it for him, and backed it liberally. Webster was vigorous, hard-working, and capable; but the end of each month showed a deficit, until Clemens was from forty to fifty thousand dollars out of pocket in his effort to save the race with chalk and brass. The history of these several ventures (and there were others), dismissed here in a few paragraphs, would alone make a volume not without interest, certainly not without humor. Following came the type-setting machine, but we are not ready for that. Of necessity it is a longer, costlier story.

Mrs. Clemens did not share his enthusiasm in these various enterprises. She did not oppose them, at least not strenuously, but she did not encourage them. She did not see their need. Their home was beautiful; they were happy; he could do his work in deliberation and comfort. She knew the value of money better than he, cared more for it in her own way; but she had not his desire to heap up vast and sudden sums, to revel in torrential golden showers. She was willing to let well enough alone. Clemens could not do this, and suffered accordingly. In the midst of fair home surroundings and honors we find him writing to his mother:

> Life has come to be a very serious matter with me. I have a badgered, harassed feeling a good part of my time. It comes mainly from business responsibilities and annoyances.

He had no moral right to be connected with business at all. He had a large perception of business opportunity, but no vision of its requirements—its difficulties and details. He was the soul of honor, but in anything resembling practical direction he was but a child. During any period of business venture he was likely to be in hot water: eagerly excited, worried, impatient, alternately suspicious and overtrusting, rash, frenzied, and altogether upset.

Yet never, even to the end of his days, would he permanently lose faith in speculative ventures. Human traits are sometimes modified, but never eliminated. The man who is born to be a victim of misplaced confidence will continue to be one so long as he lives and there are men willing to victimize him. The man who believes in himself as an investor will uphold that faith against all disaster so long as he draws breath and has money to back his judgments.

CHARLES L. WEBSTER

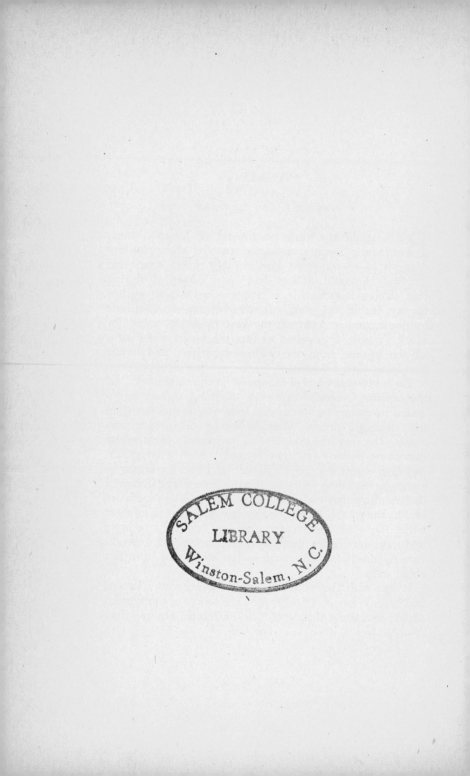

CXXXIX

FINANCIAL AND LITERARY

BY a statement made on the 1st of January, 1882, of Mark Twain's disbursements for the preceding year, it is shown that considerably more than one hundred thousand dollars had been expended during that twelve months. It is a large sum for an author to pay out in one year. It would cramp most authors to do it, and it was not the best financing, even for Mark Twain. It required all that the books could earn, all the income from the various securities, and a fair sum from their principal.

There is a good deal of biography in the statement. Of the amount expended forty-six thousand dollars represented investments; but of this comfortable sum less than five thousand dollars would cover the legitimate purchases; the rest had gone in the "ventures" from whose bourne no dollar would ever return. Also, a large sum had been spent for the additional land and for improvements on the home—somewhat more than thirty thousand dollars altogether—while the home life had become more lavish, the establishment had grown each year to a larger scale, the guests and entertainments had become more and more numerous, until the actual household expenditure required about as much as the books and securities could earn.

It was with the increased scale of living that Clemens had become especially eager for some source of commercial profit; something that would yield a return, not in paltry thousands, but hundreds of thousands. Like Colonel Sellers, he must have something with "millions in it." Almost any proposition that seemed to offer these possible millions appealed to him, and in his imagination he saw the golden freshet pouring in.

His natural taste was for a simple, inexpensive life; yet in his large hospitality, and in a certain boyish love of grandeur, he gloried in the splendor of his entertainment, the admiration and delight of his guests. There were *always* guests; they were coming and going constantly. Clemens used to say that he proposed to establish a 'bus line between their house and the station for the accommodation of his company. He had the Southern hospitality. Much company appealed to a very large element in his strangely compounded nature. For the better portion of the year he was willing to pay the price of it, whether in money or in endurance, and Mrs. Clemens heroically did her part. She loved these things also, in her own way. She took pride in them, and realized that they were a part of his vast success. Yet in her heart she often longed for the simpler life—above all, for the farm life at Elmira. Her spirit cried out for the rest and comfort there. In one of her letters she says:

> The house has been full of company, and I have been "whirled around." How can a body help it? Oh, I cannot help sighing for the peace and quiet of the farm. This is my work, and I know that I do very wrong when I feel chafed by it, but how can I be right about it? Sometimes it seems as if the simple sight of people would drive me *mad*. I am all wrong; if I would simply accept the fact that this is my work and let other things go, I know I should not be so fretted; but I want so much to do other things, to study and do things with the children, and I cannot.
>
> I have the best French teacher that I ever had, and if I could give any time to it I could not help learning French.

When we reflect on the conditions, we are inclined to say how much better it would have been to have remained there among the hills in that quiet, inexpensive environment, to have let the world go. But that was not possible. The game was of far larger proportions than any that could be restricted to the limits of retirement and the simpler round of life. Mark Twain's realm had become too large for his court to be established in a cottage.

It is hard to understand that in spite of a towering fame Mark Twain was still not regarded by certain American arbiters of reputations as a literary fixture; his work was not yet recognized by them as being of important meaning and serious purport.

In Boston, at that time still the Athens of America, he was enjoyed, delighted in; but he was not honored as being quite one of the elect. Howells tells us that:

> In proportion as people thought themselves refined they questioned that quality which all recognize in him now, but which was then the inspired knowledge of the simple-hearted multitude.

Even at the *Atlantic* dinners his place was "below the salt"—a place of honor, but not of the greatest honor. He did not sit on the dais with Emerson, Longfellow, Holmes, Whittier, Howells, and Aldrich. We of a later period, who remember him always as the center of every board—the one supreme figure, his splendid head and crown of silver hair the target of every eye—find it hard to realize the Cambridge conservatism that clad him figuratively always in motley, and seated him lower than the throne itself.

Howells clearly resented this condition, and from random review corners had ventured heresy. Now in 1882 he seems to have determined to declare himself, in a large, free way, concerning his own personal estimate of Mark Twain. He prepared for the *Century Magazine* a biographical appreciation, in which he served notice to the world that Mark Twain's work, considered even as literature, was of very considerable importance indeed. Whether or not Howells then realized the "inspired knowledge of the multitude," and that most of the nation outside of the counties of Suffolk and Essex already recognized his claim, is not material. Very likely he did; but he also realized the mental dusk of the cultured *un*inspired and his prerogative to enlighten them. His *Century* article was a kind of manifesto, a declaration of independence, no longer confined to the obscurities of certain book notices, where of course one might be expected to stretch friendly favor a little for a popular *Atlantic* contributor. In the open field of the *Century Magazine* Howells ventured to declare:

Mark Twain's humor is as simple in form and as direct as the statesmanship of Lincoln or the generalship of Grant.

When I think how purely and wholly American it is I am a little puzzled at its universal acceptance. . . . Why, in fine, should an English chief-justice keep Mark Twain's books always at hand? Why should Darwin have gone to them for rest and refreshment at midnight, when spent with scientific research?

I suppose that Mark Twain transcends all other American humorists in the universal qualities. He deals very little with the pathetic, which he nevertheless knows very well how to manage, as he has shown, notably in the true story of the old slave-mother; but there is a poetic lift in his work, even when he permits you to recognize it only as something satirized. There is always the touch of nature, the presence of a sincere and frank manliness in what he says, the companionship of a spirit which is at once delightfully open and deliciously shrewd. Elsewhere I have tried to persuade the reader that his humor is, at its best, the foamy break of the strong tide of earnestness in him. But it would be limiting him unjustly to describe him as a satirist, and it is hardly practicable to establish him in people's minds as a moralist; he has made them laugh too long; they will not believe him serious; they think some joke is always intended. This is the penalty, as Dr. Holmes has pointed out, of mak-

> ing one's first success as a humorist. There was a paper of Mark Twain's printed in the *Atlantic Monthly* some years ago and called, "The Facts Concerning the Late Carnival of Crime in Connecticut," which ought to have won popular recognition of the ethical intelligence underlying his humor. It was, of course, funny; but under the fun it was an impassioned study of the human conscience. Hawthorne or Bunyan might have been proud to imagine that powerful allegory, which had a grotesque force far beyond either of them. . . . Yet it quite failed of the response I had hoped for it, and I shall not insist here upon Mark Twain as a moralist; though I warn the reader that if he leaves out of the account an indignant sense of right and wrong, a scorn of all affectations and pretense, an ardent hate of meanness and injustice, he will come infinitely short of knowing Mark Twain.

Howells realized the unwisdom and weakness of dogmatic insistence, and the strength of understatement. To him Mark Twain was already the moralist, the philosopher, and the statesman; he was willing that the reader should take his time to realize these things. The article, with his subject's portrait as a frontispiece, appeared in the *Century* for September, 1882. If it carried no new message to many of its readers, it at least set the stamp of official approval upon what they had already established in their hearts.

CXL

DOWN THE RIVER

OSGOOD was doing no great things with *The Prince and the Pauper*, but Clemens gave him another book presently, a collection of sketches—*The Stolen White Elephant*. It was not an especially important volume, though some of the features, such as "Mrs. McWilliams and the Lightning" and the "Carnival of Crime," are among the best of their sort, while the "Elephant" story is an amazingly good take-off on what might be called the spectacular detective. The interview between Inspector Blunt and the owner of the elephant is typical. The inspector asks:

"Now what does this elephant eat, and how much?"

"Well, as to what he eats—he will eat anything. He will eat a man, he will eat a Bible; he will eat anything between a man and a Bible."

"Good—very good, indeed, but too general. Details are necessary; details are the only valuable thing in our trade. Very well, as to men. At one meal—or, if you prefer, during one day—how many men will he eat if fresh?"

"He would not care whether they were fresh or not; at a single meal he would eat five ordinary men."

"Very good; five men. We will put that down. What nationalities would he prefer?"

"He is indifferent about nationalities. He prefers acquaintances, but is not prejudiced against strangers."

"Very good. Now, as to Bibles. How many Bibles would he eat at a meal?"

"He would eat an entire edition."

Clemens and Osgood had a more important publishing enterprise on hand. The long-deferred completion of the Mississippi book was to be accomplished; the long-deferred trip down the river was to be taken. Howells was going abroad, but the charming Osgood was willing to make the excursion, and a young man named Roswell Phelps, of Hartford, was engaged as a stenographer to take the notes.

Clemens made a farewell trip to Boston to see Howells before his departure, and together they went to Concord to call on Emerson; a fortunate thing, for he lived but a few weeks longer. They went again in the evening, not to see him, but to stand reverently outside and look at his house. This was in April. Longfellow had died in March. The fact that Howells was going away indefinitely, made them reminiscent and sad.

Just what breach Clemens committed during this visit is not remembered now, and it does not matter; but his letter to Howells, after his return to Hartford, makes it pretty clear that it was memorable enough at the time. Half-way in it he breaks out:

But oh, hell, there is no hope for a person that is built like me, because there is no cure, no cure.

If I could only *know* when I have committed a crime: then I could conceal it, and not go stupidly dribbling it out, circumstance by circumstance, into the ears of a person who will give no sign till the confession is complete; and then the sudden damnation drops on a body like the released pile-driver, and he finds himself in the earth down to his chin. When he merely supposed he was being entertaining.

Next day he was off with Osgood and the stenographer for St. Louis, where they took the steamer *Gold Dust* down the river. He intended to travel under an assumed name, but was promptly recognized, both at the Southern Hotel and on the boat. In *Life on the Mississippi* he has given us the atmosphere of his trip, with his new impressions of old scenes; also his first interview with the pilot, whom he did not remember, but who easily remembered him.

"I did not write that story in the book quite as it happened," he reflected once, many years later. "We went on board at night. Next morning I was up bright and early and out on deck to see if I could recognize any of the old landmarks. I could not remember any. I did not know where we were at all. It was a new river to me entirely. I climbed up in the pilot-house and there was a fellow of about forty at the wheel. I said 'Good morning.' He answered pleasantly enough. His face was entirely strange to me. Then I sat down on the high seat back of the wheel and looked out at the river and began to ask a few questions, such as a landsman would ask. He began, in the old way, to fill me up with the old lies, and I enjoyed letting him do it. Then suddenly he turned round to me and said:

"'I want to get a cup of coffee. You hold her, will you, till I come back?' And before I could say a word he was out of the pilot-house door and down the steps. It all came so suddenly that I sprang to the wheel, of course, as I would have done twenty years before. Then in a moment I realized my position. Here I was with a great big steamboat in the middle of the Mississippi River, without any further knowledge than that fact, and the pilot out of sight. I settled my mind on three conclusions: first, that the pilot might be a lunatic; second, that he had recognized me and thought I knew the river; third, that we were in a perfectly safe place, where I could not possibly kill the steamboat. But that last conclusion, though the most comforting, was an extremely doubtful one. I knew perfectly well that no sane pilot would trust his steamboat for a single moment in the hands of a greenhorn unless he were standing by the greenhorn's side. Of course, by force of habit, when I grabbed the wheel, I had taken the steering marks ahead and astern, and I made up my mind to hold her on those marks to the hair; but I could feel myself getting old and gray. Then all at once I recognized where we were; we were in what is called the Grand Chain—a succession of hidden rocks, one of the most dangerous places on the river. There were two rocks there only about seventy feet apart, and you've got to go exactly between them or wreck the boat. There was a time when I could have done it without a tremor, but that time wasn't now. I would have given any reasonable sum to have been on the shore just at that moment. I think I was about ready to drop dead when I heard a step on the pilot-house stair; then the door opened and the pilot came in, quietly picking his teeth, and took the wheel, and I crawled weakly back to the seat. He said:

"'You thought you were playing a nice joke on me, didn't you? You thought I didn't know who you were. Why, I recognized that drawl of yours as soon as you opened your mouth.'

"I said, 'Who the h—l are you? I don't remember you.'

"'Well,' he said, 'perhaps you don't, but I was a cub pilot on the river before the war, when you were a licensed pilot, and I couldn't get a license when I was qualified for one, because the Pilots' Association was so strong at that time that they could keep new pilots out if they wanted to, and the law was that I had to be examined by two licensed pilots, and for a good while I could not get any one to make that examination. But one day you and another pilot offered to do it, and you put me through a good, healthy examination and indorsed my application for a license. I had never seen you before, and I have never seen you since until now, but I recognized you.'

"'All right,' I said. 'But if I had gone half a mile farther with that steamboat we might have all been at the bottom of the river.'

"We got to be good friends, of course, and I spent most of my time up there with him. When we got down below Cairo, and there was a big, full river—for it was high-water season and there was no danger of the boat hitting anything so long as she kept in the river—I had her most of the time on his watch. He would lie down and sleep, and leave me there to dream that the years had not slipped away; that there had been no war, no mining days, no literary adventures; that I was still a pilot, happy and care-free as I had been twenty years before."

From the book we gather that he could not keep out of the pilot-house. He was likely to get up at any hour of the night to stand his watch, and truly enough the years had slipped away. He was the young fellow in his twenties again, speculating on the problems of existence and reading his fortune in the stars. To heighten the illusion, he had himself called regularly with the four-o'clock watch, in order not to miss the mornings.[1]

The majesty and solitude of the river impressed him more than ever before, especially its solitude. It had been so full of life in his time; now it had returned once more to its primal loneliness—the loneliness of God.

At one place two steamboats were in sight at once—an unusual spectacle. Once, in the mouth of a river, he noticed a small boat, which he made out to be the *Mark Twain*. There had been varied changes in twenty-one years; only the old fascination of piloting remained unchanged. To Bixby afterward he wrote:

"I'd rather be a pilot than anything else I've ever done in my life. How do you run Plum Point?"

He met Bixby at New Orleans. Bixby was captain

[1] It will repay the reader to turn to chap. xxx of *Life on the Mississippi*, and consider Mark Twain's word-picture of the river sunrise.

now on a splendid new Anchor Line steamboat, the *City of Baton Rouge*. The Anchor Line steamers were the acme of Mississippi River steamboat-building, and they were about the end of it. They were imposingly magnificent, but they were only as gorgeous clouds that marked the sunset of Mississippi steamboat travel. Mark Twain made his trip down the river just in time.

In New Orleans he met George W. Cable and Joel Chandler Harris, and they had a fraternizing good time together, mousing about the old French Quarter or mingling with the social life of the modern city. He made a trip with Bixby in a tug to the Warmouth plantation, and they reviewed old days together, as friends parted for twenty-one years will. Altogether the New Orleans sojourn was a pleasant one, saddened only by a newspaper notice of the death, in Edinburgh, of the kindly and gentle and beloved Dr. Brown.

Clemens arranged to make the trip up the river on the *Baton Rouge*. Bixby had one pretty inefficient pilot, and stood most of the watches himself, so that with "Sam Clemens" in the pilot-house with him, it was wonderfully like those old first days of learning the river, back in the fifties.

"Sam was ever making notes in his memorandum-book, just as he always did," said Bixby to the writer, recalling the time. "I was sorry I had to stay at the wheel so much. I wanted to have more time with Sam without thinking of the river at all. Sam was sorry, too, from what he wrote after he got home."

Bixby produced a letter in the familiar handwriting. It was a tender, heart-spoken letter:

I didn't see half enough of you. It was a sore disappointment. Osgood could have told you, if he would—discreet old dog—I expected to have you with me *all* the time. Altogether, the most pleasant part of my visit with you was after we arrived in St. Louis, and you were your old natural self again. Twenty years have not added a month to your age or taken a fraction from your loveliness.

Said Bixby: "When we arrived in St. Louis we came to the Planters' Hotel, to this very table where you and I are sitting now, and we had a couple of hot Scotches between us, just as we have now, and we had a good last talk over old times and old acquaintances. After he returned to New York he sent for my picture. He wanted to use it in his book."

At St. Louis the travelers changed boats, and proceeded up the Mississippi toward St. Paul. Clemens laid off three days at Hannibal.

Delightful days [he wrote home]. Loitering around all day long, examining the old localities, and talking with the gray heads who were boys and girls with me thirty or forty years ago. I spent my nights with John and Helen Garth, three miles from town, in their spacious and beautiful house. They were children with me, and afterward schoolmates. That world which I knew in its blooming youth is old and bowed and melancholy now; its soft cheeks are leathery and withered, the fire has gone out of its eyes, the spring from its step. It will be dust and ashes when I come again.

He had never seen the far upper river, and he found it very satisfying. His note-book says:

The bluffs all along up above St. Paul are exquisitely beautiful where the rough and broken turreted rocks stand up against the sky above the steep, verdant slopes. They are inexpressibly rich and mellow in color; soft dark browns mingled with dull greens—the very tints to make an artist worship.

In a final entry he wrote:

The romance of boating is gone now. In Hannibal the steamboat man is no longer the god.

CXLI

LITERATURE AND PHILOSOPHY

CLEMENS took a further step toward becoming a publisher on his own account. Not only did he contract to supply funds for the Mississippi book, but, as kaolatype, the chalk-engraving process, which had been lingeringly and expensively dying, was now become merely something to swear at, he had his niece's husband, Webster, installed as Osgood's New York subscription manager, with charge of the general agencies. There was no delay in this move. Webster must get well familiarized with the work before the Mississippi book's publication.

He had expected to have the manuscript finished pretty promptly, but the fact that he had promised it for a certain time paralyzed his effort. Even at the farm he worked without making much headway. At the end of October he wrote Howells:

> The weather turned cold, and we had to rush home, while I still lacked thirty thousand words. I had been sick and got delayed. I am going to write all day and two-thirds of the night until the thing is done or break down at it. The spur and burden of the contract are intolerable to me. I can endure the irritation of it no longer. I went to work at nine o'clock yesterday morning and went to bed an hour after midnight. Result of the day (mainly stolen from books though credit given), 9,500 words, so I reduced my burden by one-third in one day. It was five days' work in one. I have nothing more to borrow or steal; the rest must all be written. It is ten days' work. and unless something breaks it will be finished in five.

He had sworn once, when he had finally finished *A Tramp Abroad*, that he would never limit himself as to time again. But he had forgotten that vow, and was suffering accordingly.

Howells wrote from London urging him to drop everything and come over to Europe for refreshment.

We have seen lots of nice people, and have been most pleasantly made of; but I would rather have you smoke in my face and talk for half a day, just for pleasure, than to go to the best house or club in London.

Clemens answered:

Yes, it would be more profitable to me to do that because, with your society to help me, I should swiftly finish this now apparently interminable book. But I cannot come, because I am not boss here, and nothing but dynamite can move Mrs. Clemens away from home in the winter season.

This was in November, and he had broken all restrictions as to time. He declared that he had never had such a fight over any book before, and that he had told Osgood and everybody concerned that they must wait.

I have said with sufficient positiveness that I will finish the book at no particular date; that I will not hurry it; that I will not hurry myself; that I will take things easy and comfortably—write when I choose to write, leave it alone when I do so prefer. . . . I have got everything at a dead standstill, and that is where it ought to be, and that is where it must remain; to follow any other policy would be to make the book worse than it already is. I ought to have finished it before showing it to anybody, and then sent it across the ocean to you to be edited, as usual; for you seem to be a great many shades happier than you deserve to be, and if I had thought of this thing earlier I would have acted upon it and taken the tuck somewhat out of your joyousness.

It was a long, heartfelt letter. Near the end of it he said:

> Cable has been here, creating worshipers on all hands. He is a marvelous talker on a deep subject. I do not see how even Spencer could unwind a thought more smoothly or orderly, and do it in cleaner, clearer, crisper English. He astounded Twichell with his faculty. You know that when it comes down to moral honesty, limpid innocence, and utterly blemishless piety, the apostles were mere policemen to Cable; so with this in mind you must imagine him at a midnight dinner in Boston the other night, where we gathered around the board of the Summerset Club: Osgood full, Boyle O'Reilly full, Fairchild responsively loaded, and Aldrich and myself possessing the floor and properly fortified. Cable told Mrs. Clemens, when he returned here, that he seemed to have been entertaining himself with horses, and had a dreamy idea that he must have gone to Boston in a cattle-car. It was a very large time. He called it an orgy. And no doubt it was, viewed from his standpoint.

Osgood wanted Mark Twain to lecture that fall, as preliminary advertising for the book, with "Life on the Mississippi" as his subject. Osgood was careful to make this proposition by mail, and probably it was just as well; for if there was any single straw that could have broken the back of Clemens's endurance and made him violent at this particular time, it was a proposition to go back on the platform. His answer to Osgood has not been preserved.

Clemens spoke little that winter. In February he addressed the Monday Evening Club on "What is Happiness?" presenting a theory which in later years he developed as a part of his "gospel," and promulgated in a privately printed volume, *What is Man?* It is the postulate already mentioned in connection with his reading of Lecky, that every human action, bad or good, is the result of a selfish impulse; that is to say, the result of a desire for the greater content of spirit. It is not a new idea; philosophers in all ages have considered it, and accepted or rejected it, according to their temperament and teachings, but it was startling and apparently new to the Monday Evening Club. They scoffed and jeered at it; denounced it as a manifest falsity. They did not quite see then that there may be two sorts of selfishness—brutal and divine; that he who sacrifices others to himself exemplifies the first, whereas he who sacrifices himself for others personifies the second—the divine contenting of his soul by serving the happiness of his fellow-men. Mark Twain left this admonition in furtherance of that better sort:

"Diligently train your ideals upward, and still upward, toward a summit where you will find your chiefest pleasure, in conduct which, while contenting you, will be sure to confer benefits upon your neighbor and the community."

It is a divine admonition, even if, in its suggested moral freedom, it does seem to conflict with that other theory—the inevitable sequence of cause and effect, descending from the primal atom. There is seeming irrelevance in introducing this matter here; but it has a chronological relation, and it presents a mental aspect of the time. Clemens was forty-eight, and becoming more and more the philosopher; also, in logic at least, a good deal of a pessimist. He made a birthday aphorism on the subject:

"The man who is a pessimist before he is forty-eight knows too much; the man who is an optimist after he is forty-eight knows too little."

He was never more than a pessimist in theory at any time. In practice he would be a visionary; a builder of dreams and fortunes, a veritable Colonel Sellers to the end of his days.

CXLII

"LIFE ON THE MISSISSIPPI"

THE Mississippi book was completed at last and placed in Osgood's hands for publication. Clemens was immensely fond of Osgood. Osgood would come down to Hartford and spend days discussing plans and playing billiards, which to Mark Twain's mind was the proper way to conduct business. Besides, there was Webster, who by this time, or a very little later, had the word "publisher" printed in his letter-heads, and was truly that, so far as the new book was concerned. Osgood had become little more than its manufacturer, shipping-agent, and accountant. It should be added that he made the book well, though somewhat expensively. He was unaccustomed to getting out big subscription volumes. His taste ran to the artistic, expensive product.

"That book cost me fifty thousand dollars to make," Clemens once declared. "Bliss could have built a whole library for that sum. But Osgood was a lovely fellow."

Life on the Mississippi was issued about the middle of May. It was a handsome book of its kind and a successful book, but not immediately a profitable one, because of the manner of its issue. It was experimental, and experiments are likely to be costly, even when successful in the final result.

Among other things, it pronounced the final doom of kaolatype. The artists who drew the pictures for it declined to draw them if they were to be reproduced by that process, or indeed unless some one of the lately discovered photographic processes was used. Furthermore, the latter were much cheaper, and it was to the advantage of Clemens himself to repudiate kaolatype, even for his own work.

Webster was ordered to wind up the last ends of the engraving business with as little sacrifice as possible, and attend entirely to more profitable affairs—*viz.*, the distribution of books.

As literature, the Mississippi book will rank with Mark Twain's best—so far, at least, as the first twenty chapters of it are concerned. Earlier in this history these have been sufficiently commented upon. They constitute a literary memorial seemingly as enduring as the river itself.

Concerning the remaining chapters of the book, they are also literature, but of a different class. The difference is about the same as that between *A Tramp Abroad* and the *Innocents*. It is the difference between the labors of love and duty; between art and industry, literature and journalism.

But the last is hardly fair. It is journalism, but it is literary journalism, and there are unquestionably areas that are purely literary, and not journalistic at all. There would always be those in any book of travel he might write. The story of the river revisited is an interesting theme; and if the revisiting had been done, let us say eight or ten years earlier, before he had become a theoretical pessimist, and before the river itself had become a background for pessimism, the tale might have had more of the literary glamour and illusion, even if less that is otherwise valuable.

Life on the Mississippi has been always popular in Germany. The Emperor William of Germany once assured Mark Twain that it was his favorite American book, and on the same evening the *portier* of the author's lodging in Berlin echoed the Emperor's opinion.

Paul Lindau, a distinguished German author and critic,

in an interview at the time the Mississippi book appeared, spoke of the general delight of his countrymen in its author. When he was asked, "But have not the Germans been offended by Mark Twain's strictures on their customs and language in his *Tramp Abroad?*" he replied, "We know what we are and how we look, and the fanciful picture presented to our eyes gives us only food for laughter, not cause for resentment. The jokes he made on our long words, our inverted sentences, and the position of the verb have really led to a reform in style which will end in making our language as compact and crisp as the French or English. I regard Mark Twain as the foremost humorist of the age."

Howells, traveling through Europe, found Lindau's final sentiment echoed elsewhere, and he found something more: in Europe Mark Twain was already highly regarded as a serious writer. Thomas Hardy said to Howells one night at dinner:

"Why don't people understand that Mark Twain is not merely a great humorist? He is a very remarkable fellow in a very different way."

The Rev. Dr. Parker, returning from England just then, declared that, wherever he went among literary people, the talk was about Mark Twain; also that on two occasions, when he had ventured diffidently to say that he knew that author personally, he was at once so evidently regarded as lying for effect that he felt guilty, and looked it, and did not venture to say it any more; thus, in a manner, practising untruth to save his reputation for veracity.

That the Mississippi book throughout did much to solidify this foreign opinion of Mark Twain's literary importance cannot be doubted, and it is one of his books that will live longest in the memory of men.

CXLIII

A GUEST OF ROYALTY

FOR purposes of copyright another trip to Canada was necessary, and when the newspapers announced (May, 1883) that Mark Twain was about to cross the border there came one morning the following telegram:

> Meeting of Literary and Scientific Society at Ottawa from 22d to 26th. It would give me much pleasure if you could come and be my guest during that time.
>
> LORNE.

The Marquis of Lorne, then Governor-General of Canada, was the husband of Queen Victoria's daughter, the Princess Louise. The invitation was therefore in the nature of a command. Clemens obeyed it graciously enough, and with a feeling of exaltation no doubt. He had been honored by the noble and the great in many lands, but this was royalty—English royalty—paying a tribute to an American writer whom neither the Marquis nor the Princess, his wife, had ever seen. They had invited him because they had cared enough for his books to make them wish to see him, to have him as a guest in Rideau Hall, their home. Mark Twain was democratic. A king to him was no more than any other man; rather less if he were not a good king. But there was something national in this tribute; and, besides, Lord Lorne and the Princess Louise were the kind of sovereigns that honored their rank, instead of being honored by it.

It is a good deal like a fairy tale when you think of it;

the barefooted boy of Hannibal, who had become a printer, a pilot, a rough-handed miner, being summoned, not so many years later, by royalty as one of America's foremost men of letters. The honor was no greater than many others he had received, certainly not greater than the calls of Canon Kingsley and Robert Browning and Turgenieff at his London hotel lodgings, but it was of a less usual kind.

Clemens enjoyed his visit. Princess Louise and the Marquis of Lorne kept him with them almost continually, and were loath to let him go. Once they took him tobogganing—an exciting experience.

It happened that during his stay with them the opening of the Canadian Parliament took place. Lord Lorne and the principal dignitaries of state entered one carriage, and in a carriage behind them followed Princess Louise with Mark Twain. As they approached the Parliament House the customary salute was fired. Clemens pretended to the Princess considerable gratification. The temptation was too strong to resist:

"Your Highness," he said, "I have had other compliments paid to me, but none equal to this one. I have never before had a salute fired in my honor."

Returning to Hartford, he sent copies of his books to Lord Lorne, and to the Princess a special copy of that absurd manual, *The New Guide of the Conversation in Portuguese and English*, for which he had written an introduction.[1]

[1] A serious work, in Portugal, though issued by Osgood ('83) as a joke. Clemens in the introduction says: "Its delicious, unconscious ridiculousness and its enchanting naïveté are as supreme and unapproachable in their way as Shakespeare's sublimities." An extract, the closing paragraph from the book's preface, will illustrate his meaning:

"We expect then, who the little book (for the care that we wrote him, and for her typographical correction), that may be worth the acceptation of the studious persons, and especially of the Youth, at which we dedicate him particularly."

CXLIV

A SUMMER LITERARY HARVEST

ARRIVING at the farm in June, Clemens had a fresh crop of ideas for stories of many lengths and varieties. His note-book of that time is full of motifs and plots, most of them of that improbable and extravagant kind which tended to defeat any literary purpose, whether humorous or otherwise. It seems worth while setting down one or more of these here, for they are characteristic of the myriad conceptions that came and went, and beyond these written memoranda left no trace behind. Here is a fair example of many:

Two men starving on a raft. The pauper has a Boston cracker, resolves to keep it till the multimillionaire is beginning to starve, then make him pay $50,000 for it. Millionaire agrees. Pauper's cupidity rises, resolves to wait and get more; twenty-four hours later asks him a million for the cracker. Millionaire agrees. Pauper has a wild dream of becoming enormously rich off his cracker; backs down; lies all night building castles in the air; next day raises his price higher and higher, till millionaire has offered $100,000,000, every cent he has in the world. Pauper accepts. Millionaire: "Now give it to me."

Pauper: "No; it isn't a trade until you sign documental history of the transaction and make an oath to pay."

While pauper is finishing the document millionaire sees a ship. When pauper says, "Sign and take the cracker," millionaire smiles a smile, declines, and points to the ship.

Yet this is hardly more extravagant than another idea

that is mentioned repeatedly among the notes—that of an otherwise penniless man wandering about London with a single million-pound bank-note in his possession, a motif which developed into a very good story indeed.

IDEA FOR "STORMFIELD'S VISIT TO HEAVEN"

In modern times the halls of heaven are warmed by registers connected with hell; and this is greatly applauded by Jonathan Edwards, Calvin, Baxter and Company, because it adds a new pang to the sinner's sufferings to know that the very fire which tortures him is the means of making the righteous comfortable.

Then there was to be another story, in which the various characters were to have a weird, pestilential nomenclature; such as "Lockjaw Harris," "Influenza Smith," "Sinapism Davis," and a dozen or two more, a perfect outbreak of disorders.

Another—probably the inspiration of some very hot afternoon—was to present life in the interior of an iceberg, where a colony would live for a generation or two, drifting about in a vast circular current year after year, subsisting on polar bears and other Arctic game.

An idea which he followed out and completed was the *1002d Arabian Night*, in which Scheherazade continues her stories, until she finally talks the Sultan to death. That was a humorous idea, certainly; but when Howells came home and read it in the usual way he declared that, while the opening was killingly funny, when he got into the story itself it seemed to him that he was "made a fellow-sufferer with the Sultan from Scheherazade's prolixity."

"On the whole," he said, "it is not your best, nor your second best; but all the way it skirts a certain kind of fun which you can't afford to indulge in."

And that was the truth. So the tale, neatly type-written, retired to seclusion, and there remains to this day.

Clemens had one inspiration that summer which was not

directly literary, but historical, due to his familiarity with English dates. He wrote Twichell:

Day before yesterday, feeling not in condition for writing, I left the study, but I couldn't hold in—had to do something; so I spent eight hours in the sun with a yardstick, measuring off the reigns of the English kings on the roads in these grounds, from William the Conqueror to 1883, calculating to invent an open-air game which shall fill the children's heads with dates without study. I give each king's reign one foot of space to the year and drive one stake in the ground to mark the beginning of each reign, and I make the children call the stake by the king's name. You can stand in the door and take a bird's-eye view of English monarchy, from the Conqueror to Edward IV.; then you can turn and follow the road up the hill to the study and beyond with an opera-glass, and bird's-eye view the rest of it to 1883.

You can mark the sharp difference in the *length* of reigns by the varying distances of the stakes apart. You can see Richard II., two feet; Oliver Cromwell, two feet; James II., three feet, and so on—and then big skips; pegs standing forty-five, forty-six, fifty, fifty-six, and sixty feet apart (Elizabeth, Victoria, Edward III., Henry III., and George III.). By the way, third's a lucky number for length of days, isn't it? Yes, sir; by my scheme you get a realizing notion of the *time* occupied by reigns.

The reason it took me eight hours was because, with little Jean's interrupting assistance, I had to measure from the Conquest to the end of Henry VI. three times over, and besides I had to whittle out all those pegs.

I did a full day's work and a third over, yesterday, but was full of my game after I went to bed trying to fit it for indoors. So I didn't get to sleep till pretty late; but when I did go off I had contrived a new way to play my history game with cards and a board.

We may be sure the idea of the game would possess him, once it got a fair start like that. He decided to save the human race that year with a history game. When he had got the children fairly going and interested in playing it, he adapted it to a cribbage-board, and spent his days and nights working it out and perfecting it to a degree where the world at large might learn all the facts of all the histories, not only without effort, but with an actual hunger for chronology. He would have a game not only of the English kings, but of the kings of every other nation; likewise of great statesmen, vice-chancellors, churchmen, of celebrities in every line. He would prepare a book to accompany these games. Each game would contain one thousand facts, while the book would contain eight thousand; it would be a veritable encyclopedia. He would organize clubs throughout the United States for playing the game; prizes were to be given. Experts would take it up. He foresaw a department in every newspaper devoted to the game and its problems, instead of to chess and whist and other useless diversions. He wrote to Orion, and set him to work gathering facts and dates by the bushel. He wrote to Webster, sent him a plan, and ordered him to apply for the patent without delay. Patents must also be applied for abroad. With all nations playing this great game, very likely it would produce millions in royalties; and so, in the true Sellers fashion, the iridescent bubble was blown larger and larger, until finally it blew up. The game on paper had become so large, so elaborate, so intricate, that no one could play it. Yet the first idea was a good one: the king stakes driven along the driveway and up the hillside of Quarry Farm. The children enjoyed it, and played it through many sweet summer afternoons. Once, in the days when he had grown old, he wrote, remembering:

Among the principal merits of the games which we played by help of the pegs were these: that they had to be played in the open air, and that they compelled brisk exercise. The peg of William the Conqueror stood in front of the house; one could stand near the Conqueror and have all English history skeletonized and landmarked and mile-posted under his eye. . . . The eye has a good memory. Many years have gone by and the pegs have disappeared, but I still see them and each in its place; and no king's name falls upon my ear without my seeing his pegs at once, and noticing just how many feet of space he takes up along the road.

It turned out an important literary year after all. In the Mississippi book he had used a chapter from the story he had been working at from time to time for a number of years, *The Adventures of Huckleberry Finn.* Reading over the manuscript now he found his interest in it sharp and fresh, his inspiration renewed. The trip down the river had revived it. The interest in the game became quiescent, and he set to work to finish the story at a dead heat.

To Howells, August 22 (1883), he wrote:

I have written eight or nine hundred manuscript pages in such a brief space of time that I mustn't name the number of days; I shouldn't believe it myself, and of course couldn't expect you to. I used to restrict myself to four and five hours a day and five days in the week, but this time I have wrought from breakfast till 5.15 P.M. six days in the week, and once or twice I smouched a Sunday when the boss wasn't looking. Nothing is half so good as literature hooked on Sunday, on the sly.

He refers to the game, though rather indifferently.

When I wrote you I thought I *had* it; whereas I was merely entering upon the initiatory difficulties of it. I might have known it wouldn't be an easy job or somebody would have invented a decent historical game long ago—a thing which nobody has done.

Notwithstanding the fact that he was working at *Huck* with enthusiasm, he seems to have been in no hurry to revise it for publication, either as a serial or as a book. But the fact that he persevered until *Huck Finn* at last found complete utterance was of itself a sufficient matter for congratulation.

CXLV

HOWELLS AND CLEMENS WRITE A PLAY

BEFORE Howells went abroad Clemens had written:

> Now I think that the play for you to write would be one entitled, "Colonel Mulberry Sellers in Age" (75), with Lafayette Hawkins (at 50) still sticking to him and believing in him and calling him "My lord." He [Sellers] is a specialist and a scientist in various ways. Your refined people and purity of speech would make the best possible background, and when you are done, I could take your manuscript and rewrite the Colonel's speeches, and make him properly extravagant, and I would let the play go to Raymond, and bind him up with a contract that would give him the bellyache every time he read it. Shall we think this over, or drop it as being nonsense?

Howells, returned and settled in Boston once more, had revived an interest in the play idea. He corresponded with Clemens concerning it and agreed that the American Claimant, Leathers, should furnish the initial impulse of the drama.

They decided to revive Colonel Sellers and make him the heir; Colonel Sellers in old age, more wildly extravagant than ever, with new schemes, new patents, new methods of ameliorating the ills of mankind.

Howells came down to Hartford from Boston full of enthusiasm. He found Clemens with some ideas of the plan jotted down: certain effects and situations which seemed to him amusing, but there was no general scheme of action. Howells, telling of it, says:

> I felt authorized to make him observe that his scheme was as nearly nothing as chaos could be. He agreed hilariously with me, and was willing to let it stand in proof of his entire dramatic inability.

Howells, in turn, proposed a plan which Clemens approved, and they set to work. Howells could imitate Clemens's literary manner, and they had a riotously jubilant fortnight working out their humors. Howells has told about it in his book, and he once related it to the writer of this memoir. He said:

"Clemens took one scene and I another. We had loads and loads of fun about it. We cracked our sides laughing over it as it went along. We thought it mighty good, and I think to this day that it was mighty good. We called the play 'Colonel Sellers.' We revived him. Clemens had a notion of Sellers as a spiritual medium—there was a good deal of excitement about spiritualism then; he also had a notion of Sellers leading a women's temperance crusade. We conceived the idea of Sellers wanting to try, in the presence of the audience, how a man felt who had fallen, through drink. Sellers was to end with a sort of corkscrew performance on the stage. He always wore a marvelous fire extinguisher, one of his inventions, strapped on his back, so in any sudden emergency, he could give proof of its effectiveness."

In connection with the extinguisher, Howells provided Sellers with a pair of wings, which Sellers declared would enable him to float around in any altitude where the flames might break out. The extinguisher, was not to be charged with water or any sort of liquid, but with Greek fire, on the principle that like cures like; in other words, the building was to be inoculated with Greek fire against the ordinary conflagration. Of course the whole thing was as absurd as possible, and, reading the old manuscript to-day, one is impressed with the roaring humor of some of the scenes, and with the wild extravagance of the farce motive, not wholly warranted by the previous character of Sellers, unless, indeed, he had gone stark mad. It is, in fact, Sellers caricatured. The gentle, tender side of Sellers—the best side—the side which Clemens and Howells themselves cared for most, is not there. Chapter III of Mark Twain's novel, *The American Claimant*, contains a scene between Colonel Sellers and Washington Hawkins which presents the extravagance of the Colonel's materialization scheme. It is a modified version of one of the scenes in the play, and is as amusing and unoffending as any.

The authors' rollicking joy in their work convinced them that they had produced a masterpiece for which the public in general, and the actors in particular, were waiting. Howells went back to Boston tired out, but elate in the prospect of imminent fortune.

CXLVI

DISTINGUISHED VISITORS

MEANTIME, while Howells had been in Hartford working at the play with Clemens, Matthew Arnold had arrived in Boston. On inquiring for Howells at his home, the visitor was told that he had gone to see Mark Twain. Arnold was perhaps the only literary Englishman left who had not accepted Mark Twain at his larger value. He seemed surprised and said:

"Oh, but he doesn't like *that* sort of thing, does he?"

To which Mrs. Howells replied:

"He likes Mr. Clemens very much, and he thinks him one of the greatest men he ever knew."

Arnold proceeded to Hartford to lecture, and one night Howells and Clemens went to meet him at a reception. Says Howells:

> While his hand laxly held mine in greeting I saw his eyes fixed intensely on the other side of the room. "Who—who in the world is that?" I looked and said, "Oh, that is Mark Twain." I do not remember just how their instant encounter was contrived by Arnold's wish, but I have the impression that they were not parted for long during the evening, and the next night Arnold, as if still under the glamour of that potent presence, was at Clemens's house.

He came there to dine with the Twichells and the Rev. Dr. Edwin P. Parker. Dr. Parker and Arnold left together, and, walking quietly homeward, discussed the remarkable creature whose presence they had just left.

Clemens had been at his best that night—at his humorous best. He had kept a perpetual gale of laughter going, with a string of comment and anecdote of a kind which Twichell once declared the world had never before seen and would never see again. Arnold seemed dazed by it, unable to come out from under its influence. He repeated some of the things Mark Twain had said; thoughtfully, as if trying to analyze their magic. Then he asked solemnly:

"And is he *never* serious?"

And Dr. Parker as solemnly answered:

"Mr. Arnold, he is the most serious man in the world."

Dr. Parker, recalling this incident, remembered also that Protap Chunder Mazoomdar, a Hindoo Christian prelate of high rank, visited Hartford in 1883, and that his one desire was to meet Mark Twain. In some memoranda of this visit Dr. Parker has written:

> I said that Mark Twain was a friend of mine, and we would immediately go to his house. He was all eagerness, and I perceived that I had risen greatly in this most refined and cultivated gentleman's estimation. Arriving at Mr. Clemens's residence, I promptly sought a brief private interview with my friend for his enlightenment concerning the distinguished visitor, after which they were introduced and spent a long while together. In due time Mazoomdar came forth with Mark's likeness and autograph, and as we walked away his whole air and manner seemed to say, with Simeon of old, "Lord, now lettest thou thy servant depart in peace!"

CXLVII

THE FORTUNES OF A PLAY

HOWELLS is of the impression that the "Claimant" play had been offered to other actors before Raymond was made aware of it; but there are letters (to Webster) which indicate that Raymond was to see the play first, though Clemens declares, in a letter of instruction, that he *hopes Raymond will not take it.* Then he says:

> Why do I offer him the play at all? For these reasons: he plays that character well; there are not thirty actors in the country who can do it better; and, too, he has a sort of sentimental right to be *offered* the piece, though no moral, or legal, or other kind of right.
>
> Therefore we do offer it to him; but only once, not twice. Let us have no hemming and hawing; make short, sharp work of the business. I decline to have any correspondence with R. myself in *any* way.

This was at the end of November, 1883, while the play was still being revised. Negotiations with Raymond had already begun, though he does not appear to have actually seen the play during that theatrical season, and many and various were the attempts made to place it elsewhere; always with one result—that each actor or manager, in the end, declared it to be strictly a Raymond play. The thing was hanging fire for nearly a year, altogether, while they were waiting on Raymond, who had a profitable play, and was in no hurry for the recrudescence of Sellers. Howells tells how he eventually took the manuscript to

Raymond, whom he found "in a mood of sweet reasonableness" at one of Osgood's luncheons. Raymond said he could not do the play then, but was sure he would like it for the coming season, and in any case would be glad to read it.

In due time Raymond reported favorably on the play, at least so far as the first act was concerned, but he objected to the materialization feature and to Sellers as claimant for the English earldom. He asked that these features be eliminated, or at least much ameliorated; but as these constituted the backbone and purpose of the whole play, Clemens and Howells decided that what was left would be hardly worth while. Raymond finally agreed to try the play as it was in one of the larger towns —Howells thinks in Buffalo. A week later the manuscript came back to Webster, who had general charge of the business negotiations, as indeed he had of all Mark Twain's affairs at this time, and with it a brief line:

DEAR SIR,—I have just finished rereading the play, and am convinced that in its present form it would not prove successful. I return the manuscript by express to your address.

Thanking you for your courtesy, I am,

Yours truly, JOHN T. RAYMOND.

P. S.—If the play is altered and made longer I will be pleased to read it again.

In his former letter Raymond had declared that "Sellers, while a very sanguine man, was not a lunatic, and no one but a lunatic could for a moment imagine that he had done such a work" (meaning the materialization). Clearly Raymond wanted a more serious presentation, something akin to his earlier success, and on the whole we can hardly blame him. But the authors had faith in their performance as it stood, and agreed they would make no change.

Finally a well-known elocutionist, named Burbank, conceived the notion of impersonating Raymond as well as Sellers, making of it a sort of double burlesque, and agreed to take the play on those terms. Burbank came to Hartford and showed what he could do. Howells and Clemens agreed to give him the play, and they hired the old Lyceum Theater for a week, at seven hundred dollars, for its trial presentation. Daniel Frohman promoted it. Clemens and Howells went over the play and made some changes, but they were not as hilarious over it or as full of enthusiasm as they had been in the beginning. Howells put in a night of suffering—long, dark hours of hot and cold waves of fear—and rising next morning from a tossing bed, wrote: "Here's a play which every manager has put out-of-doors and which every actor known to us has refused, and now we go and give it to an elocutioner. We are fools."

Clemens hurried over to Boston to consult with Howells, and in the end they agreed to pay the seven hundred dollars for the theater, take the play off and give Burbank his freedom.[1] But Clemens's faith in it did not immediately die. Howells relinquished all right and title in it, and Clemens started it out with Burbank and a traveling company, doing one-night stands, and kept it going for a week or more at his own expense. It never reached New York.

"And yet," says Howells, "I think now that if it had come it would have been successful. So hard does the faith of the unsuccessful dramatist die."

[1] This was as late as the spring of 1886, at which time Howells's faith in the play was exceedingly shaky. In one letter he wrote: "It is a lunatic that we have created, and while a lunatic in one act might amuse, I'm afraid that in three he would simply bore."

And again:

"As it stands, I believe the thing will fail, and it would be a disgrace to have it succeed."

CXLVIII

CABLE AND HIS GREAT JOKE

MEANWHILE, with the completion of the Sellers play, Clemens had flung himself into dramatic writing once more with a new and more violent impetuosity than ever. Howells had hardly returned to Boston when he wrote:

Now let's write a tragedy.

The inclosed is not fancy, it is *history;* except that the little girl was a passing stranger, and not kin to any of the parties. I read the incident in Carlyle's *Cromwell* a year ago, and made a note in my note-book; stumbled on the note to-day, and wrote up the closing scene of a possible tragedy, to see how it might work.

If we made this colonel a grand fellow, and gave him a wife to suit—hey? It's right in the big historical times—war; Cromwell in big, picturesque power, and all that.

Come, let's do this tragedy, and do it well. Curious, but didn't Florence want a Cromwell? But Cromwell would not be the chief figure here.

It was the closing scene of that pathetic passage in history from which he would later make his story, "The Death Disc." Howells was too tired and too occupied to undertake immediately a new dramatic labor, so Clemens went steaming ahead alone.

My billiard-table is stacked up with books relating to the Sandwich Islands; the walls are upholstered with scraps of paper penciled with notes drawn from them. I have saturated myself with knowledge of that unimaginably beautiful land and that most strange and fascinating people. And I have begun a story. Its hidden motive will illustrate a but-little considered fact in human nature: that the religious folly you are born in you will *die* in, no matter what apparently reasonabler religious folly may seem to have taken its place; meanwhile abolished and obliterated it. I start Bill Ragsdale at eleven years of age, and the heroine at four, in the midst of the ancient idolatrous system, with its picturesque and amazing customs and superstitions, three months before the arrival of the missionaries and the erection of a shallow Christianity upon the ruins of the old paganism.

Then these two will become educated Christians and highly civilized.

And then I will jump fifteen years and do Ragsdale's leper business. When we come to dramatize, we can draw a deal of matter from the story, all ready to our hand.

He made elaborate preparations for the Sandwich Islands story, which he and Howells would dramatize later, and within the space of a few weeks he actually did dramatize *The Prince and the Pauper* and *Tom Sawyer*, and was prodding Webster to find proper actors or managers; stipulating at first severe and arbitrary terms, which were gradually modified, as one after another of the prospective customers found these dramatic wares unsuited to their needs. Mark Twain was one of the most dramatic creatures that ever lived, but he lacked the faculty of stage arrangement of the dramatic idea. It is one of the commonest defects in the literary make-up; also one of the hardest to realize and to explain.

The winter of 1883–84 was a gay one in the Clemens home. Henry Irving was among those entertained, Augustus Saint-Gaudens, Aldrich and his wife, Howells of course, and George W. Cable. Cable had now permanently left the South for the promised land which all authors of the South and West seek eventually, and had in due course made his way to Hartford. Clemens took Cable's fortunes in hand, as he had done with many

AN APOLOGY FROM SAINT-GAUDENS FOR A BROKEN ENGAGEMENT

another, invited him to his home, and undertook to open negotiations with the American Publishing Company, of which Frank Bliss was now the manager, for the improvement of his fortunes.

Cable had been giving readings from his stories and had somewhere picked up the measles. He suddenly came down with the complaint during his visit to Clemens, and his case was a violent one. It required the constant attendance of a trained nurse and one or two members of the household to pull him through.

In the course of time he was convalescent, and when contagion was no longer to be feared guests were invited in for his entertainment. At one of these gatherings, Cable produced a curious book, which he said had been lent to him by Prof. Francis Bacon, of New Haven, as a great rarity. It was a little privately printed pamphlet written by a Southern youth, named S. Watson Wolston, a Yale student of 1845, and was an absurd romance of the hyperflorid, grandiloquent sort, entitled, "Love Triumphant, or the Enemy Conquered." Its heroine's name was Ambulinia, and its flowery, half-meaningless periods and impossible situations delighted Clemens beyond measure. He begged Cable to lend it to him, to read at the Saturday Morning Club, declaring that he certainly must own the book, at whatever cost. Henry C. Robinson, who was present, remembered having seen a copy in his youth, and Twichell thought he recalled such a book on sale in New Haven during his college days. Twichell said nothing as to any purpose in the matter; but somewhat later, being in New Haven, he stepped into the old book-store and found the same proprietor, who remembered very well the book and its author. Twichell rather fearfully asked if by any chance a copy of it might still be obtained.

"Well," was the answer, "I undertook to put my cellar in order the other day, and found about a cord of them down there. I think I can supply you."

Twichell took home six of the books at ten cents each, and on their first spring walk to Talcott's Tower casually mentioned to Clemens the quest for the rare Ambulinia. But Clemens had given up the pursuit. New York dealers had reported no success in the matter. The book was no longer in existence.

"What would you give for a copy?" asked Twichell.

Clemens became excited.

"It isn't a question of price," he said; "that would be for the owner to set if I could find him."

Twichell drew a little package from his pocket.

"Well, Mark," he said, "here are six copies of that book, to begin with. If that isn't enough, I can get you a wagon-load."

It was enough. But it did not deter Clemens in his purpose, which was to immortalize the little book by pointing out its peculiar charms. He did this later, and eventually included the entire story, with comments, in one of his own volumes.

Clemens and Twichell did not always walk that spring. The early form of bicycle, the prehistoric high-wheel, had come into vogue, and they each got one and attempted its conquest. They practised in the early morning hours on Farmington Avenue, which was wide and smooth, and they had an instructor, a young German, who, after a morning or two, regarded Mark Twain helplessly and said:

"Mr. Clemens, it's remarkable—you can fall off of a bicycle more different ways than the man that invented it."

They were curious things, those old high-wheel machines. You were perched away up in the air, with the feeling that you were likely at any moment to strike a pebble or something that would fling you forward with damaging results. Frequently that is what happened. The word "header" seems to have grown out of that early bicycling period. Perhaps Mark Twain invented it. He had enough experience to do it. He always declared afterward that he invented all the new bicycle profanity that has since come into general use. Once he wrote:

> There was a row of low stepping-stones across one end of the street, a measured yard apart. Even after I got so I could steer pretty fairly I was so afraid of those stones that I always hit them. They gave me the worst falls I ever got in that street, except those which I got from dogs. I have seen it stated that no expert is quick enough to run over a dog; that a dog is always able to skip out of his way. I think that that may be true; but I think that the reason he couldn't run over the dog was because he was trying to. I did not try to run over any dog. But I ran over every dog that came along. I think it makes a great deal of difference. If you try to run over the dog he knows how to calculate, but if you are trying to miss him he does not know how to calculate, and is liable to jump the wrong way every time. It was always so in my experience. Even

when I could not hit a wagon I could hit a dog that came to see me practise. They all liked to see me practise, and they all came, for there was very little going on in our neighborhood to entertain a dog.

He conquered, measurably, that old, discouraging thing, and he and Twichell would go on excursions, sometimes as far as Wethersfield or to the tower. It was a pleasant change, at least it was an interesting one; but bicycling on the high wheel was never a popular diversion with Mark Twain, and his enthusiasm in the sport had died before the "safety" came along.

He had his machine sent out to Elmira, but there were too many hills in Chemung County, and after one brief excursion he came in, limping and pushing his wheel, and did not try it again.

To return to Cable. When the 1st of April (1884) approached he concluded it would be a good time to pay off his debt of gratitude for his recent entertainment in the Clemens's home. He went to work at it systematically. He had a "private and confidential" circular letter printed, and he mailed it to one hundred and fifty of Mark Twain's literary friends in Boston, Hartford, Springfield, New York, Brooklyn, Washington, and elsewhere, suggesting that they write to him, so that their letters would reach him simultaneously April 1st, asking for his autograph. No stamps or cards were to be inclosed for reply, and it was requested that "no stranger to Mr. Clemens and no minor" should take part. Mrs. Clemens was let into the secret, so that she would see to it that her husband did not reject his mail or commit it to the flames unopened.

It would seem that every one receiving the invitation must have responded to it, for on the morning of April 1st a stupefying mass of letters was unloaded on Mark Twain's table. He did not know what to make of it, and Mrs. Clemens stood off to watch the results. The first one he opened was from Dean Sage, a friend whom he valued highly. Sage wrote from Brooklyn:

DEAR CLEMENS,—I have recently been asked by a young lady who unfortunately has a mania for autograph-collecting, but otherwise is a charming character, and comely enough to suit your fastidious taste, to secure for her the sign manual of the few distinguished persons fortunate enough to have my acquaintance. In enumerating them to her, after mentioning the names of Geo. Shepard Page, Joe Michell, Capt. Isaiah Ryndus, Mr. Willard, Dan Mace, and J. L. Sullivan, I came to yours. "Oh!" said she, "I have read all his works—*Little Breeches*, *The Heathen Chinee*, and the rest—and think them delightful. Do oblige me by asking him for his autograph, preceded by any little sentiment that may occur to him, provided it is not too short."

Of course I promised, and hope you will oblige me by sending some little thing addressed to Miss Oakes.

We are all pretty well at home just now, though indisposition has been among us for the past fortnight. With regards to Mrs. Clemens and the children, in which my wife joins,

Yours truly, DEAN SAGE.

It amused and rather surprised him, and it fooled him completely; but when he picked up a letter from Brander Matthews, asking, in some absurd fashion, for his signature, and another from Ellen Terry, and from Irving, and from Stedman, and from Warner, and Waring, and H. C. Bunner, and Sarony, and Laurence Hutton, and John Hay, and R. U. Johnson, and Modjeska, the size and quality of the joke began to overawe him. He was delighted, of course; for really it was a fine compliment, in its way, and most of the letters were distinctly amusing. Some of them asked for autographs by the yard, some by the pound. Henry Irving said:

I have just got back from a very late rehearsal—five o'clock—very tired—but there will be no rest till I get your autograph.

Some requested him to sit down and copy a few chapters from *The Innocents Abroad* for them or to send an original manuscript. Others requested that his autograph be attached to a check of interesting size. John Hay suggested that he copy a hymn, a few hundred lines of Young's "Night Thoughts," and an equal amount of Pollak's "Course of Time."

> I want my boy to form a taste for serious and elevated poetry, and it will add considerable commercial value to have them in your handwriting.

Altogether the reading of the letters gave him a delightful day, and his admiration for Cable grew accordingly. Cable, too, was pleased with the success of his joke, though he declared he would never risk such a thing again. A newspaper of the time reports him as saying:

> I never suffered so much agony as for a few days previous to the 1st of April. I was afraid the letters would reach Mark when he was in affliction, in which case all of us would never have ceased trying to make it up to him.
>
> When I visited Mark we used to open our budgets of letters together at breakfast. We used to sing out whenever we struck an autograph-hunter. I think the idea came from that. The first person I spoke to about it was Robert Underwood Johnson, of the *Century*. My most enthusiastic ally was the Rev. Henry Ward Beecher. We never thought it would get into the papers. I never played a practical joke before. I never will again, certainly.

Mark Twain in those days did not encourage the regular autograph-collectors, and seldom paid any attention to their requests for his signature. He changed all this in later years, and kept a supply always on hand to satisfy every request; but in those earlier days he had no patience with collecting fads, and it required a particularly pleasing application to obtain his signature.

CXLIX

MARK TWAIN IN BUSINESS

SAMUEL CLEMENS by this time was definitely engaged in the publishing business. Webster had a complete office with assistants at 658 Broadway, and had acquired a pretty thorough and practical knowledge of subscription publishing. He was a busy, industrious young man, tirelessly energetic, and with a good deal of confidence, by no means unnecessary to commercial success. He placed this mental and physical capital against Mark Twain's inspiration and financial backing, and the combination of Charles L. Webster & Co. seemed likely to be a strong one.

Already, in the spring of 1884, Webster had the new Mark Twain book, *The Adventures of Huckleberry Finn*, well in hand, and was on the watch for promising subscription books by other authors. Clemens, with his usual business vision and eye for results, with a generous disregard of detail, was supervising the larger preliminaries, and fulminating at the petty distractions and difficulties as they came along. Certain plays he was trying to place were enough to keep him pretty thoroughly upset during this period, and proof-reading never added to his happiness. To Howells he wrote:

> My days are given up to cursings, both loud and deep, for I am reading the *Huck Finn* proofs. They don't make a very great many mistakes, but those that do occur are of a nature that make a man swear his teeth loose.

Whereupon Howells promptly wrote him that he would help him out with the *Huck Finn* proofs for the pleasure of reading the story. Clemens, among other things, was trying to place a patent grape-scissors, invented by Howells's father, so that there was, in some degree, an equivalent for the heavy obligation. That it was a heavy one we gather from his fervent acknowledgment:

It took my breath away, and I haven't recovered it yet, entirely—I mean the generosity of your proposal to read the proofs of *Huck Finn.*

Now, if you *mean* it, old man—if you are in *earnest*—proceed, in God's name, and be by me forever blessed. I can't conceive of a rational man deliberately piling such an atrocious job upon himself. But if there be such a man, and you be that man, *pile it on.* The proof-reading of *The Prince and the Pauper* cost me the last rags of my religion.

Clemens decided to have the *Huckleberry Finn* book illustrated after his own ideas. He looked through the various comic papers to see if he could find the work of some new man that appealed to his fancy. In the pages of *Life* he discovered some comic pictures illustrating the possibility of applying electrical hurriers to messenger boys, waiters, etc. The style and the spirit of these things amused him. He instructed Webster to look up the artist, who proved to be a young man, E. W. Kemble by name, later one of our foremost cartoonists. Webster engaged Kemble and put the manuscript in his hands. Through the publication of certain chapters of *Huck Finn* in the *Century Magazine*, Kemble was brought to the notice of its editors, who wrote Clemens that they were profoundly indebted to him for unearthing "such a gem of an illustrator."

Clemens, encouraged and full of enthusiasm, now endeavored to interest himself in the practical details of manufacture, but his stock of patience was light and the details were many. His early business period resembles, in some of its features, his mining experience in Esmeralda, his letters to Webster being not unlike those to Orion in that former day. They are much oftener gentle, considerate, even apologetic, but they are occasionally terse, arbitrary, and profane. It required effort for him to be entirely calm in his business correspondence. A criticism of one of Webster's assistants will serve as an example of his less quiet method:

Charley, your proof-reader, is an idiot; and not only an idiot, but blind; and not only blind, but partly dead.

Of course, one must regard many of Mark Twain's business aspects humorously. To consider them otherwise is to place him in a false light altogether. He wore himself out with his anxieties and irritations; but that even he, in the midst of his furies, saw the humor of it all is sufficiently evidenced by the form of his savage phrasing. There were few things that did not amuse him, and certainly nothing amused more, or oftener, than himself.

It is proper to add a detail in evidence of a business soundness which he sometimes manifested. He had observed the methods of Bliss and Osgood, and had drawn his conclusions. In the beginning of the *Huck Finn* canvass he wrote Webster:

Keep it diligently in mind that we don't issue till we have made a *big sale*.

Get at your canvassing early and drive it with all your might, with an intent and purpose of issuing on the 10th or 15th of next December (the best time in the year to tumble a big pile into the trade); but if we haven't 40,000 subscriptions we simply postpone publication till we've got them. It is a plain, simple policy, and would have saved both of my last books if it had been followed. [That is to say, *The Prince and the Pauper* and the Mississippi book, neither of which had sold up to his expectations on the initial canvass.]

CL

FARM PICTURES

GERHARDT returned from Paris that summer, after three years of study, a qualified sculptor. He was prepared to take commissions, and came to Elmira to model a bust of his benefactor. The work was finished after four or five weeks of hard effort and pronounced admirable; but Gerhardt, attempting to make a cast one morning, ruined it completely. The family gathered round the disaster, which to them seemed final, but the sculptor went immediately to work, and in an amazingly brief time executed a new bust even better than the first, an excellent piece of modeling and a fine likeness. It was decided that a cut of it should be used as a frontispiece for the new book, *The Adventures of Huckleberry Finn.*

Clemens was at this time giving the final readings to the *Huck Finn* pages, a labor in which Mrs. Clemens and the children materially assisted. In the childish biography which Susy began of her father, a year later, she says:

> Ever since papa and mama were married papa has written his books and then taken them to mama in manuscript, and she has expergated[1] them. Papa read *Huckleberry Finn* to us in manuscript,[2] just before it came out, and then he would leave parts of it with mama to expergate, while he went off to the study to work, and sometimes Clara and I would be sitting with mama while she was looking the manuscript over, and I remember so

[1] Susy's spelling is preserved. [2] Probably meaning proof.

well, with what pangs of regret we used to see her turn down the leaves of the pages, which meant that some delightfully terrible part must be scratched out. And I remember one part perticularly which was perfectly fascinating it was so terrible, that Clara and I used to delight in and oh, with what despair we saw mama turn down the leaf on which it was written, we thought the book would almost be ruined without it. But we gradually came to think as mama did.

Commenting on this phase of *Huck's* evolution Mark Twain has since written:

I remember the special case mentioned by Susy, and can see the group yet—two-thirds of it pleading for the life of the culprit sentence that was so fascinatingly dreadful, and the other third of it patiently explaining why the court could not grant the prayer of the pleaders; but I do not remember what the condemned phrase was. It had much company, and they all went to the gallows; but it is possible that that especially dreadful one which gave those little people so much delight was cunningly devised and put into the book for just that function, and not with any hope or expectation that it would get by the "expergator" alive. It is possible, for I had that custom.

Little Jean was probably too youthful yet to take part in that literary arbitration. She was four, and had more interest in cows. In some memoranda which her father kept of that period—the "Children's Book"—he says:

She goes out to the barn with one of us every evening toward six o'clock, to look at the cows—which she adores—no weaker word can express her feeling for them. She sits rapt and contented while David milks the three, making a remark now and then—always about the cows. The time passes slowly and drearily for her attendant, but not for her. She could stand a week of it. When the milking is finished, and "Blanche," "Jean," and "the cross cow" are turned into the adjoining little cow-lot, we have to set Jean on a shed in that lot, and stay by her half an hour, till Eliza, the German nurse, comes to take her to bed. The cows merely stand there, and do nothing; yet the mere sight of them is all-sufficient for Jean. She requires nothing more. The other evening, after contemplating them a long time, as they stood in the muddy muck chewing the cud, she said, with deep and reverent appreciation, "Ain't this a sweet little garden?"

Yesterday evening our cows (after being inspected and worshiped by Jean from the shed for an hour) wandered off down into the pasture and left her bereft. I thought I was going to get back home, now, but that was an error. Jean knew of some more cows in a field somewhere, and took my hand and led me thitherward. When we turned the corner and took the right-hand road, I saw that we should presently be out of range of call and sight; so I began to argue against continuing the expedition, and Jean began to argue in favor of it, she using English for light skirmishing and German for "business." I kept up my end with vigor, and demolished her arguments in detail, one after the other, till I judged I had her about cornered. She hesitated a moment, then answered up, sharply:

"Wir werden nichts mehr darüber sprechen!" (We won't talk any more about it.)

It nearly took my breath away, though I thought I might possibly have misunderstood. I said:

"Why, you little rascal! Was hast du gesagt?"

But she said the same words over again, and in the same decided way. I suppose I ought to have been outraged, but I wasn't; I was charmed.

His own note-books of that summer are as full as usual, but there are fewer literary ideas and more philosophies. There was an excitement, just then, about the trichina germ in pork, and one of his memoranda says:

I think we are only the microscopic trichina concealed in the blood of some vast creature's veins, and that it is that vast creature whom God concerns himself about and not us.

And there is another which says:

People, in trying to justify eternity, say we can put it in by learning all the knowledge acquired by the inhabitants of the

Susy Clara Jean

MRS. CLEMENS AND THE CHILDREN, HARTFORD, CONN., 1884

myriads of stars. We sha'n't need that. We could use up two eternities in learning all that is to be learned about our own world, and the thousands of nations that have risen, and flourished, and vanished from it. Mathematics alone would occupy me eight million years.

He records an incident which he related more fully in a letter to Howells:

Before I forget it I must tell you that Mrs. Clemens has said a bright thing. A drop-letter came to me asking me to lecture here for a church debt. I began to rage over the exceedingly cool wording of the request, when Mrs. Clemens said: "I think I know that church, and, if so, this preacher is a colored man; he doesn't know how to write a polished letter. How should he?"

My manner changed so suddenly and so radically that Mrs. C. said: "I will give you a motto, and it will be useful to you if you will adopt it: 'Consider every man colored till he is proved white.'"

It is dern good, I think.

One of the note-books contains these entries:

Talking last night about home matters, I said, "I wish I had said to George when we were leaving home, 'Now, George, I wish you would take advantage of these three or four months' idle time while I am away—'"

"To learn to let my matches alone," interrupted Livy. The very words I was going to use. Yet George had not been mentioned before, nor his peculiarities.

Several years ago I said:

"Suppose I should live to be ninety-two, and just as I was dying a messenger should enter and say—"

"You are become Earl of Durham," interrupted Livy. The very words I was going to utter. Yet there had not been a word said about the earl, or any other person, nor had there been any conversation calculated to suggest any such subject.

CLI

MARK TWAIN MUGWUMPS

THE Republican Presidential nomination of James G. Blaine resulted in a political revolt such as the nation had not known. Blaine was immensely popular, but he had many enemies in his own party. There were strong suspicions of his being connected with doubtful financiering—enterprises, more or less sensitive to official influence, and while these scandals had become quieted a very large portion of the Republican constituency refused to believe them unjustified. What might be termed the intellectual element of Republicanism was against Blaine: George William Curtis, Charles Dudley Warner, James Russell Lowell, Henry Ward Beecher, Thomas Nast, the firm of Harper & Brothers, Joseph W. Hawley, Joseph Twichell, Mark Twain—in fact the majority of thinking men who held principle above party in their choice.

On the day of the Chicago nomination, Henry C. Robinson, Charles E. Perkins, Edward M. Bunce, F. G. Whitmore, and Samuel C. Dunham were collected with Mark Twain in his billiard-room, taking turns at the game and discussing the political situation, with George, the colored butler, at the telephone down-stairs to report the returns as they came in. As fast as the ballot was received at the political headquarters down-town, it was telephoned up to the house and George reported it through the speaking-tube.

The opposition to Blaine in the convention was so

strong that no one of the assembled players seriously expected his nomination. What was their amazement, then, when about mid-afternoon George suddenly announced through the speaking-tube that Blaine was the nominee. The butts of the billiard cues came down on the floor with a bump, and for a moment the players were speechless. Then Henry Robinson said:

"It's hard luck to have to vote for that man."

Clemens looked at him under his heavy brows.

"But—we don't—*have* to vote for him," he said.

"Do you mean to say that you're *not* going to vote for him?"

"Yes, that is what I mean to say. I am not going to vote for him."

There was a general protest. Most of those assembled declared that when a party's representatives chose a man one must stand by him. They might choose unwisely, but the party support must be maintained. Clemens said:

"No party holds the privilege of dictating to me how I shall vote. If loyalty to party is a form of patriotism, I am no patriot. If there is any valuable difference between a monarchist and an American, it lies in the theory that the American can decide for himself what is patriotic and what isn't. I claim that difference. I am the only person in the sixty millions that is privileged to dictate my patriotism."

There was a good deal of talk back and forth, and, in the end, most of those there present remained loyal to Blaine. General Hawley and his paper stood by Blaine. Warner withdrew from his editorship of the *Courant* and remained neutral. Twichell stood with Clemens and came near losing his pulpit by it. Open letters were published in the newspapers about him. It was a campaign when politics divided neighbors, families, and congregations. If we except the Civil War period, there never had been a more rancorous political warfare than that waged between the parties of James G. Blaine and Grover Cleveland in 1884.

That Howells remained true to Blaine was a grief to Clemens. He had gone to the farm with Howells on his political conscience and had written fervent and imploring letters on the subject. As late as September 17th, he said:

> Somehow I can't seem to rest quiet under the idea of your voting for Blaine. I believe you said something about the country and the party. Certainly allegiance to these is well, but certainly a man's first duty is to his own conscience and honor; the party and country come second to that, and never first. I don't ask you to vote at all. I only urge you not to soil yourself by voting for Blaine. . . . Don't be offended; I mean no offense. I am not concerned about the rest of the nation, but—well, good-by. Yours ever, MARK.

Beyond his prayerful letters to Howells, Clemens did not greatly concern himself with politics on the farm, but, returning to Hartford, he went vigorously into the campaign, presided, as usual, at mass-meetings, and made political speeches which invited the laughter of both parties, and were universally quoted and printed without regard to the paper's convictions.

It was during one such speech as this that, in the course of his remarks, a band outside came marching by playing patriotic music so loudly as to drown his voice. He waited till the band got by, but by the time he was well under way again another band passed, and once more he was obliged to wait till the music died away in the distance. Then he said, quite serenely:

"You will find my speech, without the music, in the morning paper."

In introducing Carl Schurz at a great mugwump mass-meeting at Hartford, October 20, 1884, he remarked that he [Clemens] was the only legitimately elected officer, and was expected to read a long list of vice-presidents; but he had forgotten all about it, and he would ask all the gentlemen there, of whatever political complexion, to do him a great favor by acting as vice-presidents. Then he said:

As far as my own political change of heart is concerned, I have not been convinced by any Democratic means. The opinion I hold of Mr. Blaine is due to the comments of the Republican press before the nomination. Not that they have said bitter or scandalous things, because Republican papers are above that, but the things they said did not seem to be complimentary, and seemed to me to imply editorial disapproval of Mr. Blaine and the belief that he was not qualified to be President of the United States.

It is just a little indelicate for me to be here on this occasion before an assemblage of voters, for the reason that the ablest newspaper in Colorado—the ablest newspaper in the world—has recently nominated me for President. It is hardly fit for me to preside at a discussion of the brother candidate, but the best among us will do the most repulsive things the moment we are smitten with a Presidential madness. If I had realized that this canvass was to turn on the candidate's private character I would have started that Colorado paper sooner. I know the crimes that can be imputed and proved against me can be told on the fingers of your hands. This cannot be said of any other Presidential candidate in the field.

Inasmuch as the Blaine-Cleveland campaign was essentially a campaign of scurrility, this touch was loudly applauded.

Mark Twain voted for Grover Cleveland, though up to the very eve of election he was ready to support a Republican nominee in whom he had faith, preferably Edmunds, and he tried to inaugurate a movement by which Edmunds might be nominated as a surprise candidate and sweep the country.

It was probably Dr. Burchard's ill-advised utterance

concerning the three alleged R's of Democracy, "Rum, Romanism, and Rebellion," that defeated Blaine, and by some strange, occult means Mark Twain's butler George got wind of this damning speech before it became news on the streets of Hartford. George had gone with his party, and had a considerable sum of money wagered on Blaine's election; but he knew it was likely to be very close, and he had an instant and deep conviction that these three fatal words and Blaine's failure to repudiate them meant the candidate's downfall. He immediately abandoned everything in the shape of household duties, and within the briefest possible time had changed enough money to make him safe, and leave him a good margin of winnings besides, in the event of Blaine's defeat. This was evening. A very little later the news of Blaine's blunder, announced from the opera-house stage, was like the explosion of a bomb. But it was no news to George, who went home rejoicing with his enemies.

CLII

PLATFORMING WITH CABLE

THE drain of many investments and the establishment of a publishing house had told heavily on Clemens's finances. It became desirable to earn a large sum of money with as much expedition as possible. Authors' readings had become popular, and Clemens had read in Philadelphia and Boston with satisfactory results. He now conceived the idea of a grand tour of authors as a commercial enterprise. He proposed to Aldrich, Howells, and Cable that he charter a private car for the purpose, and that with their own housekeeping arrangements, cooking, etc., they could go swinging around the circuit, reaping a golden harvest. He offered to be general manager of the expedition, the impresario as it were, and agreed to guarantee the others not less than seventy-five dollars a day apiece as their net return from the "circus," as he called it.

Howells and Aldrich liked well enough to consider it as an amusing prospect, but only Cable was willing to realize it. He had been scouring the country on his own account, and he was willing enough to join forces with Mark Twain.

Clemens detested platforming, but the idea of reading from his books or manuscript for some reason seemed less objectionable, and, as already stated, the need of much money had become important.

He arranged with J. B. Pond for the business side of

the expedition, though in reality he was its proprietor. The private-car idea was given up, but he employed Cable at a salary of four hundred and fifty dollars a week and expenses, and he paid Pond a commission. Perhaps, without going any further, we may say that the tour was a financial success, and yielded a large return of the needed funds.

Clemens and Cable had a pleasant enough time, and had it not been for the absence from home and the disagreeableness of railway travel, there would have been little to regret. They were a curiously associated pair. Cable was orthodox in his religion, devoted to Sunday-school, Bible reading, and church affairs in general. Clemens—well, Clemens was different. On the first evening of their tour, when the latter was comfortably settled in bed with an entertaining book, Cable appeared with his Bible, and proceeded to read a chapter aloud. Clemens made no comment, and this went on for an evening or two more. Then he said:

"See here, Cable, we'll have to cut this part of the program out. You can read the Bible as much as you please so long as you don't read it to me."

Cable retired courteously. He had a keen sense of humor, and most things that Mark Twain did, whether he approved or not, amused him. Cable did not smoke, but he seemed always to prefer the smoking compartment when they traveled, to the more respectable portions of the car. One day Clemens said to him:

"Cable, why do you sit in here? You don't smoke, and you know I always smoke, and sometimes swear."

Cable said, "I know, Mark, I don't do these things, but I can't help admiring the way you do them."

When Sunday came it was Mark Twain's great happiness to stay in bed all day, resting after his week of labor; but Cable would rise, bright and chipper, dress himself in neat and suitable attire, and visit the various churches and Sunday-schools in town, usually making a brief address at each, being always invited to do so.

It seems worth while to include one of the Clemens-Cable programs here—a most satisfactory one. They varied it on occasion, and when they were two nights in a place changed it completely, but the program here given was the one they were likely to use after they had proved its worth:

PROGRAM

Richling's visit to Kate Riley

GEO. W. CABLE

King Sollermun

MARK TWAIN

(*a*) Kate Riley and Ristofolo
(*b*) Narcisse in mourning for "Lady Byron"
(*c*) Mary's Night Ride

GEO. W. CABLE

(*a*) Tragic Tale of the Fishwife
(*b*) A Trying Situation
(*c*) A Ghost Story

MARK TWAIN

At a Mark Twain memorial meeting (November 30, 1910), where the few who were left of his old companions told over quaint and tender memories, George Cable recalled their reading days together and told of Mark Twain's conscientious effort to do his best, to be worthy of himself, regardless of all other concerns. He told how when they had been traveling for a while Clemens seemed to realize that he was only giving the audience nonsense; making them laugh at trivialities which they would forget before they had left the entertainment hall. Cable said that up to that time he had supposed Clemens's chief thought was the entertainment of the moment, and that if the audience laughed he was satisfied. He told how he had sat in the wings, waiting his turn, and heard the tides of laughter gather and roll forward and break against the footlights, time and time again, and how he had believed his colleague to be glorying in that triumph. What was his surprise, then, on the way to the hotel in the carriage, when Clemens groaned and seemed writhing in spirit and said:

"Oh, Cable, I am demeaning myself. I am allowing myself to be a mere buffoon. It's ghastly. I can't endure it any longer."

Cable added that all that night and the next day Mark Twain devoted himself to the study and rehearsal of selections which were justified not only as humor, but as literature and art.

A good many interesting and amusing things would happen on such a tour. Many of these are entirely forgotten, of course, but of others certain memoranda have been preserved. Grover Cleveland had been elected when they set out on their travels, but was still holding his position in Albany as Governor of New York. When they reached Albany Cable and Clemens decided to call on him. They drove to the Capitol and were shown into the Governor's private office. Cleveland made them welcome, and, after greetings, said to Clemens:

"Mr. Clemens, I was a fellow-citizen of yours in Buffalo a good many months some years ago, but you never called on me then. How do you explain this?"

Clemens said: "Oh, that is very simple to answer, your Excellency. In Buffalo you were a sheriff. I kept away from the sheriff as much as possible, but you're Governor now, and on the way to the Presidency. It's worth while coming to see you."

Clemens meantime had been resting, half sitting, on the corner of the Executive desk. He leaned back a little, and suddenly about a dozen young men opened various doors, filed in and stood at attention, as if waiting for orders.

No one spoke for a moment; then the Governor said to this collection of attendants:

"You are dismissed, young gentlemen. Your services are not required. Mr. Clemens is sitting on the bells."

In Buffalo, when Clemens appeared on the stage, he leisurely considered the audience for a moment; then he said:

"I miss a good many faces. They have gone—gone to the tomb, to the gallows, or to the White House. All of us are entitled to at least one of these distinctions, and it behooves us to be wise and prepare for all."

On Thanksgiving Eve the readers were in Morristown, New Jersey, where they were entertained by Thomas Nast. The cartoonist prepared a quiet supper for them and they remained overnight in the Nast home. They were to leave next morning by an early train, and Mrs. Nast had agreed to see that they were up in due season. When she woke next morning there seemed a strange silence in the house and she grew suspicious. Going to the servants' room, she found them sleeping soundly. The alarm-clock in the back hall had stopped at about the hour the guests retired. The studio clock was also found stopped; in fact, every timepiece on the premises had retired from business. Clemens had found that the clocks interfered with his getting to sleep, and he had quieted them regardless of early trains and reading engagements. On being accused of duplicity he said:

"Well, those clocks were all overworked, anyway. They will feel much better for a night's rest."

A few days later Nast sent him a caricature drawing—a picture which showed Mark Twain getting rid of the offending clocks.

At Christmas-time they took a fortnight's holiday and Clemens went home to Hartford. A surprise was awaiting him there. Mrs. Clemens had made an adaptation of

MARK TWAIN AND THE CLOCKS. BY TH: NAST

The Prince and the Pauper play, and the children of the neighborhood had prepared a presentation of it for his special delectation. He knew, on his arrival home, that something mysterious was in progress, for certain rooms were forbidden him; but he had no inkling of their plan until just before the performance—when he was led across the grounds to George Warner's home, into the large room there where it was to be given, and placed in a seat directly in front of the stage.

Gerhardt had painted the drop-curtain, and assisted in the general construction of scenery and effects. The result was really imposing; but presently, when the curtain rose and the guest of honor realized what it was all about, and what they had undertaken for his pleasure, he was deeply moved and supremely gratified.

There was but one hitch in the performance. There is a place where the Prince says, "Fathers be alike, mayhap; mine hath not a doll's temper."

This was Susy's part, and as she said it the audience did not fail to remember its literal appropriateness. There was a moment's silence, then a titter, followed by a roar of laughter, in which everybody but the little actors joined. They did not see the humor and were disturbed and grieved. Curiously enough, Mrs Clemens herself, in arranging and casting the play, had not considered the possibility of this effect. The parts were all daintily played. The children wore their assumed personalities as if native to them. Daisy Warner played the part of Tom Canty, Clara Clemens was Lady Jane Grey.

It was only the beginning of *The Prince and the Pauper* productions. The play was repeated, Clemens assisting, adding to the parts, and himself playing the rôle of Miles Hendon. In her childish biography Susy says:

Papa had only three days to learn the part in, but still we were all sure that he could do it. The scene that he acted in was the scene between Miles Hendon and the Prince, the "Prithee, pour the water" scene. I was the Prince and papa and I rehearsed together two or three times a day for the three days before the appointed evening. Papa acted his part beautifully, and he added to the scene, making it a good deal longer. He was inexpressibly funny, with his great slouch hat and gait—oh such a gait! Papa made the Miles Hendon scene a splendid success and every one was delighted with the scene, and papa too. We had great fun with our "Prince and Pauper," and I think we none of us shall forget how immensely funny papa was in it. He certainly could have been an actor as well as an author.

The holidays over, Cable and Clemens were off on the circuit again. At Rochester an incident happened which led to the writing of one of Mark Twain's important books, *A Connecticut Yankee at King Arthur's Court.* Clemens and Cable had wandered into a book-store for the purpose of finding something to read. Pulling over some volumes on one of the tables, Clemens happened to pick up a little green, cloth-bound book, and after looking at the title turned the pages rather curiously and with increasing interest.

"Cable," he said, "do you know anything about this book, the Arthurian legends of Sir Thomas Malory, *Morte Arthure?*"

Cable answered: "Mark, that is one of the most beautiful books in the world. Let me buy it for you. You will love it more than any book you ever read."

So Clemens came to know the old chronicler's version of the rare Round Table legends, and from that first acquaintance with them to the last days of his life seldom let the book go far from him. He read and reread those quaint, stately tales and reverenced their beauty, while fairly reveling in the absurdities of that ancient day. Sir Ector's lament he regarded as one of the most simply beautiful pieces of writing in the English tongue, and some of the combats and quests as the most ridiculous absurdities in romance. Presently he conceived the idea of linking that day, with its customs, costumes, and abuses, with the progress of the present, or carrying back into that age of magicians and armor and superstition and cruelties a brisk American of progressive ideas who would institute reforms. His note-book began to be filled with memoranda of situations and possibilities for the tale he had in mind. These were vague, unformed fancies as yet, and it would be a long time before the story would become a fact. This was the first entry:

> Dream of being a knight-errant in armor in the Middle Ages. Have the notions and habits, though, of the present day mixed with the necessities of that. No pockets in the armor. No way to manage certain requirements of nature. Can't scratch. Cold in the head and can't blow. Can't get a handkerchief; can't use iron sleeve; iron gets red-hot in the sun; leaks in the rain; gets white with frost and freezes me solid in winter; makes disagreeable clatter when I enter church. Can't dress or undress myself. Always getting struck by lightning. Fall down and can't get up.

Twenty-one years later, discussing the genesis of the story, he said:

"As I read those quaint and curious old legends I suppose I naturally contrasted those days with ours, and it made me curious to fancy what might be the picturesque result if we could dump the nineteenth century down into the sixth century and observe the consequences."

The reading tour continued during the first two months of the new year and carried them as far west as Chicago. They read in Hannibal and Keokuk, and Clemens spent a day in the latter place with his mother, now living with Orion, brisk and active for her years and with her old-time force of character. Mark Twain, arranging for her Keokuk residence, had written:

Ma wants to board with you, and pay her board. She will pay you $20 a month (she wouldn't pay a cent more in heaven; she is obstinate on this point), and as long as she remains with you and is content I will add $25 a month to the sum Perkins already sends you.

Jane Clemens attended the Keokuk reading, and later, at home, when her children asked her if she could still dance, she rose, and at eighty-one tripped as lightly as a girl. It was the last time that Mark Twain ever saw his mother in the health and vigor which had been always so much a part of her personality.

Clemens saw another relative on that trip; in St. Louis, James Lampton, the original of Colonel Sellers, called.

He was become old and white-headed, but he entered to me in the same old breezy way of his earlier life, and he was all there, yet—not a detail wanting: the happy light in his eye, the abounding hope in his heart, the persuasive tongue, the miracle-breeding imagination—they were all there; and before I could turn around he was polishing up his Aladdin's lamp and flashing the secret riches of the world before me. I said to myself: "I did not overdraw him by a shade, I set him down as he was; and he is the same man to-day. Cable will recognize him."

Clemens opened the door into Cable's room and allowed the golden dream-talk to float in. It was of a "small venture" which the caller had undertaken through his son.

"Only a little thing—a mere trifle—a bagatelle. I suppose there's a couple of millions in it, possibly three, but not more, I think; still, for a boy, you know—"

It was the same old Cousin Jim. Later, when he had royally accepted some tickets for the reading and bowed his exit, Cable put his head in at the door.

"That was Colonel Sellers," he said.

CLIII

HUCK FINN COMES INTO HIS OWN

IN the December *Century* (1884) appeared a chapter from *The Adventures of Huckleberry Finn*, "The Grangerford-Shepherdson Feud," a piece of writing which Edmund Clarence Stedman, Brander Matthews, and others promptly ranked as among Mark Twain's very best; when this was followed, in the January number, by "King Sollermun," a chapter which in its way delighted quite as many readers, the success of the new book was accounted certain.[1]

The Adventures of Huckleberry Finn was officially published in England and America in December, 1884, but the book was not in the canvassers' hands for delivery until February. By this time the orders were approximately for forty thousand copies, a number which had increased to fifty thousand a few weeks later. Webster's first publication venture was in the nature of a triumph. Clemens wrote to him March 16th:

"Your news is splendid. *Huck* certainly is a success."

He felt that he had demonstrated his capacity as a general director and Webster had proved his efficiency as an executive. He had no further need of an outside publisher.

The story of *Huck Finn* will probably stand as the best

[1] Stedman, writing to Clemens of this instalment, said: "To my mind it is not only the most finished and condensed thing you have done, but as dramatic and powerful an episode as I know in modern literature."

of Mark Twain's purely fictional writings. A sequel to *Tom Sawyer*, it is greater than its predecessor; greater artistically, though perhaps with less immediate interest for the juvenile reader. In fact, the books are so different that they are not to be compared—wherein lies the success of the later one. Sequels are dangerous things when the story is continuous, but in *Huckleberry Finn* the story is a new one, wholly different in environment, atmosphere, purpose, character, everything. The tale of Huck and Nigger Jim drifting down the mighty river on a raft, cross-secting the various primitive aspects of human existence, constitutes one of the most impressive examples of picaresque fiction in any language. It has been ranked greater than *Gil Blas*, greater even than *Don Quixote;* certainly it is more convincing, more human, than either of these tales. Robert Louis Stevenson once wrote, "It is a book I have read four times, and am quite ready to begin again to-morrow."

It is by no means a flawless book, though its defects are trivial enough. The illusion of Huck as narrator fails the least bit here and there; the "four dialects" are not always maintained; the occasional touch of broad burlesque detracts from the tale's reality. We are inclined to resent this. We never wish to feel that Huck is anything *but* a real character. We want him always the Huck who was willing to go to hell if necessary, rather than sacrifice Nigger Jim; the Huck who watched the river through long nights, and, without caring to explain why, felt his soul go out to the sunrise.

Two or three days and nights went by; I reckon I might say they swum by, they slid along so quiet and smooth and lovely. Here is the way we put in the time. It was a monstrous big river down there—sometimes a mile and a half wide; we run nights and laid up and hid daytimes; soon as the night was most gone we stopped navigating and tied up—nearly always in the dead water under a towhead; and then cut young cottonwoods and willows and hid the raft with them. Then we set out the lines. Next we slid into the river and had a swim, so as to freshen up and cool off; then we set down on the sandy bottom where the water was about knee deep, and watched the daylight come. Not a sound anywheres—perfectly still—just like the whole world was asleep, only sometimes the bullfrogs a-cluttering, maybe. The first thing to see, *looking* away over the water, was a kind of dull line—that was the woods on t'other side, you couldn't make nothing else out; then a pale place in the sky; then more paleness, spreading around; then the river softened up, away off, and warn't black anymore, but gray; you could see little dark spots drifting along, ever so far away—trading scows, and such things; and long black streaks—rafts; sometimes you could hear a sweep screaking; or jumbled up voices, it was so still, and sounds come so far; and by-and-by you could see a streak on the water which you know by the look of the streak that there's a snag there in a swift current which breaks on it and makes that streak look that way; and you see the mist curl up off the water, and the east reddens up, and the river, and you make out a log-cabin in the edge of the woods, away on the bank on t'other side of the river, being a woodyard, likely, and piled by them cheats so you can throw a dog through it anywheres; then the nice breeze springs up, and comes fanning you over there, so cool and fresh, and sweet to smell, on account of the woods and the flowers. . . . And next you've got the full day, and everything smiling in the sun, and the song-birds just going it!

This is the Huck we want, and this is the Huck we usually have, and that the world has long been thankful for.

Take the story as a whole, it is a succession of startling and unique pictures. The cabin in the swamp which Huck and his father used together in their weird, ghastly relationship; the night adventure with Jim on the wrecked steamboat; Huck's night among the towheads; the Grangerford-Shepherdson battle; the killing of Boggs—to name a few of the many vivid presentations—these are of no time or literary fashion and will never lose their flavor nor their freshness so long as humanity itself does not change. The terse, unadorned Grangerford-Shepherdson episode—built out of the Darnell-Watson feuds[1]—is simply classic in its vivid casualness, and the same may be said of almost every incident on that long river-drift; but this is the strength, the very essence of picaresque narrative. It is the way things happen in reality; and the quiet, unexcited frame of mind in which Huck is prompted to set them down would seem to be the last word in literary art. To Huck, apparently, the killing of Boggs and Colonel Sherburn's defiance of the mob are of about the same historical importance as any other incidents of the day's travel. When Colonel Sherburn threw his shotgun across his arm and bade the crowd disperse Huck says:

> The crowd washed back sudden, and then broke all apart and went tearing off every which way, and Buck Harkness he heeled it after them, looking tolerable cheap. I could a staid if I'd a wanted to, but I didn't want to.
>
> I went to the circus, and loafed around the back side till the watchman went by, and then dived in under the tent.

That is all. No reflections, no hysterics; a murder and a mob dispersed, all without a single moral comment. And when the Shepherdsons had got done killing the Grangerfords, and Huck had tugged the two bodies ashore and covered Buck Grangerford's face with a handkerchief, crying a little because Buck had been good to him, he spent no time in sentimental reflection or sermonizing, but promptly hunted up Jim and the raft and sat down to a meal of corn-dodgers, buttermilk, pork and cabbage, and greens:

> There ain't nothing in the world so good, when it is cooked right; and while I eat my supper we talked, and had a good

[1] See *Life on the Mississippi*, chap. xxvi. Mark Twain himself, as a cub pilot, came near witnessing the battle he describes.

time. I was powerful glad to get away from the feuds, and so was Jim to get away from the swamp. We said there warn't no home like a raft, after all. Other places do seem so cramped up and smothery, but a raft don't; you feel mighty free and easy and comfortable on a raft.

It was Huck Finn's morality that caused the book to be excluded from the Concord Library, and from other libraries here and there at a later day. The orthodox mental attitude of certain directors of juvenile literature could not condone Huck's looseness in the matter of statement and property rights, and in spite of New England traditions Massachusetts librarians did not take any too kindly to his uttered principle that, after thinking it over and taking due thought on the deadly sin of abolition, he had decided that he'd go to hell rather than give Jim over to slavery. Poor vagrant Ben Blankenship, hiding his runaway negro in an Illinois swamp, could not dream that his humanity would one day supply the moral episode of an immortal book.

Able critics have declared that the psychology of Huck Finn is the book's large feature: Huck's moral point of view—the struggle between his heart and his conscience concerning the sin of Jim's concealment, and his final decision of self-sacrifice. Time may show that as an epic of the river, the picture of a vanished day, it will rank even greater. The problems of conscience we have always with us, but periods once passed are gone forever. Certainly Huck's loyalty to that lovely soul Nigger Jim was beautiful, though after all it may not have been so hard for Huck, who could be loyal to anything. Huck was loyal to his father, loyal to Tom Sawyer of course, loyal even to those two river tramps and frauds, the King and the Duke, for whom he lied prodigiously, only weakening when a new and lovelier loyalty came into view—loyalty to Mary Wilks.

The King and the Duke, by the way, are not elsewhere

matched in fiction. The Duke was patterned after a journeyman-printer Clemens had known in Virginia City, but the King was created out of refuse from the whole human family—"all tears and flapdoodle," the very ultimate of disrepute and hypocrisy—so perfect a specimen that one must admire, almost love, him. "Hain't we all the fools in town on our side? and ain't that a big enough majority in any town?" he asks in a critical moment—a remark which stamps him as a philosopher of classic rank. We are full of pity at last when this pair of rapscallions ride out of the history on a rail, and feel some of Huck's inclusive loyalty and all the sorrowful truth of his comment: "Human beings *can* be awful cruel to one another."

The "poor old king" Huck calls him, and confesses how he felt "ornery and humble and to blame, somehow," for the old scamp's misfortunes. "A person's conscience ain't got no sense," he says, and Huck is never more real to us, or more lovable, than in that moment. Huck is what he is because, being made so, he cannot well be otherwise. He is a boy throughout—such a boy as Mark Twain had known and in some degree had been. One may pettily pick a flaw here and there in the tale's construction if so minded, but the moral character of Huck himself is not open to criticism. And indeed any criticism of this the greatest of Mark Twain's tales of modern life would be as the mere scratching of the granite of an imperishable structure. *Huck Finn* is a monument that no puny pecking will destroy. It is built of indestructible blocks of human nature; and if the blocks do not always fit, and the ornaments do not always agree, we need not fear. Time will blur the incongruities and moss over the mistakes. The edifice will grow more beautiful with the years.

CLIV

THE MEMOIRS OF GENERAL GRANT

THE success of *Huck Finn*, though sufficiently important in itself, prepared the way for a publishing venture by the side of which it dwindled to small proportions. One night (it was early in November, 1884), when Cable and Clemens had finished a reading at Chickering Hall, Clemens, coming out into the wet blackness, happened to hear Richard Watson Gilder's voice say to some unseen companion:

"Do you know General Grant has actually determined to write his memoirs and publish them. He has said so to-day, in so many words."

Of course Clemens was immediately interested. It was the thing he had proposed to Grant some three years previously, during his call that day with Howells concerning the Toronto consulship.

With Mrs. Clemens, he promptly overtook Gilder and accompanied him to his house, where they discussed the matter in its various particulars. Gilder said that the Century Editors had endeavored to get Grant to contribute to their war series, but that not until his financial disaster, as a member of the firm of Grant & Ward, had he been willing to consider the matter. He said that Grant now welcomed the idea of contributing three papers to the series, and that the promised payment of five hundred dollars each for these articles had gladdened his heart and relieved him of immediate anxiety.[1]

[1] Somewhat later the Century Company, voluntarily, added liberally to this sum.

Gilder added that General Grant seemed now determined to continue his work until he had completed a book, though this at present was only a prospect.

Clemens was in the habit of calling on Grant, now and then, to smoke a cigar with him, and he dropped in next morning to find out just how far the book idea had developed, and what were the plans of publication. He found the General and his son, Colonel Fred Grant, discussing some memoranda, which turned out to be a proposition from the Century Company for the book publication of his memoirs. Clemens asked to be allowed to look over the proposed terms, and when he had done so he said:

"General, it is clear that the Century people do not realize the importance—the commercial magnitude of your book. It is not strange that this is true, for they are comparatively new publishers and have had little or no experience with books of this class. The terms they propose indicate that they expect to sell five, possibly ten thousand copies. A book from your hand, telling the story of your life and battles, should sell not less than a quarter of a million, perhaps twice that sum. It should be sold only by subscription, and you are entitled to double the royalty here proposed. I do not believe it is to your interest to conclude this contract without careful thought and investigation. Write to the American Publishing Company at Hartford and see what they will do for you."

But Grant demurred. He said that, while no arrangements had been made with the Century Company, he thought it only fair and right that they should have the book on reasonable terms; certainly on terms no greater than he could obtain elsewhere. He said that, all things being equal, the book ought to go to the man who had first suggested it to him.

Clemens spoke up: "General, if that is so, it belongs to *me*."

Grant did not understand until Clemens recalled to him how he had urged him, in that former time, to write his memoirs; had pleaded with him, agreeing to superintend the book's publication. Then he said:

"General, I am publishing my own book, and by the time yours is ready it is quite possible that I shall have the best equipped subscription establishment in the country. If you will place your book with my firm—and I feel that I have at least an equal right in the consideration—I will pay you twenty per cent. of the list price, or, if you prefer, I will give you seventy per cent. of the net returns and I will pay all office expenses out of my thirty per cent."

General Grant was really grieved at this proposal. It seemed to him that here was a man who was offering to bankrupt himself out of pure philanthropy—a thing not to be permitted. He intimated that he had asked the Century Company president, Roswell Smith, a careful-headed business man, if he thought his book would pay as well as Sherman's, which the Scribners had published at a profit to Sherman of twenty-five thousand dollars, and that Smith had been unwilling to guarantee that amount to the author.[1]

[1] Mark Twain's note-book, under date of March, 1885, contains this memorandum:

"Roswell Smith said to me: 'I'm glad you got the book, Mr. Clemens; glad there was somebody with courage enough to take it, under the circumstances. What do you think the General wanted to require of me?'

"'What?'

"'He wanted me to insure a sale of twenty-five thousand sets of his book. I wouldn't risk such a guarantee on any book that was ever published.'"

Yet Roswell Smith, not so many years later, had so far enlarged his views of subscription publishing that he fearlessly and successfully invested a million dollars or more in a dictionary, regardless of the fact that the market was already thought to be supplied.

Clemens said:

"General, I have my check-book with me. I will draw you a check now for twenty-five thousand dollars for the first volume of your memoirs, and will add a like amount for each volume you may write as an advance royalty payment, and your royalties will continue right along when this amount has been reached."

Colonel Fred Grant now joined in urging that matters be delayed, at least until more careful inquiry concerning the possibilities of publishing could be made.

Clemens left then, and set out on his trip with Cable, turning the whole matter over to Webster and Colonel Fred for settlement. Meantime, the word that General Grant was writing his memoirs got into the newspapers and various publishing propositions came to him. In the end the General sent over to Philadelphia for his old friend, George W. Childs, and laid the whole matter before him. Childs said later it was plain that General Grant, on the score of friendship, if for no other reason, distinctly wished to give the book to Mark Twain. It seemed not to be a question of how much money he would make, but of personal feeling entirely. Webster's complete success with *Huck Finn* being now demonstrated, Colonel Fred Grant agreed that he believed Clemens and Webster could handle the book as profitably as anybody; and after investigation Childs was of the same opinion. The decision was that the firm of Charles L. Webster & Co. should have the book, and arrangements for drawing the contract were made.

General Grant, however, was still somewhat uneasy as to the terms. He thought he was taking an unfair advantage in receiving so large a proportion of the profits. He wrote to Clemens, asking him which of his two propositions—the twenty per cent. gross royalty or the seventy per cent. of the net profit—would be the best all around. Clemens sent Webster to tell him that he believed the simplest, as well as the most profitable for the author, would be the twenty per cent. arrangement. Whereupon Grant replied that he would take the alternative; as in that case, if the book were a failure, and there were no profits, Clemens would not be obliged to pay him anything. He could not consent to the thought of receiving twenty per cent. on a book published at a loss.

Meantime, Grant had developed a serious illness. The humiliation of his business failure had undermined his health. The papers announced his malady as cancer of the tongue. In a memorandum which Clemens made, February 26, 1885, he states that on the 21st he called at the Grant home, 3 East 66th Street, and was astonished to see how thin and weak the General looked. He was astonished because the newspaper, in a second report, had said the threatening symptoms had disappeared, that the cancer alarm was a false one.

I took for granted the report, and said I had been glad to see that news. He smiled and said, "Yes—if it had only been true."

One of the physicians was present, and he startled me by saying the General's condition was the opposite of encouraging.

Then the talk drifted to business, and the General presently said: "I mean you shall have the book—I have about made up my mind to that—but I wish to write to Mr. Roswell Smith first, and tell him I have so decided. I think this is due him."

From the beginning the General has shown a fine delicacy toward those people—a delicacy which was native to the character of the man who put into the Appomattox terms of surrender the words, "Officers may retain their side-arms," to save General Lee the humiliation of giving up his sword. [Note-book.]

The physician present was Dr. Douglas, and upon Clemens assuming that the General's trouble was probably due to smoking, also that it was a warning to those who smoked to excess, himself included, Dr. Douglas said that General Grant's affliction could not be attributed altogether to smoking, but far more to his distress of mind, his year-long depression of spirit, the grief of his financial disaster. Dr. Douglas's remark started General Grant upon the subject of his connection with Ward, which he discussed with great freedom and apparent relief of mind. Never at any time did he betray any resentment toward Ward, but characterized him as one might an offending child. He spoke as a man who has been deeply wronged and humiliated and betrayed, but without a venomous expression or one with revengeful nature. Clemens confessed in his notes that all the time he himself was "inwardly boiling—scalping Ward—flaying him alive—breaking him on the wheel—pounding him to a jelly."

While he was talking Colonel Grant said:

"Father is letting you see that the Grant family are a pack of fools, Mr. Clemens."

The General objected to this statement. He said that the facts could be produced which would show that when Ward laid siege to a man he was pretty certain to turn out to be a fool; as much of a fool as any of the Grant family. He said that nobody could call the president of the Erie Railroad a fool, yet Ward had beguiled him of eight hundred thousand dollars, robbed him of every cent of it.

He cited another man that no one could call a fool who had invested in Ward to the extent of half a million. He went on to recall many such cases. He told of one man who had come to the office on the eve of departure for Europe and handed Ward a check for fifty thousand dollars, saying:

"I have no use for it at present. See what you can do with it for me." By and by this investor, returning from Europe, dropped in and said:

"Well, did anything happen?"

Ward indifferently turned to his private ledger, consulted it, then drew a check for two hundred and fifty thousand dollars, and handed it over, with the casual remark:

"Well, yes, something happened; not much yet—a little too soon."

The man stared at the check, then thrust it back into Ward's hand. "That's all right. It's plenty good enough for me. Set that hen again," and left the place.

Of course Ward made no investments. His was the first playing on a colossal scale of the now worn-out "get rich quick" confidence game. Such dividends as were made came out of the principal. Ward was the Napoleon of that game, whether he invented it or not. Clemens agreed that, as far as himself or any of his relatives were concerned, they would undoubtedly have trusted Ward.

Colonel Grant followed him to the door when he left, and told him that the physicians feared his father might not live more than a few weeks longer, but that meantime he had been writing steadily, and that the first volume was complete and fully half the second. Three days later the formal contract was closed, and Webster & Co. promptly advanced General Grant ten thousand dollars for imminent demands, a welcome arrangement, for Grant's debts and expenses were many, and his available resources restricted to the *Century* payments for his articles.

Immediately the office of Webster & Co. was warm with affairs. Reporters were running hot-foot for news of the great contract by which Mark Twain was to publish the life of General Grant. No publishing enterprise of such vast moment had ever been undertaken, and no publishing event, before or since, ever received the amount of newspaper comment. The names of General Grant and Mark Twain associated would command columns, whatever the event, and that Mark Twain was to become the publisher of Grant's own story of his battles was of unprecedented importance.

The partners were sufficiently occupied. Estimates and prices for vast quantities of paper were considered, all available presses were contracted for, binderies were pledged exclusively for the Grant book. Clemens was boiling over with plans and suggestions for distribution. Webster was half wild with the tumult of the great campaign. Applications for agencies poured in.

In those days there were general subscription agencies which divided the country into districts, and the heads of these agencies Webster summoned to New York and laid down the law to them concerning the new book. It was not a time for small dealings, and Webster rose to the occasion. By the time these men returned to their homes they had practically pledged themselves to a quarter of a million sets of the *Grant Memoirs*, and this estimate they believed to be conservative.

Webster now moved into larger and more pretentious quarters. He took a store-room at 42 East 14th Street, Union Square, and surrounded himself with a capable force of assistants. He had become, all at once, the most conspicuous publisher in the world.

CLV

DAYS WITH A DYING HERO

THE contract for the publication of the Grant Life was officially closed February 27, 1885. Five days later, on the last day and at the last hour of President Arthur's administration, and of the Congress then sitting, a bill was passed placing Grant as full General, with full pay, on the retired army list. The bill providing for this somewhat tardy acknowledgment was rushed through at the last moment, and it is said that the Congressional clock was set back so that this enactment might become a law before the administration changed.

Clemens was with General Grant when the news of this action was read to him. Grant had greatly desired such recognition, and it meant more to him than to any one present, yet Clemens in his notes records:

> Every face there betrayed strong excitement and emotion except one—General Grant's. He read the telegram, but not a shade or suggestion of a change exhibited itself in his iron countenance. The volume of his emotion was greater than all the other emotions there present combined, but he was able to suppress all expression of it and make no sign.

Grant's calmness, endurance, and consideration during these final days astonished even those most familiar with his noble character. One night Gerhardt came into the library at Hartford with the announcement that he wished to show his patron a small bust he had been making in clay of General Grant. Clemens did not show much interest in the prospect, but when the work was uncovered he became enthusiastic. He declared it was the first likeness he had ever seen of General Grant that approached reality. He agreed that the Grant family ought to see it, and that he would take Gerhardt with him next day in order that he might be within reach in case they had any suggestions. They went to New York next morning, and called at the Grant home during the afternoon.

From the note-book:

Friday, March 20, 1885. Gerhardt and I arrived at General Grant's about 2.30 P.M. and I asked if the family would look at a small clay bust of the General which Gerhardt had made from a photograph. Colonel Fred and Jesse were absent to receive their sister, Mrs. Sartoris, who would arrive from Europe about 4.30; but the three Mrs. Grants examined the work and expressed strong approval of it, and also great gratification that Mr. Gerhardt had undertaken it. Mrs. Jesse Grant had lately dreamed that she was inquiring where the maker of my bust could be found (she had seen a picture of it in *Huck Finn*, which was published four weeks ago), for she wanted the same artist to make one of General Grant. The ladies examined the bust critically and pointed out defects, while Gerhardt made the necessary corrections. Presently Mrs. General Grant suggested that Gerhardt step in and look at the General. I had been in there talking with the General, but had never thought of asking him to let a stranger come in. So Gerhardt went in with the ladies and me, and the inspection and cross-fire began: "There, I was sure his nose was so and so," and, "I was sure his forehead was so and so," and, "Don't you think his head is so and so?" And so everybody walked around and about the old hero, who lay half reclining in his easy chair, but well muffled up, and submitting to all this as serenely as if he were used to being served so. One marked feature of General Grant's character is his exceeding gentleness, goodness, sweetness. Every time I have been in his presence—lately and formerly—my mind was drawn to that feature. I wonder it has not been more spoken of.

THE GERHARDT BUST OF GENERAL GRANT

Presently he said, let Gerhardt bring in his clay and work there, if Gerhardt would not mind his reclining attitude. Of course we were glad. A table for the bust was moved up in front of him; the ladies left the room; I got a book; Gerhardt went to work; and for an hour there was perfect stillness, and for the first time during the day the General got a good, sound, peaceful nap. General Badeau came in, and probably interrupted that nap. He spoke out as strongly as the others concerning the great excellence of the likeness. He had some sheets of MS. in his hand, and said, "I've been reading what you wrote this morning, General, and it is of the utmost value; it solves a riddle that has puzzled men's brains all these years and makes the thing clear and rational." I asked what the puzzle was, and he said, "It was why Grant did not immediately lay siege to Vicksburg after capturing Port Hudson" (at least that is my recollection, now toward midnight, of General Badeau's answer).

The little bust of Grant which Gerhardt worked on that day was widely reproduced in terra-cotta, and is still regarded by many as the most nearly correct likeness of Grant. The original is in possession of the family.

General Grant worked industriously on his book. He had a superb memory and worked rapidly. Webster & Co. offered to supply him with a stenographer, and this proved a great relief. Sometimes he dictated ten thousand words at a sitting. It was reported at the time, and it has been stated since, that Grant did not write the *Memoirs* himself, but only made notes, which were expanded by others. But this is not true. General Grant wrote or dictated every word of the story himself, then had the manuscript read aloud to him and made his own revisions. He wrote against time, for he knew that his disease was fatal. Fortunately the lease of life granted him was longer than he had hoped for, though the last chapters were written when he could no longer speak, and when weakness and suffering made the labor a heavy one indeed; but he never flinched or faltered, never at any time suggested that the work be finished by another hand.

Early in April General Grant's condition became very alarming, and on the night of the 3d it was believed he could not live until morning. But he was not yet ready to surrender. He rallied and renewed his task; feebly at first, but more perseveringly as each day seemed to bring a little added strength, or perhaps it was only resolution. Now and then he appeared depressed as to the quality of his product. Once Colonel Fred Grant suggested to Clemens that if he could encourage the General a little it might be worth while. Clemens had felt always such a reverence and awe for the great soldier that he had never dreamed of complimenting his literature.

"I was as much surprised as Columbus's cook could have been to learn that Columbus wanted his opinion as to how Columbus was doing his navigating."

He did not hesitate to give it, however, and with a clear conscience. Grant wrote as he had fought; with a simple, straightforward dignity, with a style that is not a style at all but the very absence of it, and therefore the best of all literary methods. It happened that Clemens had been comparing some of Grant's chapters with *Cæsar's Commentaries*, and was able to say, in all sincerity, that the same high merits distinguished both books: clarity of statement, directness, simplicity, manifest truthfulness, fairness and justice toward friend and foe alike, soldierly candor and frankness, and soldierly avoidance of flowery speech.

"I placed the two books side by side upon the same level," he said, "and I still think that they belong there. I learned afterward that General Grant was pleased with this verdict. It shows that he was just a man, just a human being, just an author."

Within two months after the agents had gone to work canvassing for the *Grant Memoirs*—which is to say by the 1st of May, 1885—orders for sixty thousand sets had been received, and on that day Mark Twain, in his note-book, made a memorandum estimate of the number of books that the country would require, figuring the grand total at three hundred thousand sets of two volumes each. Then he says:

> If these chickens should really hatch according to my account, General Grant's royalties will amount to $420,000, and will make the largest single check ever paid an author in the world's history. Up to the present time the largest one ever paid was to Macaulay on his *History of England*, £20,000. If I pay the General in silver coin at $12 per pound it will weigh seventeen tons.

Certainly this has a flavor in it of Colonel Sellers, but we shall see by and by in how far this calculation was justified.

Grant found the society of Mark Twain cheering and comforting, and Clemens held himself in readiness to go to the dying man at call. On the 26th of May he makes this memorandum:

> It is curious and dreadful to sit up in this way and talk cheerful nonsense to General Grant, and he under sentence of death with that cancer. He says he has made the book too large by 200 pages—not a bad fault. A short time ago we were afraid we would lack 400 of being enough.
>
> To-day talked with General Grant about his and my first great Missouri campaign in 1861. He surprised an empty camp near Florida, Missouri, on Salt River, which I had been occupying a day or two before. How near he came to playing the devil with his future publisher!

Of course Clemens would amuse the old commander with the tale of his soldiering, how his company had been chased through the brush and mud by the very announcement that Grant was coming. Some word of this got to the *Century* editors, who immediately proposed that Mark Twain contribute to the magazine War Series the story of his share in the Rebellion, and particularly of his war relations with General Grant. So the "Private History of a Campaign that Failed" was prepared as Mark Twain's side-light on the history of the Rebellion; and if it was not important history it was at least amusing, and the telling of that tale in Mark Twain's inimitable fashion must have gone far toward making cheerful those last sad days of his ancient enemy.

During one of their talks General Grant spoke of the question as to whether he or Sherman had originated the idea of the march to the sea. Grant said:

"Neither of us originated the idea of that march. The enemy did it."

Reports were circulated of estrangements between General Grant and the Century Company, and between Mark Twain and the Century Company, as a result of the book decision. Certain newspapers exploited and magnified these rumors—some went so far as to accuse Mark Twain of duplicity, and to charge him with seeking to obtain a vast fortune for himself at the expense of General Grant and his family. All of which was the merest nonsense. The Century Company, Webster & Co., General Grant, and Mark Twain individually, were all working harmoniously, and nothing but the most cordial relations and understanding prevailed. As to the charge of unfair dealing on the part of Mark Twain, this was too absurd, even then, to attract more than momentary attention. Webster & Co., somewhat later in the year, gave to the press a clear statement of their publishing arrangement, though more particularly denying the report that General Grant had been unable to complete his work.

CLVI

THE CLOSE OF A GREAT CAREER

THE Clemens household did not go to Elmira that year until the 27th of June. Meantime General Grant had been taken to Mount McGregor, near the Adirondacks. The day after Clemens reached Elmira there came a summons saying that the General had asked to see him. He went immediately, and remained several days. The resolute old commander was very feeble by this time. It was three months since he had been believed to be dying, yet he was still alive, still at work, though he could no longer speak. He was adding, here and there, a finishing touch to his manuscript, writing with effort on small slips of paper containing but a few words each. His conversation was carried on in the same way. Mark Twain brought back a little package of those precious slips, and some of them are still preserved. The writing is perfectly legible, and shows no indication of a trembling hand.

On one of these slips is written:

> There is much more that I could do if I was a well man. I do not write quite as clearly as I could if well. If I could read it over myself many little matters of anecdote and incident would suggest themselves to me.

On another:

> Have you seen any portion of the second volume? It is up to the end, or nearly so. As much more work as I have done

to-day will finish it. I have worked faster than if I had been well. I have used my three boys and a stenographer.

And on still another:

> If I could have two weeks of strength I could improve it very much. As I am, however, it will have to go about as it is, with verifications by the boys and by suggestions which will enable me to make a point clear here and there.

Certainly no campaign was ever conducted with a braver heart. As long as his fingers could hold a pencil he continued at his task. Once he asked if any estimate could now be made of what portion would accrue to his family from the publication. Clemens's prompt reply,

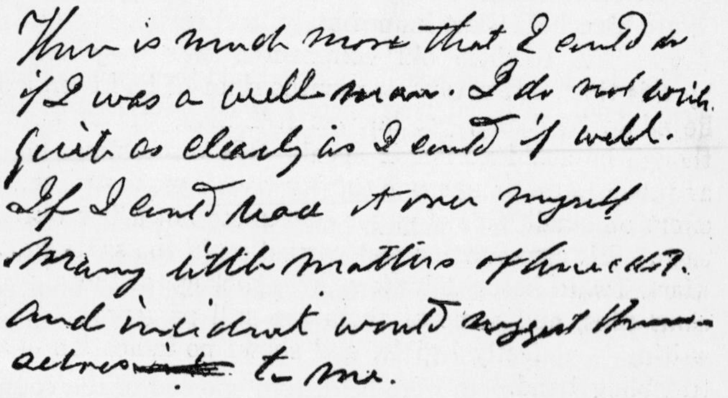
There is much more that I could do
if I was a well man. I do not write
quite as clearly as I could if well.
If I could read it over myself
many little matters of anecdote
and incident would suggest themselves to me.

FACSIMILE OF GENERAL GRANT'S LAST WRITING

that more than one hundred thousand sets had been sold, and that already the amount of his share, secured by safe bonds, exceeded one hundred and fifty thousand dollars, seemed to give him deep comfort. Clemens told him that the country was as yet not one-third canvassed, and that without doubt there turns would be twice as much more by the end of the year. Grant made no further inquiry, and probably never again mentioned the subject to any one.

When Clemens left, General Grant was sitting, fully dressed, with a shawl about his shoulders, pencil and paper beside him. It was a picture that would never fade from the memory. In a later memorandum he says:

I then believed he would live several months. He was still adding little perfecting details to his book, and preface, among other things. He was entirely through a few days later. Since then the lack of any strong interest to employ his mind has enabled the tedious weariness to kill him. I think his book kept him alive several months. He was a very great man and superlatively good.

This note was made July 23, 1885, at 10 A.M., on receipt of the news that General Grant was dead. To Henry Ward Beecher, Clemens wrote:

One day he put his pencil aside and said there was nothing more to do. If I had been there I could have foretold the shock that struck the world three days later.

It can be truly said that all the nation mourned. General Grant had no enemies, political or sectional, in those last days. The old soldier battling with a deadly disease, yet bravely completing his task, was a figure at once so pathetic and so noble that no breath of animosity remained to utter a single word that was not kind.

Memorial services were held from one end of the country to the other. Those who had followed him in peace or war, those who had fought beside him or against him, alike paid tribute to his memory. Twichell, from the mountains of Vermont, wrote:

I suppose I have said to Harmony forty times since I got up here, "How I wish I could see Mark!" My notion is that between us we could get ourselves expressed. I have never known any one who could help me read my own thoughts in such a case as you can and *have* done many a time, dear old fellow.

I'd give more to sit on a log with you in the woods this afternoon, while we twined a wreath together for Launcelot's grave, than to hear any conceivable eulogy of him pronounced by mortal lips.

The death of Grant so largely and so suddenly augmented the orders for his *Memoirs* that it seemed impossible to get the first volume printed in time for the delivery, which had been promised for December 1st. J. J. Little had the contract of manufacture, and every available press and bindery was running double time to complete the vast contract.

In the end more than three hundred thousand sets of two volumes each were sold, and between four hundred and twenty and four hundred and fifty thousand dollars was paid to Mrs. Grant. The first check of two hundred thousand dollars, drawn February 27, 1886, remains the largest single royalty check in history. Mark Twain's prophecy had been almost exactly verified.

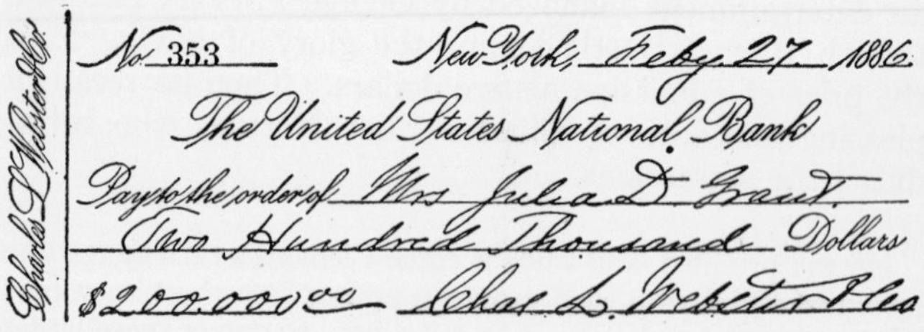
Charles L. Webster & Co.
No. 353 New York, Feby 27 1886
The United States National Bank
Pay to the order of Mrs Julia D Grant
Two Hundred Thousand Dollars
$200.000.00 Chas L. Webster & Co

FACSIMILE OF THE FIRST ROYALTY CHECK PAID BY CHARLES L. WEBSTER & CO., ON THE GRANT MEMOIR. ORIGINAL NOW OWNED BY THE PLAYERS CLUB, N. Y.

CLVII

MINOR MATTERS OF A GREAT YEAR

THE Grant episode, so important in all its phases, naturally overshadowed other events of 1885. Mark Twain was so deeply absorbed in this great publishing enterprise that he wasted little thought or energy in other directions.

Yet there are a few minor things that it seems worth while to remember. Howells has told something of the Authors' Reading given for the Longfellow Memorial, an entertainment managed by George Parsons Lathrop, though Howells justly claims the glory of having fixed the price of admission at five dollars. Then he recalls a pleasing anecdote of Charles Eliot Norton, who introduced the attractions.

> Norton presided, and when it came Clemens's turn to read he introduced him with such exquisite praises as he best knew how to give, but before he closed he fell a prey to one of those lapses of tact which are the peculiar peril of people of the greatest tact. He was reminded of Darwin's delight in Mark Twain, and how when he came from his long day's exhausting study, and sank into bed at midnight, he took up a volume of Mark Twain, whose books he always kept on a table beside him, and whatever had been his tormenting problem, or excess of toil, he felt secure of a good night's rest from it. A sort of blank ensued which Clemens filled in the only possible way. He said he should always be glad he had contributed to the repose of that great man, to whom science owed so much, and then without waiting for the joy in every breast to burst forth, he began to read.

Howells tells of Mark Twain's triumph on this occasion, and in a letter at the time he wrote: "You simply straddled down to the footlights and took that house up in the hollow of your hand and tickled it."

Howells adds that the show netted seventeen hundred dollars. This was early in May.

Of literary work, beyond the war paper, the "Private History of a Campaign that Failed" (published December, 1885), Clemens appears to have done very little. His thoughts were far too busy with plans for furthering the sale of the great military *Memoir* to follow literary ventures of his own. At one time he was impelled to dictate an autobiography—Grant's difficulties in his dying hour suggesting this—and he arranged with Redpath, who was no longer a lecture agent and understood stenography, to co-operate with him in the work. He dictated a few chapters, but he was otherwise too much occupied to continue. Also, he was unused to dictation, and found it hard and the result unsatisfactory.

Two open communications from Mark Twain that year deserve to be remembered. One of these, unsigned, was published in the *Century Magazine*, and expressed the need for a "universal tinker," the man who can accept a job in a large household or in a community as master of all trades, with sufficient knowledge of each to be ready to undertake whatever repairs are likely to be required in the ordinary household, such as—"to put in window-panes, mend gas leaks, jack-plane the edges of doors that won't shut, keep the waste-pipe and other water-pipe joints, glue and otherwise repair havoc done in furniture, etc." The letter was signed X. Y. Z., and it brought replies from various parts of the world. None of the applicants seemed universally qualified, but in Kansas City a business was founded on the idea, adopting "The Universal Tinker" as its firm name.

The other letter mentioned was written to the *Christian*

Union, inspired by a tale entitled, "What Ought We to Have Done?" It was a tale concerning the government of children; especially concerning the government of one child—John Junior—a child who, as it would appear from the tale, had a habit of running things pretty much to his own notion. The performance of John Junior, and of his parents in trying to manage him, stirred Mark Twain considerably—it being "enough to make a body's blood boil," as he confesses—and it impelled him to set down surreptitiously his impressions of what would have happened to John Junior as a member of the Clemens household. He did not dare to show the communication to Mrs. Clemens before he sent it, for he knew pretty well what its fate would be in that case. So he took chances and printed it without her knowledge. The letter was published July 16, 1885. It is too long to be included entire, but it is too illuminating to be altogether omitted. After relating, in considerable detail, Mrs. Clemens's method of dealing with an unruly child—the gentleness yet firmness of her discipline—he concludes:

The mother of my children adores them—there is no milder term for it—and they worship her; they even worship anything which the touch of her hand has made sacred. They know her for the best and truest friend they have ever had, or ever shall have; they know her for one who never did them a wrong, and cannot do them a wrong; who never told them a lie, nor the shadow of one; who never deceived them by even an ambiguous gesture; who never gave them an unreasonable command, nor ever contented herself with anything short of a perfect obedience; who has always treated them as politely and considerately as she would the best and oldest in the land, and has always required of them gentle speech and courteous conduct toward all, of whatsoever degree with whom they chanced to come in contact; they know her for one whose promise, whether of reward or punishment, is gold, and always worth its face, to the uttermost farthing. In a word, they know her, and I know her, for the best and dearest mother that lives—and by a long, long way the wisest. . . .

In all my life I have never made a single reference to my wife in print before, as far as I can remember, except once in the dedication of a book; and so, after these fifteen years of silence, perhaps I may unseal my lips this one time without impropriety or indelicacy. I will institute one other novelty: I will send this manuscript to the press without her knowledge and without asking her to edit it. This will save it from getting edited into the stove.

Susy's biography refers to this incident at considerable length. She states that her father had misgivings after he had sent it to the *Christian Union*, and that he tried to recall the manuscript, but found it too late. She sets down some comments of her own on her mother's government, then tells us of the appearance of the article:

When the *Christian Union* reached the farm and papa's article in it, all ready and waiting to be read to mama, papa hadn't the courage to show it to her (for he knew she wouldn't like it at all) at first, and he didn't, but he might have let it go and never let her see it; but finally he gave his consent to her seeing it, and told Clara and I we could take it to her, which we did with tardiness, and we all stood around mama while she read it, all wondering what she would say and think about it.

She was too much surprised (and pleased privately too) to say much at first; but, as we all expected, publicly (or rather when she remembered that this article was to be read by every one that took the *Christian Union*) she was rather shocked and a little displeased.

Susy goes on to tell that the article provoked a number of letters, most of them pleasant ones, but some of them of quite another sort. One of the latter fell into her mother's hands, after which there was general regret that the article had been printed, and the subject was no longer discussed at Quarry Farm.

MINOR MATTERS OF A GREAT YEAR

Susy's biography is a unique record. It was a sort of combined memoir and journal, charming in its innocent frankness and childish insight. She used to keep it under her pillow, and after she was asleep the parents would steal it out and find a tender amusement and pathos in its quaint entries. It is a faithful record so far as it goes, and the period it covers is an important one; for it presents a picture of Mark Twain in the fullness of his manhood, in the golden hour of his fortune. Susy's beginning has a special value here:[1]

> We are a very happy family! We consist of papa, mama, Jean, Clara and me. It is papa I am writing about, and I shall have no trouble in not knowing what to say about him, as he is a very striking character. Papa's appearance has been described many times, but very incorrectly; he has beautiful curly grey hair, not any too thick, or any too long, just right; a Roman nose, which greatly improves the beauty of his features, kind blue eyes, and a small mustache, he has a wonderfully shaped head, and profile, he has a very good figure in short he is an extraordinarily fine looking man. All his features are perfect, except that he hasn't extraordinary teeth. His complexion is very fair, and he doesn't ware a beard.
>
> He is a very good man, and a very funny one; he has got a temper but we all of us have in this family. He is the loveliest man I ever saw, or ever hope to see, and oh so absent-minded!

That this is a fair statement of the Clemens home, and the truest picture of Mark Twain at fifty that has been preserved, cannot be doubted. His hair was iron-gray, not entirely white at this time, the auburn tints everywhere mingled with the shining white that later would mantle it like a silver crown. He did not look young for his years, but he was still young, always young—indestructibly young in spirit and bodily vigor. Susy tells how that summer he blew soap-bubbles for the children,

[1] Susy's spelling and punctuation are preserved.

filling the bubbles with tobacco smoke; how he would play with the cats, and come clear down from his study on the hill to see how "Sour Mash," then a kitten, was getting along; also how he wrote a poem for Jean's donkey, Cadichon (which they made Kiditchin). She quotes the poem:

KIDITCHIN

O du lieb' Kiditchin
Du bist ganz bewitchin,
    Waw— — — –he!

In summer days Kiditchin
Thou'rt dear from nose to britchin
    Waw— — — –he!

No dought thoult get a switchin
When for mischief thou'rt itchin'
    Waw— — — –he!

But when you're good Kiditchin
You shall feast in James's kitchin
    Waw— — — –he!

O now lift up thy song—
Thy noble note prolong—
Thou living Chinese gong!
    Waw— –he! waw— –he waw
    Sweetest donkey man ever saw.

Clemens undertook to ride Kiditchin one day, to show the children how it should be done, but Kiditchin resented this interference and promptly flung him over her head. He thought she might have been listening to the poem he had written of her.

Susy's discovery that the secret of her biography was

known is shown by the next entry, and the touch of severity in it was probably not entirely unconscious:

Papa said the other day, "I am a mugwump and a mugwump is pure from the marrow out." (Papa knows that I am writing this biography of him, and he said this for it.) He doesn't like to go to church at all, why I never understood, until just now. He told us the other day that he couldn't bear to hear anyone talk but himself, but that he could listen to himself talk for hours without getting tired, of course he said this in joke, but I've no doubt it was founded on truth.

Susy's picture of life at Quarry Farm at this period is realistic and valuable—too valuable to be spared from this biography:

There are eleven cats at the farm here now. Papa's favorite is a little tortoise-shell kitten he has named "Sour Mash," and a little spotted one "Fannie." It is very pretty to see what papa calls the cat procession; it was formed in this way. Old Minnie-cat headed, (the mother of all the cats) next to her came aunt Susie, then Clara on the donkey, accompanied by a pile of cats, then papa and Jean hand in hand and a pile of cats brought up in the rear, mama and I made up the audience.

Our varius occupations are as follows. Papa rises about ½ past 7 in the morning, breakfasts at eight, writes, plays tennis with Clara and me and tries to make the donkey go, in the morning; does varius things in P.M., and in the evening plays tennis with Clara and me and amuses Jean and the donkey.

Mama rises about ¼ to eight, breakfasts at eight, teaches Jean German reading from 9–10; reads German with me from 10–11. Then she reads studdies or visits with aunt Susie for a while, and then she reads to Clara and I till lunch time things connected with English history (for we hope to go to England next summer) while we sew. Then we have lunch. She studdies for about half an hour or visits with aunt Susie, then reads to us an hour or more, then studdies writes reads and rests till supper time. After supper she sits out on the porch and works till eight o'clock, from eight o'clock to bedtime she plays whist with papa and after she has retired she reads and studdies German for a while.

Clara and I do most everything from practicing to donkey riding and playing tag. While Jean's time is spent in asking mama what she can have to eat.

It is impossible, at this distance, to convey all that the farm meant to the children during the summers of their infancy and childhood and girlhood which they spent there. It was the paradise, the dreamland they looked forward to during all the rest of the year. Through the long, happy months there they grew strong and brown, and drank deeply of the joy of life. Their cousins Julia, Jervis, and Ida Langdon ranged about their own ages and were almost their daily companions. Their games were mainly of the out-of-doors; the woods and meadows and hillside pastures were their playground. Susy was thirteen when she began her diary; a gentle, thoughtful, romantic child. One afternoon she discovered a wonderful tangle of vines and bushes between the study and the sunset—a rare hiding-place. She ran breathlessly to her aunt:

"Can I have it? Can Clara and I have it all for our own?"

The petition was granted, of course, and the place was named Helen's Bower, for they were reading *Thaddeus of Warsaw* and the name appealed to Susy's poetic fancy. Then Mrs. Clemens conceived the idea of building a house for the children just beyond the bower. It was a complete little cottage when finished, with a porch and with furnishings contributed by friends and members of the family. There was a stove—a tiny affair, but practical—dishes, table, chairs, shelves, and a broom. The little house was named Ellerslie, out of Grace Aguilar's *Days of Robert Bruce*, and became one of the children's most beloved possessions. But alas for Helen's Bower! A workman was sent to clear away the debris

ELLERSLIE

after the builders, and being a practical man, he cut away Helen's Bower—destroyed it utterly. Susy first discovered the vandalism, and came rushing to the house in a torrent of sorrow. For her the joy of life seemed ended, and it was long before she could be comforted. But Ellerslie in time satisfied her hunger for retreat, became, in fact, the nucleus around which the children's summer happiness centered.

To their elders the farm remained always the quiet haven. Once to Orion's wife Clemens wrote:

> This is a superb Sunday. . . .
>
> The city in the valley is purple with shade, as seen from up here at the study. The Cranes are reading and loafing in the canvas-curtained summer-house, fifty yards away, on a higher (the highest) point; the cats are loafing over at Ellerslie, which is the children's estate and dwelling-house in their own private grounds (by deed from Susie Crane), a hundred yards from the study, among the clover and young oaks and willows. Livy is down at the house, but I shall now go and bring her up to the Cranes to help us occupy the lounges and hammocks, whence a great panorama of distant hills and valley and city is seeable. The children have gone on a lark through the neighboring hills and woods, Susie and Clara horseback and Jean driving a buggy, with the coachman for comrade and assistant at need. It is a perfect day indeed.

The ending of each year's summer brought only regret. Clemens would never take away all his things. He had an old superstition that to leave some article insured return. Mrs. Clemens also left something—her heart's content. The children went around bidding various objects good-by and kissed the gates of Ellerslie to.

CLVIII

MARK TWAIN AT FIFTY

MARK TWAIN'S fiftieth birthday was one of the pleasantly observed events of that year. There was no special celebration, but friends sent kindly messages, and *The Critic*, then conducted by Jeannette and Joseph Gilder, made a feature of it. Miss Gilder wrote to Oliver Wendell Holmes and invited some verses, which with his never-failing kindliness he sent, though in his accompanying note he said:

"I had twenty-three letters spread out on my table for answering, all marked immediate, when your note came."

Dr. Holmes's stanzas are full of his gentle spirit:

TO MARK TWAIN

(*On his fiftieth birthday*)

Ah, Clemens, when I saw thee last,
We both of us were younger;
How fondly mumbling o'er the past
Is Memory's toothless hunger!

So fifty years have fled, they say,
Since first you took to drinking;
I mean in Nature's milky way—
Of course no ill I'm thinking.

But while on life's uneven road
Your track you've been pursuing,
What fountains from your wit have flowed—
What drinks you have been brewing!

MARK TWAIN AT FIFTY

I know whence all your magic came,
  Your secret I've discovered,
The source that fed your inward flame,
  The dreams that round you hovered.

Before you learned to bite or munch,
  Still kicking in your cradle,
The Muses mixed a bowl of punch
  And Hebe seized the ladle.

Dear babe, whose fiftieth year to-day
  Your ripe half-century rounded,
Your books the precious draught betray
  The laughing Nine compounded.

So mixed the sweet, the sharp, the strong,
  Each finds its faults amended,
The virtues that to each belong
  In happiest union blended.

And what the flavor can surpass
  Of sugar, spirit, lemons?
So while one health fills every glass—
  Mark Twain for Baby Clemens!

OLIVER WENDELL HOLMES.

Frank R. Stockton, Charles Dudley Warner, and Joel Chandler Harris sent pleasing letters. Warner said:

You may think it an easy thing to be fifty years old, but you will find it's not so easy to stay there, and your next fifty years will slip away much faster than those just accomplished.

Many wrote letters privately, of course, and Andrew Lang, like Holmes, sent a poem that has a special charm.

FOR MARK TWAIN

To brave Mark Twain, across the sea,
The years have brought his jubilee.
  One hears it, half in pain,
That fifty years have passed and gone
Since danced the merry star that shone
  Above the babe Mark Twain.

We turn his pages and we see
The Mississippi flowing free;
  We turn again and grin
O'er all Tom Sawyer did and planned
With him of the ensanguined hand,
  With Huckleberry Finn!

Spirit of Mirth, whose chime of bells
Shakes on his cap, and sweetly swells
  Across the Atlantic main,
Grant that Mark's laughter never die,
That men through many a century
  May chuckle o'er Mark Twain!

Assuredly Mark Twain was made happy by these attentions; to Dr. Holmes he wrote:

DEAR DR. HOLMES,—I shall never be able to tell you the half of how proud you have made me. If I could you would say you were nearly paid for the trouble you took. And then the family: If I could convey the electrical surprise and gratitude and exaltation of the wife and the children last night, when they happened upon that *Critic* where I had, with artful artlessness, spread it open and retired out of view to see what would happen —well, it was great and fine and beautiful to see, and made me feel as the victor feels when the shouting hosts march by; and if you also could have seen it you would have said the account was squared. For I have brought them up in your company, as in the company of a warm and friendly and beneficent but far-distant sun; and so, for you to do this thing was for the sun to send down out of the skies the miracle of a special ray and transfigure me before their faces. I knew what that poem would be to them; I knew it would raise me up to remote and shining heights in their eyes, to very fellowship with the chambered Nautilus itself, and that from that fellowship they could never more dissociate me while they should live; and so I made sure to be by when the surprise should come.

Charles Dudley Warner is charmed with the poem for its own felicitous sake; and so indeed am I, but more because it has drawn the sting of my fiftieth year; taken away the pain of it, the grief of it, the somehow *shame* of it, and made me glad and proud it happened.

With reverence and affection,
Sincerely yours,
S. L. CLEMENS.

So Samuel Clemens had reached the half-century mark; reached it in what seemed the fullness of success from every viewpoint. If he was not yet the foremost American man of letters, he was at least the most widely known—he sat upon the highest mountain-top. Furthermore, it seemed to him that fortune was showering her gifts into his lap. His unfortunate investments were now only as the necessary experiments that had led him to larger successes. As a publisher, he was already the most conspicuous in the world, and he contemplated still larger ventures: a type-setting machine patent, in which he had invested, and now largely controlled, he regarded as the chief invention of the age, absolutely certain to yield incalculable wealth. His connection with the Grant family had associated him with an enterprise looking to the building of a railway from Constantinople to the Persian Gulf. Charles A. Dana, of the *Sun*, had put him in the way of obtaining for publication the life of the Pope, Leo XIII., officially authorized by the Pope himself, and this he regarded as a certain fortune.

Now that the tide had turned he felt no hesitancy in

To Mark Twain — Samuel L. Clemens, —
on his 50th birthday.

Ah Clemens, when I saw thee last, —
We both of us were younger, —
How fondly mumbling o'er the past
Is Memory's toothless hunger!

So fifty years have fled, they say,
Since first you took to drinking, —
I mean in Nature's milky way, —
Of course no ill I'm thinking.

But while on life's uneven road
Your track you've been pursuing
What fountains from your wit have flowed,
What drinks you have been brewing!

* * * * * *

Before you learned to bite or munch
Still kicking in your cradle,
The Muses mixed a bowl of punch
And Hebe seized the ladle:

Dear babe, whose fiftieth year today
Your ripe half-century rounded,
Your books the precious draught betray
The laughing Nine compounded.

So mixed the sweet, the sharp, the strong,
Each finds its faults amended,
The virtues that to each belong
In happiest union blended.

And what the flavor can surpass
Of sugar, spirit, lemons?
So while one health fills every glass
Mark Twain for Baby Clemens!

Oliver Wendell Holmes Boston Nov. 23d 1885

FACSIMILE OF DR. HOLMES'S POEM TO MARK TWAIN
(One stanza omitted)

reckoning a fortune from almost any venture. The Grant book, even on the liberal terms allowed to the author, would yield a net profit of one hundred and fifty thousand dollars to its publishers. *Huck Finn* would yield fifty thousand dollars more. The sales of his other books had considerably increased. Certainly, at fifty, Mark Twain's fortunes were at flood-tide; buoyant and jubilant, he was floating on the topmost wave. If there were under-currents and undertow they were down somewhere out of sight. If there were breakers ahead, they were too far distant to be heard. So sure was he of the triumphant consummation of every venture that to a friend at his home one night he said:

"I am frightened at the proportions of my prosperity. It seems to me that whatever I touch turns to gold."

END OF VOL II